# SOUL & SURVIVAL

## The common human experience

# SOUL & SURVIVAL

## The common human experience

**GRANT BENTLEY**

**PUBLISHED BY GRANT BENTLEY**

First published 2008 in Australia by Grant Bentley
Copyright © Grant Bentley 2008
The moral right of the author has been asserted
All rights reserved. No part of this book may be reproduced or transmitted by any person or entity in any form or by any means, electronic
or mechanical, including photocopying, recording, scanning or by any information storage and retrieval system, without prior permission in writing from the publisher.

Bentley, Grant.

Soul & Survival

Edition: 2nd ed.

ISBN-13: 978-1514601945

Self-actualization (Psychology)

158.1

Originally produced for Grant Bentley by Allan Cornwell
Cover design by nishnish

# CONTENTS

| | | |
|---|---|---|
| **INTRODUCTION** | | 8 |
| **Chapter 1** | **THE GREATEST EXPERIMENT IN HISTORY** | 13 |
| **Chapter 2** | **THE POLITICS OF SURVIVAL** | 42 |
| | The survival instinct | 42 |
| | Learning and ability | 45 |
| | The opinion of others | 47 |
| | Appearance | 48 |
| | Personality | 48 |
| **Chapter 3** | **REFLECTIONS ON THE SOUL AND THE SURVIVAL INSTINCT** | 50 |
| | The survival instinct | 50 |
| | The soul | 53 |
| **Chapter 4** | **THE MATERIAL UNIVERSE** | 58 |
| **Chapter 5** | **THE SEVEN TRADITIONAL ROLES** | 61 |
| | Traditional roles | 61 |
| | Colours, forces and roles | 62 |
| | The trader | 64 |
| | The farmer | 65 |
| | The shepherd | 65 |
| | The warrior | 66 |
| | The priest | 66 |
| | The hunter | 67 |
| | The craftsman | 68 |
| | The life experiences of the roles | 68 |
| | Different responses | 69 |
| | Reading a force or instinct | 71 |
| **Chapter 6** | **BALANCING SOUL AND SURVIVAL** | 72 |
| | Balance | 72 |
| | Following our soul | 73 |
| | Self-denial | 74 |
| | More energy equals less stress | 75 |
| | Energy and memory | 75 |
| | Opposites and similars | 76 |
| **Chapter 7** | **INDIVIDUAL REACTIONS TO STRESS** | 77 |
| | Reaction | 77 |
| | Under Stress | 77 |
| | Contribution | 80 |
| | Frequency of stress | 80 |

| | | |
|---|---|---|
| **Chapter 8** | **HEALTH AND ILLNESS** | 81 |
| | Energy levels and the survival instinct | 81 |
| | Trauma and disease | 83 |
| | Triggers for the survival instinct | 86 |
| | Immunity and defence | 92 |
| | Breaking habits | 93 |
| | The mind not the brain | 94 |
| **Chapter 9** | **TIME CYCLES AND EPIDEMICS** | 95 |
| | Space | 95 |
| | Time | 96 |
| **Chapter 10** | **LIFE THEMES** | 99 |
| | Frequency | 100 |
| | Repeating circumstances | 101 |
| | Distinctiveness | 102 |
| | Impact | 102 |
| | Examples of life themes | 103 |
| | Yellow | 103 |
| | Red | 105 |
| | Blue | 108 |
| | Orange | 110 |
| | Purple | 113 |
| | Green | 115 |
| | Brown | 118 |
| **Chapter 11** | **UNDERSTANDING COLOUR GROUPS** | 122 |
| | Colour groups help us understand ourselves and others | 122 |
| | Colour groups help us acknowledge the effects of stress | 123 |
| | Traits in balance and out of balance | 124 |
| | Variations in colour groups | 125 |
| | What is in the colour chapters? | 126 |
| | What colour group are you in? | 127 |
| | Traits of colour groups | 127 |
| | Summary of the colour groups | 129 |
| **Chapter 12** | **THE FACE** | 130 |
| **Chapter 13** | **YELLOW — OUTWARD MOTION** | 139 |
| **Chapter 14** | **RED — CIRCULAR MOTION** | 190 |
| **Chapter 15** | **BLUE — INWARD MOTION** | 235 |
| **Chapter 16** | **ORANGE — OUTWARD MOTION AND CIRCULAR MOTION – RESISTANCE** | 280 |

**Chapter 17** PURPLE — INWARD AND CIRCULAR MOTION – SPACE  319

**Chapter 18** GREEN — OUTWARD AND INWARD MOTION – REACTIVITY  367

**Chapter 19** BROWN — OUTWARD, CIRCULAR AND INWARD MOTION – UNITY  410

**Chapter 20** - HISTORY  453
    The cycle of colour periods  453

**ACKNOWLEDGEMENTS**  472

# INTRODUCTION

When I first wrote Soul & Survival in 2008 I decided not to do an introduction. The topic was so vast it seemed impossible to do anything other than simply start. However in this second edition of Soul & Survival, I have chosen to summarise the book – just a little – for new readers.

Soul & Survival is a book about life and the patterns that influence our lives. It is about the transfer of information both genetically and energetically from one generation to the next. It is about understanding our animal instinct and recognising the difference between that part of ourselves and developed conscious thought. Through various analogies, stories, and examples, I will attempt to explain the differences between virtuous aspiration and inherited instinctive behaviour.

At a global level, I will demonstrate how energy patterns reproduce themselves in predictable cyclic time patterns. These cycles influence events and thought and separate one historical time frame from another. Once understood, these patterns explain why the reformation occurred in the sixteenth century, and why the eighteenth century became the age of enlightenment. It becomes apparent why tuberculosis and other chronic diseases have their rise and fall within certain time frames, and most importantly for our age, it explains the rise of consumerism and other modern developments such as terrorism, obesity, computers, and virtual reality. All become understandable outcomes of the energy that dominates our time.

The model of facial analysis, which I will touch on briefly, evolved out of my clinical practice as a homeopath. This facial model helped me identify people, places, and times, into what I call colour groups. It also underpins my understanding of the personality and the forces behind each group. Homoeopathy (for those who don't know of it) is a system of medicine developed by a German physician called Samuel Hahnemann two hundred years ago. It is based on the concept that what can cause a disease, can also fix that same disease if applied in a specialised (energetic) way. This process is called the law of similars. A product or poison that may cause fever, nausea, and lethargy can be utilised (energetically) to become an effective medicine for any fever, nausea, and lethargy that has been caused by illness or stress. It is the same as in mathematics where two negatives become a positive. My knowledge of the law of similars became invaluable as I began to notice that not only do similars cancel each other out when applied homoeopathically, but the resident energy within every person also attracts similar energies in order to heal and balance itself.

Everyone has a personality and this personality is made up of a set of thoughts, emotions and beliefs, likes and dislikes, fears and desires. These desires and beliefs determine what you want to achieve in life as well as the type of person you are. It is vital for the understanding of this model that you appreciate one important aspect of these traits - none of them are material. Belief, enjoyment, fear, and love, have no physical body or form. In fact once you begin to examine them, you will conclude that most of the characteristics that define who you are, are non-material by definition. The true essence of every human being is defined by the qualities you cannot see rather than by the qualities you can. Most people identify themselves by the very thing the modern world denies exists – non-physical energy. Character and personality have a non–material quality and as such are governed by different universal laws than those that govern the physical world.

At the base of this non-material law is attraction and repulsion. Personality, being energy, cannot be contained within the barrier of the physical body. Just like light from a globe, it radiates out beyond the skin and into its surrounding areas. This radiating energy influences everything it touches. Others of like mind will pick up on this energy, either consciously or unconsciously, and react to it with either attraction or repulsion.

Finally, because I do not have a scientific background outside of my training as a naturopath and homeopath, I prefer to explain my ideas in the least scientific way possible. Aspects of physics are kept to a minimum and instead are replaced by personal stories that demonstrate the same principles. I hope you will enjoy the concept and be intrigued to know more.

***

Samuel Hahnemann (1755-1843) presented the three primary motions to the world in his book Chronic Diseases (1828) – he called them psora, sycosis, and syphilis

John Henry Allen (1854 - 1925) wrote about the relationship between the three primary motions and facial structure in his book The Chronic Miasms (1908)

My patients had their facial features analysed and told me their life stories

My students shared their enthusiasm and insights, learned about facial analysis, and applied all they were taught

My four children and four stepchildren gave me an intimate understanding of their survival instincts

My love of history and spirituality led me to an understanding of the motions and time cycles

Grant Bentley May 2015

This second edition of Soul & Survival doesn't show any of the facial images. This might seem strange as the idea of Soul & Survival came from facial analysis and it still underpins all my clinical work, but the first edition only showed a selection of facial images. There are more than 70 allocations of facial structure and even more combinations. Go to www.soulandsurvival.com for an online interactive program to discover your own facial analysis or better still download the full practitioner version which is free to use for a while – this will help you identify your own facial group. Read more about the face in Chapter 12. I have also written about facial analysis extensively in my two books *Appearance and Circumstance* and *Homoeopathic Facial Analysis (companion guide to Appearance and Circumstance)* and my clinical interpretation of disease and its allocation in *How Aphorism 27 Changed The World.*

Grant Bentley 2015

## Chapter 1

# THE GREATEST EXPERIMENT IN HISTORY

*God grant me the serenity to accept the things I cannot change, courage to change the things I can, and wisdom to know the difference.*

Reinhold Niebuhr

Finally the letter arrives. You'd been telling your family and friends that you didn't really care if you were accepted or not. That it was all a bit of a joke. But that is not the truth. You desperately want to play. Privately you have been crossing your fingers and praying to be selected. Now, finally, you will know.

About twelve months ago you entered a competition. The people in charge called it a social and historical experiment, combining with the media to form a new era in entertainment. 'Histrotainment' was what they were calling it, and you wanted to be a part of the competition.

You had a vague idea what you were letting yourself in for. You had entered your name into a competition where twelve hundred people were going to replicate history. You didn't know how exactly but it sounded exciting.

Slowly you open the letter.

'Dear ... congratulations, we are pleased to inform you that your application to be part of our new and ground breaking adventure has been successful. Our cultural and historical aim is to ... '

'Yeah, yeah ... whatever!' you say to yourself, 'just get to the point.' Then you see what you are looking for – the money – and it's even more than they said in the brochure. When you first read about this event and how they were calling for volunteers, your enthusiasm was lukewarm at best, but when you saw how much money was being offered to those left at the end, you were suddenly very interested indeed.

The project itself is enormous and constitutes the largest social experiment ever funded. Government research units together with universities, professional organisations and movie makers have all come together to finance and learn from this event. The experiment will run for three years. Its aim is to see whether social evolution would repeat itself in the same manner as it already has in human history. The researchers hope to gain an understanding of how human culture developed, and why.

Participants will be isolated from family and friends for a period of three years, and then it might take another one to two years for them to re-integrate back into the community. Careers and future earning potential will be severely affected.

In return, the people taking part in the experiment will never have to worry about money again. Of course, there is a catch. Only those remaining at the end of the three-year period will be paid, the rest will receive nothing! Even if you pull out or are forced out the day before the three years is up, you get nothing. This was the incentive to try hard, and to avoid any 'I'm not doing it and you can't make me' attitudes. Anyone who doesn't try to participate will be removed immediately and paid nothing.

Trembling, you re-read the opening of the letter just to make sure you have not made a mistake. It is now the fourth time you have read it and the words are still the same – you are accepted. Suddenly your excitement vanishes and is replaced by disbelief. The sum you were told you would get is not what they are offering now. This new sum is more, considerably more. And for a special reason.

The twelve hundred participants are to be divided into four groups of three hundred. Each one of these four groups will have a team leader and one of the leaders chosen is you. 'This is insane,' you say to yourself, 'I have never managed anything or anyone in my life.' This of course is all part of the experiment, but it sends shock waves through you.

'Your duties as team leader include organising work parties, maintaining social order, health and welfare, as well as deciding who will leave the group if that need arises. Your selection as team leader is not negotiable and you have until ten o'clock tomorrow morning to inform us of your reply. Your reply will consist of a single word, either "yes" or "no". Failure to accept this team leader position means you forfeit any place in this experiment and any future dealings with it. We look forward to your reply.'

This is why you are being paid extra. After a sleepless night weighing up all of your options you finally and nervously send your decision – 'yes'.

The following week in a large hall you gather with two hundred and ninety-nine other people to listen to your instructions. The splitting up of the twelve hundred participants into four groups has already taken place and the organisers are careful to make sure that none of the groups meet.

Your group, simply called group three, listens to what the organisers have to say. A woman standing on the stage walks to the microphone and begins.

'All three hundred of you will stay together as one single group. Each group is intended to mimic the concept of a tribe as it would have been thousands of years ago. Your job is simply to survive and to do the best you can within your group. Each tribe or group has been assigned a team leader and this team leader will serve and behave in the way a tribal chief would have in prehistoric times.

'The area where you will be staying is a vast area of privately owned property given to us by a philanthropist. It is now yours to do with as you will for the remainder of your time. You do not have to be environmentally conscious, in fact you can choose to tear the whole place down if that's what you want.

'The property is vast. It is a mountain that stretches down to the sea. Being near the ocean, the mountain catches the clouds, so significant rainfall is experienced on one side but not on the other. This gives us our four diverse ecosystems, or habitats. One is the upper half of the mountain itself. This is an alpine environment. The lower half of the mountain, rich in rainfall and soil, is a heavily wooded forest environment. The third, the one in which you will reside, is a coastal environment, and the fourth is the dry side of the mountain, where it is mainly open, flat pasture land.

'As you have probably worked out, the twelve hundred participants have been divided into four groups. Once you have been assigned to a group, you must stay in that group for the remainder of the experiment. Anyone disobeying this rule will be sent home and they will forfeit any payment. We have placed cameras in every camp so behaviour and compliance can be monitored. The rest we leave up to you.

'Each group has a team leader and their decisions must be obeyed.

However, if we feel they are turning from team leader to tyrant, they will be replaced. Anyone who is asked to leave, or who leaves of their own accord, will be sent home immediately, without remuneration.

'Each group's allocated area is one of the four ecosystems. From now on the groups will be referred to by the name of the habitat they dwell in. Group one is now the mountain group or mountain people, group two is the forest group or forest people, group three – that's you – are the coast group or coast people, while group four are the plains group or plains people.

'People from each group must reside with that group. This means you are free to talk and to meet people from other groups but you cannot live anywhere else but with the group to which you have been allocated.

'Now, this map shows the zones which represent each group's territory. For example you coastal people have this area here. That means this area of beach, together with the hinterland up to and including all this area, until the next section begins. Your section includes an estuary, some marsh land, a small, open, flat grassy area and the lightly forested woods extending to the upper part of the river.

'The river as you can see, winds its way down the mountain almost cutting it in two as it flows across the mountain face before heading in a southerly route toward the ocean. This is where your land stops and the forest group's land begins. In short the coastal side of the river is yours, while the forest side of the river is theirs.

'On the mountain, the forest continues upwards until it stops abruptly. Above the tree line is the home of the mountain group. Their territory ranges over the mountain top and down the other side to the ravine. Here their land stops and the land of the plains group begins. The ravine itself is only small and there is no real problem crossing it.

'The aim is simple. Try to cooperate with each other so you survive both as individuals as well as a group. Which laws you decide to create and enforce and the etiquette you choose to adopt is entirely up to you. There will be no outside interference unless life is at risk.

'You will be given some basic non-perishable food stores such as flour and rice, but only enough to last you for a few months. We estimate that you will have enough stores to live off for one month if you choose to eat from these stores entirely, or you could survive up to three months if you use them as a supplement to other food sources you can organise. It is up to you, but you must understand that if you run out of stores and no other food sources are available, we will not risk the lives of the group, and your involvement *as a group* will be cancelled. In this case, no one will receive payment, so it is in your best interest to begin establishing yourselves as quickly as possible.

'I think that just about covers everything so I will leave you to get organised. You have one week to prepare yourselves, say your goodbyes and do what you have to do. No one selected has any physical ailment so medical supplies are not necessary, and you are not permitted to carry any sort of drug, prescription or otherwise, not even a painkiller, as that would defeat the purpose of the experiment. If someone is badly injured they will be evacuated but that also means their contribution is over. Whenever someone is removed, evacuated or expelled from the group for whatever reason, fault or no fault, it is the historical equivalent of dying or being banished, which in previous times was the same as dying but just took a little longer.

'The rules allow you to bring one change of clothes but nothing else, and I can assure you that one change of clothes is one change more than what most people had back in the past. No books, pens, paper or anything from contemporary times are permitted, and all bags will be checked. Good luck and I wish you all well.'

After the speaker has finished you are brought on stage and introduced as team leader. It is explained that your selection was random and that your decision is law. Others can question, counsel and advise but all must adhere. Once a week, a member of the organising team will meet with you to check that everything is okay and to act according to your advice, although the extent of their action is limited. Occasionally you will be called on to make the tough decision of who can stay and who must go. The organisers will enforce this decision on your behalf.

Privately, you are told of some other rules and these are not discussed with the rest of the group. The first of these concerns food. If food supplies run too short, to the point of rationing, and rationing continues for more than one month, you must select people to leave the group. If rationing is severe because starvation is imminent, you can remove however many people you consider necessary. This will continue until you feel that the group's population has reached a sustainable level.

The next rule concerns behaviour. A group is a team and the happier and more content it is, the better it operates. If you believe someone constitutes a risk to the life or wellbeing of an individual or to the group, you and you alone have the power to remove them. All you need to do is tell one of the organisers when you next meet and they will take care of it. Punishment for wrongdoing is the responsibility of the team leader. However, should you misbehave or should the group get tired of you they may have you removed, but that cannot happen without cause.

The team leader has the right to assign specific people to specific tasks. You can choose to have advisors, or you can gather together a ruling body like the senate of ancient Rome, to look after the affairs of the group, but you are not allowed to abdicate. Now, with everything established and in place, it is time for the experiment to begin.

## The experiment

One of the first things you notice is the weather. It is summer but not excessively hot, although that could be because you are near the sea. It has only been a few hours since the landing and after a period of getting to know each other it is time to look around. Someone suggests that a fire should be lit and the group agrees so a few of the group gather driftwood while others spread out to have a look around.

Your stretch of beach is long and sandy. The water's edge is divided into two parts. Half of it is open water while the other half is a rocky shelf. When the tide is out this will leave a scattering of rock-pools and that is good news. About two hours later, the group begins to reassemble to discuss their findings.

The estuary is salty and extends up to the bend in the river where it begins to freshen. That also is good news. The woodland near the river is open forest and it's extensive so timber for firewood and hut building will not be a problem. Further down the beach, the flat land rises steeply and there are five caves in the cliff face. This is where the group will spend their first night.

Some of the group go off to scout for berries and other possibilities for food but come back with the report that nothing could be found. With night approaching it is agreed that a few should try to catch some fish, while others will bring wood to the caves for the first night's camp-out. But all the plans go wrong. Firstly, after trying for nearly two hours, the fishing party returns empty handed – there will be no food tonight. Even though the group has flour and rice, no one has collected any water and the caves are far from the fresh water above the river bend. On top of that, there are no pots, pans or buckets to carry the water in, even if someone had thought of it. You do have one box of matches, so at least a fire can be lit.

Moving into the caves seems a good idea at first. However, the people carrying the wood struggle to climb the cliff face, some of them even drop their loads into the water below. Storm clouds approach and soon the wind is howling. A strong onshore gale drives rain and sea-spray into the caves which are nowhere near as deep and protected as it first appeared.

With bellies rumbling and cold, wet bodies shivering, the first night of three years passes. Hardly anyone sleeps and over the course of the night, complaints turn to bitterness and tempers fray. Some begin to take charge, telling everyone what should be happening, stating how different things would be if they were in command. By morning, alliances have been made and loyalties divided. Groups have formed within the group and enemies created due to the cross words exchanged during the night. Some are pleading for calm while others want to go home – and it has only been twelve hours.

In the morning everyone comes out of the caves, assembles on the beach and looks to you. Clearly something has to be organised. The most basic of basics is food and shelter, so you arrange the group into separate units. The first is a large hunting group and the second a group to gather wood and keep the fire going, while the third you assign to make huts.

During the second day you learn some things you didn't know before. Firstly you learn that attempting to catch fish without hooks, bait or nets is an unproductive task. Secondly you learn that chopping down trees without an axe is just as difficult. Thirdly, because you still do not have any pots, you discover that uncooked rice is revolting.

Slowly but surely the group gathers its momentum and the first week finally passes. At first a few seem to be luckier than others at catching fish but you soon realise that it is not luck at all. In the evening when the tide is low, large schools of stingrays come into the shallows to feed. A man in the group works out a way to catch them by using a branch to pin them to the sea-floor, dragging them to the beach along the bottom and flicking them on to the sand, like a scoop.

Using sharp shells as knives, stingrays are cut and skinned and thrown on to the fire. Other hunters soon follow and stingrays are being caught continuously. Some hunters are good enough to catch one or two, while others catch five or six. After a few weeks it becomes clear which hunters are good, which are average and which are not very good at all. This is important knowledge and the continuing existence of the group depends on you understanding who is most skilled.

Although in raptures over of the taste of the meat in the cooked stingray wings, a woman in the group is alert enough to realise that the barb at the end of the stingray tail would make a good spear. Next morning she sets about making spears and soon some of the hunting party have weapons. Now, not only are stingrays being caught, but so too are other fish – all due to the spears.

The introduction of the spear means you now have to make your first real decision as leader. Who will get the spears and who will not? Obviously there are not three hundred spears, but then again not everyone fishes, but even for those who could fish, there are not enough spears to go around. The woman who makes the spears has managed to make a dozen throughout the day but that is hardly enough. So who gets the twelve spears? The twelve best hunters of course.

You are pleased with yourself. At first you thought you could never manage this role, you were sure it was more than you could handle, but you are feeling confident now that you have made the right decision and what's more, it was easy. You had already noticed that some of the hunting party were 'luckier' than others but you also know that when luck is consistent it probably isn't luck at all. Some people are just better hunters than others, so when it comes to deciding who should get the limited number of spears, the answer is obvious. The people to get the spears should be the ones who can make the most use of them. A good hunter with a spear can catch ten fish, while an average hunter may only be able to catch two or three. You have made the right decision and life proves it, because the catch made by the hunters who were given the spears increases markedly. The problem is that a dozen hunters with spears cannot feed three hundred people and food stores are still dropping rapidly.

What do you do? Do you take more people off firewood collection and water gathering and throw everyone into fishing and if so, how much does it really improve matters? After all, half the hunters out there are hardly catching anything at all and a small percentage catches nothing day after day.

Finally you realise the answer you are searching for. Once the spear was made it increased the hunters' catch, so the answer is not more hunters, it is better hunters, and the best way to do that is to provide the right tools. It is time for you to make an important decision and you think, 'If I can find some talented people to make weapons and tools, the hunters can be more productive.' So you decide to take some people away from fishing, but this turns out to be a bad mistake.

There are three extremely good hunters and you reason that they are the type of people who might be good at everything. After all if they can hunt well, maybe they can make spears just as well. Then perhaps you can build some real huts rather than the leafy piles of rubbish you are all forced by necessity to live in, but this doesn't turn out to be true. Most people are not good at everything even though some are. Most people are good at one or two things, capable at a number of others and not very good at all with what's left over.

When you take your three best hunters away from fishing and put them into tool making you notice that two of them are adequate at the job while the other, the best hunter, is terrible, and the daily catch drops significantly. You will never make that mistake again. On top of it all you can see that the three of them are nowhere near as happy when making tools as they are when they are fishing.

You are learning a lot about human nature and you are beginning to recognise individual strengths and weaknesses, which makes you a good and valuable leader. Early in your life you were taught that anyone can master anything, that we can achieve anything we want to, providing we work hard enough, but now in this practical world, you realise that is not true. Anyone can become capable if they work hard and practice, but you can see first hand that some people have a natural edge that puts their results above what hard work alone can achieve. What you now know is that while hard work beats lazy talent, nothing beats talent and hard work.

A few men and women have made jugs to carry water. They are very good with their hands and now the group does not have to huddle together round the water's edge getting on each other's nerves. You bring these people together with the woman who made the spears and ask them to devote their time to weapon making, which they happily agree to do because they hate fishing. Now your hunters are free to go back to the water and the catch immediately improves.

With a small number of people entirely devoted to making weapons, the number of spears, bows and arrows increases at a rapid rate. A number of other people come to you and express their interest in joining this craftsman group and you agree. As a result, within a few weeks there are over a hundred new spears and many bows and arrows and there is so much fish that none of the stores are required.

As wonderful as this is, man cannot live by fish alone – other food sources must be found. With fewer people catching more fish thanks to the new tools, others are free to help with other tasks and you decide to send them out to look for different types of food.

In the middle of the day a few of them return with handfuls of berries, so you give them an earthen water jug and off they go to gather some more. So you make another decision. You take one of the craftsmen away from making spears and put them on to making jugs to carry water. You do this so the gatherers have something in which to bring back the berries, without taking away necessary tools from the rest of the group.

So far, your management skills have been good and the group as a whole has gained in morale and strength. At first you had the whole group fishing and gathering, but although it was surviving the group was not really prospering. Then, by taking some people who were talented with their hands away from fishing and putting them to work crafting spears, bows and arrows, jugs and now fishing hooks, you increased the amount of food caught, allowing even more people to leave the hunting role to forage and gather for other types of food.

These people become known as the gatherers and many, although not all, do a wonderful job. Over time they learn about the different species of plants that grow in the area. While there are only small quantities of fruits and berries growing in this sandy soil, a woman in your group discovers an edible root vegetable. Not very tasty, but it sets like glue, so it keeps hunger pains at bay and that's a welcome contribution to a diet based on fish and the occasional berry.

The weather is becoming colder. Summer is clearly over and it is well and truly into autumn. Then one morning the wind starts picking up and soon it blows ferociously. The winds of summer came from the west but this wind blows from the east, and fish in your bay do not come close in to shore while a strong easterly is blowing. Each time the wind blows hard from this direction, the hunters come back empty handed. So far this has not been too much of a problem because you have been able to dry and smoke fish and have some reserves.

In the past the easterly usually stopped after a few days and hunters caught fish in record numbers as hunger forced the fish to swarm back into the shallows, but now it is the fourth day in a row. The week passes and you are now well into the next week and still the wind blows from the east and the catch is small. On top of this, the berries and fruits are also disappearing as the season changes, and all that is left is the vegetable you call 'glue root' and a few leftover stores.

By the third week you have placed the group on severe rationing. As usual you meet with the coordinators of the experiment as you do each week, but this time you must discuss the food shortage. It is clear that some people must leave the group or everyone will starve. You dreaded this moment but it has to be done and you know it.

You call your council together. Two people from each craft group who represent the others working in that field. The agenda of the council meeting is simple – when there is not enough food to go around, people have to go. The task is unpleasant and turning people into numbers unsavoury. In the past you would have been revolted by people who were forced to separate others, judging this behaviour as disrespectful to the sanctity of life, but now you are in this position and there is no other way.

Centuries before, this same event occurred time and time again but in those days it was for real. When food grew short, as it always did, people were expelled and banished so the remaining members of the group could survive. Sometimes people were killed outright and in extreme conditions homicide and infanticide were common practices until a famine subsided.

Once the council sits down, you begin.

'The predicament we find ourselves in is obvious. Fish catches are insufficient, reserve stocks are already running low and the summer fruits are now out of season. Something has to be done and we cannot wait any longer, there are simply too many mouths to feed. So as I see it, we only have two options, but I will be happy to hear any other ideas. Our first option is to stay unified as a group and hope that our luck will change, or we can begin the task of eliminating people from the group.'

'How many would have to go?' someone asks.

'I am not sure of numbers, that's something we will have to discuss later. What I am after now is certainty of direction. Do we tough it out as a group or do we sacrifice a few for the many?'

'The trouble with sticking it out as a tribe,' a woman representing the craftsman group answers, 'is that the rules state that if our food supplies drop to unsustainable levels and the whole group is in danger, they will pull the plug on us all and we'll all go home empty handed.'

'That's true,' you answer, 'they were quite specific about that.'

Another of the council interjects, 'But that seems stupid. Why would they pull the whole group out, wouldn't that ruin the experiment?'

'No, not really,' the woman replies, 'it was common in the past for whole tribes to die out due to changing conditions or mismanagement. You have to remember that they are trying to replicate history so they can have a better idea of what may have happened. To us this is a game, a competition that we are all trying to win so as we can be rewarded at the end, but for them, the agenda is different. If we can't make it, maybe that means that one quarter of the population that struggled to hang on to life failed also. I don't know what it all means, all I know is we are in real trouble and my vote is that people should go.'

'This is not a democracy,' you remind them, 'there is no voting here, just opinion, the decision itself is mine and mine alone.'

'Then my advice is to reduce the number of people in the group,' the woman replies.

'Okay,' you continue, 'is there anyone who disagrees with cutting numbers and thinks we should tough it out as a group?'

No-one replies, it is unanimous, people must go.

'We cannot make this decision lightly,' you add, 'the people we choose are going to lose a lifetime's worth of money, and for some this was their last chance. You are the leaders of the different work groups so I want to know who you think should go.'

At this point you sit back and watch as talk turns to argument, and argument turns to anger, and it is here that you intervene.

'This is getting us nowhere. The problem is that we are talking about individual personalities, whether we like them or not, but I don't think that should be our first consideration. I have done a lot of thinking regarding this and it is my firm belief that personality, at least at this stage should be taken out of the decision. What we do not want is another debacle like what happened when I took the best hunters out of the water and put them on to spear making. I must be very sure in my own mind, and I can't believe I'm even saying this, that the people we send home are expendable. All of us must come together and discuss honestly who is valuable to the group and who is not. This is not a game where one person wins; we only win if *all* of us make it to the end. We must make sure that no one valuable leaves.'

'Define valuable,' someone asks.

'Well, by valuable I mean skilled. Take the hunters for example. While most people catch something every now and again, only a few people catch something every day. Surely if we have to banish someone, it should be someone who doesn't catch much. I mean what is the point of sending home someone who is good at providing us all with food?'

This type of logic is impossible to refute because deep down everyone knows it is the truth. Why would the group get rid of the skilled and the hard working? As tough and as ruthless as it seems, the least skilled and the lazy must go first.

Stores and fresh food supplies are almost exhausted and everyone is continuously hungry, so together with your council you decide on some radical measures. You are going to cut the group by one hundred people in one swift motion. This figure is agreed upon by all as the minimum number needed to get a positive effect. You now begin to understand the impact of history, where famine or disease would slash the population.

All through the night you and your council argue and debate about who should stay and who ought to go. In the end it becomes a discussion about who is the least productive and the most likely to avoid work.

While many are busy there are always some who make themselves scarce. They either don't work at all, fail to show up or work so poorly they may as well not be there. The lazy and the absent are now on their way home but they have friends who still remain, discontented and frustrated because of the departures.

A few weeks later with the fish not biting and fruits out of season, many of the remaining group take the opportunity to help build bigger and better huts from the ti-tree. Each person is down to half a cup of rice a day, some glue root and one small piece of flat bread made from flour and water. Morale is very low.

Then, as quickly as it started, the east wind stops blowing and a few days later the fish return to the bay. Many bemoan the timing. If the change had occurred earlier the group would still be complete but how was anyone to know? Soon there is a big enough catch for everyone to have at least one decent meal a day and not long after, fish and shellfish together with clams, mussels and oysters are all being harvested at a rapid rate, and you now have a surplus. Next time you will not be caught unprepared and the salting and smoking of fish is done at a frenetic pace.

The flour and rice are put away for future desperate times. You are proud of your decision and believe you were right to cut numbers. With fish and other seafood preserved, stores do not have to be touched and your group is again in good shape.

The gatherer group has been cut down in numbers and some have been reassigned into hunting and craft. Trying to do their best, some of the gatherers decide that desperate times call for desperate measures, and cross the river to scout for food in the forest group's land.

After traveling for some time, the scouting party smells wood-smoke and realises they are near the forest group's camp. Some are nervous about being on forest land uninvited, but the party agrees to make their introductions. Two of your group ask whether the forest group is short of any supplies. What each group hasn't known until now is that different supplies were allocated to each group. Everyone has assumed that all groups were given the same.

On their return the scouting party tell you what transpired. Because the forest is usually more bountiful, the organisers had decided that the forest group should receive less food but more implements. As a result they have a surplus of axes and shovels but due to low rainfall they are desperately short on food. In fact, the forest group has sent one hundred and fifty people home in order to survive, fifty percent more than your own radical measures.

The self-appointed leader of the scouting party has a long discussion with you about the possibility of trade, and when you agree, they start their return visit laden with salted and smoked fish. Three days later they return with as many axes, shovels and knives as they could carry. Up till now the craftsmen had been using axes made from shells and sharp rock but now they had real tools.

Since the gatherers' first visit to the forest group, trade has taken place regularly and now you have more axes than you need, so it is time to establish a group of traders for the purpose of trading what you require rather than making everything yourself.

Traveling without permission through the forest group's land, some of the traders go past the tree line to the mountain group, while others keep moving until they reach the plains people.

The mountain group were given no food or tools; they received goats, sheep, tents and a number of buckets. The plains people were given some food, seeds and established plants.

Over the next few months your allocated traders deal with all three other groups and build your supplies to a level where you now have some, albeit minimal, comfort. However, to keep trading your group must keep providing fish or you will receive nothing in return. On a number of occasions supplies still run precariously low and each time this occurs, people are expelled.

Those left are trying hard to not upset others in their group or to fall behind in their responsibilities; all fear the next expulsion could be them.

Throughout history this same event has occurred over and over again as groups and tribes went through periods of feast and famine. The fear of rejection that resides in us stems from this heritage; so too does a sense of responsibility, as well as the need for approval.

To the organisers of the experiment, events are moving along according to plan. Of course, society is going to develop differently in this controlled environment, so how history actually unfolded can never be really known, but so far it is a good start. The people in this experiment bring their existing knowledge to their group, something that in historical times people had to accumulate over time.

With winter's arrival, life becomes more desperate for all, but especially for the snowed-in mountain people, since much of the feed for their animals disappears. The mountain area has a supply of small tough plants and grasses suitable for the warmer months but in winter the land is infertile. Even the plants that exist in the summer time are far too few and woody for human consumption. The mountain group survive by living off the animals that live naturally in this environment, using their milk, blood and meat as food. Only goats and sheep can live from the meagre growth found in the mountains.

The mountain people and their animals are suffering. In desperation they drive the herd down the mountain onto the plains so their animals can feed, but this is not their land and the plains group had cultivated much of it. The plains people use this land because it is less arid and crops grow easily and quickly. The sheep and goats destroy a large part of their crop and the plains people demand recompense, because they too are facing hardship and shortage, but the mountain group have nothing to give. Retreating back into the mountains many of the group herd their animals back down to the plains at night; if they don't, their animals will die and they will lose everything.

The farmers know the animals are eating their crops, but the organisers can't interfere. There are often altercations both within groups and more frequently between groups. Envy and desperation develops when the traders bring back stories of access to animals, grain and implements that the others do not have. On a few occasions small parties attempt to steal from another group and all groups have to implement some protection. The plains people, left with no other choice after the invasion of the mountain pain and heal wounds. Their actions replicated history's role of the shaman and the priest.

With the coming of another spring tensions ease. The snow on the higher peaks begins to melt away exposing the grasses underneath. In the mountains goats and sheep give birth to kids and lambs and flocks increase by a third within months. At last the mountain group can relax and find food for their animals without the necessity of encroachment.

Flocks of ducks and water fowl arrive. In the forest birds, pigs and deer are abundant. On the plains the established plants are flowering ready to sprout fruit in the summer, while vegetables including corn are growing in the surviving fields.

Not content to sit back and wait, you make a very interesting decision. Bird stocks are replenishing but it will take many months to return to healthy levels especially when you take into account natural predators and hardships; eggs are eaten by snakes and chicks are taken by hawks. Ducks are a welcome change and are becoming a staple in the diet of the group. Both their meat and eggs are sought after and no-one wants to go back to just fish. You decide to domesticate ducks.

A woman in your group is used to dealing with animals. She knows how to clip wings and hatch eggs, so you put her in charge of organising a group to help her while the craftsmen get busy preparing hatcheries and fences. The people needed for this new role must be suitable if the task is to be accomplished successfully. Bird domestication requires patience, nurturing, management and protection.

After several months she and her helpers are making great progress and the operation is hailed as a success. The hatchlings, because they were raised by hand, have bonded with their handlers and now follow them wherever they go. Soon they will be mature enough to breed and other hatchlings will follow. By next winter there will be enough ducks and swans to supply meat and eggs for the entire group.

Your traders in their dealings have bartered food for seeds. As part of their original survival package, the plains group were given a large supply of seeds. This included grains and vegetables as well as a variety of established fruit trees. As a result the plains group crave meat so fish, oysters and ducks become a valued delicacy. The people in charge of the

During winter the situation looks set to explode and the organisers are ready to call the experiment off, but spring relaxes those pressures. What everybody learns is how reactive human beings are. We all like to think of ourselves as separate units, people who can cope and manage their own lives regardless of the feelings, moods and actions of others, but now everyone realises this perception is very limited. The winter shows that when one group acts, all must act in response, and if one is tense, all are tense.

It takes a while for you to realise just how important this understanding is. You had been taught throughout your life to 'get on with your own business and not to worry about anybody else.' Independence, and not letting the opinions or moods of others affect you, were regarded as virtues. But now you know that when someone living with you is stressed, then everyone will be stressed. It is impossible for human beings to not react to changes in their environment, and their environment consists not just of the physical world, but of the people around them.

The development of the warrior comes as a surprise to the organisers. They think that the threat of expulsion is enough to deter people from threatening others, and so there would not be a need for protection and security. What they don't count on is the weather. Snowfalls are heavier and come sooner than expected, leaving all the groups unprepared and although actual violence does not occur, the threat of it is very real.

Another surprise is what happens during those cold evenings by the fire when a few members of the group inspire everyone else with their stories of faith and their willingness to accept hardship along with success. A few begin to provide a counselling role and basic health services. A small, dedicated group establish a retreat. The retreat is built, maintained and supplied by supporters. This retreat gradually comes to provide essential support for the community. Not so much physical support as spiritual support. The combination of prayer and meditation, teaching, counselling and help for the sick makes the retreat a common meeting ground for people from all four groups. The organisers allow the retreat to continue because it is a part-time church and hospital that is staffed by people who continue to function as active members of their group. These people acquired an extensive knowledge of various herbs and plants, to alleviate

And so the year passes. The groups have by now become well established and trade regularly with each other. The plains people have started crop farming while the mountain people shepherd their animals; hunters still dominate both in the forest and on the coast while craftsmen and traders play an important role in the lives of all. During spring, summer and autumn, life is pretty good on the whole.

But now winter is approaching again and you realise the flimsy wood provided by the ti-trees and wattles and other light coastal shrubs is not enough for proper housing. However, thanks to a bountiful ocean and a river-estuary you have an abundance of fish, shellfish, ducks and swans as well as other water birds. Your traders now swap goods for services and the forest group send cut logs from large forest trees down the river in exchange for a variety of food. Now you have more protective shelter as well as full bellies.

As the winter worsens the forest group also establishes a security force to protect their land and stores because both the mountain and the plains groups are encroaching onto their land. When the sheep and goats eat the growing crops they eat much of the plains group's food supply. This forces both the mountain and plains people into the forest in search of food, but the forest is having difficulty supporting one group, let alone three. It is not long before your own hunters reported dwindling bird stocks from the estuary, as well as sightings of foreign hunters in your bay.

Despite the alarm, you play down suggestions of retaliation and embargoes, deciding instead to wait and see how events pan out, but when for the first time ever your hunters come back empty handed from the estuary, without so much as an egg, you have to act. You need security of your own and you need it quickly, otherwise all the bird life will be gone and there will be too few to breed up the stocks you need.

Protectors are different from hunters because the job requires a different personality. Hunters have to be quiet, subtle and patient, whereas security needs an obvious presence. They are stronger, louder and more controlling, so you pick a group of louder, stronger and more forceful people. With their determined and overt personalities protecting the stock, bird numbers once again begin to rise. Your ability to get the right people for the right task is your group's greatest strength.

people and their animals, form a security force. As happened in history, the need for the warrior begins.

The plains group now find themselves in a predicament. A sub-group has developed, consisting of a small number of people who are loud and aggressive. At their last meeting, the plains council decided the sub-group had to be broken up. Some wanted to be rid of them but others wanted them to stay as they were hard and diligent workers. The trouble was, they drove many in the group too hard and expected everyone to have the same endurance they had. They were exhausting and with their surplus of energy, competitive and driven.

The plains council thinks of banishing this sub-group, but then they have a better idea; the sub-group can become the group's security. They have the endurance to patrol the long distances required, as well as the attitude and demeanour to deal with potentially volatile situations.

The mountain people of course, reply with a strategy of their own and form their own group of 'heavies' with the express purpose of taking food. You know of all these events because your traders tell you when they return. The mountain people are not actually bad or doing the wrong thing by stealing food from other groups. Maybe the plains people are bad and selfish for not sharing?

You understand that dividing life into good and bad is irrelevant and confusing and leads to failure of understanding. The plains people are not selfish, they are protecting what they have, and the mountain people are not bad, they're hungry. If the mountain group do not get food for their animals the organisers will fail them and a lifetime's worth of money is lost, but if the plains group give them their reserve, they have no reserve of their own. One more calamity and they are out. Everyone must protect their own self interest because scarcity of resources demands it.

Even in the forest, food becomes scarce over winter but at least there is enough, when combined with the food you trade to them, to keep the forest people going. Your own tribe, the coastal group, are faring well and have developed largely because of your good management. You realised early that people have strengths and weaknesses and you put people into tasks appropriate to their skills and personality. That means your tribe is the most productive of all.

ducks, swans and water birds do such a good job that soon there are more birds and eggs than the group can use, so a number of live ducks are carried by traders to the plains group in exchange for seeds.

The vegetables the plains group had grown finished their season and turned to seed. Now that you have these new seeds, you decide to take a number of people away from foraging with the gathering group and put them in charge of growing a garden. Soon your coastal group is growing its own plant food. The soil is sandy and the garden could never provide self-sufficiency for the group but the roots added to your diet are beneficial.

As you experience the renewal of your last spring of the experiment, you take stock of the situation you are now in. For the last year or so, life has been comfortably secure. Once you had passed the half-way mark, you began to realise that things were starting to settle down. You had a sustainable food supply, and people were feeling fairly content. The threat of violence diminished as it became clear that those left would survive until the end of the experiment. You made it through the third winter with no real troubles. But how different things are now to when you set out on this adventure nearly three years ago.

At the beginning of the experiment, twelve hundred people were taken to a remote spot with a bare minimum of provisions and told to survive on their own. Three years later the experiment is concluding with four thriving, interacting, self-supporting communities. But there are no more than two hundred people left. If the experiment really does represent the development of human history then an important insight has been gained; the majority of human beings did not survive. Your group consists of just fifty people by the experiment's end, even though you had started with three hundred.

The development of sustainable resources dominated the time of the group and only by extending beyond hunter-gathering to developing tools, domesticating animals and trading goods and services were these sustainable levels reached. By the time these levels were reached, five sixths of the group were no longer present. If this figure was the same as real history, more people died or were rejected than the number who stayed and lived on.

Another insight was the necessity of skill and cooperation. Each time resources became short, somebody had to leave and it was your job to select who would stay and who would go. Because of this, the group was not a particularly happy place as people competed with each other in their struggle to remain included. Many times you contemplated what it must have been like in real history, where banishment and rejection meant starvation and death; not just losing a game. What made people in the experiment struggle and compete was the amount of money on offer, but in real life banishment meant the end.

You also learned a lot about yourself and social interaction. You learned that surviving the elements is only part of the struggle. Before the experiment, you thought survival meant shelter, food and water and protection from animals, but now you understand that survival also comes from harmonious living. You came to understand that people's greatest survival tool is each other, and as team leader it became obvious to you how much human beings depended on the skills of others.

Before the experiment you thought that being a hermit and only needing to feed yourself would be an easier life than having to provide for a group, but you soon learned this was not the case. You now realise that the reason human history is filled with tribes, towns and cities is because we are communal creatures who depend on the assistance of others.

Without hunters the group would have starved, but without craftsmen the hunters would have no weapons. Without the trader your diet would not be varied enough to survive and shelters from wood would not exist. Without the domesticating role of the shepherd, goats, so important to the mountain group's diet, would remain wild, while the farmer's fruits, vegetables, berries and grains are the staff of life. The warrior ensures the hard work and welfare of the group is protected while the priest tends to the sick and reminds people there is more to life than food. Anything less, and human beings will not survive and culture will not flourish.

As you reflect on your experience, the difference between the past and present becomes strong. You were raised in a rich and peaceful country. This means you were getting adequate pay, sick days, and food and water to spare, variety and the luxury of boredom. But your days with nothing to do stopped abruptly with the beginning of the experiment, and so too did being selective about food. Sick or not, everyone got out of bed. Not contributing meant forfeiting and going home because there was never enough food to go around and no one wanted to share with someone who gives nothing back.

Before the experiment, examples of taking and abundance were all around you. People complained about their purchases and were fussy about food. They craved and they desired and there was insatiable indulgence. You never realised how good plain fish could taste until you ate some after three days of nothing but rain water. You never appreciated the importance of a roof that doesn't leak until you spent a night in the rain, and you now understand why the refrigerator was invented.

But you also learned a number of other things. For a start you learned reliance both on yourself and others. You learned to see beyond the exterior of people and to look at their skills. You learned how to cooperate and the deep and lasting happiness of contribution. In the spoilt life of modern times it is impossible to explain the thrill of catching a fish or picking fruit that you have grown. It is almost impossible for others to understand the depth of the bonds that are forged in a group that relies completely on the skills and character of each other.

Through the course of the experiment your personality also changed. You used to be far more accepting and far more liberal but that is no longer the case. It was not long before you became intolerant of people who didn't contribute and your attitude of 'live and let live' hardened. Yet at the same time your appreciation for those who were making the most of what they had increased. Self-importance faded as quickly as excess weight and the levelling of the social status of every participant made friendships easier. At this stage you were all competing with nature rather than each other.

Then times got hard and people were expelled. It was your role to 'play God', to pick and choose. The lazy and uncooperative went first, then the unpleasant and threatening. Finally everything came down to skill and how likeable and cooperative each remaining person was. If two craftsmen had the same degree of skill at making weapons but one of them had to go, it would be the one that could not turn their hand to anything else but weapon making. If both were equally versatile, then the one to go would be the one least liked, or the one with the most uncompromising attitude. If two hunters had the same quick reflexes the smarter and more likeable would remain while the other would go home.

It soon became apparent that to protect the group was to protect yourself. The more anyone contributed, the more the group wanted them to stay, after all no one is going to remove a person who provides a valuable service and is willing to share. In a life where each is dependent on the other, contribution is everything. Sharing goods and effort is the most valuable commodity we have for our own survival. In a game where so much is at stake and contestants are being eradicated continuously, it is vital to be liked and to be held in high regard. Fear of rejection is ever present but everyone had to overcome that fear. 'Do what you have to do, no matter what,' was the chant in everyone's mind. Hard work got you through the tough times so harder work will get you through tougher ones.

You came to see that, just as in the natural world, diversity is the key to human survival and it became imperative that the remaining players find a niche that they were best fitted to. Because you were in the position where you did the choosing, you could see that the most secure people were the ones who were the best at what they did.

And so the experiment finishes. Once you have begun to settle back into the modern world, but before you lose track of the issues that have been so important to you in the previous three years, the organisers arrange a de-briefing session. They have many observations they want to discuss and are keen to hear your insights as to how your society evolved.

The organisers explain that your community, for that is what it had become, had developed all seven of the traditional roles. They had expected that only the five practical, 'productive' roles would develop as they had throughout human history. These traditional roles are the hunter, the farmer, the trader, the shepherd and the craftsman. The two other traditional roles, the warrior and the priest, historically play just as important a role, but the organisers did not expect them to develop in this experiment. They were wrong. Your community had developed both warriors and priests.

Historically, once agriculture and trading towns became established so too did an organised army. The militia, citizens who either volunteer or are drafted into the army, were no longer adequate because they could not compete against trained soldiers. Nations and cities with an organised army soon over-ran those that did not have protection, and from east to west the samurai and knight became a social class of their own. The role of the warrior is not just about war; sometimes it is not even about fighting. It is about protection and security. The warrior class flourished on every continent, but it was not the only traditional role to develop into an impregnable social class.

During the experiment, in only two short years, with food and shelter at a premium a spiritual movement began. The workers at the retreat had effectively become priests. The organisers were interested to note that the retreat was not supported by everybody and some thought it was a waste of time and resources. Only a small number were regular adherents and devotees, the majority supported the retreat because of its works, not its theology. They supported the retreat because the retreat supported others by helping with sickness and injury.

The role of the priest is about connecting with God. History is often dry and simplistic when it comes to religion, and attributes its development to a weak-minded desire for caution. The warrior creates security in this world while the priest creates security in the next. If groups have someone who can connect with God, then they have privileged access to the forces that bring a better harvest or better weather. Contemporary history views the priest as a tribal talisman, a charm to ward off evil and prevent calamity. In short, history's priest is an insurance policy.

If the definition of the priest stops here, it stops half way. Religious doctrine has God creating mankind in God's own image, as if God were lonely and needed company and purpose. 'God creates mankind, because God needs us.' However, God also exists because we need God. People need to believe there is truth and order, that life continues beyond the grave, and that life is not a waste of time. People need to believe that life did not occur against all odds but occurred because it was wanted. People want to know they are a soul as well as a collection of cells; that they have meaning and a right to exist. They want to know they are looked after and that someone cares. Whether these beliefs are a delusion or not, at a very deep level within our unconscious mind, this is what people want.

Stranded in the world of the experiment, and away from the flashing lights and instant entertainment of the modern western world, many participants began gaining what they believed was a deeper understanding and appreciation of life. Instead of being isolated from their most basic origins, people mingled with the life force of nature. They watched birds hatch and plants grow, seeds sprout and eagles fly. They watched the weather change and the sun set. At night, they saw the stars shining just as they had for millions of years, and they began to wonder. Spirituality developed as naturally and as easily as it first did in prehistoric times.

When you first came home you felt confused. At first you thought it was the endless variety and constant stimulation of modern society. In the experiment life was simple and there were few choices. Once back in the real world you felt overwhelmed by shops and supermarkets but there was something else that was making you feel puzzled. Suddenly it dawned on you.

You realised that people, here in the modern world, were competing with each other in exactly the same way as they did during the experiment. This was an epiphany, a moment of such rare clarity that you were taken aback by your own revelation. Regardless of the fact that the world now lives in surplus, people behave as if there isn't enough to go around!

During the experiment you lived through times of extreme hunger as well as through times of adequacy and sometimes plenty, so you recognised the difference each situation had on behaviour. People are different in times of famine; they are highly stressed and aggressively competitive while in feast times they are relaxed and more forgiving. Historically, as the experiment showed, more people died or were expelled than actually survived, and the ones that did survive did so by constant effort.

In the human history of feast and famine, it is famine that is most dominant and it is famine that nature must guard against. This is so obvious you wonder why you had not thought of it before. Nature does not have to protect you against good times; it only has to strengthen and prepare you against bad. When nature passes on character traits from one generation to the next, it passes on memories and helpful hints to see you through bad times, not the good ones. Good times look after themselves but bad times can put you in the grave.

Human beings have a long history of feast and famine and the odds of survival have always been slim. As a result, people compete with each other every day regardless of resources. During the tough famine times –

which was most of the time – the behaviour of people in the experiment was predictable, and that behaviour is exactly the same as the behaviour you witness at home in your contemporary society. Suddenly you understood; whether you are locked away in an experiment or it is everyday life, people behave in the same way because they have a history of scarcity in their unconscious and a survival instinct that makes them all compete whether they want to or not.

In the experiment only the last fifty people in each group were really comfortable because the available resources were adequate for the population. Before that time everyone was focussed on avoiding the next expulsion and nerves were on edge. People often displayed an attitude of, 'It's either me or you'. Competition meant you had to win the approval of others', by contributing and working hard, or perhaps by running others down; some did both. A shortage of resources meant expulsion, just as it did throughout history, when the threat of expulsion and death were always present, and life had to be managed as if calamity was inevitable. Much of the world's population continues to walk the tightrope of life and death.

Life depends on the goodwill of others because human beings cannot make it as individuals on their own. Who does the hunting while you keep the fire alight or fetches water while you sew? Who makes shelter while you plant, or utensils while you tend to the animals? Tribes, villages and cities are all testaments to the fact that we are reliant on the skill and support of others. If we could do it all we would not be communal creatures, we would be living as loners or in small family groups as bears and leopards do. Human beings could never have come this far without living in groups, but being in a group comes at a price and that means we must stay in favour. Human beings have been living this way forever; it is necessary and ingrained and it is passed on from one generation to the next as instinct.

The experiment was designed to find out how human culture developed and the organisers succeeded in their aim, but you had no such aspirations. All you wanted was to be there at the end so you could pick up a lifetime's worth of income, but you got far more than you bargained for. You were not searching for answers but you found them anyway. The organisers may know how human culture developed, but you have learned the answer to the ultimate question – what makes people do the things they do.

Every person has a survival instinct based on millions of years of collective learning. Everyone alive today is a legacy of those who survived before, and we carry inside us all the strategies nature can provide for longevity and effective competition. When times become hard, for whatever reason, we revert to this instinct because it is how we have survived the tough times of the past. The survival instinct's sole purpose is to keep us alive and help us compete for resources within a group setting. For someone living in modern western society, the threat is no longer famine – it is now all those things that we call 'stress' that trigger our survival instinct. By understanding our own survival instinct we can become better and more confident people as we learn to harness our skills. We will interact more effectively and understand the motivation behind our desires. Most of all, we can use this knowledge to truly appreciate ourselves and those around us.

During the experiment, you came to realise that just as in the natural world organisms survive by finding the niche that they are best fitted to, so too human beings survive in social groups by finding the niche that best suits them. It is these niches that we return to when we feel stressed or threatened. These niches are where our strengths become apparent to us and to others, and where we are able to do our best. They are the arena where we can best compete with others, they are our 'not so level' playing field where we have a better chance of winning.

This book tells you how to identify your own strengths as well as the strengths in others. It will identify and clarify which instincts against expulsion are still residing within your unconscious mind, why you have certain triggers that 'set you off' and why certain themes keep recurring in your life.

Perhaps you have someone you love but you find it difficult to communicate with them. It seems that each time you approach a subject everything explodes into tears or defensive anger. These things happen because you each have different forces and different memories stored in your unconscious, and unless you understand this, communication will always remain difficult. In relationships stress is frequent, and by the end of this book you will know why. The greater the difference between your unconscious memory – that is your survival instinct – and that of your spouse or partner, the more stressed you become and the more distant you grow. Soon you will know why this is so and how to manage it appropriately.

By the end of this book you will know what your natural survival instinct is, what drives it, and why. You will understand how others see you, and what you need to do in order to communicate effectively. You will understand what it is like to be in someone else's shoes.

This book teaches you a system to recognise and evaluate the fundamental forces that reside in us all, and determine how we respond whenever the pressure is on. You will be able to determine, by reading facial features, how other people look at life. You will be able to analyse and understand needs and motivations, how to keep people satisfied and how to talk in their language.

You will be able to decide which combination of seven specific categories everyone, including yourself, belongs to. This knowledge can be applied to any circumstance or environment. It can be used to enrich personal relationships and it is vital knowledge for parents. Educators can use this knowledge to improve learning by making their teaching specific to the needs of their students. Our health can improve when we understand the ancient, ingrained responses we have to stress, and the effect of living constantly with stress. In the world of business, being able to understand what is driving other people can lead to greater results in sales and marketing, or better strategies for dealing with your competitors.

The greatest experiment in history is ready and waiting for you to join.

All that remains is for you to open your mind and turn the page.

# Chapter 2

# THE POLITICS OF SURVIVAL

As the 'experiment' in Chapter 1 highlighted, individuals survive by existing in groups, while survival of the group depends in turn on individual skills. In order for an individual to become an important member of the group a talent, quality, personality or skill of value must be provided.

The ending of a friendship, the breakdown of a marriage or social revolution – all have the same basic cause even though that cause may be manifested in a thousand different ways. What they have in common is that for the people involved, the 'getting' is out of proportion to the 'giving'.

When someone gets more than they deserve, trouble begins. From a member of the nobility being beheaded to a partner walking out of a marriage, the root cause is always the same and it stems from the experience of a thousand or more generations of famine.

Inside the survival instinct rests the memory of near starvation and what was needed to outlast that close-to-death experience. Contribution is the only way social progress can develop and continue.

## The survival instinct

The survival instinct is in charge of the body. It is a force or motion that animates physical form making it reactive and responsive. The survival instinct performs two essential roles. The first is to keep the physical body in balance and the second is to defend its position. The most reactive, responsive and communicative parts of the body are where the dominant force expresses itself most. Everyone has a survival instinct. Without it we cannot live.

The survival instinct is endowed with two separate strategies. The first is an 'attack response'. The second is a 'famine response'.

The attack response is fairly well-defined and is over in a short time. It is a bit like the body's response to an acute illness. The reason for this is simple. The victim of acute disease, just as the victim of an animal attack, has only one objective, to escape or fight off the attacker. Whether it is a virus or a lion, the objective is the same – get away from it or kill it.

The famine response is more complicated. It draws on all the different ways a person has for ensuring that the group sees them as being valuable. It is a long-term response. Like the body's response to chronic disease, it requires a complex and coordinated approach. With chronic disease, whole body systems can be thrown into confusion, and to interfere with one system means interfering with others. Patients with chronic disease can testify to the problems new medicines create. Many feel as if their lives are taken over by the regimen of pills and potions, each designed to offset the negative effects caused by the other. Famine acts in the same way as chronic disease because it affects the community, not just the individual. It does not come from a single source like infection or attack, but from a complicated interplay of environment and politics. Famine, like chronic disease, results in a complete structural breakdown unless solutions can be found quickly.

Throughout human history, famine has been a more consistent and more common experience than attack. Consequently it is famine that the survival instinct has become best adapted to and it is famine for which it has evolved the most beneficial, efficient and complex strategies.

In famine, the response of the survival instinct is twofold – firstly, readjusting emotional personality and secondly, emphasizing talent and contribution.

Emotional personality includes moods and behavior that have an expressive base such as anger, weepiness or fear. When people are in balance it means their rational soul is in control of the majority of the decision making. The survival instinct can never be switched off, otherwise we would not respond to danger when appropriate and that could be fatal. The survival instinct is not always in charge but it is always on the alert, and when conditions call for it, it must respond immediately.

When energy levels remain constantly low the survival instinct moves into famine mode and a sophisticated structure of measures and actions is immediately put in place. What the survival instinct is trying to achieve is the same result, regardless of the variations in methods it takes. At its most basic, the situation is this:

- Individuals can only survive in groups.
- When famine is severe the group cannot sustain the same number of people as it did when food was abundant.
- The first measure is the rationing of food but if famine continues and food becomes desperate, it is more beneficial for a few to have enough, than for everyone to die a slow death from starvation.
- The group must decrease its numbers, otherwise everyone will die.
- The first to go are the sick and the weak.
- The next are those who take more from the group than what they give to it.
- Those who provide as much as they take are expelled before those who can provide more than they take.
- Of those who provide more than they take, the people most socially accepted and liked are better protected than those who are socially awkward or loners.

In modern times these strategies still exist and shape how we react in difficult situations. The more tired we become and the harder we work, the more our energy reserves run down allowing the survival instinct to take command. In this lowered state we are back in famine conditions and anyone we think is 'taking it easy' becomes the enemy. To those whose survival instinct is positioned second to their rational consciousness, our behaviour is considered as bad tempered and unwarranted, but the person in 'famine mode' is not thinking at all. Famine conditions make people hostile, creating 'us or them' behaviour and everyone is forced to comply – there are no exceptions.

People who are strong or skilled survive much better than people who are not, while people who are social as well as skilled are more highly regarded than those with skill alone. To be loved, liked and wanted is not just a desire of the soul. It is an important component of the survival instinct.

Contribution is the memory that lies in the survival instinct and this memory is the cause of both divorce and revolutions. Individuals survived famine times by remaining in the group, and they were allowed to remain because they contributed something of value. When individuals contribute to a group, it is in the best interests of the group to keep them around. Deep in our unconscious instinct rests the understanding that effort and security are related. The harder we try to work and contribute, the more food and security we expect in return. When someone does not contribute we get angry because it elicits a response deep in the survival instinct. Existence without contribution is a drain on the group's resources and the more the survival instinct is dominant the more it reacts to this type of behaviour.

There are a number of common ways in which individuals can make their position in a group more secure.

## Learning and ability

Knowledge can be divided into two categories; primary knowledge that forms part of the survival instinct and secondary knowledge which consists of learned skills. The ability to learn is a primary attribute and is passed down as a survival tool. The skills learnt during life are secondary information and that depends on being taught.

While every person has the ability to learn, personal attributes are also important. Each person can be taught how to build but not everyone can build with equal finesse. Desire and willpower are vital ingredients to success in any given area but a good work ethic combined with natural ability is better than a solid work ethic without talent. It is nature that gives natural ability and it is up to the individual to then recognise and improve upon this talent. We are all born with the same muscles in our legs but we are not all born with the same desire to run or endure the pain required to complete a marathon. We can train ourselves to complete a marathon if we set our heart and our mind to the task but this does not mean that we are on our way to the Olympics.

One problem we face is that life is finite and the time needed to become proficient in everything simply does not exist. The benefit of living in groups is that each individual can use the natural skill of others to supplement the shortfall in themselves. In this way a craftsman skilled at making weapons but average at hunting can complement a proficient hunter who is poor in using tools. A tribe is like a rainforest that survives by diversity. There are plants that can only continue to exist by the birds and insects they attract; they are pollinated by bees or their seeds are spread in the droppings of birds. Human groups, like the rainforest, flourish from cooperative diversity.

Natural attributes make us adept at the tasks which the group needs to survive. Gathering requires endurance and strength, while hunting needs alert senses and patience; scavenging requires a mind that can put two and two together, while tool making demands dexterity and consistency. For groups to survive through hard famine times, they need individuals who are skilled, not people who are just adequate. In good times people can relax and adequacy can be tolerated, but adequacy is dangerous when the group is in crisis and shedding numbers due to a shortage of food. Sharing always comes first, but rationing cannot continue if there is no food to share. Rather than everyone dying a slow death, like lost sailors in a drifting boat, the decision is made and someone must be sacrificed. However unlike the sailors there is no drawing the short straw. Survival in a group is not a game of chance; it is an environment where people earn their right to stay. In order not to be expelled by the group, each individual must contribute as much as they take. If they don't contribute, then they are taking food from someone else's allocation and during famine conditions such division is not permissible; they will be forced to leave.

Intelligence and proficiency come in a variety of forms. Natural talent is not just being academic. There are different types of 'IQ'. There is the common academic IQ, a technical IQ, a social IQ and a conceptual IQ. The non-academic IQs are often not as highly regarded, but natural talent should never be ignored. Whatever that talent may be it will provide some advantage to the group.

A conceptual IQ for instance means a person can easily grasp abstract constructs such as art or mysticism. This makes it easy for them to use their imagination to write, compose, and comprehend the obscure.

Technical IQ relates to building and problem solving while social IQ is how successfully and easily we relate to others. Healthy individuals are balanced in a minimum of two of these IQs but many find one of these qualities difficult to master. When we are low in one of these areas we lack confidence and try to avoid it because we feel silly and inadequate. These areas of skill or weakness often become themes in our lives because they have such a profound effect on us.

Each of these four different IQs is important for survival and the continuation of society. Without an academic understanding we could never make sense of the world around us. Technical expertise helps maintain and build, while conceptual thinking explores who we are. Social skill and effective communication is what brings others together making the swapping of ideas possible.

For millions of years cultural development stagnated because every individual was needed to search and hunt for food and this left little if any time for personal specialisation. Specialisation is not always successful in an evolutionary way because it makes a species vulnerable to change. Human beings are unique because general adaptability is achieved by the specialisation of skills from individuals within the group. The specialisation of skills creates interdependence in the group as each member relies on another to fulfil their own role. If the other does not do what is required, the entire group can be put at risk.

## The opinion of others

We like to think we are self-contained and couldn't care less what others think of us. Not only is that untrue, it is a dangerous way of viewing our relationship to others. It is imperative that we care how others view us, because our survival rests on their good opinion. If others are indifferent, or even worse, if they dislike us, it places us in a perilous social position should famine once again cause expulsions to occur.

Human babies are completely helpless, they are not like other animals that can run and feed on their own in a matter of weeks, days or even hours after birth. Human babies only have one survival defence and that is parents who love them. Without this protection they would never survive. Deep in the unconscious survival instinct is the knowledge of reliance and it is a knowledge that never goes away regardless of how long we live. Reliance on other people for help and protection, based on the love they feel toward us, is the oldest and most primal interactive social drive.

Staying alive is a complex business where only the fittest survive; the fittest being the most socially adaptive not just the physically strong. A survival instinct that can be of worth by contributing and caring for others in the group is even better served if sex appeal, happiness, a keen intellect or loyalty is also offered. When others want us to be around, our place in the group becomes more secure.

## Appearance

People like to associate with good looking people. Glossy magazines display beautiful faces like masterpieces hanging in the Louvre. Human beings love beauty whether it is the natural environment or a perfectly formed face or body. Spectacular waterfalls surrounded by forest entice more people to visit than flat open grass land. It is much easier for environmental groups to raise money to save baby harp seals than it would be to save an endangered vulture. At Christmas children ask for cute little kittens or a golden retriever puppy rather than a spider or a toad.

## Personality

We feel more comfortable around people who are stable, warm, considerate and friendly than people who are sullen, uncommunicative, depressed and withdrawn. Personality is an attribute that can help or hinder an individual's chances of remaining in the group when times get tough.

The survival instinct has devised a number of tactics to increase the chances of longevity. Happiness is a natural response and an emotion we all experience and like to express. The survival instinct has capitalised on this and used happiness to serve its own ends. By being happy and friendly a person becomes someone fun to be around, and as a result makes many true and loyal friends. The survival instinct can use this trait to produce a person who under stress demands smiles and happiness no matter how false or painful that display of happiness may be. There is a difference between genuine happiness which everybody experiences and survival happiness which only a few employ.

When a joke is funny we are happy and laugh but when we pretend to be happy when someone is being vindictive or mean, happiness is coming from the survival instinct, not from the soul. The survival instinct understands that a person who is happy and liked, as well as being a valuable contributor, is more likely to survive than a person just as valuable but less liked. As a result this type of person will react to stress in a happy-go-lucky manner or in a conciliatory way, even though circumstances may be anything but happy. Survival instinct happiness is not real happiness but a way of calming a tense situation in an attempt to gain protection from physical harm.

When the people around us are content and relaxed, our own security is assured because no one is threatening or angry. A placid type of survival instinct has adopted the techniques of happiness and playfulness to defuse threatening situations. When such an individual is high in nervous adrenalin or consistently low in energy, their survival instinct unconsciously makes them smile and act meekly as a way of escaping danger.

For hundreds of thousands, perhaps millions of generations, the survival instinct has struggled to find its own unique niche. Not everyone can display the same behaviour otherwise only the ones who were the best in that conduct would survive. Human culture relies on diversity for survival, so while some become placid others become aggressive. We need different aspects of character to complete the totality needed for balance. If everyone was happy and gentle, the first person to become aggressive would dominate the world. We all have different sides to our character because life requires different responses. Anger when anger is required and compassion when compassion is needed. To be in balance is to be adaptable and employ the correct emotion at the correct time. Out of balance is the opposite, meaning incorrect responses at inappropriate times or the same response regardless of circumstance.

# Chapter 3

# REFLECTIONS ON THE SOUL AND THE SURVIVAL INSTINCT

## The survival instinct

The survival instinct clings on to anything that works; it never lets any successful characteristic pass it by. As a result the traits, skills and personal attributes that helped our ancestors flourish and prosper remain as an unconscious reaction to be utilised again when circumstances require.

Nervous adrenalin or consistently poor energy can arise from a variety of causes, not just famine or attack, but the survival instinct does not understand the difference. Under stress we will either become agitated and nervous or tired and run down, both of which make the survival instinct dominant. Once this state occurs, the actions and manner of our survival mode come to the fore and move beyond our conscious control. We behave as if we are in danger and fighting for our lives in the only way we know how. The survival instinct is provided by nature to suspend the conscious thought of the soul in preference for instantaneous reaction. Nature has decided on this course because conscious thought takes time and contemplation. It is a process of acquired wisdom where the individual learns as they go along. A dangerous situation is not the time or place for contemplation because threat requires an immediate response.

Over time the survival instinct has amassed an array of time-tested responses specifically dedicated to getting us out of trouble. Instinct can only assume that the most common dangers of the past will be the most common dangers of the present. The modern world with its modern safety nets has not existed for long enough in comparison to the danger of animals, war and famine. Our survival instinct cannot tell the difference.

The survival instinct is filled with memories from the past, and while at the moment times are good, the instinct is driven by the cycle of boom and bust and it 'knows' that bad times are just around the corner. Stability is an impermanent state because conditions always change. The survival instinct is aware we cannot rest on our laurels; we must have more than we need to safeguard the future. Too much today can mean barely enough tomorrow, stockpiles and reserves are paramount. 'Live for today for tomorrow we die,' to the survival instinct should read, 'If we just live for today we will definitely die tomorrow – and I can't let that happen.'

As energy condenses into matter, the survival instinct exists at the last stage before actual matter forms; its role is to animate and to protect. It is too refined for the eye to see but too gross to fall under the influence of non-material law. It stores experience to use as instinct when the need arises.

In a human being the survival instinct manifests as an animate life force that connects events and circumstances, with emotions and outcomes to form patterns. This creates an instinctive response that comes into play when a person feels stressed.

Matter in all its forms both organic and inorganic, including human beings, has a survival instinct specific to its needs. Every creature strives to stay alive and the will to live is the same.

The survival instinct is protective by nature; its only concern is you. It is a program provided by nature to secure your physical future and longevity, to help you and your offspring survive. It is not concerned with happiness or contentment and whether you enjoy your life or not is not of consideration. Breathing is more important than happiness and food and shelter are primary issues.

To the soul the primary concern is learning, love and experience, but these experiences can never take place while the survival instinct is dominant. The survival instinct makes us fight for the last piece of food or the last breath of air, it makes us do whatever it takes, to whomever it is necessary just so we can live another day. If the survival instinct cared about love and compassion, it would compromise its objective by limiting its function. Longevity at any cost is the function of the survival instinct.

Whenever there is tension, tiredness or stress, the survival instinct automatically becomes dominant, which forces us to compete or cooperate. If the survival instinct is dominant for too long, those we love become our worst competitors and we project our inner turmoil on to them.

# Rejection

Deep in the unconscious survival instinct lies the universal terror of rejection. The need to be accepted is embedded within all of us because survival depends on the consent of others. We cannot survive if we are left on our own which is why rejection is our primary social fear.

Many people enjoy living on their own, they cope well and relish their privacy but this is not the same as rejection. To be rejected is to be banished, pushed aside and cast-out. There is no communication with anyone in the group and the person rejected must fend for themselves. In tribal times there was no social security, no shops, no plumbing and no medicine. To be alone was to die; it was just a matter of time.

The survival instinct is programmed to respond to energy levels and the experience of stress is the most influential factor. Instinct is not governed by rational thought nor is it managed by conscious control. We may be consciously aware of the way we are behaving but that is not the same as having enough conscious control to stop that behaviour. Willpower is implemented by the soul to try to regain control over the survival instinct. This is a Catch 22 situation because it takes vast amounts of energy to control the survival instinct. The more energy that is used the more the survival instinct is dominant and soon the willpower of the soul becomes inadequate and the survival instinct again takes control. In everyday situations this is the breaking of a resolution or the slipping back into old habits. Willpower or soul does not have enough energy to control the survival instinct indefinitely. What is required is a lifestyle change that takes the survival instinct away from the belief that it is under threat.

Stress is the enemy of willpower because it draws on so much energy. The survival instinct is a program that is not designed to think, only to respond. Danger and stress are interchangeable states because they both have the same effect on energy levels. In this context, stress is any situation or circumstance that causes a rise in nervous energy or a continuous depletion of vitality. Because the outcome is exactly the same, the survival instinct reacts as if it is the same events causing the response. Whenever nervous energy rises, the survival instinct interprets that rise as a sign of attack, when energy remains at a chronically low point, it behaves as if it is in a famine situation.

To the survival instinct, all stress is the same stress and it reacts accordingly. The survival instinct has no idea whether our blood pressure has gone up due to an argument, trouble with a partner or because of being chased, and the reaction is always fight or flight. When energy levels remain consistently poor for whatever reason; late nights, being overweight or excessive workload, all drain the body of its vital energy and the survival instinct acts as if famine is present.

The survival instinct is designed to protect against outside attack whether virus or human, irrespective of personal relationship. Commonly the biggest stressor is a family member, because the family home is a confined space that causes competitive behaviour. Family members are also the people in whom we have the most emotional investment. The workplace is another competitive environment but in this situation competitive behaviour is often encouraged and rewarded.

Regardless of whether the stress is a spouse, child, sibling or a work colleague; the survival instinct does not examine relationship, it simply responds to danger.

Out of balance a dominant survival instinct may do anything to conform and be accepted. The group will follow whoever they believes has the authority. History is full of groups and communities that behaved in a manner now considered immoral. Crusaders from every corner of the globe cut and slaughtered their way into heaven, while slave traders and owners never questioned for a moment, their right to abuse and work another person to death. Fitting in with the group may mean doing your best, but it may also mean being the best at being the worst.

Many tribes lived by stealing from others, while kidnapping and rape were commonplace for any victorious army. There is no morality in the survival instinct, just the drive to win and take. Morality is the soul crying out, 'Enough!'

## The soul

It is natural to link the soul with religion. The soul is not bound to material form, while the survival instinct is. The survival instinct cannot continue an independent existence after physical death. Human beings can act independently of instinct; in fact we often over-rule it. People are motivated by virtue, a desire to do what is right and truthful, and not just what is profitable and expedient. Sometimes this can place us in physical or social danger, which is contrary to the role of the survival instinct. Actions like these come from the soul in its desire to do what is principled and in the best interests of all.

Many of us have experiences outside the physical world. This type of event is a common human occurrence, such as the déjà vu phenomenon. This happening is a dream, where we experience the future and watch like a spectator as a sequence plays itself out in the present. The soul has left the material body, moving through time and space, bringing back the memory of a possible future that in the present has come to pass.

The survival instinct is bound to matter and cannot separate from physical form. It exists in human beings, animals, plants as well as inorganic minerals, but it cannot exist independently on its own.

Anything that can transcend time must be non-material or energetic by nature; it must also be independent, conscious and self-aware. The survival instinct is none of these things; it is only our soul that can exist independently of the body. The soul is not bound to material structure and therefore not tied to time and space.

The soul is conscious and self-aware, as many who have experienced a near death episode will testify. Rather than being obliged to reside in the body, the description given by those who have momentarily died, is one of the soul's liberation and release. The soul is immortal because it has no physical ties. People who experience a near death episode, remain conscious of who they are, never losing their memory or their sense of self.

The agenda of the soul is different to that of the survival instinct. The soul is not petrified of death, nor is it interested by worldly drives. The survival instinct is our support system while we exist here on earth. It makes sure we survive, prosper and contribute to the continuance of human civilisation. The soul is creative, evolving and able to think outside of itself. It can understand and integrate. The soul embraces wisdom, self-reliance, willpower and responsibility. It is tolerant of others and expects tolerance in return.

When the soul is in balance with the survival instinct, it can utilise the survival instinct and this interaction is what makes us human. We can think outside pure instinct, using the willpower of the soul to temper the survival instinct's demands, yet at the same time employ the skills it has developed.

The soul is special because it can differentiate, it is our individuality. The survival instinct of one person can be much the same as the survival instinct of another.

Everyone has natural talents, thoughts and ambitions they wish to pursue. Genius is working hard at being yourself.

The nature of the survival instinct can cause a number of different problems because its purpose is often contrary to the purpose of the soul and human beings must try to fulfil both. The survival instinct tries to keep time the same and make life as small as possible. The soul is trying to expand horizons and be in a constant state of movement and learning.

## Exclusively living in the soul

When the survival instinct is dominant life is unhappy and exhausting, but an exclusive focus on the soul makes us forget our material responsibilities.

Material life is not to be shunned, we are here for a reason and that should not be disrespected. Many mystics of the past shunned earthly life. They treated the body with contempt by torturing themselves and treating happiness as a sin. Some believed material life was an illusion, a testing ground or hell itself. They believed that no good could come from earthly life and that the sins of the body led the soul to hell; suffer in this life and you will be rewarded in the next. Suffering meant salvation in the world beyond.

If God didn't approve of earthly existence we wouldn't be here at all. Whatever occurs does so for a reason. If the soul didn't require earthly experience, it would have no need to incarnate into a material body. The soul is here and it is here for a reason; everything has meaning.

## The existential soul

The soul is existential and immortal. The soul is not bound to material form, while the survival instinct is not designed for anything but material form. The survival instinct cannot continue an independent existence after physical death, because it is not designed for any other function than to animate material form.

Human beings can act independently of instinct; in fact we often overrule it. People are motivated by virtue, a desire to do what is right and truthful, and not just what is profitable and expedient. Sometimes this can place us in physical or social danger, which is contrary to the role of the survival instinct. Actions like these come from the soul in its desire to do what is principled and in the best interests of all.

Human beings are unique because we fluctuate between, the soul and the survival instinct. Part of our time is spent in the non-material universe of the soul, while the rest is spent in the physical. Every time we create, think, develop or laugh, love, pray or plan, we are in the world of the soul; mind is soul. Conversely, whenever we are stressed tired or upset, threatened or hungry, we are in the world of the survival instinct.

Human beings compete because nature compels energy to push for influence and dominance. In order for the soul to be in balance, we must first un-clutter and de-stress. It is impossible to think, be creative or spiritual at the same time as feeling tense or under threat.

The survival instinct is responsive, not analytical. It does not examine the cause of stress it simply reacts when it exists. Threat to survival can be environmental, physical or biological so to guarantee the best response, the survival instinct acts in the same manner to all.

## The role of the brain

The mind, because it is non-material, cannot age or die. Its self-awareness and knowledge, continues for all time. The mind gains knowledge and experience and changes and evolves. It can expand upon its own knowledge but can never undo what it already knows. The brain not only manifests the will, it also filters and keeps the soul centred. The brain ensures that the soul stays focused and fixed inside the body. Physical form dictates the survival instinct's function, and the brain does the same for the soul. The brain impedes the soul's connection to the spirit world, anchoring it to the here and now.

## Partnership and procreation

Human beings are a species where both sexes get to choose their partners. In many animal groups it is only the dominant male who chooses when and with whom to breed. Choice creates diversity and promotes individual skills and personal qualities.

Being able to take an active part in the selection of a partner has far reaching consequences beyond sex. It is valuable for the human soul in its quest to understand itself and to interact with others. Choice of partner means assessing other people. When there is only one dominant male there is no need to observe or assess the personality or qualities of others. From the humble step of choosing a partner, deep bonds and relationships are able to form. Understanding good and evil, experiencing both love and pain and the ability to grasp abstract concepts like death, have their origin in the evolutionary step forward of choosing a partner.

By using the body and the survival instinct that animates the material being, the soul can feel what it is to be alive. It begins to understand what is important and what is not, what makes it happy and what is irrelevant but most of all it learns about others and a partnership choice is a crucial step in this process.

When the physical body dies, the soul moves on to a world of energy while the survival instinct is absorbed back into the collective unconscious. The collective unconscious is like a cloud that releases a million raindrops. Each raindrop is individual yet all of them come from the same cloud. When water evaporates, it returns to the cloud and falls as rain again. Individual survival instincts return to the collective cloud when the physical body dies and are then reborn into another life form. The individual survival instinct is not at liberty to infuse itself to the nearest available body, only nature has the ability to redirect and instil this life force into soon to be born form.

When this survival instinct once again animates a human, the person it animates will inherit the experiences of the people that came before them. The survival instinct can once more express these reactions, because human beings have a physiology sophisticated enough to express and apply them.

## Chapter 4

# THE MATERIAL UNIVERSE

There are three primary forces of motion in the material universe and all physical life is made from them. We live in a world that has three dimensions. Not only height, width, and depth but also time, space and matter, proton, neutron and electron and the three types of movement; outward motion, circular motion and inward motion.

Outward motion continually expands, pushing the universe forward. Circular motion is a rotational force that makes the planets revolve around the sun as well as spin on their axes. Third is inward motion which draws other forces and keeps the universe fixed. Gravity is a good example of inward motion.

Unlike outward or inward motion, circular motion revolves in a continuing cycle. In nature all three forces are required for physical life to begin. These forces create time and distance, and matter is the ultimate outcome.

The three forces of motion have distinct and separate qualities and are expressed in a variety of names and ways. At an atomic level, outward, circular and inward motion is manifested as repulsion, attraction and bonding. Once two forces are joined, atoms and molecules do their best to remain stable. Two dissimilar particles like a proton and an electron will be drawn toward each other because opposites attract. Attraction is inward motion. However, two protons will push each other away because similar forces repel. Repulsion is outward motion. In order for matter to grow, similar forces must be neutralised by an equally strong force without direction. The equally strong force cannot push away like outward motion, nor can it attract like inward motion. To neutralise these motions a third force must exist that absorbs but does not contribute to either inward or outward force. Circular motion is the buffer between the two, going around rather than in or out. Circular motion neutralises inward and outward motion so more force can accumulate.

Within physical matter, the electron is characterised by outward motion, the neutron by circular motion and the proton by inward motion. Matter forms by the particles gathering to build the elements needed for physical life.

These forces can only move according to their nature. Outward motion moves forward sweeping whatever is in its path in the same direction. Only when outward motion comes up against an equal or stronger opposing force can it be stopped. The same is true of every primary motion.

Material form is in a constant state of change, because each of the three forces continually exerts itself in a struggle of strength, each vying for superiority. Not in a conscious way – force is not trying to achieve anything in particular – but in a mechanistic way like water running downhill.

Because each is an opposing force, it must compete when it comes into contact with the other. When outward motion meets circular motion, it will either be strong enough to push circular motion aside and sweep it into its path, or if circular motion is stronger outward motion will be overpowered and swept up to become part of the circle.

When a strong force comes into contact with a weaker force the stronger force dominates the weaker. Attraction, repulsion and bonding create the outcomes of competition, cooperation or separation. In a confined space equal forces will continue to interact while a stronger force will become dominant. The only other option is to remain independent and not be drawn into the influence. In a confined area where separation is not possible only the law of dominance and interaction applies.

Dominance and interaction in people is recognised as competition or cooperation. Competition is the fight for dominance while cooperation creates interaction.

Competition occurs when similar forces of equal strength meet in a confined space. In particles two protons repel each other but will accept a neutron or electron. In human beings when famine conditions are present two people with the same skills compete for their position in the group. Those who are highly skilled in a separate but allied area retain their specialised place. Stronger forces dominate weaker ones.

Human beings also are governed by these laws when the survival instinct takes control. These are the laws that govern the material universe and the survival instinct is part of that process. The soul lies outside these laws and is not compelled to comply but the survival instinct is bound by them.

When stress reaches the level where the survival instinct becomes dominant, the home or office becomes a closed environment that forces the survival instinct of others to comply. When the survival instinct of one person is dominant, their competitive behaviour forces others to conform. It is impossible to remain in a confined space and not be affected.

The survival instinct is reactive, it responds to danger in all its forms. When a person is aggressive because they are stressed and they take it out on those around them, the survival instinct of those who are attacked responds accordingly. Separation is removing oneself away from a charged environment so the laws of dominance and interaction do not apply.

The three primary forces of outward, circular and inward motion exist so creation can begin. Circular motion traps outward and inward motion into a confined space making them interact. All three energies must be of equal strength otherwise they could not be caught. If one force was significantly stronger, it would dominate and overwhelm the others. When two or more forces of equal strength come together, all three must cooperate which creates something new.

Human beings react in the same manner. When two opposing forces of equal strength come together, cooperation takes place and something new begins. This can be a relationship, children or a new business arrangement. Cooperation and unity of opposite forces is the most creative power in the material universe. Competition builds resilience but it is not always creative.

## Chapter 5

# THE SEVEN TRADITIONAL ROLES

Everyone alive today, exists because of the success of the survival instinct they have inherited. No one will ever know how many prototypes have come and gone through history. All we know is that each of us has beaten the odds and is a survivor.

Human beings have been in competition with each other since communal living began. The key to surviving is to provide the group with a service it needs. Working with our natural talent makes a gift out of character.

If a person is born with naturally acute senses and quick reactions, then hunting is a task they will be good at because their natural talents are suited to the role. As a result, provided they are not lazy, they will become a successful hunter, live out their life, reproduce and pass on their skills.

Every person belongs to a single colour group and has the memories and reactions of a traditional role as part of their survival instinct. The colour group we are born into is the group we belong to for life. The survival instinct of each colour group is a predictable response to stress. It does not represent a person's soul or their creative potential.

## Traditional roles

For civilisation to flourish, diverse tasks must be performed by different people simultaneously. Some build houses while others gather food, some hunt while others scavenge. In this way the whole tribe gets food and shelter. These are the traditional roles vital to every society. Traditional roles have evolved from the ways in which fundamental needs have been met by using natural skills.

It is important to understand the traditional roles, not just because they were essential for personal and group survival, but because they form *the basis of unconscious reaction.* Traditional roles are based on natural talents and attributes that extend from their dominant force.

Everyone has a dominant force that comes from one of the three primary motions, outward, circular or inward motion. A dominant force can also result from the *interaction* of two primary motions. These interactions are resistance, separation and reaction. Unity is the dominant force that comes from the *interaction* of three primary motions.

Traditional roles are *stress reactions* based on repetition. Traditional roles share common goals and experiences and employ common skills and ways of thinking. Inside the brain of every human being is the ability to learn and adapt and combined with this capability are the survival tactics gained through repeated experience. When we are born a large part of our brain is ready for the experiences new life will bring, but there also exists an even larger part with remembered reactions to the past. Here, neurons are already assembled to make responses and talents instinctive.

The more we practise a topic or activity the more intrinsic that activity becomes. In time if we practise enough we can perform even complex actions automatically with a limited amount of concentration.

The human brain is wired to learn. However like everything material, its capacity is finite. While the brain has billions of cells, it also has billions of activities and thoughts to process. When we focus on something continuously, the brain begins to re-channel itself, creating deeper and stronger pathways. The brain is like every other system in the body; the more we use it the stronger it becomes.

When we focus on the same task consistently, it is equivalent to exercising the same muscles every day. The brain is governed by the same rules as the body; both are transformed by routine.

Survival reactions are gained and stored in response to attack and famine and because stress is how they are acquired, stress also triggers them. The more we become embroiled into a dangerous or stressful moment, the more we return to our inherited reactions lying ready for us to draw upon. This can be seen as a part of the unconscious mind; a collection of neurons already in place, based on the frequent events and dangers acquired while performing a traditional role in the past.

## Colours, forces and roles

As with many concepts, simple analogies can be used to convey complicated messages. Each primary force has been given a primary colour. Outward motion is yellow, circular motion is red, while inward motion is blue; three primary colours to represent the three primary forces. Each primary motion through dominance or interaction will either remain independent and dominant, or be forced to interact with another primary motion of equal but opposite strength. A small amount of blue mixed into a canvas of yellow, is not enough to turn the entire canvas green. In order to turn a backdrop from yellow into green, enough blue must be added to change the yellow.

All the seven forces of motion result in natural talents, which are employed as specific traditional roles. The dominant force together with the memories and responses of the traditional role is collectively called the survival instinct. Each dominant force is separate and distinct and creates skills and attributes that are utilised by human beings into valuable traditional roles. There are seven traditional roles that come from the seven dominant forces, creating seven distinct types of survival instinct. Each of us has one of these survival instincts as a natural response to stress.

The primary and combination forces of motion and their associated traditional roles are represented by the following colour groups.

## The forces of motion

| Type of motion | Energetic purpose | Natural skills and attributes | Traditional role | Colour |
|---|---|---|---|---|
| **Single motion** | | | | |
| Outward | Progress | Opportunity | Trader | Yellow |
| Circular | Growth | Productivity | Farmer | Red |
| Inward | Stability | Support | Shepherd | Blue |
| **Interaction of two motions** | | | | |
| Outward - Circular | Resistance | Determination | Warrior | Orange |
| Circular - Inward | Separation | Creativity | Priest | Purple |
| Outward - Inward | Reaction | Perception | Hunter | Green |
| **Interaction of three motions** | | | | |
| Outward – Circular - Inward | Unity | Equality | Craftsman | Brown |

Colour groups incorporate the dominant force together with the memories and reactions of their own traditional roles. Yellow for example represents the force of outward motion, combined with the responses to life events throughout history of people fulfilling the traditional role of the trader. The dominant force combined with the reactions of the specific traditional role of the trader is summarised as 'yellow'. Similarly, 'red' embodies the results of the historical role of the farmer interacting with the dominant force of circular motion.

Every developing group or society relied on the functioning of the seven traditional roles. Each role performed a vital task upon which everyone else in the group relied. Each traditional role has existed in some form for thousands of generations. The skills, traits and dangers faced by each traditional role, have been engrafted into the survival instinct. These traits can be employed in a variety of different ways. What profession a person chooses is not as important as the skills they employ. Skills are what the survival instinct passes on, not the 'know-how' of an actual profession.

## The trader

The trader evolved from our need to scavenge which rewarded the skills of investigation and opportunity. As the trader, these same skills were applied to the development of markets and trade routes. Trade made peaceful interaction between different cultures possible and the world opened up as a result. Outward motion is the dominant force behind the trader and it is no coincidence that for thousands of years traders from all races, creeds and colours, have explored the world for goods. Outward motion means progress. Outward motion continues to find ways of moving forward to expand the boundaries of the material universe. Outward motion in the form of the trader is exactly the same; stretching the boundaries of the known world into the boundaries of the unknown, creating trade routes, outposts and communication lines.

Analysis, inquiry and an intrepid nature are traits the yellow survival instinct retains. The yellow survival instinct knows how to bargain, how to balance the books and what goods are valuable regardless of profession, hobby or lifestyle.

## The farmer

The farmer evolved from the gardener, who in turn evolved from the gatherer. In prehistoric times, the gatherer was the person who collected and prepared fruits, nuts, seeds and vegetables. The gatherer acquired an intimate and proficient understanding of plants and how to prepare them. They understood the cycles of nature, what plants grew where and how to collect them. Understanding life cycles allowed the gatherer to obtain food all year long by utilising different environments as well as varieties of plants. Understanding cycles also enabled the gatherer to turn the forest into a garden as they learned how to cultivate rather than collect. Later the garden turned into the farm.

The farmer laboured long and hard, clearing the forest and turning the soil. Circular motion, like a ring on a finger travels in a direct and continuous line. Circular motion removes any obstacles because if anything breaks its flow, circular motion is no longer a circle. The doggedness of the farmer comes from circular motion and the traits of determination and effort continue in red today. Their single mindedness and steadfast drive can make red a high achiever.

## The shepherd

Domestication of animals for labour, their hides or food was one of the most important steps in history. It helped wandering tribes gain a stable food source as they made a lifestyle out of following the herd. For the follower, living continuously with the herd provided a more secure lifestyle than the existence they left behind. Following the herd eventually led to domestication of the animals they trailed and the traditional role of the shepherd began. Blue continues the unconscious reactions of the shepherd in their survival instinct.

The shepherd survived by living in communities developing beliefs, culture and an extensive social framework. Many blue people continue to carry an instinct for communication and co-operation. A high social IQ has developed from generations of communal living making blue likable and well respected with a desire to contribute to their community.

The shepherd moved their herd and tended them with care relying on the symbiotic relationship of the individual, community and animals.

Management, nurture and the ability to organise, together with a supportive nature are some of the traits a person who is blue may exhibit as part of their personality. Each is an extension of the traditional role of the shepherd.

## The warrior

The differentiation of skill from profession applies to every colour group. The warrior does not have to be in the army or the military. They may be a carpenter, cleaner or astronomer, but when their survival instinct is dominant, everyone who is orange will act in a similar way. The warrior developed from the need to protect and moved into a class specifically aimed at defending. In time, instead of just warding off attackers, the warrior formed part of a successful order that was rich and highly esteemed. As the difference between part time defender and full time warrior grew, war developed into an art form. The warrior reached the pinnacle of this living art, through precision, drill and mindset. They dedicated themselves body and soul to becoming the epitome the warrior represented. From the knights of Europe to the samurai of Japan, the warrior trained and moulded their character in pursuit of the perfection their profession embodied.

This same attention to detail and practice continues to exist in orange. If they are a cleaner they make sure that every nook and cranny is perfectly clean and sparkling or if they are a carpenter, their work is precise, efficient and quick. The warrior protects the underdog and believes in important causes.

## The priest

The priest began life as the tribal shaman; the witchdoctor, wise woman, witch or medicine man. Today there is a gap between healing and magic but for most of history this was not the case, and the two were inextricably linked. The traditional healer, clairvoyant and counsellor were merged into one in the role of the priest. Over time, medicine and spiritualism parted ways and religious and spiritual belief became the most powerful and dominant force. Doctors never developed into a privileged class but remained, once separated, as a learned vocation rather than a position of birth and rank. Today some may argue that medicine has become the religion of modern times, but whether mysticism, medicine or magic, the essence of the priest dominates them all.

In historical times it was viewed that people became sick because they were cursed. Chronic disease was caused by spirits or other shamans, who placed curses that could only be removed by someone equally as powerful. Shamans always had a foot in both worlds; from heavenly appointed rulers to a person who transcended the living and the dead. The priest dealt with death and disease on a regular basis. They witnessed this transition as they ministered to the sick and continued their function as a guide to the spirit world, after illness had claimed its victim. The shaman for centuries induced transitions, through hallucinogenic drugs and trances. They crossed the threshold of this world and the next. The priest continued this transcendental tradition through fasting, prayer, meditation and solitude, specifically designed to release the mind from the body. This continues in purple.

Priests, like warriors, became a class of their own, a generational profession that was rewarded and esteemed. Businesses and professions stayed within families passed down through generations. Priests, also like the warriors, gained privileges and titles and became rich as they secured their position by birthright.

## The hunter

The hunter was the bedrock of human existence, providing food for the group. They had sharp senses due to the reactivity caused by their dominant force. Working alone or in small, tight groups the hunter endured harsh climate and terrain to perform their role for the benefit of all.

Endurance, skill and perseverance are traits still alive in green. Hunters relied on outsmarting their prey because they were generally smaller or weaker than the animals they hunted. Under stress, green returns to these skills and thinks quickly and decisively under pressure. Their acute senses and perceptive mind allows green to assess situations and make judgements with a high degree of accuracy.

In the forest knowledge is a collage of information drawn together by logic. When a twig snaps as a bush moves while a scent is in the air, all come together to tell the hunter that an animal is nearby.

Today green still employs the hunter's thinking to analyse and develop ideas. Traditionally the hunter only worked until the kill was made, after which they returned to the tribe to feast on the animal they had killed. The hunter worked when it was necessary and relaxed when it was not. Acute senses, clear communication and a quick thinking brain were the hunter's greatest weapons. With these three qualities the hunter helped make human beings the unapproachable kings of the jungle.

## The craftsman

The craftsman's role became increasingly more complex as each traditional role developed. Making spears and arrows gave way to building houses, tools and roads. As the shepherd emerged, wagons and tents were made from the hides of animals, the warrior needed weapons made from metal, while the trader required measuring devices and ships. The craftsman was needed by everyone. This imposed the need to be all things to all people and continues today in brown.

Craftsmen were skilled at finding solutions, developing ideas and understanding the difficulties of others. They had an eye for detail and a determination to continue to advance and make life better. Finding new and improved ways of supporting and helping others was the role of the craftsmen and they continue to be of benefit to everyone who needs them.

The brown survival instinct will still try and meet the demands of those around them. When in balance, problem solving and finding solutions is one of their more positive traits. Out of balance, brown can become overwhelmed by demands, feeling anxious and not up to the task.

Each traditional role requires a number of skills to complete its function. The more these skills and qualities are repeated, the more deeply etched in the brain they become until the common reactions experienced by each traditional role form part of the survival instinct of that colour group.

## The life experiences of the roles

Each traditional role experienced repeating circumstances and dangers. The warrior faced battle more often than any other role, while the trader had to withstand long periods away from home. The hunter employed camouflage, while the craftsman sought perfection. The farmer needed brute force and perseverance, while the shepherd required management and caring. Hunters often came face to face with animals, larger or more dangerous than themselves. The priest rarely encountered this predicament but dealt constantly with problems of disease, death and the afterlife.

Common experiences that are life threatening and dangerous are embedded into each survival instinct to serve as a warning and an alarm. Not only are these events burned into the survival instinct's memory but so too is any successful response.

## Different responses

The hunter cannot be cornered. If they are trying to kill an animal it is imperative for their safety that the hunter remain free to move around and escape. Often the animals hunted were larger than themselves; mammoths, buffalo or elk. To be cornered by one of these massive beasts meant being crippled or killed. In modern times green still hate to be cornered, it is a situation their survival instinct tries to avoid.

The more fearful or exhausted green becomes, the more their survival instinct is dominant and the more they revert to their ancient instincts. People standing too close or strangers who wander into green's personal space can put them on edge because it makes them feel trapped and vulnerable. Green needs open space and time on their own, without someone beside them. They are not anti-social. They love company and an intimate relationship, but many feel stifled if they do not have enough personal space, because their survival instinct links closeness to danger.

The priest by contrast does not have these traits because the priest did not hunt. Generally their survival instinct has nothing to fear by small places or confined relationships. Instead the priest is happy to share the trials and tribulations of emotional entanglement. Their survival instinct does not demand to escape, because it does not have the etched memory of a charging boar or buffalo. Green are happy to lend support, to be there to comfort and to shoulder a burden, but they also need time away otherwise they feel caught.

The priest is used to suffering and emotion; they are used to listening and sitting by the bedside. However if they become run down and out of balance and people begin talking about them, the table turns and now it is the priest who does not feel so secure. When others start talking about them, the priest becomes nervous. History is full of disgruntled masses turning their anger and directing it upon the church. The past is abundant with stories about burning witches and desecrated temples.

This is the difference between the survival instinct of one colour group and another. Green hate to be trapped and confined, but when slander and gossip begins they try their best to ignore the insults. Purple on the other hand starts to feel paranoid. Their survival instinct understands what can happen during mob rule. Taking on a larger group is not a situation green is frightened of. They are used to it because for most of the time their prey was bigger than them, but to purple, taking on a group or feeling the target of a group's scorn, is their survival instinct's worst nightmare.

Open space protected the hunter so open space is what green craves. This can occur in a variety of ways and is generally more metaphorical than literal. A job or business where green is in charge, or a relationship that is not emotionally needy are examples of open space. Every colour group has in their survival instinct, the imprint of the dangerous events that frequently occurred, together with the responses that saved them. Each colour group is different because the traditional roles varied and the situations they faced were unique to each group.

The trader did not take confession, nor did they comfort the sick. They found foreign markets, battled bandits and sailed the seven seas. The warrior did not plough the earth but they did face death and emotional suffering.

To the warrior, loyalty is of prime importance. Without being able to depend on their comrades the warrior is certain to die. Only by sticking to the oaths that were made, can there be any hope of the warrior winning and returning to their home. The warrior is compelled to place trust in others; trust is a stronger requirement in them than it is for any other traditional role. Today loyalty, trust and commitment are what orange demand in their home and work. As a boss they demand commitment and in relationships fidelity to the highest degree.

Knowing the differences between the survival instincts of each colour group helps make sense of how people behave, by understanding what is at work deep in their unconscious. This understanding helps us comprehend why people react differently in similar stressful situations. It also explains why a situation that barely affects one individual, can be totally devastating to another.

## Reading a force or instinct

Every aspect of the survival instinct is expressed in the body's defence system, because that is the area the survival instinct influences most powerfully. The nervous system and the immune system, together with the emotions and the face all manifest the drive of the survival instinct. Although we can see the effects of both nervous and emotional strain, we cannot learn to read and predict them because they do not have material form. The face however can be read in reference to the survival instinct because it is physical and therefore observable. Facial analysis will be examined further in Chapter 12. A complete facial analysis can be undertaken on the soul and survival website <www.soulandsurvival.com>.

## Chapter 6

# BALANCING SOUL AND SURVIVAL

*Thousands of candles can be lighted from a single candle, and the life of the candle will not be shortened. Happiness never decreases by being shared.*

Buddha

## Balance

When the survival instinct is dominant, relationships are poor. The survival instinct is entirely selfish and there is no room for anyone else. Instinct will turn your closest friend into your competitor. Harmony results when the soul and the survival instinct are in balance.

It is important for our emotional well-being that we balance our survival instinct with our soul. As discussed previously, living solely in our survival instinct makes us unhappy and exhausted, but an exclusive focus on the soul makes us forget our material responsibilities. The more we try and deny earthly life the more our survival instinct rebels, and soon we are at war with ourselves. Material life is not all there is, but that does not mean it is irrelevant. However, the more we give in to the demands of the survival instinct, the more shallow, unfulfilled and hedonistic we become. When the survival instinct is dominant, discontentment is strong, because the survival instinct is never contented with enough. Too much is never enough because its role is to secure the future.

The way that the soul attempts to regain control is by using willpower. The best way to break the habits of the survival instinct is to re-channel energy back into the soul. Concentrating on breaking habits through self-control and effort, while successful at times can also be difficult and draining of energy. Focus on the soul does not replace willpower, but it is a valuable adjunct to it. Doing something you love is how the soul gets energy. Willpower is the soul at work.

Enjoying our life is how we find balance, regardless of what we love to do. Reading, sailing, sport or friends, walks in the country or a long distance run; whatever it is that makes us lose track of time, makes us energised and full of life, is what we must make time for. Balancing soul and survival, means finding the blend of what is required and what we find pleasing. It is balancing what we have to do, together with what we want to do.

The body must be harmonious and responsive to the wishes of the mind. Whether we want to sit or run, laugh, cry or build, it is the job of the brain to send the right signals and to orchestrate a coordinated and appropriate response. The brain is the go-between that links the wishes of the mind with the functions of the body.

No connection to the soul can ever result when the survival instinct is the dominant force. The soul desires to learn, grow and love, while the survival instinct is driven to accumulate and possess. Relationships where the soul and survival instinct are in balance are independent, loving and fruitful. Relationships where the survival instinct is dominant are volatile, dependent and inhibited.

Human beings are both soul and survival instinct, and the balance of the two is difficult to achieve. If we do not acknowledge the survival instinct as a valid part of our nature, we will always be at war with ourselves. We are both angels and devils; neither one nor the other. Human beings are capable of acts of great sacrifice, benevolence, kindness and love, but we are also capable of wickedness, selfishness, cruelty and pain. Human beings are both a soul searching for elevation as well as a survival instinct ready to sacrifice everyone and everything for one more breath.

Keeping the soul in balance with the survival instinct is life's primary challenge. Becoming the person we want to be depends on understanding the interaction of these two sides competing inside us continually. The survival instinct can never be switched off and the soul can never be our single dominant force. Balance is the best objective we can aim for and to find it we must have self-understanding.

## Following our soul
The soul converts feelings into deeds, while the survival instinct drops what is no longer of value. When the emotions that the survival instinct

demands are no longer being supplied, the person who first supplied them becomes as dispensable as the emotion itself. The soul understands complexity and the soul understands another person's point of view. Emotions, like the survival instinct, are self-centred and potentially addictive.

Soul love means a helping hand, taking time to be with someone, to comfort or understand. Survival love is bells and whistles, the elation of desire and of being desired. Survival love is power; it is needy, demanding and uncompromising. It can also be unconditional. Unconditional love; where a partner can do whatever they like, in any manner they wish, while the other person promises to accept their behaviour, is fear masquerading as love.

The soul does not want to be belittled, it wants to reach out, explore and experience life. Putting up with bad behaviour because of an underlying fear of rejection, is nothing more than the survival instinct remembering the past, where expulsion meant an early grave. Out of balance the survival instinct can be so terrified of being alone, that it allows the worst degradations to occur, as long as it can prevent being rejected and starving to death.

We can only observe our own survival instinct because we have a separate soul. Animals always act according to their instinct but this is not the case for human beings. We constantly fight ourselves in an attempt to modify, enhance or develop the part of our character that lets us down. Most people are aware of their repeated shortcomings, and make promises to be more patient, helping, open or active. The list of what we try to change is endless, but it always belongs to the survival instinct. Knowing how the survival instinct works and when and why it takes charge, allows us to manage our own energy reserves so we can experience a balance between soul and survival.

## Self-denial

Denial of food makes energy levels fall and the survival instinct dominant. So too does hardship and stress. Self denial and self-reproach is a difficult way to bring the soul in balance. Buddha tortured himself to achieve salvation before he realised the middle way.

## More energy equals less stress
When we say, 'I must try to be less angry, more communicative, demonstrative, stronger or happier', what we are really saying is, 'I need to be less stressed'. The emotional responses we try to change are our survival instinct's natural reaction to stress. The survival instinct is using aggression, compliance, or a closed-off demeanour as a way of protection against attack or expulsion, because our current energy levels are mimicking the conditions of danger or famine.

Rather than trying to change the survival instinct, it is easier to boost energy levels and lower the danger response. Changing a program that is firmly set in the brain takes time and is often arduous. Raising energy levels is considerably easier and even if not a complete replacement, is often a valuable addition. Increased energy calms the survival instinct because it no longer believes it is in danger.

## Energy and memory
The role of the survival instinct is to provide safety and longevity, and its function is linked to energy. The more erratic energy levels become, the more the survival instinct reacts, as if it were in danger of attack. The more exhausted energy levels become, the more the survival instinct believes it's in famine.

Emotion is linked to memory. The more emotion that is involved during an event, the more the survival instinct commits that event to memory. Adrenalin and exhaustion are vital triggers, and any event that is strong in either is immediately turned into instinctive reaction. The more a danger has repeated itself, the more the survival instinct expects it to reoccur in the future and it waits in readiness for warning signs.

Dangerous situations are remembered by the survival instinct to help avoid making the same mistakes in the future. When a number of people all experience a similar dangerous event, the memory becomes part of the collective experience shared by everyone in that colour group. This is what makes the history of the traditional role so important.

## Opposites and similars

The laws that govern the world of the soul are opposite to the laws that govern matter and the survival instinct. In the material universe opposites attract, but in the world of the soul it is similars that attract. The laws that govern matter do not have jurisdiction over the soul.

In the world of matter the more you give away the less you have, but in the world of the soul, the more you give away the more you accumulate. Take a material substance like money. The more money that is given away, the less there is to keep. However if we apply these same rules to an energetic force like love, we find the results are exactly the opposite. The more love we give, the more love we have. Conversely, the less love we give, the less love we have. If we have a pile of oranges, each time we give an orange away our pile becomes smaller, but with each person or child there is to love, the more love we have to give them.

Relationships, like motion or force, are governed by the rules of attraction. If the survival instinct is the dominant force we attract forces that are opposite to ourselves. When the soul and survival instinct are in balance we are attracted to and attract similar minds.

## Chapter 7

# INDIVIDUAL REACTIONS TO STRESS

## Reaction

Reaction to danger is instinctive. When a car or truck is speeding down a road that you happen to be crossing, you jump instinctively when it beeps its horn or at the sound of screeching tyres.

If you are outside and a bee or a wasp lands on your skin, you immediately try to shoo it away or jump in response. You do not stop to think things through; it is an immediate reaction because your reaction is driven by instinct.

When circumstances become dangerous our instinct takes over. Instinct is nature's way of ensuring the best result in a tight situation. Quick reaction is vital in order to escape danger. Attack is not the time for conscious deliberation so nature has put in place a system where an automatic response takes over when life is threatened, handing back conscious control once the danger is over.

How many times, once a stressful situation is over, do you wish you had handled it differently? How many people have said to themselves, 'If only I had said … at the time?' Inside us lie two separate traits; one is the soul, which is conscious rational thinking, the other is the survival instinct which is our natural predetermined automatic response to danger.

When the wasp attacked or the truck tyres screeched, conscious thought was abandoned and instinct took over. This is the design of every human being; consciousness can only occur when there is no external threat to life. When a circumstance become dangerous, instinct takes charge and becomes the dominant force, while consciousness is suppressed and relegated to the background. The more dangerous the situation the more instinct is dominant.

## Under stress

Human beings get along well when life is good but under stress we fight and compete. Stress is a generic term that signifies the state when the survival instinct has become dominant.

The word 'stress' is used to describe both being in immediate danger and competing to avoid expulsion. The survival instinct does not analyse or rationalise and cannot examine cause. Only the soul is self aware, conscious of subtlety and difference. The survival instinct has no brain so it cannot think; it is entirely linked to energy levels. When energy is suddenly unusually high, from a rush of adrenalin, the survival instinct becomes dominant to counter attack or to flee. When energy has been slowly drained the survival instinct becomes dominant to compete for resources. Everyone has experienced the phenomenon of losing sleep and becoming exhausted from overwork or worry. Personality begins to change and normally content people become aggressive, over-sensitive, apathetic or withdrawn. When we experience a lot of tension or pressure our personality changes and we can become revengeful, competitive or spiteful, or else we aim to please and attempt to conform. Then, when the pressure is over or we have caught up on our sleep, we return to normal and our mood settles.

How many people state how different they feel while on holiday, or how many women during their periods experience headaches or personality changes because of this drop in energy?

When we are stressed we become selfish because instinct is designed for self-preservation. The way we behave when stressed is due to the force and reactions inside us. If we belong to the orange colour group, the force of resistance is the primary drive along with the reactions and memories of the warrior. When stress reaches a stage where the survival instinct takes control, people who are orange will react in a predetermined manner in accordance with what helped them survive in the past.

Under stress people behave in different ways because of the different forces, reactions and memories inside us. A person in whom inward motion is dominant will behave differently to a person who has outward motion as dominant. Combined with this difference are the reactions of each traditional role. The life and experiences of the outward motion trader is completely different to the experiences of the inward motion shepherd.

Babies have different personalities because they are born with different survival instincts. As adults become conscious, they learn to modify their behaviour but under stress everyone reverts to the instinct inside them. People who have experienced hardship and pressure say that you never know how someone will react until they face that situation.

If you have a gentle, friendly survival instinct, the greater the danger the more accommodating you will become. If you have been given the instincts of the hunter, the greater the danger, the more you will hit and run in retaliation, or camouflage yourself. If you have inherited the warrior, you will fight back or cause as big a disturbance as possible when stressed.

Our greatest common problem is that life is stressful. The more stressed we become the more selfishly we act and the more selfishly we act, the more we compete with those around us. In times of attack or famine, to compete with others is important but when this competition is applied to our family and the people we love, the results can be disastrous.

When a person is stressed and their survival instinct is dominant, they are critical and judgmental of others because the survival instinct makes them see enemies everywhere. The survival instinct sees the flaws in others and makes it too irresistible not to highlight these faults. The reason we do this is to show other people how flawed and weak our competitor can be. When times become hard or famine returns, the others in the group would be foolish to choose that person over you.

The survival instinct has no concept of right or wrong, it also has no understanding of time or conditions. The consciousness of the soul can see why it is appropriate to be angry at one person but not another, but when the survival instinct is dominant we become angry at everyone.

The survival instinct is petty and immature because in times of crisis this behaviour works. It does not take long for bloodshed and primeval behaviour to break free in countries that regard themselves as sophisticated. As soon as the soul is replaced by the survival instinct due to famine, war or natural disaster, the law of the jungle prevails. The survival instinct can make beasts out of otherwise decent human beings.

The survival instincts of individuals cannot be the same because the needs of the group vary. If the entire group needed only the strength to fight, then just the most vicious would survive. However a vicious personality soon turns on others because it is not selectively vicious. Civilisation cannot take place when people behave like wild animals, but wild animals are all that we are when conditions evoke the survival instinct to extremes.

Human beings do not survive by strength and aggression alone because protection is just one aspect of survival. Acute senses are needed for hunting but so too is patience and solitude. Careful planning is required by the shepherd as well as a nurturing demeanour. The trader is astute and creates opportunity while the farmer has endurance and sees projects through. The priest is compassionate, creative and giving, while the craftsman is inventive and accurate. The warrior is structured, self-disciplined and protective and does what is necessary for others to flourish.

By contributing in different ways, individuals secure their position in the group by supplying the diversity of its needs. Temperament and traditional role go hand in hand and as a result each of us acts differently when stressed.

## Contribution

Human beings have learned to make themselves indispensable to the group during famine. As food stores disappear, so too must people in proportion to the food. The group removes the old and the sick first because they contribute the least. Expulsion is judged on contribution and character. The more others want or need us, the more we remain part of the group and the greater the chances of personal survival.

## Frequency of stress

Nature never gambles on long shots; she always plays the odds. The most common experiences of the past will be the most common experiences of the present. Frequency is how nature works like practice in a human being. The survival instinct always tries to stay in its comfort zone and keep circumstances in a realm where it has the most experience. Traditional roles require constant repetition and they experience similar events. The survival instinct repeats the events of the past regardless of whether they were positive or negative.

# Chapter 8

# HEALTH AND ILLNESS

## Energy levels and the survival instinct

Health results from a balance between the soul and the survival instinct.

Balance occurs when the soul is equal to the survival instinct, leaving the mind free to develop and explore without being inhibited. The soul can over-rule the survival instinct, creating acts of charity, illumination and inspiration. However if the soul or mind is the dominant force for an extended period of time, physical health suffers. When the soul is dominant it disregards earthly needs of food, companionship and acceptance. People who are in their mind exclusively can forget to eat, sleep or wash; many lose contact and find it difficult to relate or make conversation with others. Their mind is away in the clouds, leaving their material life ungrounded.

It is difficult for the soul to consistently remain dominant, because life is filled with stress. Physical need and danger brings the survival instinct out of its state of readiness, back into a dominant position. A dominant soul makes a person naïve and easily taken advantage of. Living in the soul creates a childlike innocence and a total focus on a subject, person or objective, to the exclusion of anyone and everything else. The soul makes a person live in a world of their own, which is why we need and have a survival instinct.

The survival instinct ensures that we mix with others and do not stay totally in the world of ideas and creation. The survival instinct not only alerts us to danger, it helps us gain wisdom, compassion and understanding through interaction with others. The soul will neglect the physical body because it is not dependant upon anything material. The universe disagrees otherwise it would not make the soul incarnate. The soul continues after the body wears out, so it feels no necessity to keep the physical part of us healthy. As a result, people who live constantly in their soul to the exclusion of everything else, often become reclusive, unkempt and unhealthy; the archetypical mad professor.

When the survival instinct is dominant, it uses vast amounts of energy.

If the survival instinct is dominant continuously, due to exhaustion or danger, chronic disease is the inevitable outcome. When we are in danger, adrenalin is released to give us the extra energy needed to escape whatever may harm us. When danger is continuous or chronic, the same physical response occurs but there is no relaxation afterwards. In fight or flight the body is thrown into a state of alarm. Adrenalin causes the senses and nerves to become more alert than normal, while the muscles tense in readiness to run or fight back.

When danger is continuous, due to an abusive house member, aggressive boss or fear of losing a job, the physical response of fight or flight occurs, but no fight or flight activity takes place. Consequently there is no action telling the survival instinct to return to normal. Adrenalin stays elevated in the body, causing high blood pressure, muscular tension, sleeplessness and anxiety. The body remains in a constant state of readiness.

Exhaustion is also energy expensive because the survival instinct must borrow from the future. Reserves from outside sources can no longer supplement daily requirements, so the survival instinct extracts energy from the reservoir nature has given it. Every person is born with a finite amount of energy. However we do not always use energy from our stores and can take energy from other sources. Fresh food is full of energy we can utilise, instead of draining our own supply. Supplementing energy means taking less from our reserves.

Energy, like fresh water, is ready to use but most fresh water is locked away underground. Energy and life force are the same. Energy reserves are contained and locked within the muscles. The muscles are the body's energy vault, because the muscles are what we use to fight or run away. When we use our muscles, energy is released that would otherwise remain trapped and dormant. This is why we feel better after exercising. Sedentary living makes us tired and hungry because we are not releasing the energy, that has been given to us to use. The less we use our muscles the less energy is released, and the more we look to outside sources, high in the energy and life force that we are searching for.

The soul is pure energy – the more freedom it is given the brighter it becomes. Consequently the soul can radiate and supply extra energy to the body, which is then stored in the muscles. Involving ourselves in art, enjoyable pursuits or thought can enthuse, inspire and supplement our energy. However if physical exercise is limited or absent, the energy our soul or mind has supplied remains locked and unused. Balancing soul and survival is more than finding a balance between doing what we have to and doing what we want to; it is also <u>finding a balance between thought and physical activity</u>.

We gain energy and life from outside sources in the form of nutritious fresh food. Chronic exhaustion means operating under famine conditions. Either the survival instinct will borrow from future reserves or it will slow the body down to conserve energy.

If the survival instinct borrows from the future, daily energy levels are maintained by eating into reserves. There is enough personal energy to last to old age without signs and symptoms of disease, but when we are stressed we use large quantities of energy and begin to drain our reserves. By the time a stressed person reaches middle or old age, there is not enough life force to keep the body operating at an optimum and pain free level; now disease develops.

## Trauma and disease

Illness and pathology can be divided into three types

- trauma
- acute disease
- chronic disease

Trauma describes accidents and mishaps which includes falls, car accidents, broken bones, bruises, sprains and injuries. The effects of trauma on the body are the same regardless of colour group. There is no individuality in the trauma response; a broken leg is a broken leg.

Acute disease includes viruses, fungal and bacterial infections. Chicken pox, measles, colds and flu, are common examples of acute infection. Acute disease has a limited time period, with distinct patterns and stages. The common cold or flu for example has a number of stages starting with fatigue, which develops into fever or chill. Then lethargy, muscle aches and headaches begin, as well as an excessive accumulation of mucus. Acute disease generally lasts between one to twenty one days, depending on the illness. Acute disease has defined limits and either survival or death results.

Each viral or bacterial infection affects the body in its own unique way. Every germ causes a particular set of signs and symptoms that displays the character of the infecting agent. This is the basis of the germ theory. Acute disease tells us more about the germ than it does about ourselves.

There are two types of chronic disease, acquired and congenital. Acquired chronic disease is very different to either trauma or acute disease and can tell us a lot about the life we are leading. Chronic disease does not have a limited life span; it can begin in childhood and continue into old age, growing increasingly stronger and more debilitating as energy levels fall. Chronic disease includes arthritis, cancer, asthma and a multitude of other life-long pathologies. A number of factors, including inheritance, lifestyle and stress, influence the severity and impact of chronic disease.

Acute diseases such as chicken pox do not continue for years at a time, let alone for decades. Chronic diseases such as asthma or migraines can afflict the sufferer for a lifetime. Chronic disease grows stronger as time progresses and natural energy levels fall. Chronic exhaustion leads to chronic disease when the body is unable to supply itself with extra energy to the inherently weak areas that need it most. Energy loss makes weaker areas incapable of maintaining organic function within healthy normal limits. Every person is born with weak areas that may ultimately develop into pathological conditions when energy levels drop too low.

When energy is in balance with demand, good health is the result. When demand for energy outstrips supply, we feel tired and run down. If demand continues to outweigh supply, the weak areas of the body, like the weak links in a chain, start breaking down.

Weak areas of the body need extra energy to keep pace with normal functioning. If a person is born with a twenty percent deficiency in their liver, they need twenty percent more energy to supply the natural shortfall. Energy deficiency does not mean a specific pathology exists and this shortage is rarely recognised by conventional testing. When energy levels drop, the body is no longer able to supply the extra energy that weak areas or organs need. When the survival instinct is dominant, energy for bodily functions is rationed until the survival instinct returns to a balanced state. When our survival instinct perceives an immediate threat, whether real or imagined, energy is withdrawn from other areas to deal with the danger, and so maintaining extra function to a weaker area becomes a lower priority and that area misses out.

When danger threatens, the survival instinct takes what it needs. Day to day bodily functions must make do with the energy left over. However, if the body only receives sixty percent of its energy, compared to its usual one hundred, a weak organ that is already under-functioning can no longer remain healthy. If this state continues for an extended period, signs and symptoms of organ dysfunction manifest. If it continues indefinitely, pathology and organic breakdown occurs. Many people experience signs and symptoms before tests show pathology has begun.

When the survival instinct believes it is under attack, energy is used to keep adrenalin levels high. When the survival instinct believes famine is present, it conserves energy and only provides what energy is necessary for the body to operate and nothing more. In contemporary times, an aggressive and competitive environment is the situation most commonly interpreted as 'attack', while overwork and a poor diet are the situations most commonly interpreted as 'famine'.

Weak areas cause the signs and symptoms that manifest when we are tired. Over-work or loss of sleep, poor diet or emotional stress – any of these create predictable signs and symptoms that each of us recognise as common indicators, telling us to slow down and rest. Many women notice this during their menstrual period. The hormonal cycle, requiring more energy than normal, leaves their body with a shortfall of energy, creating distinctive signs and symptoms that would only occur outside their menstrual period if they were overworked or rundown.

Signs and symptoms of a weak area are different to natural function. If a woman experiences abdominal cramping during her menstrual cycle, it does not mean there is any reproductive weakness because discomfort is a natural outcome of contraction. However if the same woman experiences severe abdominal discomfort, whenever she becomes tired or stressed, this signifies a weak area depleted of energy.

When a person becomes tired, stressed or overworked, weak areas exhibit themselves with signs and symptoms because they are no longer functioning normally. In some people stress becomes physical pathology while in others an emotional response arises; many individuals experience both. If energy is reduced but still sustainable, functional disturbance is common. When energy drops to consistently low levels where maintenance is no longer possible, structural pathology occurs. Functional signs and symptoms are the aches and pains a person experiences without any detectable organic breakdown. Structural disturbance means there is a change in the architecture of an organ or joint. For most people, chronic disease is a condition that develops as life progresses, accompanied by sustained energy loss. Weak areas, even though present from birth, remain dormant while energy is high. Chronic disease is the result of energy being used by the survival instinct instead of for the body. This redirection of energy turns a weak area into a health condition. Chronic disease is chronic exhaustion.

## Triggers for the survival instinct

In health and illness cause and effect can be a revolving cycle. Initial energy loss creates organic dysfunction which can then cause breakdown and pain. Pain caused by pathology can in turn create further pathology by draining the body of energy. Pain uses high amounts of energy depriving weak areas even further. Pain is not the only condition that is a cause and effect of energy loss. The commandeering of energy by the survival instinct can also be due to:

- worry and anxiety
- tense environments
- overwork
- poor nutrition
- alcohol and drugs
- negative self-belief
- emotional trauma
- physical trauma and exertion

## Worry and anxiety

Worry develops from a survival instinct that is in a permanent state of alarm. Energy levels are erratic, telling the survival instinct that attack remains likely. The brain is designed to make connections; neurons work by joining pathways. Making connections is how we link cause and effect together. When the body feels a particular way for an extended period of time, the brain attempts to link that feeling to an appropriate action that can cause it. This is projection.

If a person is nervous, worried or anxious, without a good cause to be feeling that way, their brain will try to link this feeling to a reason. A worrier may state that their primary fear is not having enough money, but if that problem was magically fixed they would worry about something else. Continuous anxiety, panic or worry is the survival instinct in a state of permanent fight or flight.

## Tension

A tense environment, one that is aggressive, competitive or demanding, does not permit the survival instinct to relax.

When tension is consistent, energy levels become erratic and the survival instinct responds as if it were under attack. An aggressive or belittling home environment, a workplace that is demanding or a school environment with social or academic competition are common causes. Many workplaces still use fear as a primary motivator. These are 18th century business ethics that employ the fear of expulsion in the same way that overseers during the slave trade made use of the lash. Whipping never made workers more confident or competent and the threat of termination as a motivating force has the same negative affect. Workers are never at their best when stressed because the survival instinct suppresses the soul.

For some, home is a dangerous place because of violence, addiction or competition. Chronic disease often plagues individuals who live in homes like this because energy is exhausted by fear. Most of the time, fear of attack is legitimate, but sometimes it can be a projection. Often the most aggressive person, because their survival instinct is dominant, will see other people's response to their own aggressive behaviour as an attack against them rather than as a reaction to them.

## Overwork

Overwork can create energy exhaustion because working not only takes effort but overwork deprives us of time that would be spent pursuing revitalising activities. Survival is based on contribution and whenever the survival instinct is dominant the tendency to overwork is strong. Unconsciously under stress we revert to overwork as an attempt to secure our position by making ourselves indispensable. Exhaustion drives the survival instinct into proving its self-worth by production, however the more we overwork to improve our security the more exhausted we become.

Not taking breaks or grabbing a snack instead of a nutritious meal are common additions to overwork. So too is the limited time that is left to share and gain happiness from our family and friends. Overwork is a state of imbalance because 'over' anything implies that a task is being completed to the detriment of other activities. The constitution becomes drained because energy is going out without any taking its place.

## Poor nutrition

Junk food which is usually highly processed can be a trap because it can be both a cause and a consequence of low energy reserves. When we are run-down or working late, it is easy to buy take-away instead of cooking a meal, but this in turn can lead to lowering our energy levels, and so a downward spiral begins. Processed food often supplies little in the way of organic nutrients. Even if fortified with vitamins and minerals, processed food has very little life force. Junk or heavily processed food is dead food, leaving the body with a loss of energy by comparison to fresh natural food. Home cooked food has higher energy levels than processed food because it is made with fresh ingredients. Even home cooked fried chips have some goodness in them if they are made from freshly peeled potatoes.

Eating foods without life force gives immediate gratification but leaves the body with little in the way of sustained energy. Heavily processed food can even leave the body with a net loss of energy by the time metabolism takes place.

Plants and animals have a life force. Animals store energy differently to plants. Life force can remain in the muscles of animals for only a short time after death. Plants store life in seeds, kernels and grains, dormant yet ready to grow again. Fruit and vegetables can remain alive after they have been picked, although only for a limited time. Nature has enabled plants, through seeds, fruits and tubers, to store their life force until conditions become conducive to grow again. This allows grains and seeds to be dispersed by wind or animals. Fruits, grains and vegetables are excellent sources of life force that can be utilised as energy.

Eating food containing a life force is vital because it supplements our own reserves. Processed food may satisfy hunger in the short term but only natural food makes us feel alive after eating. The benefits of eating natural foods are two fold:

- Natural food has a life force which is absorbed into our own
- It takes less energy to metabolise natural food than it does to metabolise processed food

Processed food must be able to sit for longer periods in storage than natural foods from the garden. Biscuits and buns and numerous other snacks may sit on the shelf for weeks or months. After being opened some processed foods do not decompose for days or even weeks. Compare this to a freshly picked apple straight off the tree. An apple picked off the branch begins to go brown within minutes, often even less. Some apples begin to turn brown even while you are eating them.

Fruit, vegetables, meat and fish begin to decay rapidly. Our stomach has to work harder breaking down processed foods, because it is used to food that decomposes quickly. Processed food is made for longevity, not to decompose. Processed foods not only supply less energy than natural, they also require greater energy to breakdown and digest. Processed foods, to meet nutritional guidelines contain supplements to meet these levels, but they still lack that spark of life that only natural food can provide.

For the soul to be in balance with the survival instinct, energy through fresh foods is a vital addition along with a balanced lifestyle.

## Alcohol and drugs

People use mood altering substances to change the way they feel and have done so for thousands of years. Alcohol relaxes the drinker, making them feel less tense and inhibited. Alcohol has evolved to become socially accepted because human beings in a large group are naturally tense. Alcohol as a relaxant calms the survival instinct's wariness. However, alcohol like any drug is poisonous to the body, making the system work hard to balance itself and to eliminate poisonous residue. Alcohol, like all relaxants, induces sleep, but the sleep it provides, because it's unnatural, is neither adequate nor refreshing. As a result alcohol leaves people feeling drained, dehydrated, tired and poisoned. This makes energy levels plummet and the survival instinct becomes dominant, accounting for hangovers, overly acute nerves and senses, aggressive intolerant behaviour and wanting to be left alone to sleep.

Hard depressing drugs such as opiates destroy the body and throw the survival instinct into disarray. Most obvious is the impact of the drug itself on the body and the effort involved to restore equilibrium. Those addicted to opiates rarely sleep or eat well. Many will go for days without eating much at all. Opiates incapacitate, making productive labour impossible and as a result, money and work is limited or impossible for those who are addicted. Food choices become whatever is most readily available and are usually the cheapest and quickest options. However the cheapest and quickest food option is rarely high in nutrition.

Stimulating drugs throw the survival instinct into attack mode by causing a surge of adrenalin. These drugs are taken because of the heightening of strength, endurance and the senses; the same situation as being under attack. When we are under attack we become violent in an attempt to escape. Our strength is momentarily increased and rational consciousness suppressed. At this point we become trapped animals losing the independence of being human. Under continued use these drugs result in paranoid and aggressive behaviour.

Drugs destroy lives because the survival instinct inhibits the soul. Our life loses its individuality and is replaced by routine desperation and struggle. Happiness is a feeling the survival instinct does not understand because happiness comes from achievement. Feelings of euphoria are different from the genuine contentment of the soul.

There has never been an addict who does not wish to have their life back, but for many it is gone forever. The longer an addiction is continued, the more difficult it becomes for the soul to regain its position. Generally the body is so energy depleted that the survival instinct constantly fights to maintain control. Addiction can only be replaced by contentment and meaning, by doing something the soul enjoys, so energy levels can rise again. Abstinence alone through willpower is difficult to achieve. Good food, trustworthy family and friends combined with an activity that is loved, ensure the best chance of success when incorporated with rehabilitation.

## Negative self-belief

Poor self-esteem is a term to describe a sense of unworthiness; a conviction that we are unlovable, dirty, dumb, weak or ugly. This can develop during the course of life, or exhibit itself from birth. These feelings have their origin in the survival instinct, and are designed to make us work harder to maintain our material life. Out of balance these traits can have the opposite effect, but the original intent is to act as a spur, securing our place in the group. We make ourselves valuable by the extra effort caused by feeling inherently a lesser person.

Some people are born with their survival instinct dominant and act in a terrified or aggressive manner from birth. For many this instinct is triggered when they encounter their first stress; going to school, another child coming into the family or a family problem.

## Emotional trauma

The death of a loved one is a common example of emotional trauma that drains energy to unsustainable levels. Emotional trauma is an event that creates a 'life will never be the same' effect. Before the death, a family member or partner is content and confident but after they may become withdrawn, depressed or sullen.

## Physical trauma and exertion

Childbirth and accidents are the most common forms of physical trauma. Accidents affect energy levels due to shock and physical damage. After childbirth some women can experience a number of negative responses. They feel as if they are going mad with over-protective reactions and anxiety. Other women become severely depressed or have emotions that are out of proportion or unrelated to the events happening around them.

If soul and survival are balanced and there is energy in reserve, childbirth presents no unexpected after effects. However if energy levels are precarious childbirth can project the survival instinct into becoming the dominant force.

Physical pain depletes energy. Pain is energetic by nature and continued pain affects the survival instinct profoundly, causing snappy and intolerant behaviour. When pain is consistent and draining, energy becomes exhausted.

Exercise is important to release available energy. However everyone has a personal level where exercise becomes detrimental. Exercise only releases energy up to a certain level and once this level is reached, a level specific to each individual, exercise burns more energy than it releases.

## Immunity and defence

Each of the primary forces has a defence system unique to its motion. The defence system's only purpose is to secure and protect us from danger, prolonging longevity at any cost. Each part of the defence system has its own specific task. The immune system is designed to protect the body against invading germs and the nervous system heightens the senses to alert us to the presence of danger. The more acutely we can see and hear, the less chance of being taken by surprise. Emotions provide the stimulus the body needs to react, while the face sends messages to other human beings to display our feelings and intentions.

Emotions such as anger help us to fight and defend ourselves while fear helps us to run away faster. Envy drives us to compete with others, while avarice eradicates the danger of contentment. Contentment is good for the soul but it is the survival instincts worst enemy. Sadness draws us to others and guilt makes us contribute and work harder. Hormones convey these emotional messages so that every cell acts appropriately to the emotion. When energy is irregular and the survival instinct dominant, hormones go haywire, which is why many women suffer mood swings, sadness or tantrums during or before their menstrual period.

The face is there for others to see and is not designed to look at itself. Our face lets other people recognise the emotions we are feeling; whether someone is angry or friendly, sexually interested or disinterested, enthusiastic or bored. The face is linked to the emotions but not to the soul. The face does not display ambition, belief or what it is we are thinking. The face is part of the survival instinct and an integral link in our defence system. Emotions and the face are complementary to each other, so expression can be interpreted by others.

## Breaking habits

When action is performed along with thought, the imprint in the brain is doubled, because the job of the brain is to coordinate both thought and action. The more a thought is repeated, the easier the development of that thought becomes, because of the network of neurons that have developed to support its continuance. When action is put into place the brain coordinates both the mind and body around a single purpose. Thought is important but action doubles the ability of the brain to be proficient. In order to break a habit, restructuring neurons is vital, otherwise the pathways of the brain stay strong. Re-channelling neurons into a new activity, means cutting off the energy supply of the habit. To break a habit it's important to do something else in its place.

When someone conveys to us a piece of wisdom that makes perfect sense, we have a moment of enlightenment. But that enlightenment is soon forgotten if we do not act or try to understand it, by linking it to our own experiences.

The more a single piece of knowledge connects with other avenues, the more profound and integral that piece of information becomes. Knowledge that remains separate to action or personal experience is destined to stay an independent yet isolated piece of advice.

## The mind not the brain
The soul is our mind, our conscience and our sense of self, but the soul or the mind is not the brain. The brain is organic and its purpose is the physical coordination of the body. One of its functions is to transport commands, thoughts and feelings so the body remains whole, ensuring that the body is in harmony with the soul and the survival instinct. The brain is designed to turn thought into action making desire and ambition a reality. Human beings are both physical and non-physical although the essence of our character is without form.

Chapter 9

# TIME CYCLES AND EPIDEMICS

## Space

When Newton held up a prism to the light he witnessed that the spectrum of colours recombined to form the whole. Inside white light are the colours of the rainbow which we see when the sun refracts in the raindrops. The same is true for the primary forces. They exist throughout the universe in one of their seven forms as part of the backdrop of space.

In microcosms like animals, plants and human beings, the confined borders of matter make one of the forces dominant, but in macrocosms such as planets, space and time dominance does not play such a specific role but instead moves in cycles. The earth being a macrocosm is large enough to contain the seven forces of motion – the three primary and four interactions – without them having to dominate or interact.

In the confined space of a nucleus, plant or human being the governing law of compete or cooperate through attraction, repulsion or joining is the dominant rule of nature. When space is large or infinite, these laws do not come into action because the primary motions do not get near enough to each other to trigger these laws into effect. In an area as large as the size of the earth, the seven forces of motion can co-exist in their own defined space, without being compelled to interact or vie for dominance. As a result the earth contains pockets or regions where one of the seven forces is most influential without the planet being at war with itself.

The material universe comprises time, space and matter, all of which are influenced by the forces flowing within them. Just as space or light holds the spectrum of motions and colours, so too does time. Time is also a macrocosm with a large enough space for all the forces to co-exist without dominance. However unlike the macrocosm of the earth, time has no material borders and rather than designated areas the seven forces that exist in time, flow from one to another in cycles.

Competing or cooperating is seen in the force of a magnet where the positive and negative poles attract or repel each other, but the interaction only occurs when the magnets are close. Trying to force magnets together is an example that the closer or more confined the space the more the governing laws apply. Distance is the triggering force to the law of attraction, repulsion or joining. In a human being there is always a dominant force due to the boundaries of structure, while the size of the earth allows the seven forces to remain independent entities.

## Time

Time has no physical structure so the seven forces move in cycles. Whichever force is dominant at the time will influence the environment and culture of that moment. Social morals, thinking and action become influenced by the nature of the force that is dominant within that cycle. Human culture shifts in cycles of ethics and thinking, in harmony with the resonant force of the moment. Each force governs over approximately 150 years and its impact can be seen throughout history.

Outward motion is yellow and the trader influences human activity through travel, trade and the development of law. The last yellow cycle that was dominant was between 1200 and 1350 AD. During this time Genghis Khan swept through and conquered the known world. It is also during this time that parliament and the Magna Carta were both constructed in England. The major events of history are influenced by whatever force is at the peak of the ongoing cycle. History, like knowledge, never unlearns, so once a thought or activity is brought into effect, it does not disappear when the cycle is over. The majority of the world was unified under the rule of one leader due to the influence of outward motion but that does not mean that exploration ceases after outward motion has concluded its time. When a motion becomes influential it is not to the exclusion of the other forces but remains the governing drive.

Preceding the yellow period from 1050 till 1200 AD was the orange time. Orange is the result of the interaction between outward and circular motion. This interaction results in resistance and competition, and provides the natural attributes for the traditional role of the warrior. As a result it is not surprising to find during this period that the ethic of the crusades and the development of chivalry and the ultimate Christian warrior, became the most influential and respected aspiration of the time.

Each historical timeframe looks back on previous periods confused at how such thinking could be so generally accepted. Moral codes and principles as well as laws and social behaviour are an outcome of the force most prominent at that time.

When the cycle changes and a new force takes control, a different social philosophy emerges that differs from the one before it. Human history is an evolutionary process each cycle building on the other, changing and adapting the past to the evolving needs of the present. When the orange time changed into yellow, the crusades continued to exist but they were given far less support by royalty and commoners alike, and lost their social appeal. As the yellow cycle moved into purple, social attention turned from general earthly concerns to trying to understand the temperament of God. The purple time began in 1350 and continued to 1500 AD. In 1348 the black plague began throwing the western world into death and confusion. Purple is represented by the priest who embraces spiritualism as well as earthly healing. Both these concepts became a dominant force during the plague. The plague continued and in some places on earth still exists today, but its strongest social impact occurred during the purple time.

Just as chronic disease is a manifestation of a survival instinct that is draining energy, so too does an epidemic epitomise the cycles of motion. In the yellow time leprosy became part of the social language as its influence dominated the charity, ethics and fear of society. In Europe by the end of yellow's 150-year cycle, leprosy had died a natural death without medicines, simply because its time was over. By the 1340s hospitals throughout Europe formerly dedicated to the treatment of lepers, were almost empty as the disease declined. Then in 1348 the black plague appeared taking control of the fear and consciousness that leprosy used to govern.

Moving forward in time another 150 years, a new disease enters Europe in 1493 when Columbus and his sailors return with news of the new world and syphilis. In the 1700s smallpox, a disease which had been around for centuries developed into a new and fatal form killing millions worldwide. The end of the 150-year cycle of the red era (1650–1800AD) coincides with Jenner's discovery of a vaccination for smallpox in 1796. In the

1800's smallpox was replaced as the world's number one killer by tuberculosis. Tuberculosis, the dominant epidemic of the green time (1800–1950AD) reduced dramatically with the discovery of antibiotics in the 1940s. The way an epidemic disease concludes is not as relevant as its timing. Whether a disease concludes by running its natural course or is brought under control by medicine, the fear it created and its influence on society diminishes as the cycle ends.

Since 1950 the influencing force has been brown. Brown has within its nature unity and development as well as destruction. The rise of many autoimmune disorders and diseases like cancer have replaced the fear of acute epidemics. The fear of cancer dominates the minds, emotions and cheque books of modern culture. Cancer is not the only disease that exists in the modern world and more people worldwide die of heart disease and malaria but it is cancer that strikes the most fear and it is cancer that gets the publicity. The values and fears of brown dominate the landscape of contemporary thinking. They do not exclude other avenues of thought nor does prior knowledge disappear. Accepting force as influence rather than exclusion is the only way history can be understood in regards to the seven forces and time.

Chapter 10

# LIFE THEMES

Life themes are the threads that run through the events and circumstances of each individual's life. For some people life themes are plain and obvious but for others they can be subtle. Themes can be positive and rewarding or negative, causing us pain and grief. Life themes can be defined by time spent either by choice or through necessity or by their distinguishing and unique qualities. They can be an event or a way of thinking, or a part of your personality that defines you. Life themes can be something you love to do, or a belief in how the world works.

For instance, many people would regard themselves as spiritual; believing in 'something'. However when someone devotes their life to the pursuit of spiritual understanding, the amount of time they spend thinking about it, or their degree of dedication, separates the intensity of their spiritual quest from the time the average person invests. Religion or spirituality becomes a life theme for this particular person whereas for others, spiritual thinking is just part of the general human condition.

Parents see life themes in children. They separate one child's personality from another. One child loves to build and design while another likes music or fantasy games. One is boisterous while the other is sensitive. One loves the water while the other is scared of nearly everything.

Life themes are commonly the circumstances that surround a person rather than their emotional response. Emotions are generic. Everyone experiences anger, sadness, remorse or happiness in relation to the events that occur in their lives. This means emotional reaction is not a good guide to understanding the motivation of the survival instinct. Circumstances and repeating events show the survival instinct at work as it tries to reproduce what has been successful in the past.

What is successful to the soul is not always what is successful to the survival instinct. To the soul, success is happiness, contentment, learning and interaction. To the survival instinct it is accumulation and security.

Survival instinct life themes can be negative compared to the desires of the soul because the survival instinct's focus is to repeat the events of the past that it successfully survived. This can include emotional trauma, negative behaviours and addiction. The survival instinct draws to itself the people and circumstances needed to re-create the conditions of the past. As the person in the middle, you may hate the events that are occurring but they continue to occur despite how you feel.

These negative events will continue while the survival instinct is dominant but will stop when the soul is in balance with the survival instinct. It is imperative that anyone caught in the web of repeating negative events, energises their soul through healthy habits and constructive pursuits.

Life themes are set apart by:

- frequency
- repeating circumstances
- distinctiveness
- impact

## Frequency

Frequency is the easiest life theme to observe and the majority of themes are based on rate of occurrence.

People find time for what they really want to do. Trading free time is a necessity because there is simply not enough time available. It is important to spend these free moments on the people or activities we love the most.

Family, music, building, painting and playing sport are all positive life themes, but not all life themes are constructive and they can be socially negative or personally destructive. Negative life themes may include fears, phobias, addictions, negative self-beliefs and a range of other behaviours that inhibit or destroy active life. Personality traits are another manifestation of a life theme because of their frequent and dominating influence.

What puts an activity or routine into the category of a life theme is the degree of prominence it takes.

## Repeating circumstances

Place yourself in the survival instinct's position. Your allotted task is to watch over somebody and keep them alive regardless of cost. You are commissioned to go to any lengths to get the job done, you have no other agenda. You are a guardian, a samurai, not a mother. Your task is to feed and protect, not to love or nurture, educate or entertain. The survival instinct is our samurai; bound to its designated function it is both committed and unquestioning.

Imagine you are a tennis player and you are through to the grand final. All you are waiting for now is to find out who you are playing. A semi-final match will decide who you play in the grand final. Of the two people playing the semi-final one you have played before. The second is unknown. The first has weaknesses you know how to exploit in order to win the game, the second is a mystery. You do not know their style or their game plan; you will have to learn on the day and hope you can match them. You really want to win the grand final. The question is, who would you rather face, the person who is unknown, or the person you know you can beat? This is not about testing yourself; this is about winning. The answer is, you would rather face the person you know you can beat and walk away with the trophy, than face the person you do not know and possibly be beaten.

The survival instinct works in exactly the same way. It will always face a situation it knows it can win, before risking a new situation and possible defeat. This means your survival instinct will do its best to reproduce the conditions it knows it can already survive. If you have lived through a circumstance once, the survival instinct knows you can live through it again.

Reliving positive situations is easy to understand, but why the survival instinct repeats adverse circumstances is more difficult to grasp. Happiness or contentment is not the survival instinct's role. Longevity is the only concern the survival instinct has. When the survival instinct is dominant it creates the circumstances it already knows it can survive. By ensuring that the past is repeated the survival instinct stays in known territory because this gives it the best chance of winning. The survival instinct will do its utmost to draw towards itself the same events, people and conditions to replicate the past.

Every colour group has a number of traits. Repeating or distinctive traits are life themes. When reading about your colour group you will relate to a number of the traits that form part of your character. We rarely have only one life theme and commonly people have three or four.

Sometimes we find ourselves in positions and circumstances that are best represented by life themes of another colour group. Many people relate to the red theme of effort while others relate to the yellow theme of money. One life theme does not complete the full picture; only by combination does the whole image emerge.

## Distinctiveness

Distinctiveness means something in your life that stands out. However, that something cannot become a life theme just because of its distinctiveness. It also has to be a recurring theme to some extent.

Distinctive life themes can be idiosyncrasies, peculiarities, quirks or unusual habits. It is something unique to a person's character. A trait can be distinctive because it is rare, such as the belief that half the world's population has been sent by the future to spy on the remaining half; or it can be something out of place like a fifty year-old man with childish habits.

Distinctiveness is uncommon – behaviours you do not expect or hear about everyday.

## Impact

A single event can be so influential that its effect can extend for years. A death or a severe fright, an accident or even a dream, anything that has a long-lasting or life changing influence, is also a life theme. Impacting events bring back emotions as vividly as when they first occurred. Impacting events leave an emotional scar as a constant reminder of the past. For an impacting event to become a life theme, this scar must be present; an old romance that brings tears to the eyes twenty years after its break-up, or a business betrayal from years ago that still makes hands curl into fists.

# Examples of life themes

## Barry – 48 years old

### An example of some yellow life themes

Barry has always been ambitious and full of energy. As a boy he was a happy-go-lucky type and always had plenty of friends. He was a keen sportsman and played football and cricket. As an adult, Barry still enjoys sport although he no longer plays competitively.

At school, he was academic and achieved high marks. His childhood home was stable and happy and his parents were caring and available with their time. However in later times Barry would recall that he never saw his parents relate in any intimate way. They never openly hugged or kissed. On the other hand, he can never recall them arguing either. To him they were just parents.

On completing his final year of high-school, Barry was eager to get out into the workforce. He enjoyed excitement and physical activity, so at nineteen he joined the police force.

At twenty, he became engaged to his wife Lorraine and they married when he was twenty-six. He and Lorraine had been friends for years before deciding to date. Barry and Lorraine had the first of four children when Barry was twenty-seven. Lorraine remains a stay at home mother, a position both she and Barry wanted. For extra income Barry worked part time with a local concreter making paths and driveways.

Lorraine is Barry's first and only relationship and he is content with her. Life revolves around the children, their schooling and extra-curricular hobbies, which take up every minute of the day.

Barry and his three boys are all members of the local football team. The boys play, while Barry is the fitness coach for the team. His daughter does not like football but is dragged along by her mother anyway because she is trying to teach her to be supportive.

Ten years ago, Barry left the police force to start his own garden maintenance and concreting business. Recently he bought the business he worked part time for and now has more work than he can handle. Lorraine helps by doing the books. They recently agreed to put an extension on the house, which Barry is doing himself when he gets the time. He and Lorraine enjoy entertaining their extended family and friends.

Lorraine suffers from mild depression and is prone to mood swings. Barry believes it is 'poor little rich girl syndrome' and thinks she should be more grateful. As a couple, they are compatible and rarely argue. The only time they fight is when Lorraine gets bored and moody, which is only occasionally. They had a significant argument about seven years ago which ended with Lorraine demanding they see a marriage counsellor. Lorraine believes Barry is unaffectionate and preoccupied with business. They rarely have sex due to Barry's work commitments, tiredness and time constraints. The counsellor suggested Barry should try to work fewer hours and set aside some specific times in which he and Lorraine could go out to dinner.

Barry complied, but thought the idea was a load of rubbish and couldn't see why he should date his wife – in his mind they were married with children, not teenagers – and they had just two dinner dates. He could not understand why Lorraine was complaining; life had never been better. In his opinion their marriage was solid, even though it was not romantic or sexual. Their children were healthy and doing well in school, they were extending their house and putting in a pool for next summer. Business was good and there was a chance he could be involved in an opportunity to develop it even further.

Barry admits he spends too much time at work but he also believes Lorraine is being silly and ungrateful. He cannot understand her feeling that he is being cold and sees her as being too needy. To him love comes in many forms, not just romance.

There are two main life themes in Barry's life story:

- intimacy
- business

The major life theme for Barry is his practical approach to marriage and romance, which is only causing a problem because his wife does not share the same values. During childhood he never saw his parents display any romantic affection, and he has carried this behaviour into his own adult relationship, not only because it is learned behaviour but because it suits him. Others from the same background who felt uncomfortable with their parent's lack of affection would actively seek a different relationship to their parents.

For Barry, intimacy comes in many guises and relationships revolve around compatibility. His need for romantic and sexual intimacy is not as strong as his focus in other areas such as business and family.

Business is Barry's strong point. He enjoys it, is successful and as a result is well rewarded. He gets pleasure from his family life and is happy to contribute to the local football team and to support and provide for his family. Barry has always had a strong work ethic; it is part of his personality and a comfortable environment for him, which is why he spends so much time at work.

Although in Barry's mind there is nothing wrong, his story shows that he is not fully in balance otherwise he would be considering the needs of Lorraine. Finding balance between who you are as well as the needs of your partner is the same as balancing soul and survival in yourself.

Barry's story also shows how repeating patterns can exist but in a mild enough form not to dominate or ruin life. Another person can have the same themes as Barry but find themself unable to relate to any partner or unable to find employment, be distraught and live life alone. The same life themes of business and intimacy are still occurring but in a more dramatic way. The key to understanding life themes is the frequency of the same event, not always its magnitude. Often the impact of similar events will depend on how stressed the individual is.

## Janice – 37 years old

### An example of some red life themes

Janice lives with her second husband Ron, her two daughters and her stepson who lives with them part-time.

Her upbringing was volatile and her earliest memories were of her mother and father fighting. Home was always turbulent until her mother took Janice and her sister to live with her new partner. Janice was ten and life became relatively stable. At fourteen her mother packed up her and her sister, and all three moved in with another man.

Time spent with her father was stable; he was a happier and more secure person than her mother. Janice spent time with her father every second weekend and whenever else she could.

School life was steady with no ups or downs and Janice was a sensible student. Her social life was good and although she was shy, she had a small, intimate group of friends. She preferred small groups because she was daunted by larger crowds.

She started dating boys at fifteen. Although she was painfully shy, boys found her attractive so she never had to seek them. When she was sixteen there was a terrible row and her mother's partner kicked them all out of the house. He had caught her mother with somebody else.

At seventeen Janice fell madly in love with a boy who left her for her best friend. She felt betrayed and humiliated and as if she had lost both her boyfriend and her circle of friends. Her ex-boyfriend and her ex-best friend were integral members of the one group; she on the other hand felt left out and awkward and so she left. This event was an enormous upheaval because she was shy and uncommunicative. She felt she had lost everybody and now was alone without the social skills to develop a new circle of friends. It took her years to recover.

After high school, Janice went to university and studied education. After completing her degree she took up a teaching position in a small outback school for two years.

Returning to the city Janice continued to teach and slowly gathered a new circle of friends. She had a number of dates and the occasional boyfriend but not a serious relationship. At twenty-three her closest friend accused her of flirting with her boyfriend, then of trying to seduce him. Janice was mortified at the time and as usual was lost for words. Her best friend left their group and even though Janice remained, she continued to feel upset and embarrassed by the accusations. She started feeling paranoid that the remaining friends were suspicious of her, and felt the women were watching her around their boyfriends. Many started going out as couples and Janice felt left out.

A relationship started around this time, which she believes now with hindsight, was driven by her desire to be in a relationship rather than any real love on her part. Janice and Tom married five months later.

The following year Tom was retrenched and had difficulty finding work. Although she knew he was a jealous man, she was unprepared for the accusations of infidelity every time she went out. It became so terrible that Janice stopped going out with friends and refused to go anywhere without Tom beside her. Not because she wanted him around, in fact she was beginning to resent him, but she could not tolerate explaining that she had not had an affair while out shopping.

At thirty, she was pregnant for the second time and felt a prisoner in her home. After the birth, Janice went back to work because Tom had still not found a job. Janice drew the attention of one of her workmates and began an affair with her now second husband Ron. He was also married. Twelve months later, each separated from their partners and moved in together.

They have now been together for more than five years and Janice describes her relationship as stable and wonderful.

The life themes for Janice include:

- infidelity
- suspicion
- difficult communication

Infidelity is the strongest life theme around Janice because:

- her mother left her father to move in with another man
- later her mother left again to move in with another boyfriend only to be told to leave for adultery
- as a teenager not only was her boyfriend unfaithful, so too were her friends.
- in her twenties, she was accused of trying to seduce and steal her best friend's boyfriend and her other friends started excluding her
- she married a man who constantly accused her of infidelity
- she had an affair with a married man

Many of these circumstances involve suspicion and Janice herself became suspicious of others. Throughout her life as both a teenager and young adult Janice was unable to communicate effectively, which left her out of her group, unable to defend herself against others' suspicions.

Although Janice's story has life themes of adultery and infidelity, Janice herself has only been unfaithful once when she met her then married, current husband. This affair and her subsequent marriage only took place because of the intolerable suspicion of her previous husband. Life themes are not always the actions we take but can also be the events that occur to us or around us. One life theme such as infidelity is never enough to identify a person as belonging to a colour group. Understanding the influence of the survival instinct comes from grouping a number of life themes together. On its own infidelity belongs to any colour group. It is the totality of themes that define the colour group.

Colour groups can have as many as thirty different traits, a number of which will become life themes. Many of these qualities will stay as attributes but not become life themes. Life themes are determined by frequency, impact and distinctiveness.

Janice did not cause her mother's infidelity, nor did she give her previous husband any cause for suspicion. Life themes come from the survival instinct which drives unconscious behaviour. Consciousness belongs to the soul. People do not consciously make life themes happen.

## David – 50 years old

### An example of some blue life themes

David's family home was relatively normal although his mother needed to go away every six months or so to be treated for depression. His father was a clerk in the public service and family life was a typical middle class environment. At twelve, David entered and won a scholarship to a prestigious private school. His two brothers teased him relentlessly for his uniform and studious nature. After finishing high school, he joined the army officer's training program. For David the army was a way to study for his degree and earn money at the same time. This meant leaving home and moving interstate which suited him.

At twenty-two David suffered bouts of depression but found if he kept himself busy, they would lift after a week or two. He still employs this technique and is thankful he is not like his mother was and his youngest brother is now; not able to get themselves out of their depression no matter what measures they take. This is the same now for his twenty-year-old son who is bedridden for months at a time. David feels guilty because sometimes he feels he has given depression to his son, David describes depression as the 'family curse'.

David married when he was twenty-five. He was a lieutenant with a degree in marketing and commerce. He and his wife had three children. After the death of his mother-in-law his wife Anne had a breakdown. David continued his job as an administration manager in the defence force, as well as looking after the children. He believes his eldest son went into his first deep depression due to his mother's breakdown.

Trying to keep his head above water, David took up running as a way of relieving stress. Within twelve months, he was running 'fun-run' marathons. When his second son was seventeen he also took up running and together they ran up to seventy kilometres a week. David's daughter enjoys being active too and they have both taken up ballroom dancing on Thursday nights.

Anne never recovered from her breakdown and was moved to a high care facility. David is responsible with money. He manages the accounts for his wife, father, brother and one of his sons. David's mother died five years ago and his brother is on a disability pension due to the incapacitating nature of his depression. He recently tried to commit suicide.

David hopes to retire early and take some well-earned time off to travel. Above all things he is a family man, and feels compelled to look after his children and siblings.

There are four main life themes in David's biography:

- depression
- management
- exercise
- family

The life theme of depression is obvious, his mother suffered from it, so too does his brother, wife and eldest son. He himself had occasional although generally manageable bouts.

Management is a life theme because not only is David in a management role at work, but has voluntarily taken the management role for his wife, father, brother and son.

The next theme is exercise. Many people enjoy going for a walk or to the gym, but few take up marathon running. Exercise has become a family affair; running with his son and dancing with his daughter.

Last is David's commitment to his family. Some may say he is too soft, and even being exploited, but he is not resentful and is happy to provide the support needed by his family.

David highlights the difference between life themes that are in balance and those that are out of balance. Each colour group has a number of qualities that can be used by the soul for a beneficial purpose. David's endurance and caring nature is being channelled into exercise and managing the affairs of his family. Out of balance, these same qualities, with erratic and scattered energy levels, could make him incapable of holding down any position and dependent on the management and care of others.

It is how a person uses their inherited qualities that determines whether they are in balance or out of balance. Sometimes life themes can seem contradictory. How can one person so capable and caring share the same life theme with another who is depressed and helpless? Management is the life theme of both. For the capable and caring, managing others has become a life theme, while the helpless person cannot look after themselves and needs the management of others.

Life themes cannot be seen in black and white. They are lateral rather than literal. There are numerous ways a life theme can manifest.

## Sue – 50 years old

### An example of some orange life themes
Sue is the third of four girls. As a child she got along well with her sisters and the family was a close knit group until her eldest sister was killed in a car accident when Sue was fifteen. Sue said the family went quiet, and she was personally grief stricken for years; she still cries when she thinks of their loss.

Sue became withdrawn for the remainder of her high school years, although she had a few close friends. On completing school, Sue enrolled in secretarial college for twelve months, and then found work as a personal assistant.

At twenty, Sue came out of her shell, socialising with friends and going to clubs. At twenty-one she met the love of her life, a man named Charlie. Unfortunately, Charlie was dating one of her friends, so the relationship never developed. At twenty-three she took out a loan to buy a one-bedroom unit and she also bought herself a small dog. Sue became involved in dog training and obedience, and it was here she met her first husband Max.

She and Max married and at twenty-five their first daughter Sarah was born. After the birth, Sue haemorrhaged and needed a total hysterectomy. While the safe arrival of Sarah was wonderful, Sue was also devastated that Sarah would be her one and only child.

When Sue was in her thirties, her mother was diagnosed with Alzheimer's disease which progressed rapidly. This left Sue and her family heartbroken as her mother had been the core of the family. Sue watched as her once strong mother gradually reverted to an infant. Her father could not cope and began to deteriorate, becoming needy and dependent rather than the resourceful man she used to know.

Sue went back to work part time, and she and Max bought a larger house with all the modern conveniences. A few times a year they went out to dinner and caught up with old friends, one of whom was Charlie, and he still made her heart race.

She and Max led a comfortable lifestyle. They owned a beautiful home and were able to afford an occasional overseas holiday. Max was on a very good wage and expecting another promotion. Sue's mother was put into a high care nursing home where she died after a few years. Her father passed away when she was forty-five, three years after her mother.

Sue is now fifty and life is peaceful and calm. Her biggest disappointment is how infrequently she sees her daughter. Sarah moved away after leaving school early, to move in with her boyfriend. Sarah fell pregnant to her boyfriend Mick at seventeen, the result of a whirlwind romance while Mick was visiting from interstate. Sarah moved to be with him when she found she was pregnant. They now have a little boy who Sue rarely sees.

The life themes in Sue's biography include:

- grief
- disappointed love

Grief is a life theme because the early death of her sister affected her intensely making her withdrawn and quiet. Decades later Sue would still burst into tears, thinking about the impact her sister's death had on the family.

Disappointed love is seen in the loss of expression the family experienced after her sister died. Later came the heartache caused by the unrequited love she felt for Charlie. Next was the disappointment of only being able to have one child and then, when her only child Sarah became pregnant, she moved away, making contact difficult and rare.

Life themes come from the traditional roles. The traditional role of orange is the warrior. The warrior not only trained and committed themselves to the protection and care of the group but also suffered grief and loss at a level greater than other traditional roles. This does not mean that orange experience more grief or loss than others through life but for many, loss or grief will have an impact that is more profound.

Someone from another colour group would have forgotten about their first love Charlie, to focus on the life they have with Max. Sue however still considers Charlie her primary love. The death of her sister can be seen in exactly the same way. Many people experience death in their childhood but not all are moved to tears thirty-five years later.

The behaviour of people in a particular colour group can only be really understood by someone who belongs to that group. For others outside the orange colour group behaviour like Sue's can seem foreign.

Each traditional role has a variety of experiences that it passed on to the survival instinct of that colour. The warrior experiences trials and pain, death, commitment, grief and honour. All these qualities exist in orange but not every orange person will have all of these qualities as their life theme. Most have only a few. In Sue's story loss and grief are the two life themes of orange that are strong. Life themes can be what we are most sensitive to or what we fear at our core.

## Marcia – 42 years old

### An example of some purple life themes

Marcia came from a family that struggled emotionally and financially. Her father drank heavily and often gambled away what little money the family had. Her mother was also an alcoholic, diagnosed as bi-polar with depression. Despite this, Marcia always described herself as a happy person.

At primary school, Marcia had a number of close friends and in high school this trend repeated. She matured early and attracted unwanted male attention, which made her embarrassed and withdrawn. Marcia described herself as sexually prudish, unlike her sister who was far more liberal.

At sixteen she met her first boyfriend and fell madly in love. He was part of the 'wrong crowd' at school – they smoked marijuana and drank excessively and later became involved with hard drugs. Her boyfriend constantly harassed Marcia to join in with them, but she just as constantly refused. She found the idea of drugs and their potential side effects frightening. Drugs and alcohol became a constant irritation and the couple began to argue. When her boyfriend started using speed, Marcia decided that was enough and ended their relationship.

When she was nineteen, Marcia moved out of home with a friend and visited her parents as infrequently as possible. They were drunk most of the time and arguments and violence were common.

Her mother was becoming delusional, suspecting people of watching her and of authorities tapping her phone. When Marcia was twenty, her mother threw herself under a bus, either deliberately or by accident, trying to run away from the spies she believed were chasing her. Her mother was badly injured and hospitalised for six months. During this time her father cut back on his drinking and he and Marcia became the closest they had ever been; a direct result of sharing the care of her mother. Three months after being discharged from hospital, her mother and father were drinking again and within six months were as bad as ever.

At twenty-two, Marcia married Tom. A year later she had a daughter and at twenty-five their son was born.

Marcia and her husband are ardent non-drinkers. They met at a church social club soon after Marcia had become a Christian. Tom is an accountant and an active member of the local Methodist church. Now, at 42, Marcia is a full time mother and a trained church counsellor. The church is the cornerstone of their family; they are happy together and have a solid social network.

Two life themes that repeat are:

- drug and alcohol addiction
- religion

Drugs and alcohol have been a constant factor and continue to strongly influence the decisions Marcia makes. Both her parents are alcoholics, so too was her first boyfriend. Marcia not only found religion but chose the Methodists, who generally abstain from alcohol. Marcia and her husband don't drink.

Having a particular attitude to something does not necessarily make it a life theme. It is the frequency of recurrence and impact on a person's life that makes an issue a life theme. Whether a person is anti-alcohol or an alcoholic, the life theme is alcohol in both cases.

Religion is also a life theme as it provides Marcia with an outlook on life, as well as a set of personal values to live by. Religion gave Marcia a suitable husband as well as a guide to raising her family. Religion dominates Marcia's thinking and work, and decision-making is made in reference to its teachings.

The traditional role of purple is that of the priest. Marcia moved away from a life surrounded by self-absorption and addiction, to a life more meaningful and constructive where she helps those with the same problems. Drugs and religion belong to the traditional role of the priest.

The priest is more than a local minister. The priest was the shaman, the witchdoctor and wise-woman. The shaman relied on drugs to take them from this world into the next. The priest moderates self-indulgence to focus on matters of the spirit. The drugs and addiction that surrounded Marcia's early life, and the sobriety and religion that resulted are both life themes of the priest. Some within a colour group will exhibit life themes that come from the traditional role, while others have reactions and outlooks formed by the events of that colour group's time.

## Phil – 60 years old

### An example of some green life themes

In his early years Phil was an easy going, live-for-the-moment person. His upbringing was stable and he was the eldest of two. Phil hated school work although he loved the company and the social experiences school provided. School was a place where he and his friends organised their social life for the weekend. He was popular and had a number of friends as well as a few romantic relationships. No longer wanting to study, much to the concern of his parents who by this time were despairing of him, Phil got a full-time job at the local supermarket.

At eighteen Phil was bored with the supermarket and decided to travel. He was a good saver and worked two jobs. His second job was as a part-time barman at the local pub. Unlike the supermarket, Phil enjoyed bar work because it allowed him time to be friendly and social. The supermarket was strict and he hated how official and structured it was. The management at the pub did not care if he was social, in fact they encouraged friendliness as it kept the patrons happy. Provided he was quick, filled the orders and balanced the till, he could be as chatty as he wanted.

By nineteen Phil had saved enough money to travel around Asia and the Pacific. Travelling mostly by bus and free rides he also managed to find work as a barman in a number of tourist hotels. Phil also worked in youth hostels but the pay was poor and sometimes he worked for only food and board, but he was young and it helped him get around. Phil returned to Australia when he was twenty, met a girl and had a relationship with her for a year.

On his return Phil went back to his old job at the supermarket. He also began a course in hospitality. Unfortunately he did not do well in the course and dropped out after three months.

Phil left his job at the supermarket and took a position as a sales representative selling time-share apartments. However, after six months he failed to meet his sales target and he was sacked. Determined to try something new, Phil took a clerical position in the shire council offices but hated the environment so much that he resigned shortly afterwards. Phil went back to the supermarket and pub and started saving for his next trip.

At twenty-four Phil had enough money, and left to travel in Europe. He worked in London for twelve months as a barman before spending another six months travelling around the continent. When he was twenty-six Phil returned home and met Jan. They were married six months later.

After four years Phil and Jan bought a milk bar, where they both worked for the next two years. Even though they were busy they only just managed to scrape through and make a profit. Phil enjoyed getting to know the regulars but after the two-year lease ran out they decided to sell the business. Phil went back to full-time bar work; Jan was pregnant with their first child.

By the time he was thirty-five, the couple had two children. Phil was working as a cocktail barman in an up-market hotel. While his wages were low, the tips were good and he was back doing work he enjoyed. Jan worked part-time in a local sandwich bar.

Financially they were getting by, but emotionally they were not doing well. At thirty-seven the marriage broke down and Phil moved in with a woman named Di. Phil and Di had a daughter before their relationship ended when Phil was forty. At forty-one Phil met and moved in with Tanya.

His forties were tumultuous both personally and professionally. Phil changed employers a number of times, before finding work in an exclusive hotel at the airport. The tips made up for any shortfall in wages and Phil became manager of the bar. He still lives with Tanya.

Phil's life themes include:

- change
- socialising
- stimulation

Change is the dominant life theme in Phil's life. He left school early because the routine was dull, although he enjoyed the social interaction. Travel is an expression of change, and in his early years Phil had itchy feet. Change of partners is another example, as is the number of times Phil changed jobs.

Phil had the 'gift of the gab' and was happiest when talking to people. His ability to stick to one job, place or person was limited by his need for change. Socialising was a positive way to get the change he needed. As a barman at an airport he was in contact with new people. Although his personality made him unsuitable for a number of occupations, his high social IQ made him perfect for this kind of job.

A desire for stimulation is a strong life theme in green. There are a number of different events and circumstances that have occurred to Phil in his life. Life themes are the common thread that links events together.

It is easy to view life themes as traits that are *lacking*, rather than looking for traits that *exist*. To an outsider, Phil is incapable of holding down a steady job or committing to a long-term relationship but this describes what is absent. What is present is Phil's need for change and to socialise. Einstein is known for his contribution to science, not because he *didn't* play football.

Life themes must explore *what is*. Each colour group has a number of traits of which only a few will become life themes. No-one displays every trait.

Patience is another trait of green. Phil doesn't have any aspect of patience in his life story. He will not relate to the green trait of patience because it is not his repeating pattern. Another green person may have patience as their life theme but not relate to or exhibit the trait of change. Both are still green.

In the colour group chapters, single word descriptors are used to highlight life themes. Phil's constant need for stimulation and change makes him a person who is referred to as 'stimulation green'. Phil would also be defined by the sub-category of 'social green'. These two sub-categories come together to explain the core of Phil's character.

## Rachael – 54 years old

### An example of some brown life themes

Rachael has always been a high achiever. At school, she was in the top ten percent, not only scholastically but also in sport. Rachael is now, as she always has been, vibrant and dynamic. She is one of three children. Her parents and sisters are good friends and for years she saw them regularly, even though her parents divorced when she was eight. Neither she nor her sisters believe there were any long-term consequences from the divorce. Her mother was her role model and the strongest person in the family. Her father confided once that her mother's dominant personality was the reason the marriage fell apart. Her father was softer than her mother; she always 'wore the pants' and had the final say. Her mother pretended to be diplomatic but in the end always pushed until she got what she wanted.

Rachael went to private school, immersing herself in the life it offered and loving every minute. She was an active member of her school house and became house captain in her final year. Her marks were high and she was popular with everyone regardless of their background. She was and still is friendly and always ready to help and listen. Rachael played music and excelled in both debating and drama.

After completing school, she studied teaching and had ideas of saving the world; she wanted to teach poor communities to the same level as privileged ones. However, life did not work out as she had planned, and at twenty-six she left teaching.

A year earlier Rachael met John who was her second long-term relationship. Rachael left teaching, annoyed by the restrictions and narrow mindedness of the education department, as well as the apathetic way many students and parents approached learning. After leaving Rachael got a job as a sales representative, selling a range of kitchenware. A year later, she left that company and became regional sales manager for a pharmaceutical firm.

Rachael was serious about her work and wanted to be financially secure and established before starting a family. She regards herself as a career woman, determined to break through any glass ceiling that impedes her ambitions.

Rachael studied law part-time and in her thirties had a job prosecuting equal opportunity claims. Her hours were long, especially when combined with the workload needed to finish her degree. She was working day and night but she always kept Saturday night free. Rachael was later given the position of assistant manager for all equal opportunity claims.

Her relationship with John ended after an ongoing personality dispute because he believed she was too controlling. Six months later she met Rob.

At forty, Rachael's health began to suffer, nothing major but enough to be of concern. Being a perfectionist, highly motivated and extremely competitive, she would burn herself out making sure her work was faultless. Knowing that stress was the cause of the break-up between herself and John and not wanting it to happen again with Rob, Rachael took up tennis as an outlet. Soon she was in charge of the social committee as well as captain of the team representing her age.

Rachael began to suffer depression so her doctor recommended anti-depressants that have become a routine of life. Rachael also needs sleeping tablets as her mind never switches off. A few years back she tried breaking her dependence but found there was no way she could manage. Rachael hates this dependency because she likes to feel she can accomplish anything and that every situation is within her control.

At forty-two Rachael heard the ticking of her biological clock and for the first time felt the need for a child. Rob however did not want any more children as he already had three from a previous marriage. Rachael wanted a family of her own but Rob argued that corporate demands and a career were the common ground that drew them together and to change these terms would be unfair. They argued for twelve months before deciding they were at an impasse; then their relationship ended. Rachael threw herself into her job in an effort to forget about having a family.

A year later Rachael met a man named Harry and began a quick but serious relationship. The couple decided to start a family but Rachael couldn't conceive; the couple tried IVF but to no avail. Rachael decided not to continue treatment and left it to fate to decide; she did not have any children. Harry wanted to marry Rachael but Rachael believed that marriage represented property and refused, saying that living together demonstrated a commitment to the relationship.

At forty-eight Rachael became manager at her workplace and her hours increased considerably. She and Harry still get along well but their time together is less. Harry also works long hours and there is an expected social life that goes with his job, so he spends a lot of time away from home.

The main life themes for Rachael are:

- perfection
- equality

Rachael does her best at everything she attempts and generally succeeds. Rachael aims for perfection or as close as she can get. She was a high achiever academically as well as being exceptional in sport, a skilled musician, debater and house captain. Rachael rarely caused problems or rocked the boat and gets along with everyone. Rachael is a person who others describe as perfect. Even when she took up tennis to relax, she ended up in charge of the social committee and captain of her team. At work she tried to accomplish her tasks with the highest degree of efficiency.

Her next life theme is equality. In her earlier years Rachael had ambitions to give underprivileged children a level of education equal to that of the privileged. After becoming disillusioned she moved out of the teaching area and into equal opportunity.

Barriers and stereotypes create divisions and that is the opposite of equality. To Rachael any label is limiting, even marriage meant a role and expectations that she believed were subservient.

Every colour group has both positive and negative qualities, as well as traits that can be either positive or negative depending on timing and how they are applied.

Rachael has ambition and drive which she has constructively applied to her work. These same qualities in brown, when out of balance can lead to a controlling and dominating nature. While Rachael's zeal has been successful in helping her career, gaining a law degree and becoming manager of her department, she continues to apply these same qualities at home where they are not as beneficial.

Circumstance and timing are important factors in whether a quality becomes a positive or negative influence in a person's life. At work a competitive and driven attitude is what employers are looking for, but home is a refuge away from work where the same competitive behaviour has negative effects.

While the qualities of a colour group remain the same, how they are used depends upon stress. When a person is highly stressed their survival instinct employs traits for the purpose of attack and defence. When the soul is in balance with the survival instinct, these same traits are used by the soul to interact and learn about life.

# Chapter 11

# UNDERSTANDING COLOUR GROUPS

## Colour groups help us understand ourselves and others

The types of behaviour people exhibit when under stress vary enormously, yet there are enough similarities for them to be classified into distinctive groups. These similarities are explained in the chapters on 'colour groups'.

The concept of colour group traits helps explain the repeating patterns we face in our lives. The knowledge that they are built into our deepest memories – our survival instinct – makes us realise that we are the way we are for reasons that may well be outside our own control. Understanding this helps us to realise that it is often a waste of time telling someone to change. Even if they can change, the change will only last while life is going well. As soon as they are under stress, they will revert to their instinctive behaviour patterns.

Understanding colour groups will lead you to better relationships, by giving you the strength to tolerate and accept personality. As the serenity prayer says, we must have the wisdom to know what we can change and what we cannot. Instinct cannot be changed but stress levels can.

By knowing our colour group traits we acknowledge diversity and understand that while not everyone is good at everything, everyone is good at something. Colour groups help us to understand our natural traits and attributes. Working with the skills we have gives us confidence and places the soul in balance with our survival instinct, secure in the knowledge we have something to offer. Parents can use colour group knowledge to understand their children's personalities and to guide them into areas that are conducive to their character and skills.

Frustration and bad feeling are the usual result when others continually fail to behave in a way we expect. It is a common misconception that we are all aspiring to the same things. This misconception leads us to believe that what makes us happy is the same as what makes others happy. By understanding colour groups and how they arose over the course of human history, we can learn the values of those we love and the things they consider important, and accept those traits for what they are, knowing they cannot be changed. At the same time we can also make others understand our own basic needs and why they are important to us.

Some people when they are under stress and their survival instinct is dominant try to find solutions or become aggressive, while others stand mute. Some people act on the plans they have made while others have no plans at all. These reactions have a basis in the traditional role that belongs to each colour group. The survival instinct has absorbed the events of the past that created danger and exhaustion as well as the reactions that kept us alive. The survival instinct is an ever changing, ever absorbing entity whose sole purpose is to adapt and evolve and give each generation the best possible chance of longevity and of having children.

## Colour groups help us acknowledge the effects of stress

When a partner or family member displays a number of the negative traits of their colour group it is important to acknowledge their stress levels are high. Lowering the degree of stress is more effective than trying to change instinctive behaviour. No one would expect or try to train a child out of their instinctive reaction to jump from harm's way, but the colour group reactions to social stress are just as instinctive and as unconscious as running away from danger. It is common to seek advice or counselling over relationship traits that have become habits. While both parties agree that they are going to change, the moment they get back home they return to old patterns. Instinct reacts to environment and threat and cannot be counselled away. For better relationships stress must be reduced so the soul can begin to communicate and reason at a level beyond survival. Before a relationship can be repaired, the individuals in it must be content. Energy levels must be high enough for the soul to become active. Energy levels rise from wholesome food, enough sleep, exercise and enjoyment from doing the things we love.

The information in the following colour chapters provides an understanding as to why people behave in the manner they do. When both parties in a relationship are happy and content they can communicate about any subject or feeling, but when people are stressed and the survival instinct is dominant, the relationship becomes polarised. Stress turns a relationship from 'you *and* me' into 'you *versus* me'. Colour groups make clear the motivations of behaviour, giving an historical context as to why they are important and why the survival instinct employs them during stress.

A household under stress is a household that is not communicating and the reason they are not communicating is because the survival instinct cannot think. We can explain our point of view as much as we like but it will still fall on deaf ears if the other party feels threatened. Understanding colour groups means recognising stress in yourself and in the people around you.

## Traits in balance and out of balance

The human condition includes the basic needs for happiness and physical survival. When a trait is in proportion it is regarded as *in balance*. When a trait is out of proportion it is regarded as *out of balance*. Each colour group has an out of proportion response to *particular* stresses because of the history of their traditional role that lies in their colour group's survival instinct.

By knowing the different survival needs of each colour group we can understand the differences that exist in those we love. When a partner or family member is stressed we do our best to console and counsel but sometimes our words not only fall on deaf ears, they can be more of a hindrance than a help. Often this is because the language we are speaking is different to that of the survival instinct of the person we are trying to communicate with. There is no use telling a devastated orange person to forget about being betrayed. An orange person cannot forget that easily because betrayal cuts a deeper wound for them than for a person from any other colour group.

Colour group traits are the issues that are *devastating* to that group while only *upsetting* to others. Colour group traits are reactions of increased intensity to particular events by comparison with other colour groups.

Every group throughout history has survived by diversity of skills and labour. In order to provide these skills our survival instinct has developed different traits and personalities so we can contribute and enhance our chances of longevity through security. The negative consequence of diversity is that each of us feels separate from others. We feel different because *we are* different. Knowing that difference is a valuable asset. Instead of being an impediment to group acceptance, it makes individuals feel more comfortable being themselves.

A mother who is orange, with a lot of drive and ambition, can become frustrated by her blue son who continually withdraws whenever she begins to push him. He will tell her anything she wants to hear provided she leaves him alone, even though he may have no intention of ever fulfilling these promises. Because the son is blue and dominant in inward motion, the more threatened he feels the more he will withdraw into himself. Forcing him to have drive and energy does nothing but make him turn inwards and the relationship may be ruined for years, or possibly forever.

Therapists' couches are filled with people recalling how their parents never 'understood them', while pharmacies dispense anti-depressants at a rate quicker than factories can make them. Forcing others to behave in a manner that is conducive to the needs of *our* survival instinct is counterproductive and dangerous.

The difference between a trait being in balance and out of balance depends on how frequently it recurs and the circumstances that bring it out. An aggressive, dominating attitude can be a helpful trait at work but a destructive trait when applied to others in an environment like the home. The more stressed we become the more the survival instinct is dominant making a distinction between environments impossible.

## Variations in colour groups

Traits in a colour group are like colours themselves. The colour green can range from lime to turquoise to emerald and yet all these shades are still green. In each colour group there are a number of traits but these traits have variations. Variation can make traits seem contradictory but all share a common foundation. In the yellow chapter, money is discussed as a theme, but the spectrum of money ranges from wealth at one end, to poverty at the other with charity in between. One person talks about business continually and how much money they make, while another argues that accumulation of wealth is destroying the planet. Both have money as their central theme even though their attitude to money is different. These two people lead different lives and have different ambitions and values, yet both display the central theme of money. These variations in each trait are specifically titled or referred to as 'this type of' colour. In this instance these two people would both be referred to as 'money yellow'.

Here is a way of understanding the difference between colour group traits and the variations within them. Imagine a group of friends gathered together, and the topic of religion comes up. Some of the group believe in God while others view religion as a fairy tale. Among the disbelievers there are a number of reasons as to why they believe religion is valueless. Some even believe it is dangerous. Of the believers many have a different interpretation of what spirituality is. Colour group traits are the issue being discussed. Variations are the different opinions.

## What is in the colour chapters?

As well as discussing traits that developed from traditional roles each colour chapter has analogies and stories to capture the essence of each group. At the beginning of each chapter metaphors are discussed using the seasons, climate and types of terrain that help describe the nature of that group. They are not literal interpretations but valuable adjuncts to understanding. Describing personality in words, together with motivation and desire, is an almost impossible task unless we employ the imagery of symbolism. The sun is used as a symbol of yellow the way the jungle is used for green. Red is represented by the desert, while the nature of blue is characterised by the ocean. Fire epitomises orange and the soil represents brown, while the ethereal quality of ultra-violet light captures and symbolises purple.

Along with symbolism, actual events will be discussed that have embedded themselves into the survival instinct of each colour group. The survival instinct is formed by stressful historical events and reactions. These events can come from disease, climate or the traditional role. These circumstances are not symbolic but actual events that occurred in the past so frequently that our survival instinct feels it needs to protect us from them in the present.

## What colour group are you in?

In some people one or two traits can be so dominant they become life themes to the exclusion of all other traits. This means a reader may not necessarily relate to every trait in their colour group but, like everything in life, it is what *you have* that counts, not what you don't have. It is important to see yourself in the traits you display and not exclude yourself from your colour group because of the traits *you do not have*. What is lacking is not of concern.

Every trait in every colour group belongs to the human condition but not every trait has the same impact or influence. Everyone has stages of life where circumstance causes different aspects of the human condition to rise to prominence. Colour group traits are qualities that express themselves in repeated patterns. Someone under financial stress will naturally talk about money no matter which colour group they belong to. But not everyone will continue to discuss money or keep it as their driving force, once their financial position has become stable. Traits in the human condition can be satisfied but colour group traits are insatiable when the survival instinct is dominant. To understand colour groups we need to look at the totality of traits and subsequent life themes. A single life theme viewed on its own is not distinctive to a particular colour group. Behind every survival instinct action is an unconscious motivation. Life is an expression of character but can never be fully understood by the examination of single parts. Character reproduces itself in every aspect of life. Actions and deeds may be similar but the survival instinct motivation is not.

As you read the colour group chapters, you will find yourself wondering, 'Is this me?' The only way to accurately find out which colour group you belong to is by facial analysis. Chapter 12 has more about this. Also see <www.soulandsurvival.com>

## Traits of colour groups
- Each colour has as many as thirty or more distinctive traits.
- Each person will relate to as few as seven or as many as twenty-five of these traits from their colour group.
- Life themes consist of two to five consistent traits.
- Some traits are exclusively negative and some exclusively positive.

- Some traits can be both negative or positive depending on the situation.
- Some traits are displayed consistently throughout a person's life, while others are only displayed occasionally.
- People demonstrate many of these traits only under stress.
- Individuals rarely have all the traits of their colour group.
- Traits have their basis in the dominant motion or interaction of motions within that colour group.
- These traits form the skills that are the basis of the traditional role that represents that colour

# Summary of the colour groups

| Colour | Type of motion | Energetic purpose | Natural skills and attributes | Main traits | Traditional role |
|---|---|---|---|---|---|
| Yellow | Outward | Progress | Opportunity | Independence Business Flexibility | Trader |
| Red | Circular | Growth | Productivity | Relationships Effort Completion | Farmer |
| Blue | Inward | Stability | Support | Nurture Community Simplicity | Shepherd |
| Orange | Outward – Circular | Resistance | Determination | Idealism Loyalty Competition | Warrior |
| Purple | Circular – Inward | Separation | Creativity | Spirituality Devotion Expectation | Priest |
| Green | Outward – Inward | Reaction | Perception | Sensitivity Intellect Skill | Hunter |
| Brown | Outward – Circular – Inward | Unity | Equality | Perfection Abundance Productivity | Craftsman |

Chapter 12

# THE FACE

Human beings are communal creatures. We require assistance and help with tasks and we need other people's company. When we talk with others we are relaying ideas. Speech is the only way apart from writing to communicate our thoughts to another. The face cannot communicate thought because the survival instinct cannot think. The face is not designed to convey ideas or to discuss plans for the future. The face is part of the survival instinct. It does not belong to the mind or soul. The face is designed to express emotion in a way that makes others understand how we feel. Words cannot convey anger or sorrow if our face remains deadpan as we speak. On the other hand we can tell when someone is nervous, upset, dangerous or sad, just by their face and body language without them uttering a word.

To make another person react emotionally, using the face is imperative. The survival instinct does not come up with solutions nor does it have good ideas. When we communicate verbally it is soul meeting soul. Emotion is the language of the survival instinct and the face is how we communicate that emotion. The vocal chords are not exclusive to the soul and can express the needs of the survival instinct but communication of ideas and concepts comes directly from the soul.

What we feel internally is expressed on the face whether we are conscious of this expression or not. It is a successful social survival tool because it expresses our emotional needs. When we are sick or frightened, our face displays our need for help. When we are sad or upset, the face displays our need for comfort. Whether we feel lost, helpless, lonely, frustrated, tired, angry or sad, the face conveys our emotion, making other people react. The defence system benefits from facial expression by frightening away intruders or imploring others to come to our aid, attracting people to bond and showing others our confidence and skill.

A human face is familiar to all of us and yet faces present in many different forms. Identical twins aside, we can safely say there are more than six billion different faces in the world. Some are very similar to others but each has its own distinctive look.

The look that comes together to form your face is not an accident of birth. Faces are determined by the genetic information passed on by your parents, grandparents and other distant relatives. The face also provides information about the energetic forces within us.

These forces are the three primary motions – outward, circular and inward. All of these energies exist within us but when one or more of these energies is *dominant* it will shape our appearance and how we behave under stress.

The three primary motions have different natures and they will form distinctive facial features. To analyse a face a number of different facial features need to be examined. In order from top to bottom they are:

- hairline
- eyes
- nose (front and side)
- cheeks
- mouth
- lips
- teeth
- chin (front and side)
- facial lines
- forehead (side)
- bridge of nose (side)
- ears (front and side)

Each of these features can present in a multitude of ways – large, medium, small, sloping down, turned upward, outward, inward, round and straight. The way our features are arranged and their shape and size show us which force is dominant within us.

Most people have a mix of outward (yellow), circular (red) and inward (blue) features but *all of us* have one, or a mix of two or three forces, that are dominant in us.

Whether we are considering a planet, a geographical area, a plant, an animal or a human being, dominance is the law of the universe that allows for one energy or substance to have influence over another. Our face will display the effects of the dominance of one or more of these three forces.

Infants commonly display only six to ten discernible features. It is rare for them to have lines, and teeth have not yet developed. However we can still see the shape of their hairline, the shape of their forehead, the size and shape of their eyes and the size of their mouth as well as the placement of their chin and ears. As children get older their features establish and lines begin to appear. It is much easier to determine the internal force of children from the age of three and even easier again once their teeth settle after the age of twelve.

Teenagers and young adults usually have between ten and sixteen features that clearly show the force that forms them. From thirty to middle age there can be as many as twenty or more features. Older people display their internal force even more clearly, with a multitude of lines added to their facial appearance.

There is no standard number of facial features for any particular person; we are all individuals and our appearance and presentation of features will vary enormously. However the dominant forces that have resulted in those features will be discernible in all but the very young. Even as we age and our features vary or in some cases disappear (freckles are a good example) new lines will appear or an existing feature will enlarge, shrink or change shape slightly. If we compare an image of ourselves at a young age to an older age, these differences will be apparent. However the dominance that indicates our internal force will still be the same.

Although we look at other people's faces all the time we are usually less familiar with our own, depending on how much time we spend in front of the mirror. None of us are familiar with our own profile unless profile photos have been taken, as the average family snapshot is taken front on. For the purpose of correctly analysing our facial structure a series of properly angled photos need to be taken.

Once these images are taken we can commence to look at each feature to determine one or more of the following:

- shape

- size
- placement

Each feature will be either distinctive enough to show the force that moulded it or will fall into an 'average' category; that is the size and shape are so common we cannot determine the exact force behind that particular feature. Each of us has a number of 'average' features. All of us have at least a few (or as many as fifteen or twenty) features that are so distinctive we can evaluate the force behind them.

In general the three forces shape our features in the following ways.

- **Outward motion** (yellow) – small, close-set, sloped downward, fine lines
- **Circular motion** (red) – large, round, straight
- **Inward motion** (blue) – inward, crooked, upturned, deep set

All of these features have been determined through clinical analysis of over a thousand people over an eight-year period. Knowing which force is dominant is based on an easy mathematical formula where each feature is rated as being yellow, red, blue or average. Only yellow, red or blue features are included in the analysis. Dominance is determined by the following basic principle:

*Where a group of features is two or more points ahead of any rival group of features, dominance is evident.*

For example, a person has these features:

- hairline – straight
- hairline – high
- eyes – small
- eyes – – down-turned
- nose – average size and shape
- mouth – average size and shape
- lips – – thin
- teeth – crooked
- smile – compact

- chin – receding
- ears – small
- ears – set high
- bridge of nose – indented
- lines under eyes

Once each feature has been classified we arrange the features as follows to determine the dominant internal force of the individual – each feature receives one point – we only count the yellow, red and blue points. Average features receive no points.

**The above patient would have their features rated as follows -**

| Yellow | Red | Blue | Average (no points) |
|---|---|---|---|
| Eyes small<br>Eyes down-turned<br>Lips thin<br>Smile compact<br>Chin receding<br>Ears set high<br>Lines under eyes | Hairline straight | Hairline high<br>Teeth crooked<br>Ears small<br>Bridge of nose indented | Nose<br>Mouth |
| 7 points | 1 point | 4 points | 0 points |

This person is dominant in outward motion (yellow). Even though they have other features that are classified into red and blue, seven points of yellow is three ahead of blue and six ahead of red. The yellow force is dominant and this person will live their life and respond to stress in a 'yellow' way.

Another example of a person with similar but slightly different facial features could be

- hairline – straight

- hairline – high
- eyes – small
- eyes – upturned
- nose – average size and shape
- mouth – average size and shape
- lips – thin
- teeth – crooked
- smile – average
- chin – receding
- ears – small
- ears – average
- bridge of nose – indented
- lines under eyes
- dimples

**The patient above would have their features rated as follows -**

| Yellow | Red | Blue | Average (no points) |
|---|---|---|---|
| Eyes small<br>Lips thin<br>Smile compact<br>Chin receding<br>Lines under eyes | Hairline straight | Hairline high<br>Eyes upturned<br>Teeth crooked<br>Ears small<br>Bridge of nose indented<br>Dimples | Nose<br>Mouth<br>Smile |
| 5 points | 1 point | 6 points | 0 points |

This person has yellow and blue within one point of each other. Even though the blue is one point more, the yellow is still holding its place. Again the red is so far behind it cannot exert any influence. The average features don't count. This person is not dominant in yellow or blue but the *two* forces in virtually equal proportion, indicating they are dominant in *green* reactive force.

Very different looking people can belong in the same colour group and very similar looking people (with a few feature differences) can belong to a different colour group. Facial analysis isn't about a look; it is based on classifying each feature to one of the primary forces or placing it in the average group.

There are seven colour groups and each of us belongs to one. If we are dominant in a single primary force we will be either:

- yellow
- red
- blue

If we are equally dominant in two primary forces we will be either:

- orange (yellow and red)
- purple (red and blue)
- green (yellow and blue)

If we are equally dominant in all three forces we will be

- brown (yellow, red and blue)

This facial information was gathered over an eight-year period in a clinical setting with more than a thousand participants. The facial analysis method which developed through the interviews and facial research has elicited more than seventy facial shapes, sizes and positions, that are classifiable into one of the three primary forces. It can take a practitioner six months to both recognise and learn the classification of these features. To help you determine which features you have and how they are rated, an interactive web-based program has been developed. To use this program please go online to <www.soulandsurvival.com>.

Remember to have pictures taken that fully match the criteria outlined on the website. Poorly taken photos may produce an incorrect result.

## Facial analysis – now or later?

You may wish to have your facial analysis completed now before reading the chapters that describe the characteristics of each colour, or you may wish to read all the chapters first to determine your resonance with a specific group. A correctly done analysis will overrule your personal interpretation of yourself. Humans have an inclination to relate to themselves with psychological interpretations based on feelings and projection. Sometimes these are true and sometimes they are what we or another person, would like us to be. Your true interpretation of yourself will be accurately determined through facial analysis.

## Racial or cultural groups

Many racial or cultural groups seem to have a similar look, making individuals instantly recognisable as belonging to that group. This does not mean that everyone from the same race or culture belongs to the same colour group. The earth has regions more dominant in one of the primary forces, which accounts for stereotypical features such as

- down-turned nose (yellow) – commonly seen in Europe
- wide nose (red) – commonly seen in Africa
- recessed lids (blue) – commonly seen in Asia

The total number of features must be taken into account and individually rated before dominance can be established. Never let a 'look' fool you into imagining you know the colour group of an individual without a detailed analysis.

Facial analysis proves that human beings regardless of race or culture are linked more by colour group instinct than by the region in which they were born.

## Cosmetic surgery

If you have had cosmetic surgery to any feature then clearly you must analyse that as it was before the treatment. Most of us can remember what the feature was like, as in most cases it was a disliked feature. If you are unsure use old photos to determine the correct analysis. The same applies to teeth. Take into account what they were like before the braces, bridge or plate.

Chapter 13

# YELLOW - OUTWARD MOTION

*Flexibility*            *The sun*
*Heat*                   *Summer*
*Exchange*               *Leprosy*
*Wealth*                 *Outcast*
*Trade*                  *Detachment*
*Independence*           *The trader*
*Natural drives*         *Sharing*
*New ideas*              *Rational*
*Leadership*             *Urbane*
*Autonomy*               *Enterprise*
*Repulsion*              *Isolation*
*Attack*                 *Value*
*Foreign*                *Escape*
*Law*                    *Home*
*Freedom*                *Sense of inferiority*

As one of the three primary forces, outward motion is driven to pursue a relentless course of expansion. The material universe needs to expand because expansion creates opportunity. By continually pushing forward, the material universe is not restricted by the confines created by limited space, and the struggles and pressures that accompany these boundaries. Without space, the universe would be crowded and violent due to the competition created by restriction. Outward motion and restriction are opposing forces.

## Flexibility
Outward motion cannot be restricted and it cannot be contained, although it has the potential to change direction and be flexible should the need arise.

Flexibility allows outward motion to move around obstacles without being stopped and without wasting energy trying to push an obstacle from its path.

The universe is expanding because it is driven by unlimited creative potential. As it increases in size, space opens new frontiers and endless possibilities for new life. Humming with energy, the material universe develops planets, suns, galaxies and life, from the forces of outward, inward and circular motion.

The material universe is based on threes, because matter is three dimensional. All material life rests on the interaction of three varying properties:

- time, space and matter
- solids, liquids and gases
- height, width and depth
- attraction, repulsion and bonding
- electron, proton and neutron

The electron, proton and neutron form all manner of life from animal to vegetable and mineral. Electrons, neutrons and protons are the first representations of outward, circular and inward motion respectively. There is one primary colour for each primary force and each particle.

- yellow – electron – outward motion
- red – neutron – circular motion
- blue – proton – inward motion

# Heat

Outward motion manifests itself in a variety of different forms including light, repulsion and heat. Heat is an expression of outward motion because it causes liquids, solids and gases to grow and expand. Many yellow people display this excess of heat through physical signs and symptoms that result from too much warmth in the body. These physical signs and symptoms include, but are not limited to, eczema, hyperthyroidism, hot flushes, high blood pressure and a fast metabolism that creates an insatiable hunger.

An overactive immune response is common, because the excess of heat fools the defence system into believing that a microbial invasion is occurring. This happens because excess heat mimics the action of a fever. Immunity, like the entire defence system reacts to triggers; it does not think circumstances through. The immune system of yellow, believing it is under attack due to the artificial fever state, begins to hit back without discrimination, as there is no actual germ to target. The end result is multiple allergies.

Immunity is a display of how the entire defence system works. When we are first invaded by germs and bacteria, we attack foreign invaders with a non-specific defence. This includes white blood cells that go out into the body on a search and destroy mission. During the battle specific immunity begins. When an invading germ is finally identified, specific cells designed to target and kill this one type of germ are produced by the body.

The entire defence system works in this same way; firstly with a generalised response then a specific reaction, followed by retaining the memory of what worked. This response is the same, regardless of whether the defence system is reacting to a person or germ. The defence response is triggered by physical reaction, not calculated reasoning.

Many yellow people are worse in the heat and crave the open air. Yellow may still feel the cold, yet prefer to wear warm clothing and turn the heating down, rather than the modern trend of light clothing with the central heating on high. Being surrounded by enveloping heat does not suit the hot yellow and many of their hay fever and allergy symptoms are aggravated because of it. Itchy skin and blotches, sneezing and other allergy responses can be stable throughout the remainder of the year, yet flare as soon as the heating comes on.

Humankind, throughout its history has been driven by outward motion and by our desire to find new lands and markets to expand our acquisitions. Yellow exhibits these traits, in a personality that enjoys building and developing new ideas and products. Whether for a family or business, yellow is a person full of ideas of how to expand their horizons. Development and progress is the human expression of outward motion.

## Exchange

Sharing and exchange is the character of yellow, just as electrons are shared and exchanged by atoms in order to form more complex molecules. By sharing electrons, atoms form molecules so life progresses to become increasingly complex. Without this sharing life no longer adapts and changes form.

In yellow people these same concepts of exchange, sharing and adaptability apply, and are expressed as the ambition behind the production and division of wealth.

## Wealth

Wealth has been a life theme for yellow from earliest times. Money is one of the most basic concerns of the human condition and the need for it exists in everyone. One type of yellow person however, takes money one step further and uses wealth as their main tool of survival.

Money, love, family and work, as well as food and shelter, are the essentials of life for everyone regardless of colour group. These fundamentals also include personal self esteem gained from acceptance and contribution. Through contribution individuals acquire the respect and good opinion of others as well as a sense of personal value. Knowing that we have certain skills gives us comfort that we can survive. From contribution we gain our power, both individually as well as socially. Socially we learn to trade our skills in exchange for comfort, security and the companionship of others.

Money is part of the human condition because it is vital to life. Security from wealth as well as status becomes a primary focus when yellow is out of balance. In balance yellow people are capable money managers with an even-handed approach to finance and leisure. Out of balance they become a one-dimensional caricature and money is all they talk about.

Outward motion is the force behind the electron that drives it to change fields and exchange. People who are dominant in outward motion have this same drive when stressed. The more their energy becomes scattered or low, the more they are driven by their primary force to move, adapt and exchange. For yellow people movement and exchange are survival techniques their defence system puts to good use whenever they are stressed and times become difficult.

## Trade

The drive of outward motion gives yellow people a set of natural skills based around this force. This has led to the development of yellow's traditional role of the trader because it is natural for yellow to move, exchange and to forge new ground.

Inward motion is designed by nature to co-exist, while circular motion is designed to bond. Outward motion is meant to be free and independent, otherwise expansion could never take place.

## Independence

Beginning with the scavenger, the trader evolved from the same traits that sought out opportunity, and discovered a way to capitalise on the efforts of other animals. Often moving far from home, the scavenger followed the trails left by nature and utilised the skills and risks taken by other creatures and adapted them for the benefit of the group.

Yellow is usually independent and is happiest making the decisions. Independent yellow is content to survive without the help of anyone's guidance. Independent yellow cannot stand outside interference and becomes agitated whenever they feel constrained. Out of balance they can become dictatorial and bullying to get their own way. Out of balance, independent yellow ensures that the home and relationship runs according to their rules.

Even at the beginning of a relationship, when romance is supposed to take priority, independent yellow, when out of balance, will voice their expectations clearly and decisively like the trader's terms and conditions. Yellow people out of balance see no problem in this type of behaviour, while for others this type of yellow conduct can seem more like a business proposal than a marriage proposal. If love is the spice of life, yellow is the pre-nuptial agreement.

Independent yellow can seem cold and pragmatic, almost anti-romantic in their approach, but love comes in many forms and it is impossible to judge the emotions of others. Love cannot flourish unless certain basic needs are met. For some, love means excitement, while for others it means compassion or stability. The deep love we have for another human being, where there is enjoyment and acceptance of character, comes from the soul. Romantic love which is an amalgam of both the soul and the survival instinct is generally accompanied by some basic survival needs. 'I could never love someone who didn't …' or, 'I could never love someone unless they …' are examples of the survival instinct intruding into the love of the soul.

Independent yellow can often find intimacy and romance difficult, because independence is based on detachment, while love and relationships are founded on attachment. When in balance, yellow people are warm and loving, but when stressed enough to make the survival instinct dominant, they revert to their primary force and detachment over-rules attachment.

Bonding is the task of other forces; it is not what nature intended for yellow. Outward motion is designed to detach, to remain separate and to move when required. In many ways the ties that bind people together are contrary to the nature of outward motion. This can create problems for yellow because it can make intimacy difficult and complicated. When out of balance, relationships are not a natural state for independent yellow; in balance they find meaning and fulfilment in the family and friends who surround them.

## Natural drives

When stress pushes us back into the primary force and we experience scattered energy or exhaustion, we begin to display the qualities of the dominant force inside us.

The primary force of outward motion acts as a defence as well as a desire. The survival instinct is our protection. It is a collective term for the defence system as well as the animation of life. Whenever we feel attacked or exhausted, instinct becomes the dominant force and our actions follow its lead. Instinct is nature taking control, enhancing our chances of survival. Instinct replaces the motion of life with reaction rather than thought.

Inside the survival instinct of every colour group, lie the memories and reactions for the most common experiences that colour group has faced. Survival instinct reaction is based on the dominant primary force, in this case outward motion, as well as reactions to the common 'energy' events each traditional role encountered most frequently. For yellow this was the experience of the trader.

Energetic events are the circumstances that evoked an extreme defence system response. The defence system is triggered by fluctuating energy and it responds through immunity, nerves, the face and the emotions. Any event that brings to the fore the immune system, nervous system or creates emotional turmoil, is instilled into the survival instinct of that individual. When vast numbers of individuals from the same colour group experience the same event and reactions, those events and reactions move beyond the individual, into the collective survival instinct shared by everyone in that colour group.

Highly emotional events evoke the deepest response. The dangers experienced in a traditional role are common, energetic and emotional. Immunity normally remains individual unless there is a common experience, and then it becomes collective. Epidemics are an example of disease that is so widespread, cellular memory moves beyond the individual and into the collective. What happens to one aspect of the defence system happens to the survival instinct as a whole.

In contemporary times the legacy of the traditional role can be a difficult concept to appreciate. Freedom of choice is now taken for granted. However, for most of human history the younger generation followed in the footsteps of the older. Each generation lived out their lives by the skills they were taught from their parents. The hunter taught their children how to hunt, while the trader taught their children the art of trade. The tradition of passing on skills continued for countless generations.

The survival instinct reacts to energy and imprint; the deeper the imprint the more the survival instinct will respond to the same triggers. The depth of an imprint depends on how many times a task or circumstance is repeated. The more a single event takes place, the more the memory of that event becomes etched into the survival instinct.

When an event is charged with energy, the memory of that event is committed to the unconscious of the survival instinct. When that same event or something similar is repeated, the survival instinct knows what reaction is appropriate, further deepening the imprint of its action and reaction. Like the immune system the survival instinct at first responds, then it remembers and prepares by keeping reaction alive but dormant, ready to use in case it is needed. In the immune system this reaction is called antibodies; in the survival instinct it is unconscious reaction.

The more a reaction is needed and used, the more prepared the survival instinct becomes for that particular stress. Finally the survival instinct becomes entwined with the anticipation and reaction to a specific circumstance. This is unconscious instinctive reaction.

The survival instinct becomes so filled with memories that a hierarchy of importance is formed; the deeper the impression the higher up in hierarchy the reaction to that impression becomes. In this way nature ensures that life's most common dangers have an instinctive response at the ready. The more frequently an event or reaction occurs, the deeper the impression and more instinctive the reaction.

When people are in balance, the soul is conscious and we can solve problems more easily. When the survival instinct is dominant, conscious thought becomes suppressed and natural instinct takes over. Immediate situations need immediate responses, making instinct vital. When energy levels are chronically low the survival instinct takes over reducing our ability to think.

Outward motion like every other force resides in all of us, but not in equal intensity. When a force is dominant it creates a controlling authority; no other force has influence. The dominant energy suppresses the weaker, and because they are suppressed weaker forces do not have enough power to influence structure or response. When someone is dominant in outward motion, yellow has suppressed the two other primary forces, leaving them unable to influence yellow in any meaningful way.

## New ideas

Outward motion is required by nature to increase and expand the material universe. With every passing moment outward energy creates new horizons ready to be filled. The purpose of outward motion is to progress, create and develop through expansion.

People who are dominant in outward motion express these same characteristics. They can be dynamic, curious and keen to explore new and original places. Open to new ideas, many are self motivated in their hunger for enterprise or to expand their own horizons. Whenever a new idea arises it is often yellow people who see it's potential.

Yellow people like having plans and goals. Progressive yellow is always on the lookout for new projects or new places to go. Being tied down to one role, job or person will upset their character when yellow is out of balance, and they may suffer terribly, feeling trapped and constrained. This type of yellow is a student of life, enjoying politics, religion, culture and new destinations. Travel is a medium where yellow can experience the new and unfamiliar. Whether on business or just for fun, progressive yellow loves to explore and build on new and exciting ideas.

Often in a hurry to get on with their life, progressive yellow can leave school early in search of adventure or enterprise. Yellow people are prepared to learn by trial and error, rather than sitting in a classroom being told what to do. If they falter or slip they get back on their feet, undaunted by error and unafraid of mistakes. Yellow, in balance, treats every experience as a learning tool that makes them a better more complete person. This is one of yellow's greatest strengths. Not everybody can see a good idea from the beginning, most have to wait and give it time to sink in. Yellow's instincts are superior when it comes to embracing ideas because their minds are quick and alert.

## Leadership

Progressive yellow is often a leader in business or the home and many yellow people are comfortable laying down the law. Not everyone likes to be in charge, and generally people feel more comfortable being friends rather than the boss. The leader makes decisions on behalf of the group but in order to be effective, they must put friendships aside and consider what is best for all. This type of yellow person is natural at this role, because they are able to detach, a benefit of outward motion.

Outward motion leads by character. Its job is to forge and open up areas that did not exist before. Outward motion acts independently without backup or support and leadership yellow does the same, unafraid to take the reigns should the challenge arise.

Out of balance, this type of yellow person becomes less of a leader and more of a dictator. A good leader is a benevolent dictator but when the survival instinct is dominant benevolence disappears. Normally, yellow people are strong and commanding but out of balance they can become unfeeling and ruthless.

## Autonomy

Some yellow people are prepared to step up and take control, remaining impartial and detached, serving the needs of all and prepared to do whatever it takes to ensure the job gets done. But, when out of balance they can be hard, cold, unsympathetic and aloof.

Yellow people are instilled with the energy of autonomy and generally it is a trait that serves them well. If autonomy turns to detachment because of stress, the yellow person can go from decision maker to demander. When out of balance, the yellow person is no longer performing in the best interests of the group or family, but dominates the home with their self importance and rules. Rather than being part of a group and being there to help, out of balance yellow see the family or group as an impediment to their desires.

## Repulsion

Outward motion clears the way by repelling everything in its path. When two similar forces come into contact within a confined space, the force of repulsion ensures each is separated or the stronger takes control of the weaker. This is the basis of competition and survival of the fittest. Competition ensures that the strongest survive while the weak fall by the wayside. Through constant competition, species jostle for position in ebbs and flows that make some disappear leaving the sturdy and stable to flourish.

There are three laws that govern the material universe and these laws act upon every substance. The first law is attraction, while the second is repulsion; the third is the law that makes equal forces bond. Each of the three primary forces is a representation of one of these laws.

- yellow is repulsion
- red is bonding
- blue is attraction

Repulsion is designed to push out or away and repulsion is the action of the defence system of yellow. Repulsion works by driving away any threat, pushing out an invader threatening the body. The yellow immune system takes the offensive as would be expected from outward motion. Its role is to push to the edges of the body any substance that does not belong. The periphery of the body is the area that yellow is prepared to sacrifice so the vital organs are protected.

## Attack

The repulsion of outward motion makes the yellow defence system come out to meet any incoming invader. Other systems under stress wait to react once altered. The more out of balance yellow becomes, the more outward the projection of their defence system against stress. In balance, yellow responds when necessary and acts in accordance to the stress. Out of balance their defence system attacks unnecessarily causing physical allergies or emotional isolation.

If the centre of their imbalance resides in the physical, severe and multiple allergies can result, as they attack and push away anything foreign. If the centre of their imbalance resides in the emotional, yellow will push away, like a foreign invader, anyone with a difference of opinion. Outward motion is an attacking force and out of balance everything is dangerous. Normally the immune system breaks down foreign invaders with a minimum of effort and fuss, but out of balance yellow attacks with venom and force. For the individual this creates allergies to even the most natural and benign of substances, or a personality that drives others away.

From pollen in the air to pet hair and dust, even foods that are normally healthy and easy to digest; all become enemies that cause discomfort and pain when yellow is out of balance. Sneezing, tears, bloating and pain, vomiting, hives, asthma and welts; out of balance yellow attacks everything in an effort to repel and protect. Yellow may be emotionally stable but their body reacts to everything. This is a sign of an over-stressed state even if the person does not feel stressed in themselves.

Socially, attacking yellow are just as reactive as their immune systems when the centre of disturbance is located in their emotions. In balance, yellow people are as welcoming as anyone; they are warm and friendly and happy to see company. Out of balance, their survival instinct behaves in the same aggressive manner to other people as their immune system does towards allergens. Outward motion under threat can create a demeanour that is overbearing and tyrannical, as the survival instinct attempts to repel any opposing force.

At its most extreme, out of balance yellow will attack anything foreign. In this state yellow stay with the known and refuse to go outside their routine. They eat the same things and listen to the same music, they have the same holiday spot they have gone to for years, meet with the same friends at the same restaurant and always order their same favourite dish. Out of balance yellow people may reject anything new and can be openly aggressive to any opposing force including a contrary opinion. Attacking yellow is highly confrontational and many are unsociably blunt.

## Foreign

The foreign, whether microbe or man is to be feared and will be attacked. In the yellow time (1200–1350 AD), the Mongols conquered the world. In their wake they left a trail of dead with just enough people left alive to warn the next town of what was in store should they resist. The world was gripped by panic and fear at the cruelty of these foreign invaders. So much of the world was affected that the memory became part of the collective unconscious and continues in the survival instinct of yellow.

With an unstaring glare, yellow people will challenge the opinions of those around them. Others must justify their opposing position and account for their difference of opinion. In balance yellow people are the opposite, they embrace the new and enjoy the stimulation that foreign cultures provide. In an out of balance state, attacking yellow become judge and jury – always finding the defendant guilty.

Those around attacking yellow often feel intimidated, precisely the protective defensive strategy their survival instinct wants to achieve. Social etiquette expects that we smile and be friendly to other people. It requires us to be gentle and accepting of different ideas. Attacking yellow, when they are out of balance refuse to comply with these social expectations. Instead they use challenging and scoffing behaviour, calculated to publicly and openly demean.

If attacking yellow is very out of balance, their defence system will make them lose everybody dear and close. Their family is no longer able to tolerate such a continuously opinionated personality. Consequently others are driven away by a survival instinct out of control. Attacking yellow may pretend they don't care if none of the family visits, but this is usually not the case. Laying down the law may help yellow survive but it can cost them their happiness.

## Law

Yellow and the law go hand in hand because outward motion leads the way. A leader is not a leader unless they make the rules. The law is vital to the life of the trader because without it there is no reimbursement for loss. The more yellow are stressed the more likely they are to bend and twist the law to achieve their aims. Out of balance, yellow people use the law like the warrior uses the sword. Law suits, legal challenges and industrial tribunals all form the way yellow fights back.

## Freedom

Freedom yellow enjoy their own company and a life that is unconstrained by others. While freedom yellow enjoy the company of friends they don't always want a relationship that is going tie them down. If they are already in a relationship, they prefer a liaison less romantic and preferably not with anyone who is needy of too much time. Out of balance freedom yellow wants a companion but not a spouse. They are not looking for the intimacy that goes with marriage, nor the lack of liberty it demands.

Freedom yellow people are pragmatic. A husband or wife is seen as useful because they provide companionship, protection, a second income and children. Freedom yellow, when out of balance, may not be looking for a partner, but many still have a ticking biological clock. To a freedom yellow person who is out of balance, a husband or wife is burdensome, especially when they expect intimacy and exclusivity. Exclusivity is imposing because it means time with the same person. Freedom means not being constrained, while exclusivity is denial of anything or anyone else.

Intimacy, whether emotional or physical, requires a closeness that is unnatural to the nature of freedom yellow. The electron remains outside the confinement of the nucleus. Used to being uncontained, yellow allow themselves a freedom of expression and a naturalness for promoting ideas. Yellow people are innovative in business, science and art.

In a relationship many individuals give themselves over to an image of who they believe they should be. Freedom yellow are not image bound and their independence is a release from the group behaviour which ties so many into a personality that does not belong to them. Freedom yellow people are less susceptible to peer-group pressure, making them stable and not easily tipped off balance. As a result their relationships with partners and friends are often happy and stable. The best relationship is always the one where those involved are themselves.

The concept of love is as important to yellow as it is to anyone else. Freedom yellow, when out of balance, want the feeling without the commitment. Romantic love is based on the intimacy of closeness, but out of balance freedom yellow people will experience opposite feelings. Having the same person around is more of a noose than a comfort. The idea of one person playing the role of lover and friend is too stifling to bear.

Yellow find personal fulfilment from variety rather than one person fulfilling all their needs. Freedom yellow people often think of their spouse as a spouse and nothing more. They do not expect nor do they want their spouse to be their best friend. Other individuals are their friends and their spouse is their spouse; the two are separate and not interchangeable. The concept of the lover, confidante and best friend is a nightmare this type of yellow will try and avoid. Friends are who they turn to when they feel the need to escape.

To some freedom means ranking friends over and above their partner; the more friends the better. Friends are more highly regarded because of what they represent. Partners mean chains while friends represent freedom; any partner who wants to be the total package is a partner who is on shaky ground in their relationship with freedom yellow.

Some do not want a partner, because their personal needs are met by blood relations, children or work. If they are social they do not need a spouse as they will only impinge on their desire to mix with different people. This type of yellow may go out for dinner with a work colleague on Thursday, an old friend on Friday, a social group on Saturday then lunch with neighbours on Sunday.

Diversity of events and people is where freedom yellow is at home; a partner may limit this lifestyle considerably. A partner requires one on one time, moments alone and an escape from others. A spouse means forsaking all other people, including friends and family. A committed relationship goes against the grain of how freedom yellow is made.

The electron 'builds' molecules by interaction and exchange and yellow enjoys interacting with a variety of different people. Anyone who limits this interaction is viewed by their survival instinct as the enemy, when yellow is out of balance. Interaction and exchange is a primary force and the security of the trader depended on these traits. Freedom yellow is not prepared to forsake all others for one person; over time many will leave their millstone at home, while they go out to interact with friends.

Forsaking all others is the basis of marriage because it places the partner as the primary consideration. All other loves, ambitions and people, including friends and family are expected to take second place. Freedom yellow often finds this pledge too difficult to keep and many return to the single life in one form or another; being single is often a life theme for yellow. Yellow are not always the instigator of the break-up, separation or divorce. However once removed from the ties, few marry again. Some may never commit themselves to another romantic relationship; their survival instinct is happy to be free and it has no intention of changing.

Partnerships come with expectations that extend beyond practical matters. Out of balance freedom yellow wants a partner that is just as independent. Ideally they should earn independently and live independently, have their own hobbies, friends, bank account and ambitions. They should be a partner who does not impose on them or need them in any way, yet at the same time provide loyalty and half their earnings. In balance yellow enjoys their partner for the person who they are; they not only value but encourage personal freedom, releasing the pressure other relationships may have.

Freedom yellow under stress plans their day without consideration or approval. In balance they want to spend time with their spouse and are happy with the person they've chosen. Out of balance their partner is the pair of old slippers they come home to. Good to relax in but certainly not good enough to take out to dinner.

## The sun

The sun is the natural symbol of yellow. Life cannot exist without the sun; it warms, nourishes, feeds and energises. It is strong, consistent, and dependable. The sun provides light as well as heat and is the power supply on which everything relies. However the sun is also relentless and life must shield itself from its full force because too much sun is scorching.

Plants use the energy of sunlight to photosynthesise and produce oxygen and carbohydrates. Carbohydrates are a major source of food energy. Carbohydrates are so packed full of energy that carnivorous animals can still gain enough energy by eating the animals that have eaten the plants.

All of this energy comes from the sun and it shows the importance of yellow. Without outward motion life cannot exist.

Culture needs input from every colour group in order to develop and flourish. A lack of one means the collapse of all. If the sun were to vanish all life would cease as most creatures come to life with the sun. Cold dark winters mean hibernation and seclusion, but with the return of the sun comes the energy of spring. Trees bud and begin to flower, while animals and insects carry on their post-winter routine.

The sun takes command and controls its environment but the sun also warms and provides life-giving comfort. It is a central force that can always be relied on; a source of energy, light, food and power.

## Summer

Summer is a time of activity, feasting and storing for the winter. Summer is the time of the harvest and making hay while the sun shines.

Summer is like the electron, with everyone moving, trading and sharing. The cycle of summer is kind, rich, rewarding and highly productive. Yellow people in balance are exactly the same. They are active, full of life, bountiful and sharing. They love nothing better than to open up their home for friends and family to share. Today 'the harvest' means barbeques and parties and yellow loves to share their home and food, in the same way communities have done for generations.

Summer is the time for markets. Today we are divorced from the cycles that bind us to nature; feasts and celebrations full of well-earned gluttony were appreciated because they were rare. Now gluttony is not satisfying because we indulge whenever we like. In days gone by when times were harder, filling your face with blackberry pie, bobbing for apples or tasting a peach were events that left nostalgic and lasting memories.

All through the winter people survived on leftovers and foods that could be stored, especially grains and pulses. Spring showed the promise of things to come but it was summer that delivered and made the good times arrive. These same attitudes exist in yellow as they enjoy the harvest of their work, loving to share the abundance of what they have. Summer is also a time to prepare, making jams and bottling fruits, shearing sheep and making hay. The trader is the traditional role of yellow and their origin begins with the cycle of the sun.

Stockpiling food for when times turn hard is the nature of the trader. Understanding the cycles of life and how to protect the future by planning the present has kept the trader alive for centuries. Summer is the time when exchange takes place, swapping excess for other needed goods. The bounty of summer created the market place and the development of the trader.

Summer is a celebration. Today we continue to love the summer because it is a time for holidays, catching up with family and friends as well as relaxing. We still enjoy the bounty of summer, eating fruits and entertaining outdoors. Summer is the time of profitable return. In the past it was the time when effort literally bore fruit. Today it is when we catch up and relax for all the effort we have put into the year. Profit and return are the expectations of summer, the expectations of the trader and of everyone yellow.

The sun however is not always so benevolent. When there is too much sun, energy is depleted rather than increased. When they are out of balance, yellow, like an excess of sun is relentless, overwhelming and demanding. Yellow's dictatorial behaviour can force those around them to submit and adopt the lifestyle they command. Rather than risk the lectures and moralising that comes from defiance, family and friends tell them what they want to hear whether it is truthful or not.

Out of balance dictatorial yellow is head of a family held together by fear. Yellow are proud of their families' achievements and they love each one of them dearly but when their repelling action is strong, their children believe they are suppressed. In their desire to give their children the skills they need for life, out of balance yellow has forgotten to have fun and freedom along the way. As a consequence this type of yellow delivers one opinionated theory after another.

Relentless sun evaporates moisture, leaving the earth dry, sore and cracked. Emotionally, yellow people can lose the moisture needed for flexibility. Without this dampness they can become dry and rigid, set in their ways at too early an age. This type of yellow is old before their time both in their thinking and judgmental manner.

Physically their skin can be itchy and dry, and many suffer from eczema and other related skin complaints. Their joints become dry and immovable, as does their lower back. Sometimes yellow are unable to even straighten after being in a bent over position because their body has become too rigid and inflexible.

Yellow people who are in balance talk easily and freely with everyone without trying to control. Apart from the general ups and downs of life, yellow people in balance take life in their stride, moving around obstacles and embracing ideas with a high degree of acumen and flexibility.

Sunny days are cheerful and uplifting and everyone feels better when the sun is shining. 'Too good to be inside' is a saying that goes with a sunny day because it makes us want to get up and get out into the outdoors. This is the personality of yellow in balance.

## Leprosy

Time revolves in cycles, each colour group coming to prominence approximately every one hundred and fifty years. Frequent, energetic and highly emotional events that occur during a particular time frame are absorbed by the colour group that is prominent at that time; the same way reaction is absorbed by the survival instinct of the individual.

When a similar event occurs to a large number of people belonging to the same colour group, the impact of that event together with the circumstances that caused it, become part of the unconscious instinct of everyone in that group. The same occurs when emotional and traumatic events occur on a grand scale during a time period, because the prevalent force of the time creates and absorbs reaction.

The last yellow time period occurred between 1200 and 1350 AD. During this cycle an epidemic occurred of such emotional magnitude that its consequences still continue to form part of our social vernacular, such as being called a social or moral leper. The memory of its reaction lies inside the yellow survival instinct and surfaces under stress.

Leprosy had existed for centuries and was written about in the Bible. In 13th century Europe, something significant took place. Leprosy suddenly shifted from a known and feared disease, into an epidemic that infected countless numbers and changed the culture of the time.

It is not leprosy itself that lies dormant in the yellow survival instinct, but the legacy of the emotional and social reaction that occurred to the people who suffered leprosy. In later times many people would suffer tuberculosis or cancer, but these people would never be ostracised or hated like lepers. At no other time in history has an entire subculture developed solely because of an illness.

Lepers lived in communities, not support groups or in small collectives, but in towns, hospitals or entire islands dedicated solely to their existence. Being ostracised was in part due to fear of the disease and also to religion. In the Western world leprosy was the punishment for sin and righteous people were virtuous in rejecting all sinners.

The common human fear is the terror of rejection. Tuberculosis sufferers in the 19th century were moved to sanatoriums, but this is not the same as the social rejection of leprosy. The survival instinct is highly reactive to any circumstance that causes expulsion. We will adapt our behaviour and adopt common fashion to keep us part of the group. When leprosy became synonymous with social rejection, the survival instinct's worst fear was realised. This is why leprosy above all other illnesses has left such an impact on the collective yellow survival instinct.

When people became sick, especially with diseases such as the plague, the fear of infection was extreme. Sufferers were hospitalised or quarantined in their homes and as much as this separation must have added to the torment, it was leprosy that created social and moral horror, causing repulsion and rejection from the world.

Even today leprosy is used to highlight behavioural repugnance or gravity. To call someone a moral leper is to accuse them of being without principles. To call someone a social leper is to highlight their isolation, their inability to mix, or the rejection others have towards them. Leprosy has more emotional connotations than any disease in history. Leprosy has not been the world's biggest killer and leprosy is not the worst biological disease, but it is history's worst social disease and its legacy continues. 'I was treated like a leper,' is a common phrase that epitomises belittlement and rejection.

Leprosy spotters were in every town, trained to diagnose the signs. Once a leper was identified, a funeral mass called 'the mass of separation' was held, to signify they were dead to the world. After the service the leper was cast out to drift with the other living dead. They were given an alms bowl, sent to a colony or home and dressed in leper's clothes. Not until the Jews in World War Two, would another group of people be forced to identify themselves by dress. Lepers of the time had to separate themselves so the unclean would not blemish the clean.

According to the belief of the time, leprosy was a punishment from God. Suffering in this life meant lepers would receive their due reward in heaven. Many thought it sacrilege to assist a leper in anything other than the giving of alms. To alleviate suffering or provide any medicine was to go against God's plan.

Leprosy evoked this terrible social response because it was associated with Biblical sin. No one wanted to get smallpox either but it was leprosy they feared, because it wasn't just a physical mark, it represented a moral disfigurement of the soul. In the 18th century when smallpox mutated into a more hostile killer than ever before, sufferers were not cast out in the street, stoned or shunned away. They received a level of compassion that lepers were always denied.

> It is 1278 and you are a woman in your twenties, married with two young children. The eldest, a boy is two years old and your baby girl is ten weeks. Your husband is a farm labourer for the local baron. You live with your family and a number of others in small huts on the baron's property. It is a collective lifestyle that suits you, because you

enjoy the company of others. Times are hard because it's the middle of winter and food is scarce and bland. Oats and boiled water are the main winter fare. In summer there is fruit and honey but in winter there are no tasty delights, so the family munches with unappreciative faces over yet another bowl of soggy grain.

You have been more tired than normal these last few weeks, ever since the birth of your daughter. This last child seems to have taken your energy and you find it hard to get out of bed. Sometimes you feel like crying for no reason and the other women tell you to smarten up. 'You have young ones depending on you,' they say whenever you drag your feet. Lately your joints have been aching, and your energy is lower than when you had your son. Perhaps you are getting better because the last few days have not been as bad.

There is a churchman in the village sent by the local authorities to check on all the townsfolk. They are checking everyone's skin for immoral blemishes because leprosy has spread far and wide. You look yourself over but can find nothing unusual apart from the normal rashes and marks.

No one in the village ever has clear skin and many have lice and scabies. Sleeping on straw and wearing coarse clothes makes most of the villagers itch. Washing is regarded as something to avoid because of the potential germs in the water. The combination of being unwashed, sleeping with vermin and an unhealthy diet, make the villagers a biological smorgasbord.

Leprosy checkers know what to look for and claim they can tell the difference between a skin disease and sin. As the bell rings everyone stops work and lines up in file to be checked. As you enter the church where they have set up office, you are overcome by dread. You have not always been as Christian as you should have, and God can see into your thoughts. You take a deep breath and calm yourself, you have not been immoral, in fact immoral thoughts have been the furthest thing from your mind since having your last child.

As you reach the head of the line, two men check your skin; they look at your neck and around your arms, then on your legs and toes. They pull hair from your head as well as from your eyebrows then tell you to go into the room on the left, where you and two others must wait. After a few hours one of the checkers enters and pronounces you all lepers.

'God has found you deserving of punishment and to suffer for your sins. However, if you decide to live moral lives, repent and pray for forgiveness, a reward will await you in heaven. You are not to go home to your families so put them out of your mind. You cannot expect to live anymore in the homes of decent God-fearing people. Like Adam and Eve from the garden of Eden, you are now cast out.'

You scream, 'I have a child! A daughter I still need to feed. She will die if I am not there to care for her!'

'You may take your daughter with you,' one of the checkers replies, 'but you must leave the rest of your family behind. Tell me in the morning what you wish to do.'

With that the door was locked as he left and you spent your first sleepless night as a leper.

No amount of pleading was going to change their minds; there was nothing you could do. The authorities would not accept your opinion that they were making a terrible mistake. You knew you had to accept their decision as they have the power and you do not; you are now dead to the world.

By morning you had made your decision. You would not take your daughter but leave her behind. There were other women who could wet nurse her, and your husband is a good and caring man. Living with you would isolate her from life and condemn her to leprosy in the end.

It was a week before you saw your family again, through a veil covering your face. That morning you were brought into the church wearing funeral black. The priest blessed your soul as he committed you to God. This is a symbolic funeral service performed for lepers that represents their social death to the world. Later outside you stand in an open grave. Covered in black you look like a spectre and watch as your husband weeps. Your son keeps asking, 'Is that really mummy?' while your daughter sleeps peacefully in her father's arms. Looking into the grave the priest begins the Separation Mass as your family and friends watch on.

'I forbid you to ever enter a church, a monastery, a fair, a mill, a market or an assembly of people. I forbid you to leave your house unless dressed in your recognisable garb and also shod. I forbid you to wash your hands or to launder anything or to drink at any stream or fountain, unless using your own barrel or dipper. I forbid you to touch anything you buy or barter for, until it becomes your own. I forbid you to enter any tavern; and if you wish for wine, whether you buy it or it is given to you, have it funnelled into your keg. I forbid you to share house with any man but your husband. I command you, if accosted by anyone while travelling on a road, to set yourself downwind of them before you answer. I forbid you to enter any narrow passage, lest a passerby bump into you. I forbid you, wherever you go, to touch the rim or the rope of a well without donning your gloves. I forbid you to touch any child or give them anything. I forbid you to drink or eat from any vessel but your own'. (Actual Separation Mass)

After the mass you are re-dressed into the clothes of a leper. As an act of compassion you are given an alms bowl and a bell to warn others when you are near and as an act of charity the priest who 'buried' you also puts money into your bowl. With your two new friends and a coin in your bowl you brace yourself for the life that awaits you, and cry as you watch your family say goodbye and walk away without you.

After months inside the house you can bear it no longer. Everything you had is gone. The family you cared for and all your possessions were suddenly ripped away from you. Hospitals and homes made especially for lepers, 'pest houses' they are called, are springing up everywhere and you are free to move to any of them, provided you do not speak or touch a respectable person on the way.

Passing the outskirts of the next village, it dawns on you that this is the furthest you have ever travelled. As you turn to speak to the friend walking with you, a rock slams into the back of your head, making you fall to the ground. Blood is pouring from the wound as you rise to your feet. Your friend has been hit in the eye and is screaming from the pain. The two of you were walking quietly as you discreetly passed the town. What you should have been doing was ringing your bell, warning the clean to stay away.

Townsfolk come running from every direction, gathering stones and throwing them at you. They call you sinners and human refuse, swearing and promising to punish you both cruelly. The cut to your head is a reminder of what others think of you. You never knew people could be so cruel, and never before have you felt so despised. Now you know what rejection feels like and you hate the people who make you feel this way.

Many years pass and you become hardened and learn to use the fear of others to your advantage. As you wave your alms bowl and sit by the road, passersby search in their purse for the smallest change they can find. As you walk closer towards them, they begin to panic and tell you to go away, but that just makes you walk closer. Finally through fear they throw all their money and run as fast as they can; you loath their fear and are happy to exploit it.

You would like to make friends but the clean push you away, throwing stones and calling you names. You used to be a friendly person but that has all changed. Now you are as jaded as the other lepers you live with, and say and behave in whichever way you please. Some lepers have earned a reputation for cursing at cleans as they pass them by. What did the cleans expect, to take everything from you, bully you into tears, torture and twist you into a different person yet still be treated with courtesy?

You live as a leper until you finally die of bitterness and bacteria. Living off charity made you cling to your money and possessions as if they were the meaning of life. Others did not understand that these possessions were your whole life. Beggars value money to the point of spiritual worship. 'When you have nothing, you have nothing to lose,' is a rich man's view of poverty. To the begging leper having nothing means being treated as nothing until you feel like nothing. Nobody knows the importance of money until they are denied gainful employment and forced to sit on the side of the road holding out a bowl.

Yellow has these emotional events gnawing at their unconscious. Today many have a burning ambition for wealth or status. Yellow under stress is always reminded of the value of money and qualifications. Education is the way out of the gutter and nothing is more valuable to a beggar than this opportunity. By turning a leper into a beggar, yellow had come full circle; civilised people were forced to revert to the scavengers from which they came.

## Outcast
Under stress, outcast yellow returns to the feelings of the leper. To others, their habits can seem too eccentric to understand because the survival instinct of outcast yellow is used to a life alone.

Being outcast is a legacy of the yellow time. At its peak in the 13th century, there were nearly twenty thousand leper houses scattered across

Europe, yet by the middle of the 14th century – the end of the yellow period, hardly any were left. Leprosy simply died out as an epidemic.

Leprosy does not exist in the survival instinct of yellow, but the social reaction to having leprosy does. Hundreds of thousands were rejected and expelled to live on their own in a threadbare existence and this has made outcast yellow unaware of how blunt they can be to others. The leper was mistreated and shunned from place to place. They had no need or desire to be courteous, and no interest in pleasantries. To the leper nothing worse could happen than exclusion, and yellow often acts as they please, caring little for social etiquette.

Yellow people can be accused of being pompous, rude or lacking in social etiquette. Their intent is not to upset; their intent is to speak their mind. If you become offended, that's your problem but certain yellow people are going to say it anyway.

This type of yellow is a 'come as you are person', they do not bend and they do not accommodate. The outside world has been cruel, so they have no desire to fit in. Outcast yellow speak their mind irrespective of whether it is offensive. They do not care what others think about them; in their survival instinct they have already been rejected.

Outcast yellow are not looking for acceptance and as a result they do not receive it. Rejection and being made outcast continues in yellow because the group frowns at individuality. School can be a difficult time and the outcast yellow person can be a target for bullying. Outcast yellow don't care if they fit in so the group finds them strange. Even as adults this trend can continue because outcast yellow are seen as eccentric, refusing to bend or meet half way.

Leprosy is a disease that affects the nerves damaging the periphery of the body. Without a sense of feeling, lepers injure their fingers, toes and nose, allowing further infection to set in making external parts turn black and fall off.

In the 13th century the social response to leprosy was in part driven by outward motion. The yellow survival instinct pushes away because it is designed to repel. Attraction, repulsion and bonding are the building blocks of life. Outward motion is repulsion, always pushing forward. When an epidemic of leprosy occurred the continent was thrown into fear. The survival instinct was dominant in so many people all at the same time, that a collective reaction was created. Outward motion was the prevalent force of the time so the social reaction was expulsion.

When out of balance, yellow people can reject others or unconsciously cause others to reject them. Some try hard to be friendly, but still end up being misunderstood, judged harshly and then turned away.

Charity is an aspect of life as an outcast. Unable and not allowed to find gainful employment, lepers relied on the goodwill of others and the money they provided. While some felt angry at being made beggars, others were grateful for the benevolence they were given. Charity remains a life theme for many yellow people.

The world no longer was a place of wonder when someone became a leper, instead it became hostile and people were objects to avoid. Outcast lepers did not mingle because they were not allowed to by law. A sense of ruthlessness was instilled into some, stemming from the experience of having no-one to trust.

In the yellow time when leprosy was rife and outward motion was strong, leaving the home was dangerous because lepers were shunned and stoned, some were even killed. Carrying their charity bowl others were robbed and left to die by the road. As a result some outcast yellow people have no desire to ever leave their home. If they go on holiday it is often somewhere local or someplace they have been before. Some only travel to see their family or holiday in groups. In modern times yellow people can have a strong tie to their community and their family; much of that tie stems from this heritage. The home, family or community, was the only safe place. Everywhere beyond this border was unpredictable and hostile territory. The survival instinct absorbs action and reaction not just from the trader but from the leper as well.

When the woman was cast out from her home and sent to a leper house, she lost everything life had to offer, including her dreams. She lost her family and her ten-week-old daughter and never saw them again. She could never rejoin 'the land of the living' or be reunited with her husband. While her home was humble it was still the place where she and her family lived. She not only lost all she loved, she lost her social self-respect, by never being allowed to contribute and provide productive labour.

## Detachment

At the beginning the outcast woman used to lie awake crying for what had been taken. Then she began to detach from her feelings because to keep them alive was torture. Detachment comes from necessity and was reinforced by the trader. Rejection is when society forgets you and detachment is when you do the same back; both are the energy of yellow.

It becomes understandable why yellow people have such a strong attachment to possessions. Today people lead a disposable life throwing away anything that has outlived its purpose, but outcast yellow values possessions and the comfort they provide. Some when out of balance can become selfish and materialistic, placing a price on everything including the people around them. Others maintain their perspective while still respecting the commodities they own. Perspective is determined by the level of stress they are under.

Detachment has its origins in the role of outward motion. The trader legitimised and strengthened this trait by switching off their emotions until the job was complete. However the capacity to switch off entirely, becoming virtually emotionless, is a legacy of necessity caused by losing everyone and everything. Rationalising life is the only way outcast yellow could cope. Under stress, yellow people can resort to this same emotional detachment because it helped their survival instinct live through the trials of the past.

Outcast yellow relied on charity and the legacy of this experience is two fold. The first is a drive to acquire position through education, money and power. Charity makes a slave out of people and the yellow person's survival instinct understands that wealth and position mean freedom. Out of balance, outcast yellow are unrealistic about education, business and the importance of making money. The yellow person can seem a miser to others but they do not have the instinctive history of Lazarus, surviving from the scraps off the table.

The second legacy is a survival instinct that understands charity is a gracious act. This personality is grateful for what they have been given. Rather than being angry at the rich who only gave them scraps, this type of yellow person is happy they have been given scraps at all. Most people would be bitter being forced to be an outcast, but this type of yellow has a survival instinct that believes charity was their salvation. When the rich scoffed or covered their noses or told the leper to move, this type of yellow person smiled, then agreed and did what they were told. To upset anyone in authority meant their supply line could be cut, and then they would have nothing to eat at all.

The gracious yellow person bows and scrapes to anyone in authority. The educated and the moneyed have power over life and death, and gracious yellow make certain they are always in good favour. Making the right connections and trying to please everybody, this type of yellow person always agrees so no one is upset with them.

## The trader

The trader, like all traditional roles, is vital to the security and prosperity of the group. The trader barters and swaps surplus items for needs in short supply. An excess of one substance can be used as trade to buffer the shortfall in another. In this way an excess of fish can be used to trade against a shortage of furs. Trade gives the group a better chance of survival by securing against hard times through supplying basic needs.

Success in trade not only helps secure the group, it also secures the trader as an individual. The more an individual can help secure the group, the more the group will protect them. Those who could trade most successfully were in demand and rewarded. As always, survival was a competition where only the best were allowed to remain when famine rationing began.

> The weather is turning cold once more and the ground is beginning to freeze. The hunters must travel further each day to find enough food for everyone; times are hard and stomachs are empty. Babies cry and tempers fray. Every available minute is spent securing food, while other activities are pushed to the background.

> As the weather becomes colder it also begins to rain. The group is without appropriate clothing and shelter in their desperate search for food. If things don't change soon, just hanging on to life will become

difficult.

In the past everyone lived in huts and life was settled, but colder, longer winters are changing this lifestyle. At the moment you and all the other able-bodied people are searching and hunting for anything to eat. You are a successful scavenger, because you can read the signs of nature, but now there are fewer signs to read because all life is struggling.

Over the next few months the shortage of food becomes dire. A neighbouring tribe lives on the coast at the base of the mountain you live on. Their tribe lives predominantly on fish as well as the vegetables and fruits that grow nearby. Your tribe does not have access to the sea because the coastal group is hostile and will attack anyone on their land. You know they are managing through this exceptionally cold winter because you have watched them from a distance while out scavenging food.

Previous contact had been made with the coastal group through a chance meeting. The meeting was tense and nerve wracking, spears were pointed and stabbed in the air; everyone yelled and pulled fierce faces.

You noticed one of their group looking at the knife you had in your hand. The coastal group had spears but none of them had knives and it was at this point you realised, this was the first knife they had seen. Quietly and calmly you walked over and offered it for closer inspection. Taking it hesitantly he looked at the knife and was instantly impressed because he could see how useful it would be. The person you handed the knife to had a dead rabbit hanging from his side. You pointed to the rabbit then back to the knife, until finally there was an understanding. An exchange took place and the hostility between the two groups calmed as each went their separate ways.

Back at the village you explained to the others how the knife was exchanged for food. Everyone in the group looks thin and desperate and now you realise what you can do to help. The knives that are made by your group come from a type of flint that is common to your area. You gather a few knives from others in the group for the purpose of exchange. The knives to be used can easily be remade so the group loses nothing of real value. At the first meeting you were lucky because the coastal group had a level headed and inquisitive person as their leader, and both sides were evenly matched. On this next journey you will be alone and outnumbered.

As you appear over the hill and walk into their camp, the coastal tribe sees you and becomes agitated and nervous. Everything inside tells you to run but you gather your courage and slowly move forward. The coastal group begins to crowd around and some of them look angry and deliberately intimidating. Your heart is pounding and you feel like you have made a very dangerous mistake, when suddenly you spot the man you traded with before. He yells something at the group and the crowd moves back to give you room. You can tell immediately that the coastal group is in better physical condition than your own group. They show none of the hallmarks of starvation but they are freezing cold. The man you traded with stands in front of you and says something you cannot understand. You reach into your bag and show him the knives and he begins to smile.

A debate takes place and voices rise as the group becomes more animated. The other trader does a lot of the talking then walks away and returns with a basket of dried fish. He takes the knives and walks away and so does the rest of their group. The trade is complete. Returning to your village, you are treated like a hero because you have brought back food for everyone to share.

## Sharing

Sharing is a trait that is instilled in yellow. To share and accommodate is part of the yellow character and they do so willingly when their life is balanced.

There is a difference between sharing and giving away. To share means to distribute what you have so everyone can benefit. To give away means to give all you have, but you end up with nothing. The trader shares and exchanges but does not give things away, that is not in the trader's best interest.

When out of balance, the normal yellow desire to share vanishes and miserliness takes its place. When the trader is out of balance everybody suffers including yellow themselves. If a yellow person doesn't share it is contrary to their nature and results in agitation and unhappiness as their survival instinct panics.

Sharing is not just an instinct of yellow people; it is a vital survival tool of the trader. When the trader returned to the group with the fish he was rewarded with praise and protected from expulsion as the famine grew more severe. The group never expels someone who contributes more than they take.

When the survival instinct of yellow becomes dominant it creates the impulse to share, because sharing has been a successful way of creating security and need. Sharing is both a protection and a desire when a yellow person feels stressed. Many will share what little they have to gain respect and security. The more people the trader can share with, the greater the amount of appreciation. In times of famine when expulsion took place, individuals survived by numbers. The more wanted and needed an individual became, the greater their chance of survival, because know one wanted to cast them out.

At the other extreme is the miserly yellow person who refuses to share anything. Sharing can be both positive and negative. If the famine is mild, sharing is beneficial because it endears the trader to the rest of the group. If the famine is severe and long-lasting, sharing can be negative because it becomes self denial. The more the trader shares, the less they have for themselves.

The survival instinct remembers that sharing can also cause personal difficulty and when energy is consistently low, sharing is a hindrance to life rather than a help. Consequently the out of balance yellow person can squirrel away money as if the world is coming to an end, then pretend and moan about being poor. Miserly yellow begrudge even the most basic needs. From the price of school uniforms to the high cost of food, this tight yellow searches high and low to ensure they get the best price. Time is not important, only money is of value. Miserly yellow will spend hours each week to save a few dollars. Yellow never waste a purchase and they expect fifteen dollars worth of value for every ten they spend. If begging has taught their survival instinct anything, it is the value of money.

As time passes the cold continues to worsen and food becomes even scarcer. The winds are bitter as they cut through the skin, making your eyes weep. The hunters finally return but again their catch is small and there is not enough food to go around. The group is already on severe rationing and the small and frail are suffering terribly. Sickness is widespread with more people dying and becoming bedridden daily.

You have been back twice to the group by the coast, but each time they offer you less for your knives. The final trip was hardly worthwhile. Something must be done. The group is fighting and yesterday one of the warriors killed an old man in a dispute about effort. The old man defended himself saying he was trying his best to find food, while the warrior accused him of being lazy. In his fury the warrior killed the old man with a blow to the head.
Scraps have become currency and people gnaw on the same bone incessantly. Some have been made outcast because they became sick and no longer of any practical value. Rationing has given way to starvation and only those who contribute are allowed to stay. The old and the sick and even the young are starting to be expelled, because they eat more food than they can provide. You have supplied the group with food on a number of different occasions; you and your family are allowed to stay.

Always searching for opportunities, the product of a mind used to scavenging, you take the fur coats from those who have died and gather them all together. In a desperate attempt, you carry them over to exchange with the coastal group. Their village life is unbearable.

They have enough to eat but they are freezing. The coast does not have any large mammals, so their access to winter clothing is minimal. You noticed how cold they were during the last few trades and understand they may not need any more knives but they do need furs.

This time you have brought supporters with you because you intend to drive a hard and profitable bargain. The worst that can happen is they will either drive you away or try to steal your furs without paying, but you hope to be one step ahead. The furs you have brought are few in number so you can increase the price in the next trade. If you brought enough fur for everyone, the coastal group could steal what you have and then refuse to trade. Bringing a small number ensures trade continues.

The coastal group is not particularly pleased to see you, mainly because they think you are bringing more knives. When you pull out the furs their faces light up and their trader is quick to go and get a bucket of dried fish. This time however you are not so easily paid off and you demand three buckets, not one, for each pelt. The men in the group behave as if you have asked for the world; they yell and wave their arms in the air. Then the women start yelling at the men because the children are sick from the cold. Eventually the yelling subsides and your group carries the fish, twenty-seven buckets full, back to the tribe.

Over the following months, all available pelts are exchanged for food and the remainder of the tribe stays together and fed. Finally winter recedes, and spring on the mountain means animals and food. Next winter you will be prepared for trade by stockpiling extra pelts. In the meantime there is an abundance of berries and fruit and you are keen to trade once more.

These events and a thousand more like them are the foundation of the yellow survival instinct. When the trader went into the coastal village, he had no idea whether they would attack or steal. The environment was foreign and tense. As a consequence adrenalin was at fever pitch, just as it was during the first meeting.

Events such as these imprint themselves heavily upon the survival instinct because of the danger and adrenalin surrounding them and the reaction to famine and continuously low energy. Whenever the survival instinct is dominant, it absorbs circumstance and outcome, committing to memory the dangerous event and the reaction that was successful in overcoming it. Traditional roles share a similarity of circumstance, forming a common memory, which becomes part of the collective survival instinct of yellow due to the frequency of occurrence.

From events such as these the survival instinct of the trader imprints the traits of

- **Analytical skills** – developing and creating opportunity
- **Opportunity** – seizing the moment
- **Risk** – weighing up pros and cons
- **Control** of emotions – remaining calm and stable
- **Something to offer** – exchange means material survival
- **Self-assuredness** – trusting your own judgment
- **Give and take** – both must exist for long-term survival
- **Planning** – entering the seaside tribe's village may have resulted in a dire outcome if you had not brought what they needed

Ten years ago you saved the group from starvation by swapping pelts for food. It was then you realised a precarious cycle; when times are good everyone prospers and life becomes easy, but times never stay good. When life becomes hard, it is every man for himself. Consequently friendships fall apart and family ties disintegrate. In these conditions you must contribute as much or more than you take. Life during stress is simple; if you don't work, you don't eat and if you don't contribute, you don't stay.

Years ago you realised the need to stockpile against future famine, so you had the hunters search out more pelts than they needed. This winter is as cold as the one a decade earlier and knowing the coastal group will be suffering, you begin trade once more. In addition you have established trade with the people on the plains. They pay well for the variety of food as well as the jewellery you bring. Trade ensures everyone has a better chance of surviving.

When times were good there was a surplus. Hunters celebrated as every hunt brought them success. Craftsmen could barely keep up with the demand for arrows but you were relegated in your social importance. In your role as a trader you buffered the group against hard times by supplying need. You did this by exchanging surplus for shortfall, but in good times shortfall is non-existent; as a result your social position dropped.

It would not be in your best interests to go from being the best trader in the group to a mediocre hunter, so you took up trade in desired goods rather than just necessities. There are a number of tribes with whom you trade as well as the coastal group. Exchanging goods with a number of tribes diversifies stock. In good times no-one needs scraps or old pelts but they do want jewellery, tools, spices and weapons.

The collective experiences of the trader resurface as instinctive reactions to stress. Instinctive reaction is calculated gambling. Nature bets that the most frequent events that have occurred in the past will continue to be the most likely events to occur in the future. From thousands of lives over thousands of lifetimes, each new yellow child is born with these reactions in place.

- **Security** through **diversity** – never put all your eggs into one basket
- People are **skilled** in other primary areas and it is difficult to compete – yellow security comes from possessions and the **accumulation** of goods
- **Commitment** – survival comes from being prepared to do whatever it takes and that means **perseverance** and **endurance**
- **Loopholes** and **niches** – spotting strengths and weaknesses means

creating opportunities
- Supply and demand – these are short-term solutions unless **wealth** can be accumulated and wealth can only be accumulated if you **gain** from each trade

# Rational

Many yellow people are cool in a crisis and detached from the fervour of the moment. The trader relies on being calm and rational. To be caught in emotion is detrimental to their traditional role. The trader battles the elements and keeps guard for marauders and thieves; they must remain calm when difficulties occur around them.

As merchants and traders, yellow people have an instinct for opportunity, planning, stockpiling and ideas. The traditional role of the trader is not one that is emotionally or energetically charged. When energy fluctuates it is always because of trouble. It may be a storm while the trader is at sea or under attack by bandits. The daily life of the trader rarely involves emotion or exhaustion. The role of the trader is consistent and calm unless calamity strikes. Yellow people do not like fluctuating energy because historically it always meant trouble. Some traditional roles thrive on fluctuating energy and need it to fulfil their function, but not so with yellow; consequently they avoid emotional situations.

In an out of balance state yellow people project danger, because their survival instinct always perceives a threat is occurring whenever emotions are high. Their survival instinct seeks one of two reactions; to detach and cut off emotion, or give themselves over to a more rational person. The survival instinct has no recognition or understanding and appropriateness of emotion is irrelevant. Emotions are a response to danger, so when yellow people are upset, danger is present and the survival instinct becomes dominant. The more emotional a yellow person becomes, the more dangerous the world is perceived to be.

The trader survived by calculated planning; emotions meant danger. When this type of yellow person becomes highly emotional even today, the survival instinct becomes dominant trying to stop the emotion and the danger. If a yellow person feels incapable of doing this they search out someone who can. Cool in a crisis is how yellow people survive and as long as there is a cool head nearby the yellow survival instinct is happy. If rational yellow is very out of balance they will avoid anything emotional at all. Rational yellow tries to remove the emotion from a stressful situation but this is not the same as the conscious control of the soul where positive solutions are generated.

> It's been a thousand years since trading pelts for fish with the coastal tribe saved your group. Towns and villages exist in every corner of the globe and traders from all over the world deal in spices, gold, dried foods and slaves. Anything of value is traded, regardless of difficulty or price. Traders come in a variety of forms from shopkeepers to travelling merchants. The one thing they all have in common, is they are all prepared to go out of their way to provide whatever the customer is prepared to pay.
>
> For the first time in history, desired goods are stockpiled because there is value in luxury items. With stockpiled wealth comes the need for protection as rogues and thieves are far and wide. The soldiers who are meant to protect property cannot be trusted any more than the thieves; they strut and do as they please. Law and order is needed as a priority, or property cannot be protected.
>
> This is not modern times and access to the law is difficult. There is no concept of 'justice for all', while protection and compensation are only for those who can afford it.

## Urbane

The development of the town created a new hierarchy of wealth. Hunter-gatherer tribes do not have this type of social structure because theirs is not a culture of property. Hunting and gathering is a subsistence lifestyle where needs are met as required. The development of the town and the trader go hand in hand; both flourish on excess.

The town is still the natural environment for yellow people and many are attracted to the image of culture and sophistication. An urbane yellow person likes the trimmings of life because the traditional role flourished from luxuries. Luxuries earned the trader money and luxuries defined their success. Luxuries symbolise to the yellow person's unconscious how removed from scavenging they have come. To the survival instinct of the trader, necessities symbolise desperation, while luxuries symbolise the protection of wealth. Urbane yellow people are 'men about town', refined – never flashy, well educated and remunerated. They enjoy the arts and city culture, coffee in street cafés and dinner after the theatre. Out of balance, urbane yellow people flaunt their wealth and are 'snobs'. They walk with their noses in the air, using cultured privilege as a weapon against others to make them feel humble and small. In balance, yellow people are confident, unafraid to spend money yet discreet at the same time. Not everyone is born with the same talents and opportunities and when in balance, yellow people are aware of the gifts they have been given so they appreciate what they have.

> Culture can only flourish from law, but in these times those who make the law come from a position of privilege. They are moneyed and educated and keep power in their circle. The poor and uneducated have no hope of meeting people in this social class, let alone receiving the support they need to protect their rights and assets.

> Your ambition is to help develop a class equal to the privilege of birth. Through money you now can buy enough influence to change the law and use it in your favour. This secures your future prosperity. With the money you have your family is tutored and now they have professions that will always secure them and keep them in positions where they are one step ahead of the rest.

Money yellow is driven by the ambitions of wealth, influence and position. The more their survival instinct is dominant the more these ambitions become a holy quest. How much they are prepared to sacrifice, in the struggle for wealth and power depends on how out of balance they are. Not everybody in a powerful position is dominated by their survival instinct. Some are driven by social conscience in an attempt to give something back to their community. Many do not have money as their goal; they simply focus on their passion and money follows as a result.

## Enterprise

Traders travelling in ships and caravans must quickly become acquainted with the customs of the land. They must find and befriend those who can provide the goods and security they need. The trader has developed an instinct for finding the right people at the right time. Networking is natural for many yellow people and no one is better at setting up connections. The role of scavenging created a mind that was quick to seize opportunity. When scavenging turned to trade, the same qualities were put into place but the results became far more profitable.

Traders are foreigners without invitation. They are intruders and their role has placed them in danger on countless different occasions. The reactions to these dangers lie in the yellow survival instinct because of the adrenalin of danger combined with the consistency of experience met with by foreign traders.

Confidence is vital for a foreigner without invitation. Making connections with the right people keeps the trader's head attached to their shoulders. The trader does not travel to make friends, they travel for adventure and enterprise, and while many yellow people are friendly by nature, they also must get to the point.

Out of balance yellow people do not even try to be socially discreet. They want to get to the point and get there fast; 'If you want to say something – say it!' The survival instinct has no time to entertain; getting to the point was a matter of life and death. Time is money and when out of balance, enterprise yellow live their lives as if they are foreign traders on hostile soil; no time to waste and who is in charge? Enterprise yellow with the spirit of the trader, constantly works to a deadline. They only want to speak to people who count and have no time for idle chitchat.

> The caravan is stocked and overflowing with goods so the journey home will be difficult and dangerous. Once more the age-old problem of trust arises. People steal from you constantly and that is why you never travel alone. Wherever you go, your family goes with you, improving protection and keeping the profits. No one can be trusted

the way you can trust blood family.

People today are free to follow their ambition but in the past this was not the case and families were lucky to have an income at all. A successful business was something to be kept within the family circle. To a yellow person's survival instinct family is everything and while ties through marriage are important, blood ties are stronger.

Last year on this same trade run you had a windfall and it looked as though it was going to be a good year. In exchange for cutlery and china from Europe you received jewels and spices from North Africa worth ten times as much as the initial purchase. On the return voyage, your son-in-law disappeared along with most of the jewels, and the family was left with less than when they started, although the spices could still be sold for a good price in Europe.

Never again would you trust anyone outside your blood family, nor would you give anyone access to your wealth without watching them like a hawk. From now on profit will be private. The business accounts, payments and stock must be known and handled by as few people as possible, otherwise you become a target.

You still laugh and have fun with other people at a social level but in business you are a different person and always on the alert.

Yellow people in survival mode, continue this trait and are private people who prefer to keep personal matters to themselves. Their survival instinct lives by the rules of

- **Nothing for nothing** – everyone expects some **reward** so the trader must have more than enough
- Easy conversation – the trader must be **direct** but friendly
- **Bottom line** – the conversation must have a point and sometimes the trader can be **blunt**
- **Uninfluenced** by the environment – the trader is a foreigner and

separate to the culture so they have learned to remain **sensitive** but **detached**
- **Fixed** and unwavering – the trader is there for a reason and regardless of pleasantry they must always remain **focused** if they are to successfully complete their goal
- The long distances involved in trading means extensive time away from loved ones
- **Networking** – it is important for the trader to make contact with key people for **safety** and access to markets
- Family – **blood relations** are the most trusted because dealing with family is the same as dealing with yourself. In the past, trades and professions ran in families handed down from one generation to the next. 'Blood is thicker than water' is the trader's motto, and the more distant someone is from their bloodline the less they will be trusted. **Parents**, **children** and **siblings** share the same blood so are most valuable, while **partners**, extended family and friends come next.

It is the late eighteenth century and trade is flourishing in foreign ports all over the world. These days you sail rather than travel overland by caravan, but the business of foreign trade remains just as dangerous. The same old threats continue. Wherever there is money or goods there are people who want to steal them. In the past the trader faced bandits, now on the sea these bandits are called pirates, but a thief is a thief irrespective of title.

# Isolation

Isolation yellow has the memory of loneliness deep in their survival instinct. It is an instinct first forged by the pain of leprosy and rejection, then reinforced by the role of the trader and the years where business kept them away from home.

Being away for extended periods ingrained even more deeply their friendless feeling and the despair of being alone. Isolation yellow has a survival instinct of heartache caused by separation from the people they love. This type of yellow may not want to travel, some don't even want to go on holiday. For isolation yellow, home represents safety and security; when they are out of balance isolation yellow want to stay where they are and stop time from moving. They don't want their partners to ever leave or their children to grow up. This type of yellow becomes depressed if they are away from their family for even one night. The isolation yellow survival instinct is filled with the pain of loneliness to such a degree that they never want to let go of the people they love and home becomes their only sanctuary.

When they are out of balance it does not matter if their family is around them. The despair that originates from the outcast leper and the isolated trader means yellow people can experience a sense of separation even while surrounded by family. Old memories and old reactions rise to prominence when energy is erratic or exhausted. Isolation yellow feel alone, left out and rejected. They cry, withdraw and become cold or sullen, responding to the emotions of a distant past that is trying to protect them in the present. These emotions remind the survival instinct that independent strength must be sought. For yellow, putting all their hopes into the hands of other people is an action fraught with danger, as the leper's history testifies. Isolation yellow, when their energy is out of balance will weep and beg but cannot be comforted. Their survival instinct is full of memories of stolen families and homes, voyages away for years at a time and coming home to find life has moved on without them. Single and homesick, even when at home, become life themes for yellow people once more.

Many turn to anti-depressants and some have counselling for years. The sensation of homesickness and rejection is real but the event does not belong to them. These feelings occur because their energy is low or scattered due to stress. Their survival instinct is dominant and no amount of talk will persuade or comfort an instinct, which cannot hear or understand. If this state continues, those around them will leave because they feel smothered or over-whelmed. The survival instinct's drive is to make sure yellow people are independent and strong in case rejection occurs. Yellow people can be uncomfortable and refuse any intimacy, ensuring rejection does takes place. The survival instinct if left to its own devices creates the environment to match the emotion, making history repeat itself. Out of balance yellow people, like everyone else, must find their peace and energy. Exercise, eating healthy food that contains life force, and immersing themselves in activities they like, must be part of their day. Otherwise their out of balance survival instinct will create the outcast state once more.

## Value

The trader needs to travel because value is linked to demand. The most expensive goods are goods that are rare. Laden ships leave for foreign destinations, returning equally as laden. Goods common at home are bought at low prices and shipped to distant lands, where rarity and difference increases their value. With the extra money made by the sale, the trader purchases stock common to that foreign country, bringing it home as rare and expensive. Each trip makes more than enough profit to pay for the lease of the boat, as well as the time spent away.

> You are a trader and you make your living by sailing to distant ports. Here you buy and sell goods before sailing home with the cargo that will secure your family financially.
> 
> The last time this journey was made only two of the original three ships came back. Half way into the journey, the fleet was hit by a massive storm and one of the ships was sunk. The two ships that survived did not meet again until three days after the storm was over, so furiously were they blown off course.
> 
> On this trip prayers are said while others cross their fingers. Superstitious sailors wear talismans around their necks, while the priest you hired makes it known the ship has now been blessed.
> 
> Each journey takes months to reach its destination so you say your goodbyes to your family. This is always heart wrenching but you know once you are at sea you'll be fine. You have seen others on these long voyages suffer terribly. Some miss their homes so much they become physically or mentally ill. When this occurs they are useless but you are stronger because you have the survival instinct of

the trader and can detach yourself from the pain. Enjoying home while you are there but getting on with business when you are not is how trade is conducted.

Two months into the journey and many of the crew are sick. Food is the best it can be but its nutritional value is poor. The sea, while not dangerous has a constant swell that makes life unpleasant. Those without endurance are beginning to crumble, creating anxiety and discontent among the crew.

You remain confident. You have a strong natural endurance and a determination to see the expedition through. Experience has taught you that when everyone is busy and acting according to their station, business runs smoothly but when people become lost, lazy or confused danger begins to escalate. Everyone must do what's expected to ensure the success of the voyage.

At last the first sea leg of the journey is over and the ship has docked on land. For the next two months you buy and sell and make the necessary contacts. Finally the ship is stocked and ready for the long journey home.

Two weeks out to sea, swell gives way to storm. The cargo begins to shift and strain and the sound of groaning beams rises. Boxes break loose as waves crash over the hull, while the noise of shattering wood and china becomes as loud as the sound of the storm itself. Sailors panic as the fleet separates. Trying to keep the ships together proves useless as the storm takes control. Ropes break and the wind through the sails moans like an army of ghosts. No longer able to compete with the strain, bindings and ropes snap while boxes slide over the rails. Sailors hold on for dear life to masts, ropes or anything secure. Some sailors scream while others pray, only a few fight the storm. Many more are frozen with fear, unable to move.

The smell of salt is in your nose and your face and eyes sting with the pain of sea water whipped by gale force winds. Splinters of wood fly around the deck causing cuts and injuries. Panic takes over as control is lost so together with the captain you have to take charge. Swaying over to some cargo you tie it down to make it safe. Doing your best to maintain your footing you move over to a sailor clinging to a rail and ask him in a calm voice to come and help you. The sailor stares back as if you are mad then rises to his feet and joins you. Others soon start joining in and the ship springs back to life. As calmly as possible, almost in monotone, you give them your instructions. Inside you are trembling but on the surface you are calm. Your voice has no lilt or tone; it is flat, dry, serious and consistent. It is out of context with what is occurring but that is deliberate.

This same tone and approach to life continues to dominate rational yellow. They are serious people with a serious job, natural leaders because of outward motion. In the storm, rational yellow took control and issued commands naturally, remaining free of emotion and staying calm and clear. In the heat of emotion the rational yellow survival instinct uses its ability to detach, separating emotion in order to think, and this trait is the trader's greatest survival asset.

In the morning steady rain replaced the gale of the night before. The lost ships are searched for. A whole day passes but there is no sign of them anywhere. Hearts sink when you see the abundance of wreckage and the sight of sailors dead in the water. You know the ships are lost, even though the search continues for two more days. The worst is no longer feared; it is realised. The storm was costly both in lives and goods but at least most of the cargo on your ship was saved. Your family may not be rich beyond their dreams, but enough was salvaged to make the trip financially worthwhile. This does not help the families of the lost and injured but the survival instinct does not care.

The trader saw fortunes turn at a moment's notice. In one fire, storm or robbery everything could be lost. Twenty-four hours could mean the difference between wealth, destitution and the graveyard. Trading ships and caravans faced dangers of this type constantly and due to these experiences and the energy involved, these events and reactions become part of yellow's survival instinct.

- **Unpredictability** – the trader's experience is that nothing is secure until it is safely at **home** and this can translate into home being the only environment that can be trusted.
- **Command** – taking control and keeping **emotions to a minimum** is vital for security and well-being. No matter what happens, especially in a crisis, making sure your head and not your heart guides you.
- **Lack of expression** – being seen to be **emotionless** gives the impression of **control** and command
- **Focus** – without a **determined** focus the trader could never sustain the endurance they need.

Yellow people are practical. If a trader had lost control of their emotions they would also have lost their ship. Only by detaching could the trader perform their role with success. Yellow people are analytical and put in place strategies that counteract danger ahead of time. Rather than reacting emotionally to stress, the trader prioritises and considers their options. The more tired or stressed yellow people become, the more their rational instinct takes over.

The yellow instinct to rationalise can create personal difficulties. Life demands that people interact with more than rational thought. Emotional problems take time to solve and occur because of stress. However emotional stress makes the yellow person's survival instinct rationalise to get out of danger. The daily life of the trader was not filled with highs and lows, except during travel when danger could occur. For yellow people, emotion is related to danger and is something to avoid. The more tense or emotional the situation becomes the more a yellow person will want to rationalise. This is a problem for the partners because they feel they cannot express their feelings without the yellow person becoming cold and analytical. Yellow can avoid emotion by being either analytical or through seeking another person who can be analytical on their behalf.

## Escape
Outward motion is made to be flexible otherwise it would be stopped by the first barrier it came into contact with. Outward motion cannot be contained because that is contrary to its nature. Whatever outward motion cannot push aside; it must go around. This means problems that cannot be solved, are left behind.

Partnerships and their emotional difficulties can be lengthy and complicated to solve. Many have years of troubled water under the bridge and it can take just as long to smooth it all over. This is contrary to the nature of rational yellow who have a tendency to drop the unsolvable, as outward motion pushes them away from any situation stagnant or containing.

## Home
Yellow are family and community minded people who enjoy helping at a grass roots level. They contribute locally by involvement in committees and clubs. They volunteer for kindergarten duty, help with the canteen at school, contribute to local sports and organise clean-up campaigns. They become scout leaders, throw street parties and make costumes for ballet recitals.

Charity begins at home and yellow people in balance are happy to share what they have with their family. They work to send their children to the best school they can afford, and buy the safest car available so the family is protected.

Out of balance, yellow people are never happy unless they have the upper hand. The trader survived by making sure they profited from each transaction. In daily life out of balance yellow people ensure they get just a bit more than others, because their out of balance survival instinct demands it. Whatever you have plus ten percent is this type of yellow person's attitude to life. They are accustomed to getting whatever they want. To others they can seem petty or cheap as they manipulate and struggle to get more than their 'competitor', even if their competitor is a work colleague or spouse. Out of balance yellow want ten percent more money, time, attention, or recognition. Their survival instinct cannot stand the thought that someone is getting the same or more.

## Sense of inferiority

When the survival instinct of yellow people is dominant, the primal fears and reactions of the past return and become active in the present. The security of the trader rests on independence, wealth, social position and a mind for opportunity.

The insecurities of yellow people include a fear of poverty as well as a social phobia; a throwback from being outcast in the past. The begging leper was the lowest of the low, regardless of personality or talent. No one cared about their potential, only that they had leprosy. Yellow through illness was untouchable, socially rejected and the bottom of the barrel. Today when yellow people are out of balance many feel instantly out of their class with anyone more qualified or rewarded. Yellow can become tongue tied, nervous and stumbling around people they feel are 'better' than them. Successful people draw a comparison that makes their survival instinct resurface their memories of rejection and their low social rating. These were painful and disturbing times that continue to make yellow feel unworthy, even in the present.

Always ready to chip in and help, yellow people are involved in their community, and work to make it happy and prosperous. Whether through business or public service, yellow people are prepared to do the small things that count; coaching a football team or providing money, helping an elderly neighbour change a light globe, or cooking a meal for a friend in distress.

Along with the history of wealth comes philanthropy and charity to the poor. Yellow is happy to share what they have through donation or contribution. If yellow people are prosperous they happily give money, provide someone with a job or pass on experience. They are people who love to see ideas or opportunities develop because that is the instinct of the trader. To watch a small business grow, or a sporting team mature, warms the yellow person to the core.

Like anyone else when the survival instinct is dominant, yellow can be hard and ruthless; they are self protective and play to win because material existence demands it. Every colour group competes in their own unique way because life is survival of the fittest.

The modern world is dominated by the ethics, desires and the values of the trader, which proves how successful the yellow survival instinct has been despite the historical odds. From the humble beginnings of the scavenger, to the stigma of sin and illness, yellow people, like the phoenix, have risen to a class and prosperity of their own that in turn has influenced the world. Yellow is a true rags to riches story.

## Facial features

Outward motion is designed to move forward, to travel as far as it can go and to forge new ground for the material universe to fill. In nature yellow is aerodynamic. The facial features of yellow people are equally aerodynamic and are also represented by features that are small. The electron is the smallest of the three particles and the smallness of the eyes and the thinness of the lips is representative of this relationship. Heat is another expression of outward motion and it influences facial features through the lines created by dryness.

## Outward motion

The following features express the outward motion of yellow:

- the hairline sweeps back on each side from the centre creating a widows peak or M-shape
- the forehead slopes back on a straight angle
- the lids fall over the eyes (as if to protect them from the wind)
- the nose is angled downward
- the ears slope backwards
- the chin recedes

## Heat and dryness

- the brow is wrinkled
- two lines between the eyes
- multiple fine lines seen under the eyes or around the cheeks

# Small

- the eyes are smaller or close set
- the lips are thin
- The dental arch is compact

# Chapter 14

# RED - CIRCULAR MOTION

| | |
|---|---|
| *Solutions* | *The desert* |
| *Work* | *The farmer* |
| *Fixed Ideas* | *Busy* |
| *Mistakes* | *Labour* |
| *Anger* | *The worker; the slave* |
| *Social difficulty* | *A time of slavery* |
| *Activity* | *Injustice* |
| *Cradle of life* | *Contentment* |
| *Deadpan* | *Memory* |
| *Contribution* | *The slave master* |
| *Multi-skilled* | *Privilege* |
| *Puberty* | *Gratitude* |
| *Matter and barriers* | *Defiance* |
| *Growth and bonding* | *Physical* |
| *Appearance* | *Effort and energy* |
| *Insular* | *Love and friendship* |

Circular motion is the motion of form. When we think of time or distance we generally think in linear terms. We see time and space as representing forward and backward direction, usually described as past, present and future. But there is a third force of nature separate to outward motion or inward motion and that is the force of circular motion. Circular motion solidifies and brings form to otherwise shapeless energy, like the action of a churn, forming liquid cream into solid butter. It is the force that brings energies together to create solid matter. Nature uses circular motion to turn energy into substance, and its influence can be seen from a pebble to a rose.

Circular motion brings consistency to life. Even if the rest of our lives are unpredictable, we can rely on the cycles of nature. We know spring will follow winter and day will follow night.

Red people are dominant in circular motion, which makes them think and act in predictable ways when they are under stress. The more red is stressed the more the survival instinct of circular motion comes into play. The circle is a continuous shape. It is symmetrical in every direction. Red is the same, and when out of balance they are predictable and direct in their approach. The more confusing a situation becomes, the more difficult red finds it to cope. Their survival instinct needs to force things into a familiar shape. However, sometimes successful outcomes lie in the middle ground of tact and compromise. Red, when out of balance can lack these compromising traits because circular motion pushes through barriers, it does not go around them. Obstacles and impediments must be removed – they are not something to go around or to accept. To travel in a circle means to stick to a uniform and undeviating path, and to come back to territory you have seen before.

Circular motion's purpose in the material world is to capture and secure opposite forces so matter can form. When circular motion is direct and strong, weaker forces get caught in its path and swept up as in a tornado. If the opposing forces are stronger, they block circular motion like a dam in a river. When this happens the ends of the path of the motion fail to meet, and it is no longer a circle. Out of balance, red refuses to yield and either fights to become the dominant force or else surrenders themselves entirely.

Love is a common example of red's willingness to surrender. In love, or even in a close friendship, red can sacrifice their personal character to adopt the personality of another. Copying their traits, red will mimic speech, attitude, dress and manner. They act the same, vote the same and like the same things. They become a human shadow, impersonating whatever the other person does.

The red survival instinct has kept mimicry alive because it works as a survival trait. When we copy someone else's behaviour we unconsciously make them feel at ease, because the person we are most comfortable with is ourselves. By mimicking another person's manner, red builds an intimate rapport, but only with that one person. Out of balance, their mimicking behaviour can be more annoying than flattering. A pirated personality, like a pirated movie, is never as good as the real thing. It is a cheap imitation, without the strength and substance derived from the experiences that formed it.

## Solutions

Obstacles and red are like oil and water; they are totally incompatible. To circular motion obstacles are dangerous and must be overcome. To any other colour group obstacles are an annoyance but to red they are a threat to existence. Problem solving is a trait that is strong in red and no one can find solutions more effectively. Discovering a way to get from 'A' to 'B' in the best and most direct way is what many red people do best. The red brain is designed to push through barriers, because barriers block the continuity of circular motion. Every problem must have a solution and solutions red is prepared to give it their all until they reach a result. This character trait gives red a natural ability for study and analysis. 'There must be a better way,' epitomises this type of red personality and it has great benefits at work and at school, because problem solving is a fundamental requirement of both.

## Work

Work suits solutions red well, because business always relies on problem solving. Many earn scholarships while at school or rise to the top of their professions. This type of red is often multi-skilled because a talent for problem solving can be applied to any area of working life.

Work is the medium where solutions red excels. They enjoy the challenge and love finding answers. Work is also a social setting where solutions red can interact comfortably. Socially, some can be blank and withdrawn but at work they can interact easily because work provides a focus for them.

## Fixed ideas

Life is full of unexpected difficulties and arrangements rarely run to plan; disruptions, delays and even minor problems can have red fuming and cursing as if the world has come to an end. The more out of balance red becomes the angrier and more impatient they are. They cannot roll with the blows of life because circular motion does not allow for flexibility or compromise.

In history, the red time (1650–1800 AD) embraced the idea of benevolent despotism. This was the belief that enlightened people should make decisions on behalf of the less enlightened. Benevolent despotism meant no compromise or consultation and this trait returns when red are stressed. Out of balance red firmly believe they can see solutions more clearly and accurately than anyone else. However they can also be so totally focused on the problem in front of them that they miss the big picture.

Obstacles are dangerous to them because they disrupt the continuity of the circle. Fixed red is serious about efficiency and treats mistakes with emotional gravity. To others it seems as if fixed red gets angry over the slightest inconvenience, but this is because red, more than any other colour, is threatened by what they perceive as obstacles.

## Mistakes

Driven by a survival instinct that cannot allow anything to stand in its way, fixed red is obsessed with overcoming or avoiding mistakes. The more out of balance red becomes the more they react to simple mistakes as if they were serious. Out of balance, they do whatever is necessary to ensure they do not make a single mistake. They are intolerant of inefficiency, whether in a machine or in a person. In an out of balance state they consider anyone who is not helping to solve a problem as contributing to it. Red will yell and scream for support until others feel forced to help. In balance, they are calm and rational, and make provision for problems by allowing extra time. When fixed red is out of balance they cannot be calmed or advised. The only opinion they want to hear is the opinion that agrees with their own. Fixed red want help but not suggestions because they have already decided what action to take. In their haste to make everything right, red can act and make decisions too quickly and as a consequence make more mistakes.

Out of balance, red can focus on what's wrong instead of what's right. Their survival instinct is designed to remove obstacles, but under stress they see obstacles everywhere.

## Anger

It is not a green rag that is waved at a bull, nor is it purple, it is red that makes them charge. The colour is irrelevant to the bull but it does make a difference to us. Human beings project qualities onto inanimate objects and colours are included in this projection. People are said to be green with envy, have a yellow streak, or the blues. A red rag that is waved at a bull for the same reason we go 'red with rage'. Red is the colour of anger and impatience and impulsive red have a reputation for their quick temper, excessive swearing and sassy remarks.

## Social difficulty

Circular motion is the only primary force that does not make contact with other forces. It is self-contained and does not absorb like blue's inward motion, nor does it reach out like yellow. Circular motion stays on its predictable path and does not mix or accommodate. Red can pay a high social price when their survival instinct is out of balance.

The more introverted red becomes under stress the less they can relate to others. To them it is not about being rude or discourteous; they just don't know what to say or how to behave. Others will see their behaviour as rude, as they can be so quiet, aloof and self-contained, but it is not rudeness, it is circular motion responding to stress. Some introverted reds are aware of their impact and how they make others feel, but most are not.

Not every red stumbles for words. Some are very social. They are loud, brash and ostentatious; a legacy of the continuous push behind circular motion.

In private, even quiet red speaks freely but in public they go as blank as their face. A smile does more than just say 'hello'. A smile says, 'I wish you no harm'. Walking into a room with a blank, unsmiling face sends a signal of wariness and alarm to the survival instinct of other people. The face communicates feeling. When it is blank it makes others suspicious. It makes others feel red has something to hide, because a concealed face means concealed intentions. For many this trait can haunt them because they cannot understand why others don't trust them. This is especially a problem when it comes to fidelity in relationships.

Character traits are positive or negative depending on the

circumstances. Inflexibility makes red's brain join the dots and tie up all loose ends. To every beginning there must be an end and to every question there is an answer. Philosophy and pondering life's mysteries without trying to find a solution has no appeal to red.

Social interaction depends on the ability to accommodate the opinions and expectations of others. Social adaptability is the basis of communal existence and any shortfall in this area will require major input from another area to offset it. When functioning well, red's unchanging personality can provide a solid and stable platform to establish a lasting personal or business relationship.

## Activity

When active red isn't thinking, they are solving. When they aren't solving they are planning and if they aren't planning then they are doing. Without thinking, solving, planning or doing, their life will be out of balance.

Excessive activity can be unproductive and frustrating. This type of red is always busy, yet has precious little to show for their efforts. Like circular motion, they go around and around but never actually get anywhere.

## Cradle of life

Circular motion does not change the character of other forces; its role is to capture and attach to them. When opposing forces are caught in circular motion all three forces remain unaltered and continue to maintain their character. Nature has designed circular motion this way for its function as the cradle of life. As outward and inward motion become trapped within circular motion, each begins to build in strength as more of each force is added. Soon an equal amount of each force exists and using circular motion as its womb, the material universe begins. The necessity for circular motion to remain uninfluenced by outside force is vital for the development of structure.

## Deadpan

The unfaltering steadfastness of circular motion is the basis for one type of red whose character is as predictable as the force that lies inside them. Expressionless red is monotone, their face is deadpan and their answers are brief. To others they can seem like a human mannequin; they are there but they do not interact. They talk but their face is expressionless, they think but they do not share their thoughts. Out of balance, their unchanging face and style is viewed by others as arrogant and cold. Red believes this is unfair and may become disillusioned by this opinion. Our face is our only medium for conveying emotion and others judge us by our expression, whether we like it or not. A deadpan face conveys no emotion, and its owner will be thought by others to be aloof and icy. Red can end up not trusting other people because of how others misjudge their demeanour.

## Contribution

Because many have difficulty communicating socially, red tries to prove their worth in other ways. What they cannot display by words and expression, they deliver in deeds and effort. What they lack in vibrancy and social interaction, they give back in competency and achievement. Reds are doers rather than talkers. Their survival instinct competes against others by competence, not social appeal. Their drive to be constructive is strong because that is their gift to the group. Unsure of whether they are liked or not, red make themselves indispensable.

## Multi-skilled

Everyone has their special talents but red are one of the few who can turn their hand to almost anything. Academically gifted, many are also good at sport, trade and art. Skilled red may not communicate well but with such a variety of talents they don't need to. Gifted red is structured and linear in the way that they think. They piece problems together effectively and quickly and they never give up until the task is complete. This is compensation for their lack of social grace, and it is here that the red survival instinct returns when threatened or exhausted.

## Puberty

High school can be a competitive place with people crammed into a confined space, the survival instinct of many on alert. For some, rather than being the best years of their life, their high school years are the worst, with everyone being assessed and consigned to their social groupings.

The hormonal changes of puberty are a massive drain on energy and for many this change alone is enough to make the survival instinct dominant. As well as puberty, there are the social and academic pressures and for some it all becomes too much. Personality changes as the soul is suppressed and the survival instinct takes control.

As the survival instinct becomes dominant, rational thinking becomes suppressed. This means that reaction is strong but planning and decision making are weak. Red's teenage years can be a pivotal time as instinct drives them to form deep connections with one person or a small select group. Their drive to bond is linked to stress. The more threatened or exhausted, the more the survival instinct is dominant and the more unhealthy bonding takes place. Regardless of whether it is a romantic relationship or a cliquey tight knit group, the emphasis is on the small, intimate and exclusive.

## Matter and barriers

Circular motion is represented by the neutron. Mass is gained by the accumulation of protons in the nucleus but protons cannot accumulate to gather mass without the buffering action of the neutron. In human terms, a neutron is both a barrier and a bonder.

The defence system of circular motion surrounds with a wall any threat whether biological, environmental or human. Barriers and walls form part of the circular motion's defence system by creating blockades in the body that prevent systemic infection. Harmful invaders are confined in an encapsulated cyst or tumour, or by inflammation. The red immune system also makes germs immobile by surrounding them with mucous to capture and confine. Emotionally red can put up a barrier when under stress creating a personality that is blank.

## Growth and bonding

Out of balance red are driven by instinct to partner up quickly. Love is the most common reason people bond but when red is out of balance, their relationship is not based on love but dependence. Out of balance we do the right thing but for the wrong reason.

When red is in balance they have a healthy desire to bond and attach to others. Their relationship with their partner is even handed and based on give and take. Once attached this type of red feels free to move their attention into other areas of life. They do not let go of the attachment but use its base to fuel confidence to experience other avenues of life.

Emotional investment in a partner is high for everyone regardless of colour group and the future depends on getting along. Partners can cause the greatest amount of stress, because they are the people we rely on most and the ones who are linked to our future. With partners we share children, money and a home; all the responsibilities of life. Half of everything we hold dear is in their hands. When a partner is also your greatest stress, life is difficult and the pressure relentless. There is nowhere to relax or rejuvenate when the home is cold, tense or dangerous.

Continuous stress makes the survival instinct dominant and when bonding red is stressed, attachment becomes a primary survival need. When in balance, their attachment will be to their spouse but when that person is causing the stress, red will withdraw and put up a wall, or bond with somebody else. Bonding red is designed to attach themselves to one person. If that person makes themselves unavailable they will switch their attention elsewhere.

Under stress, bonding red falls in and out of love easily. Their survival instinct is unconsciously searching for a new partner to bond with. Red does not know why this is happening, just that it does. If conditions at home do not improve, someone will come into bonding red's life because the survival instinct draws them in. Often there is little a partner can do to salvage the situation once a new bonding has occurred.

## Appearance

Appearance is vital for attachment so red take their appearance seriously. Even if they have no desire for a partner, appearance red, both male and female, go to extraordinary lengths when it comes to their looks. Males can be obsessed with fitness and muscle building, while females spend hours making sure every hair is in place and their face is perfect. Appearance is part of the human condition but for red it is likely to become a life theme.

To join and attach is how red creates growth, and it has helped them survive since the dawn of time. Physical attraction is important because it helps us appeal to others. People like being around attractive people, as glossy magazines prove.

Attraction is a double-edged sword because while the red survival instinct needs to be desired, this is offset by the barrier it puts in place when it feels the need to protect itself. Appearance red desires to be found attractive yet panic if somebody approaches them. Unable to be at ease socially, many find physical attraction embarrassing or even disturbing.

Without a partner or a group of intimate friends, red can become edgy and depressed. They spend their time sulking and alone wishing someone would take them away. This instinctive red response puts them at odds with the concept of independence. Others feel it's immature the way red needs a group or partner before they can feel good about themselves. However nature doesn't care what other people think and will respond despite what they say. This type of red may put up a barrier and keep everything hidden inside. They may even pretend they are free and independent to keep in step with the modern trend, but this is not true for their survival instinct, regardless of how they like to think of themselves.

## Insular

Circular motion can be like a tornado, spinning so rapidly that the person loses the ability to reflect. In some cases red becomes caught, unable to feel, think or even move. Life becomes a dreamlike state, where reality is separate and untouchable. A barrier is in place and red have become disconnected from the world.

The more stress insular red is under, the more of a barrier they create. Some have such a division from others they find it impossible to understand another person's feelings or opinions, leaving them unable to relate at all. If this life theme is combined with appearance, red becomes narcissistic. Insular red is the only person who exists because they have bonded with themselves.

Out of balance, the barrier created by the survival instinct suppresses empathy and understanding. Once energy levels regain their balance red becomes rational and interactive once more. In some cases the survival instinct never lets this barrier drop.

## The desert

The environmental symbol of red is the desert. Not only are many of the world's deserts red in their colour, they also display red qualities. As a result the desert is a good metaphor for understanding the red survival instinct.

On the surface the desert seems barren, infertile and isolated. In reality the desert is a vibrant and delicate environment, teaming with life and diversity. In true red style, most of what happens occurs under the surface. Desert survival is constant and unrelenting; it is not like the rainforest where fruit dangles from the trees. The desert requires planning and its own brand of management. There is no waste in the desert and the people who call it home are resilient and resourceful. The desert, like red itself, exists in a number of forms, ranging from sandy dunes to spectacular rocky canyons.

The desert is misjudged and misunderstood; it is hard and unforgiving. Incapable of compromise and unwilling to bend, it destroys anyone who does not respect it. Others must adjust to the desert's rules and it is intolerant of mistakes; only the most resourceful can ever hope to survive. However the desert is also unique and special, it is romantic and captivating and the source of sensual stories. The desert is the setting for numerous novels of fantasy, adventure, sex and seduction. With its backdrop of full moons, warm desert nights, harems and isolation, the desert is the personification of everything exotic like the attractive appeal of red.

The desert is also where many of history's sages have gone to gain their wisdom. From Moses to Jesus to Mohammed, the desert has always been a place of contemplation. Its quiet isolation gives it a spiritual quality and it is symbolic that the desert is used as a barrier, to separate the sage from the rest of the world.

Deserts are places of extremes. Many red people exhibit this trait of extremes when it comes to their moods. Generally consistent and stable, red like the desert can become suddenly volatile when upset or out of balance. One moment they are quiet and subdued, the next they are a desert storm blinding and cutting anyone in their path. From extremely warm to extremely cold, red and the desert move between both.

In rockier deserts where water holes exist, wildlife and wildflowers spring into life every time it rains. Artists go to the desert in search of inspiration and beauty and are drawn by its colour as well as its light, isolation and peace.

## The farmer

While agriculture is a relatively recent industry, gathering is as old as time. History uses the term hunter-gatherer to describe early societies, but the two roles were separate and were performed by people specialised in each. Hunters were a class of their own and their role was to hunt, not to gather. Gatherers performed a different and complementary role by supplying the tribe with vegetables and herbivorous food. Together hunting and gathering sustained the human race until the agricultural age began. In prehistoric times, hunter-gathering tribes were all that existed. The environment was harsh and finding food was a full time job that prevented the development of anything else.

> You are a gatherer. It is your job to supply the tribe with as much herbivorous food as you can find. Meat is the most sought-after food because it fills the stomach but its supply is unreliable. Vegetables, fruits, berries and nuts are the tribe's true source of nutrition because gathering is far more consistent and reliable.

> Making your way through the forest, you examine the plants hoping to recognise something familiar. Thousands of years of trial and error have taught you that some plants are enjoyable and nutritious while other plants make you sick or kill you. Sometimes plants resemble each other so closely it is difficult to be certain what is tasty and what is toxic and this places great responsibility on your shoulders. You must pick the right food and prepare it correctly. That way everyone remains fed and healthy and you maintain your position in the tribe regardless of what hardships may come.

> Several plants, tubers and fruits are only safe if they are prepared in a certain way. Some must be boiled for a specific length of time while

others must be left to soak in water before cooking. A number of plants only make good eating once a certain part is removed, while others are an edible-toxic combination where pulp can be eaten but the kernel or leaves are poisonous.

In these times people are few and there is lots of space. This provides you with a large area to roam which in turn gives you access to a variety of plants and grasses, all of which flower, seed or fruit at different times and seasons. Berries and fruits are ready in the summer and autumn, while tubers and root vegetables are available in winter and spring. Access to large uninhabited areas of land is important because the plants are dispersed.

One of the main problems is that vegetable food, while nutritious, is short lived when it comes to satisfying hunger. This means constant foraging. Root vegetables are good because they are rich in starch and that means fullness in the stomach. Fruits and berries on the other hand are digested quickly so it takes lots of effort to gather enough for others to feel full and satisfied. Even then, the satiation is momentary and soon they begin to feel hungry again and that means an endless cycle of work for you.

You cannot get angry or tell them to go and find their own food, because gathering for others is how you stay in the tribe. You supply them with fruits and vegetables and they supply you with the security you need. The traditional role of the gatherer is vital because it is the backbone of food supply. Hunters are sometimes gone for days; occasionally even weeks can pass during the winter before they return with anything substantial. In the meantime you and the other gatherers supply the group with enough food to keep everybody alive.

Your day is long and arduous because the plants that are needed are dispersed over a large area. Fruit trees are dotted amongst an array of other species while other edible plants are just as scattered. These vast areas must be covered to gather what is necessary. Then, laden with stock, you take a deep breath, lift the heavy load onto your back, hoist yourself up with a groan and begin the long journey home.

When you arrive you are tired and it is getting late. Your muscles ache from the long walk and your back is sending sharp currents of pain shooting down your legs from carrying the heavy weight for such a long time, but your day is not finished. Arriving home you must now start cooking.

In modern times we pick and choose food that is easy to prepare. We buy a packet of cashew nuts as a snack without thinking of the laborious process of growing, picking and preparing them. Driving home in the car we just open the packet; we don't have to remove the nut's highly allergenic exterior, nor do we have to go through a number of other required processes before we can put that one small nut into our mouth, but the gatherer had to.

In the forest, you notice that new life comes from the seeds that have fallen on the ground. You also observe that many of the seeds thrown away after a meal are sprouting new life. With this knowledge comes the beginning of the garden. By learning how to sprout seeds and grow plants, your task of providing food becomes easier as gathering turns into growing. Planting an apple tree means not having to search for apples. Cultivating means the labour of distance is overcome and time can be better spent.

Unfortunately while you have solved the problem of travel and distance, the garden does not solve the problem of effort. Growing a crop means creating a space and that means clearing the land. Even after the trees have been felled, unwanted plants take over your garden and compete with the plants you need for food.

The rest of the group values you highly because you provide them with a stable supply of food. They protect you and nurture you and when famine times arrive, you are protected from expulsion. This memory provided you with a valuable and deeply entrenched life lesson – the more productive and efficient you are, the more others will want you. The red survival instinct is entrenched with this memory and it knows that to be busy is to be safe.

## Busy

The busy red finds it difficult to relax because their survival instinct is aware that security comes from toil. The more out of balance this red becomes the harder they work and the less they can physically relax. Many will state that finding time to relax is their aim but when that time comes they get jittery and restless. The more energy they expend, the more control the survival instinct takes, until the point is reached where red may even become physically ill whenever they attempt to lie down or relax. They may have headaches or stomach cramps or all manner of pains and many of these aches are relieved by being active. The more they move the better they feel. This out of balance red has a survival instinct that is forcing them to keep on the move, causing pain, anger, stress or guilt to ensure they keep busy and active. The gatherers who relaxed were the gatherers who were rejected. This is the memory instinct holds on to.

> It is no longer pre-history and towns and villages are everywhere, thanks mainly to farming. You now grow a variety of crops including grains such as wheat and barley. You have come a long way since the fruits from the forest and the garden is now a farm. You are self-sufficient in food and you employ every bit of land for the growth and cultivation of all that is edible. Growing changed the labour of gathering but it did not solve the problem of backbreaking toil. Now, instead of walking miles carrying food back to the camp, you spend your days turning the fields by plough.

The farmer has traded security for effort. In the days of the hunter-gatherer, life was difficult but leisurely. It is true that long distances were covered but they were covered at a relaxed pace. Now in these village times that same relaxed pace is no longer possible.

All change in life is a trade and the farmer has chosen to trade leisure for a full stomach. Life in the past was hard and precarious and more than once you were unable to sleep because of your empty and rumbling stomach. However this is no longer something you need to worry about. Irrigation, cultivation and your own backbreaking labour has ensured that you always have a full belly. As for any thought of sleeplessness, no-one who works as hard as you ever has to worry about not sleeping.

The traditional role of the farmer is an extension of circular motion because:

- The cyclic quality of farming and the seasons depicts the nature of red
- The farmer is a grower and growth is the essence of circular motion
- The farmer is a traditional role concerned with efficiency and production and circular motion in its nature, removes obstacles to make things run smoothly

## Labour

Labour as always remains a major issue on the farm. Life may have changed from the early gathering days but the need for labour and physical effort has not. In town, people are becoming increasingly more specialised. Food is so plentiful that there is even a surplus and grain stores are overflowing. Armies now have professional soldiers and craftsmen and traders have all manner of goods. Countries have become rich because of the surplus of food, and to ensure this trend of wealth continues, society has solved the problem of the labour shortage by capturing slaves as well as a creating a social hierarchy that ensures labour is always available.

Town is a vibrant and energetic place, full of activity and liveliness but the farmer rarely takes part in any of these events as they do not live close to town. Townspeople crowd together so they can make the most of their resources but the farmer needs land in order to grow food.

'Many hands make light work,' is the saying and serfs, indentured labourers, convicts and slaves are all examples of how farmers get their necessary workforce. Large families also for the first time in history have become a trend because they provide the workforce the farmer needs.

The memories that rest in the unconscious survival instinct are the memories most affected by emotion, danger, fatigue and pain. Memory is linked to adrenalin and adrenalin is linked to emotional experience, the most basic of all being the experience of danger. These chemical messengers remind the survival instinct of what is important. The survival instinct cannot think and it cannot sort out what is important from what is not, so adrenalin and exhaustion become the link for the priorities made by the survival instinct.

Unfortunately for human beings regardless of colour group, the experiences stored in the survival instinct are predominantly negative. Memories of pain and torment, danger and suffering are mixed with memories of escape and reward. All come together to form the survival instinct's drives and fears. The more an event is painful or dangerous, emotional or rewarding, the more it forms part of our reaction to stress. Each of us carries, according to the colour group we belong to, the collective memory of the experiences of the traditional role that precedes us.

The survival instinct of red is filled with experiences that have caused the greatest threat and exhaustion during the numerous lifetimes of the farmer. The more an experience is repeated, the greater the likelihood of that experience turning to memory. Each time an emotionally charged memory is repeated it goes into the unconscious collective memory of that colour group. Every time that same experience is relived, it travels up the hierarchy of importance within the survival instinct.

Like the forces behind matter, dominance is the key to understanding this outcome. The more an emotional experience is relived, the more dominant it becomes, replacing less dominant memories. The strength a memory has depends entirely on how often it is relived. The less it replays itself, the less energy it has and soon it will be replaced by one that is stronger. In this way nature ensures that the most common experiences – the ones that are the most frequent and needed – are also the ones best served.

Day to day life for the farmer, whether sowing, reaping or ploughing the fields rarely has the emotional impact required to turn experience into instinctual memory, with the exception of exhaustion and the reward of the harvest.

By far the most common memories do not belong to farming itself, but to the hardships faced by those *forced* into farming. The farmer who worked their crops and their land does not share the pain of someone forced into servitude. A long and turbulent history of peasantry and serfdom is embedded into the survival instinct of red. For tens of thousands of years, millions of human beings have been born or sold into the role of the human horse.

## The worker, the slave

If reincarnation is really true, most of us have been peasants for more lives than any other. For every noble there were a thousand serfs and it is the memory of servitude, charged with emotion that is the unconscious instinct of red. The survival instinct of the farmer comes from the shared experience of the people who worked the land. The red survival instinct has the experience and memory, emotion and ambition of not only the farmer but of the serf, convict and slave. Farm labourers were forced to work under the same horrific conditions with the same ball and chain, the same starvation and the same lash.

Which has more emotional impact – planting a crop and watching it grow, or being kidnapped and beaten, torn from the people you love, to work and die on a piece of land that isn't yours? This is the memory in the survival instinct of red.

> Nineteen years of age, and you have been sentenced to seven years hard labour for stealing. Six months ago you were talked into helping move some meat from a cart by your friend. Like everyone else you were poor and badly paid for the work you did. Thinking you had a lucky break to pick up some extra money just for helping unload some meat, you had no idea both the meat and the cart were stolen. When you were caught the police didn't care what story you had to tell and neither did the judge.
>
> Hearing the sentence you stood dumbstruck in the dock. 'Seven years!' It was a nightmare and for a while you were confused as to whether the events were real. Life had taken on a dreamlike quality

because you were in shock.

You stood there open mouthed as the judge passed sentence. He called you part of the criminal class and said that he would not be happy until the country was rid of everyone like you. You could hear your mother screaming and crying and your father yelling, 'You'll be fine son.'

Back in the cell you were beaten to a pulp because the guards threw you onto a violent man who became angry at being disturbed.

When you awoke, it was to the swaying of the ship and the groaning of the injured. You could barely see, your eye was badly damaged and you faded in and out of consciousness. You were sick from concussion, the motion of the sea and the stench of others. The heavy chains around your wrists and ankles kept you fixed to the spot, they were tight and they were brutal and they cut deeply into your skin. All around you was vomit, diarrhoea and wailing. Scared beyond belief you prayed, struggled and sweated. The people around you were so close they were almost on top of you. You needed to urinate but you couldn't move, you let go and felt it run down your legs. The indignity of this act was more than you could endure; you shut your eyes and cried.

Convicts started being transported to Australia toward the end of the eighteenth century at the same time as revolutions replaced aristocracies with democratic governments. This was the age of reason; the enlightenment where human beings threw off the dictates of both church and state to adopt the ethics of fraternity, egalitarianism and justice for all. 'All' of course discounted the poor, the black and the hungry.

## A time of slavery
While slavery had always existed, the heights it reached during this red time were unprecedented and unparalleled. Ten to twenty million black African slaves were shipped to the Americas during the red time. Along

with these slaves must be included the millions of ordinary people forced by necessity into 'service' in Europe and across the globe. Lastly there were the convicted felons who spent a great part of their lives struggling and toiling in penal servitude.

Every time period, like every individual has its good and bad attributes and the red time period is no different in this regard. Surgery and medicine reached new heights, while music was written by composers such as Mozart, Handel, Beethoven and Bach. Science bred Newton and exploration was expanded by Cook.

> In this new country everything looks different, even the plants. The soil is different and the smell of eucalyptus in the air is something impossible to describe. There are animals that hop on their hind legs and flightless birds as big as a man. As you step ashore you hope it is summer in this country because the heat seems as if it will melt your bones. The only thing that has stayed the same is the chains that bind your hands and your feet.

In the world of the survival instinct, conscious experience becomes a future unconscious response. From this experience of being used and mistreated come the egalitarian ideals of equality and dignity, unhampered by discriminating and unjust laws. Red ideals are not about courtesy and they are not about manners to make other people feel comfortable, they are a struggle against oppression and a victory over bigotry.

The experience of savagery and intolerance, brutality and injustice, struggle, liberty and eventual freedom is a memory that is deeply ingrained in everyone who is red. The convict experience has replicated itself millions of times in only a hundred years. The convict, the servant, the peasant and the slave share a common experience and a universal ideal.

## Injustice

A red person with this inherited reaction searches for mistreatment and seeks out injustice. This unconscious drive when out of balance makes red jump into fights that are not theirs to jump into. They defend people whose actions deserve to be punished and they fight for causes that affect them only marginally. They fight for the sake of fighting. In balance they are benevolent and loyal, always ready to give their support through the toughest of times. Out of balance, their actions are not thought through and their mouth can be ahead of their brain, making them aggressive and loud. Rather than being a well trained guard dog, when out of balance the egalitarian red is a snappy little terrier barking at everyone who passes, not because it's justified, but because they can.

> You have been assigned to your work gang and you have the task of felling trees and clearing roads. Marching into the bush you crunch through the dry grass in your bare feet, your issued canvas slippers masquerading as shoes fell to shreds in the first month.
>
> This is dangerous work. You hate walking barefoot in this place because two people you know, one of them was even chained to you, have died due to snakebite. This place is not like England. It is hot and dry and the snakes are deadly. The man chained to you died an excruciating and horrible death, salivating and talking all manner of gibberish, behaving as if he was having a nightmare. The whole experience was terrifying.
>
> After a day clearing land and chopping down trees, the convicts are chained into rows to pull a number of the large trees back to the prison to be milled.
>
> Like human bullocks the prisoners pull and drag the heavy timber over the uneven land. The man next to you has been here four years longer than you; he is thirty-five but looks seventy. His face is lined and drawn and his body is nothing but skin and sinew. Under the strain he collapses and you stop to help him to his feet, bringing a lash to your back and the butt of a rifle to your head. Lying on the ground you watch as the guards beat the fallen man. His head has caved in on one side because of the repeated stomping of the guards' feet on his skull. He will not survive this beating and everyone knows it; probably he is dead already.

The shock and the anger of experiences like this, repeated thousands of times over hundreds of lifetimes, is embedded into the survival instinct of red. The sense of injustice and the anger of abuse have led to a survival instinct that refuses to be dominated. The egalitarian red is savage against any situation they consider unjust or excessive. They will fight for their rights and they will serve the community. When in balance they will set up schools for the poor and feed the homeless. They are driven to do something good for the world and to defend those who cannot defend themselves.

Circular motion gives this type of red the ability to overcome hurdles and to see a task through. When they commit themselves to a project, they see it through to completion. When in balance, red are driven to contribute and to do something worthwhile and because they are in balance, they will not burn themselves out trying to save other people but instead keep themselves stable and healthy so they can enjoy and be enriched by their contribution.

> You nursed the dying man in your arms as he moaned and groaned throughout the night until you fell asleep. While you slept, he died. For helping him you received a punishment of thirty lashes because the overseer had told you not to – but you did anyway.
> The time in prison is strict and harsh and cruel penalties exist for the slightest transgression of the rules. Silence is absolute and any communication with another prisoner can mean solitary confinement, locked in a dark room for a month. Silence is enforced because talk is how human beings organise and plan. Without communication no uprising is possible and that is what the exploiters of other people fear the most. Silence and hard work are the qualities that see you through this miserable nightmare and they are the qualities that continue to influence the survival instinct of the withdrawn red.

## Contentment

To be content with their life is a trait that red has beyond all other colour groups. No-one is more appreciative of what they have than contentment red; the more they profit and the more they succeed, the more grateful and satisfied they become.

To know hardship is to appreciate success. Never taking anything in life for granted, this type of red values everyone and everything in their life regardless of how meagre that may be. There are a number of things a serf, slave or convict have in common. One is the memory of suffering and hardship; the other is the appreciation of freedom and a place to call their own.

In prison all activities are accomplished in silence. The cell is solid stone and the door made of heavy wood. Guards patrol the walkway outside the cells all through the day and night, making escape almost impossible.

Some prisoners have escaped in the past but the majority did so while outside the walls as part of a work gang, not by breaking out of their cell. Outside there is a country the size of Europe to hide in, but it is harsh and unforgiving. You don't know how many prisoners have actually escaped and you nearly took part in one breakout attempt yourself.

Five of you decided that you had all had enough. It was after the man you were chained to had died and it was in that moment you decided that anything was better than this mindless servitude. However at the last moment you did not go through with it. Not because you were afraid but because there was nowhere to go. To get away from captivity was to get away to what? The others decided they would go ahead and another man eagerly took your place. In the breakout a guard was killed and a manhunt was launched. The man-hunters didn't need to try too hard, unless there was a bounty on one of the prisoner's heads, because they knew the terrain was foreign and too harsh to survive in. Sooner or later most would give themselves up, half starved and too weak to continue.

Two months after the five had escaped, only two remained and they were both caught. They had survived by eating the three others and now they were captured and soon to be hanged.

The morning of the hanging you and all the others were marched as usual to watch. Wherever you went silence was enforced. The only time that noise was allowed was during church with the singing of hymns. Hessian bags prevented any contact with others and were only removed to view the hanging. Silently you watched as the backs of the captured men were turned into jelly under the savagery of the lash. From here they were hanged and left to struggle and swing.

After five years of hardship and trial you are near the end of the sentence. In one more year you will be given a ticket of leave allowing you to work for money. Your plan is to work and to save so you can get back to England. Memories of home have been vital for your sanity and for many years they have been your only warmth and tenderness.

## Memory

Memories of the past are strong in red. When the present is difficult and their survival instinct is dominant, the reminiscing red drifts easily into the memories of the past, in an attempt to find comfort and solace as a way of managing the hardships of the present.

The other extreme of forgetting the past is also present in red. Their survival instinct forgets the past as quickly as it happened. They can have no recollection for any memories longer than a short while ago. Some fear they are going mad or going into early dementia but for most it is neither. They do not have dementia but are just experiencing stress. Often their memory for facts and figures is sound, while the memories linked to emotion pass quickly.

In this respect the red survival instinct is working against the laws of conventional memory. In every other colour group the more emotionally charged the circumstance the more it is committed to memory, but red through the experience of the convict, slave and the serf has a survival instinct that works in the opposite way. Under normal circumstances, emotion and adrenaline helps a person escape but for red there was no escape and the emotion of the moment only serves to increase their pain, not deliver them from it.

When the present is harsh and the future too miserable to contemplate, the past is all that remains. As a way of surviving, some reds have learned that to forget is best, while others keep their hearts alive by maintaining their focus in the happiness of the past. These are the two ends of the scale but both are the same way of interpreting an inability to escape.

Out on the work gang it is another day of brutality and another day of survival. There are only a few months to go so you must make sure that nothing goes wrong. The guards are always looking for an excuse so you must not give them one. You did nothing to deserve your sentence in the first place; to have it extended over something petty would be too much to bear.

The sweat pours from your body as you swing the mallet breaking rocks into stones for the new road being built. The overseers yell abuse and the whip breaks open the backs of many around you but you do not flinch. Your face shows no emotion and your mouth is sealed tight. The guards will find no reason to report you.

The survival instinct of red carries the imprint of this moment. Refusing to look or take part in the moment keeps you invisible to the overseer's eyes and helps you survive. Others may scream and protest, but you are unchanging and unmoved. Those who protest will be flogged or starved, while you remain strong and get to eat. The survival instinct of red carries this experience because it is one that has worked a million times over.

Surviving conditions such as these takes its toll on your physical and emotional health and the lessons your survival instinct learned stay with you for life. In the future you will live a rich and independent life, but the instinct to clam tight, put your head down and work as hard as you can, when you are under stress, never leaves you.

## The slave master
There is another type of survivor in this harsh agricultural world; those who

are lucky enough to be born into rich landowning families. These people have a survival instinct that has learned to prosper by the efforts of others. Historically this group is vastly smaller than the labourers they exploited but the trait to domineer when under stress still belongs in the red survival instinct.

The slave master has a survival instinct of exploitation and the willingness to sit back and let others work on their behalf. Not just content to let others do the work, slave master red expects them to labour on their behalf. Slave masters were demanding and overseeing, harsh and judgmental and thought nothing of watching another person labour, then be both critical of their efforts and unappreciative of the outcome. The slave master red is rarer than all the other red types because workers outnumbered the aristocracy more than a thousand to one. However the tendency for red to revert to the master and become cold and dictatorial still exists if limits are pushed too far.

The survival instinct of the slave master red has flourished and prospered by using others. While the workers fell by the wayside and dropped to their knees from exhaustion, this type of red watched them from the window and ate another cake. Annoyed because it meant the expense of another worker, the breakdown or death of a human being was an inconvenience instead of a moral outrage.

Natural law means a natural food chain and all the survival instinct cares about is eating rather than being eaten. The slave master red is a predator rather than prey and they fully intend to hold on to this position. Many people working for the comfort of a few is abhorrent to a sophisticated mind, but it has been the way of the world for most of civilised history. Unfortunately in many places the trend of exploitation still exists where women, minorities and the poor are just modern day slaves by another name.

When this type of red is out of balance they once again revert to the slave master instinct, because it is what helped them survive for thousands of years. When chronically tired or threatened, the tendency to view people as property resurfaces once more. Under stress those around them are called into action, to drop what they are doing and to come and help. Whether those called were involved in other activities is totally irrelevant and if any protest is uttered, the slave master red will yell and scream and go into a rage until those around them capitulate and do their bidding.

In this state, dissatisfaction with the quality of the help is almost guaranteed. It is in the nature of the slave master to never thank or reward but to criticise and demand more. Harsh rules with even harsher penalties bind those around them in captivity. In First World nations it is against the law to beat or enslave, so this out of balance red snares others with their moods. They may no longer be physically violent and those around them are not servants in the true sense of the word, but the intention to coerce and demand and to treat others poorly is the same. Making other people too frightened of the consequences to say no is the tactic of the slave master instinct. If laws of the land allow beating or starvation then that's what the slave master will do. If they are illegal, the slave master will use emotion and anger in their place.

For slave master red, the survival instinct they have will turn them into an animal, hated by everyone including their own soul. They must not allow themselves to fall into this state as it runs contrary to everything that humanity and decency demands.

## Privilege

Historically red was often a colour of the rich. Ornate decorations, carpets and rugs, even the colour of the walls was a rich deep red. When Hollywood stars step out of their limousines, it is a red carpet that they walk down because red is both prestigious and rich. There are two shades of red; one is brash, bright, ostentatious and loud, the colour of a Ferrari with a platinum blonde driver. The other is like burgundy, warm, deep and exclusive. It is this latter shade that represents the privileged red and they are comfortable and used to the fineries of life. They have an eye for beauty and a taste for style. They are attracted to clothes, jewellery and architecture that is ornate and striking. They are tasteful and elegant with a refined finesse; this type of red is the embodiment of old money.

Inside every human being, a savage animal waits ready to defend and ready to attack. Understanding this side of human nature places the responsibility of a beneficial and conducive environment firmly on our own shoulders. Knowing that certain environments produce predictable responses, means accepting responsibility for the environment we create.

With a privileged environment comes responsibility. Those in the past lucky enough to be born one of the lords instead of one of the serfs, have an obligation to treat the less fortunate with care and decency. The survival instinct of the privileged red is divided into two distinct parts; the first is the type that thinks nothing of using others as if they belonged to them and to treat them like they wish. Out of balance, they are the slave master who uses people like machines, demanding from them what they could never supply themselves; only to cast them aside once their productivity is exhausted.

However a kinder, softer survival instinct also exists in the privileged red. This person is a soul that has seen the cruelty and hardship that others have endured, and is saddened by the knowledge that they have contributed. This privileged red has the same liberal values as the egalitarian type but lacks the hardness that comes from the oppression of servitude. As a result, they share the same ideals but are neither blunt nor aggressive in their approach to achieving them. They exhibit the perfect balance of soul and survival.

## Gratitude

Hard times breed hard personalities, something that the privileged red has not had to endure. While the first exploitative type does not appreciate their position, the second more benevolent type understands they have been blessed. Thousands of lifetimes of crawling into a warm bed, while labourers slept on the dirt or hay, has left thankfulness in their spirit for all that they have. They know there is hardship and they know there is hunger, but the privileged red does not suffer these trials and they praise and give thanks for the life they've been given. They are determined to give back and to improve the lives of others as gratitude to God for their blessed position. They know they are lucky and they appreciate their life and everyone in it.

## Defiance

There are two primary avenues of defiance. The first is non-compliance and the second is open hostility. The survival instinct of red has seen thousands collapse from exhaustion, from being pushed beyond endurance only to die from fatigue. The job of the survival instinct is to avoid death at all costs, so anything that is known to cause it en masse becomes a fear or avoidance.

The defiant red that is non-compliant has no desire to prove their existence by work because they have seen too many of their fellow workers fall. This type of red only works when necessary. The more tired and out of balance they become, the greater their desire to do nothing at all.

Avoiding being seen is of prime importance because historically the only way to avoid being worked to death was to be away from the gaze of those overseeing you. This type of red is not avoiding work because they are inherently lazy, they are avoiding being worked.

The defiant red who is hostile will not tolerate the slightest demand placed upon them. Every demand sends their survival instinct back into chains and they defy and attack anyone attempting to tell them what to do. This type of red is always right. They cannot be told what to do or accept another person's opinion. To agree that another person has a point, is to accept the requests that person is asking of them and this is contrary to what the survival instinct is trying to achieve. Complete and full autonomy is the only way red achieve freedom, and in an out of balance state, they view any form of compromise, no matter how slight, as threatening.

> Near the end of your sentence you were given a ticket of leave. This meant you could work on other landowners' farms but you were no longer captive. You received payment for your work and there were laws regarding your working conditions and treatment. Not everyone was given a ticket of leave before the end of their sentence, but you were chosen as someone to receive it because you were a model prisoner and a hard worker. The new country of Australia needed people like you, but it needed you free, independent and prosperous, not locked away in chains. You worked hard and you kept your mouth shut and now you have been rewarded. Receiving your freedom validates to the survival instinct the importance of silence, compliance and work as a survival strategy.

During your ticket of leave, you purchased some land to supplement your income from grazing sheep and growing vegetables. It was also during this time that you took a wife. She was transported as a convict and was red like you. Marriage was encouraged for the female prisoners and was seen by many as a way out of their sentence. A married woman was freed and this is what happened with your wife. Like you, her survival instinct has also been rewarded and now will elevate what made her free in the hierarchy of instinctive response.

What attracted you to her were her looks and her sense of quiet determination and you were right on both counts. She was beautiful and she had purpose, she was focused and driven by the force of circular motion to see things through.

You never made it back to England. Instead you married and had ten children, eight of whom survived.

## **Physical**

The role of the farmer is a physical one regardless of gender and farmers survive by the sweat of their effort. Working in such a manual way century after century has created a survival instinct based in the physical.

It is not just the male who relies on the body. Red females also have a traditional role that is physical. They need the same endurance for their tasks of sowing, reaping and collecting the water. There is also the cooking, the child-rearing and tending to the garden.

Farming requires more muscle than many of the other traditional roles because the farmer turns forest into pasture. The hunter and the shepherd both work with the land and adapt themselves to their environment. The farmer is the opposite because they change the environment to suit their purposes. The farmer works on the land but the farmer does not work with the land.

Males with muscles and good planning skills generally made the most successful farmers. Childbearing females who were determined and resourceful were just as successful. Human beings as a species survive by having children. Nature instils sexual desire to ensure that the chances of survival for both the individual and the species are enhanced. The best natural advantage to fulfil this childbearing role is to be desirable and found sexually attractive. Physical attraction is part of the human condition for both males and females alike, but not every colour group relies on attraction as their primary survival tool.

The physical red is dominated by the memory and importance of the body. Males are driven to increase their strength while females spend hours making themselves attractive. Muscles and attraction are the survival tools of the physical red and when out of balance they can become an obsession. While everyone likes to be found attractive, out of balance physical red defines themselves by their looks. Physical red are no more attractive than people from any other colour group but they will spend more time than most making themselves desirable.

> With every muscle of your body tense and every nerve on edge, you crouch like the animal you are considered to be. Frozen in this moment everything could have ended differently. It is the middle of the night and you are finally cornered. After two weeks on the run you are completely exhausted and feel you cannot take another step; either way it doesn't matter, you are caught.
>
> You are a black woman in her twenties so early 19th century America is no place to be. You are not in this country by choice; you were born here on a farm only twenty miles away. Your mother and father are both African, brought to America as slaves.
>
> Now you are surrounded by four fuming men. Slave catchers who specialise in returning runaways. If you give them any trouble they will abuse you before they kill you, if you give in quietly you may be lucky and just be beaten before being returned.
>
> The family on the farm where you were born and worked took it personally that you ran away. In their mind they had treated you reasonably, fed you well and had not abused you. Their children liked

you and sometimes you were trusted with their care, but that will never happen again.

At this moment you are bitter at the expectation that you should ever have been grateful to people for not beating you. No one should have that kind of power over another human being. There is no such thing as benevolent slavery, a person is either free or they are not.

You grew up with stories of the homeland and freedom as your parents sat and reminisced about their youth. Swimming in streams and hunting with the other boys, or cooking with the women and getting into mischief. How can you accept slavery when you have heard about freedom?

Two weeks ago an opportunity arose and you packed your meagre belongings and ran. You had heard about a group that helps runaway slaves. You didn't know how to find them, so you hoped they would find you.

Like salivating dogs the four men now surround you. Two look angry while the others are laughing. One of the laughing men has a net that he wants to seize you with, mocking and teasing you as he imitates your fear.

He takes one more step before the sharp end of a spade breaks his spine below the base of his neck. The gurgling of another catches your attention, as he struggles to release the chain, pulled tight by the man who had crept up behind him. The other two slave catchers are already dead.

There are many who disagree with slavery and do all they can to help slaves that have run away. Some work in the municipal offices in town and hear when a slave has run away. They send word to an underground movement that tries to find runaways before the slave catchers do. Tonight your prayers have been answered.

Quietly you walk with the small group of saviours through the dark and arrive at a safe house where you are given food and a bed. You are told to be quiet and to remain hidden. In a few months when the hunt for you dies down, you will be moved north.

As you look around the room, there are others staring back at your huddled form. Everyone is silent; no one is smiling or being friendly. They are all like you, runaways waiting for events to calm down. In time you will get to know these people better, but for now you are scared and suspicious. The survival instinct of each person in the room is on high alert, no one able to think or speak.

A few days later everyone is beginning to relax and there is conversation among the group. Each knows they must trust the other, you are all in the same situation and the group is all you have. The days roll into weeks and you come to know the other slaves well. Each has their own story but all have the longing for freedom.

As you sit at the table with all the others, you look around the room at your new circle of friends. First is Alice who is quiet but nice, a hard worker who only speaks when spoken to. Initially you wondered whether Alice could talk, but now six weeks later she has become your friend and you find it hard to shut her up. With anyone else, especially if they are new or unknown Alice never opens her mouth.

Alice ran away because she felt everyone had turned on her and there was no one left to trust. Alice is pretty and has a strong sexual presence, she is also embarrassed by the attention she receives and is painfully shy. On the farm where she lived, a number of men, white and black alike had tried to 'befriend' her.
Two men, both of whom she thought she could trust, eventually won her favour, but both turned on her and ended the relationship. The first man was black and treated her badly; the second was white and promised her the world. Now Alice is twenty and angry at being tricked. When she was sixteen her bonding red survival instinct was

in charge and she was easily taken advantage of. The others on the farm spoke of Alice's reputation. Behind her back they gossiped and to her face they treated her badly.

The red bonding instinct achieves its aims through romance which is often linked with sexual desire. Everyone needs protection and comfort, and we use any means to attach to a partner when our survival instinct is dominant. Togetherness is safer than isolation. When the survival instinct of bonding red is dominant, it can create its own social problems. Sexual desire draws attention from not only those who desire the admired, but also from others around. Individuals of the same gender can feel threatened or even jealous of the attention a bonding red can receive.

Alice found herself the victim of a number of hurtful accusations. She was not the first to be accused of such things and she certainly won't be the last. It is unfortunately a far too common experience but for Alice this sort of reaction is part of her life theme, because it continually occurs with every new group or prospective partner she comes across.

The origin of the slander was not with the men. Although they created the problem by their unwanted attention, the real difficulty was with the other women. They spoke about Alice and called her names. She felt they had betrayed her and were looking for any excuse to cast aspersions, and slander her morals. Alice kept quiet and worked as hard as she could, trying to make herself as inconspicuous as possible.

Alice did not look for attention and her survival instinct had created within her two different feelings. The first was excitement and pleasure, because sexual attention means potential bonding, making her survival instinct feel safe and at home. The other was agitation because for Alice, romantic attention always meant trouble. When the white men on the farm started showing her attention, the other black women accused her of all sorts of impropriety and when her black male colleagues did the same, the slander grew even worse. Alice felt trapped either way, and became paranoid by what others were saying about her.

Alice felt she was being judged harshly. She had done nothing out of the ordinary yet felt condemned. She had no idea that other women felt threatened or looked on her as competition. She did not feel that way about others, so she did not suspect it was happening to her. She was already insecure but when a friend told her that others were jealous she completely withdrew, hardly spoke to a soul and worked even harder. Alice kept her head down and busied herself with her duties trying to avoid making eye contact with others, particularly anyone of the opposite sex. Alice did not notice how others looked at her but others continued to notice Alice.

When she was seventeen Alice decided to marry a man who strongly desired her. Alice believed it was love. She was convinced that she loved him back but in hindsight she is not so sure. Marrying him offered her a way to escape the slander and backstabbing. By making herself 'legitimate' and 'off the market', others would have to accept the fact that she was not the names they were calling her. She hoped marriage would make them stop talking behind her back but what happened after was even worse. Her survival instinct remained dominant because she was working to exhaustion, so it continued to send out a strong sexual presence. However, instead of the other women, the accuser of infidelity became her husband.

Her new husband accused Alice of indiscretion, either actual infidelity or her desire to commit it. Alice argued as strongly as possible that the accusations were not true, but her husband felt he had history on his side. Everyone knew Alice could not be trusted; now her husband 'knew' it also. Sex, infidelity and false accusations are a life theme for Alice. When her husband was killed in an accident two years later, Alice decided there was nothing left for her so she ran away.

Your thoughts move from Alice's story back to the present. Next to her sits Campbell, a tall lean man with an abrasive demeanour. Campbell is a man looking for trouble. He was best friends with Harry, the cousin with whom he escaped. Unfortunately Harry was caught after they both became separated and lost in the night, now Campbell is on his own, a state that is unfamiliar. The survival instinct of Campbell is also one of bonding, but Campbell has a rebellious streak that Alice does not have, and although their driving force is similar they are both quite different people.

Inside the survival instinct of all colour groups are numerous memories and survival strategies. Just because two people belong to the same group does not mean they will be similar in nature. The more a person is in conscious control, the less they resemble any of the personalities locked within the survival instinct.

Both Campbell and Alice have a strong bonding energy but Campbell is rebellious whereas Alice is compliant. The more Alice feels threatened, the harder she works to show she is good, but Campbell approaches issues differently. The more he feels he is under threat, the more threatening he becomes in return. Campbell is a man who attacks before thinking. Those at the table can understand why, yet at the same time feel he should direct his anger at the people who deserve it, rather than at the individual most convenient.

The red rebellious streak seems unnecessarily hard and confrontational and Campbell does not let anyone tell him what to do. Although he is becoming more rational as his survival instinct calms, when he first arrived he was unreasonable and always looking for a fight. If life was calm Campbell would go out of his way to stir up trouble, creating arguments where none existed and defending people who were not being attacked. Campbell calls it fighting for justice but to others he is simply a man with a big mouth.

Inside the unconscious red survival instinct, lie the memory of a thousand generations of domination; regardless of skin colour or race, some were called slaves while others were called coolies, serfs, peasants or indentured labour. No matter the name, the reality of slavery is that one group lives off the hard work of another.

The injustice of domination is strong in red and for Campbell the focus on inequality is dominant. Campbell does not make romantic connections because his rebellious instinct does not allow for compromise. Romantic relationships are based on give and take but compromise is not possible when 'the rebel' is dominant.

Campbell needs to bond, but the rebel does not, so Campbell bonds with friends. Friends accept and have fewer expectations. There is no personality adjustment or concession to be made such as within a deeper relationship. As a result Campbell makes one or two very close friends but pushes away everyone else. The closeness of the bond he makes with his friends also makes Campbell easily led.

People will do anything to stay in their group when their survival instinct is dominant. Only when the soul is in balance are they free to be themselves. Rebellious red is an outcast, belonging to a counter-culture forced to exist separately to mainstream society. However, when a person lives in a small group they must adopt its culture. In a small group freedom is limited and a group ethic will dominate. Fewer people create greater reliance and rather than being independent, rebellious red is forced to be a follower because there is nowhere else to turn.

When rebellious red is out of balance they are drawn toward the irreverent. Whatever they believe will annoy polite society, they will indulge in. Decent society is historically the only class moneyed enough to exploit the average worker. From royalty to the rich, the landowning classes were the only ones who could afford to buy and sell people. Everything the rich symbolise, from their manners to their money to their good education, is held in contempt by rebellious red, because of who and what they represent.

> Campbell is smart and picks up skills quickly but acts tough and uncouth because it suits him. He knows the habits of the gentry that enchained him and he makes certain that he displays the opposite. He is inflexible, loud, brash and brazen, doing whatever it takes to shock or disturb. Campbell is an anti-culture radical.

This much anger leaves Campbell exhausted and sometimes he is tired before the day begins. However, once he gets moving he is a hard worker. On the one hand the farm where Campbell belonged was happy to finally be rid of him; he was a loud mouth who always stirred up trouble and the more he was punished the more defiant he became. On the other hand the farm owners were sorry he had left, not because Campbell cost them money to buy, but because despite all his aggressive talk, he was a good and diligent worker.

Elizabeth is sitting next to Campbell and as usual has nothing to say. She sits at the table day in, day out, expressionless and blank. Circular motion turns on itself, it does not come out to meet, nor does it draw in. It captures what comes to it by keeping it imprisoned and a red individual can be exactly the same, self-contained and locked.

Elizabeth is this type of red, finding it difficult to think outside herself. Understanding another person's feelings is almost impossible for her. It took you a long time to understand Elizabeth, like everyone else you thought she was rude and arrogant. When you spoke to her she replied, but only in monosyllables. You were new to the group and keen to make friends. Going up to Elizabeth you smiled and asked questions but a blank face was her main response.

For a while you thought she didn't like you, and soon you became angry at her hostile attitude. Later you came to realise she did not feel that way at all. She only answered 'yes' or 'no' because she literally could not think of anything else to say. Once she had got to know you, when you were alone, Elizabeth would talk freely, but would go mute again when another person walked into the room.

Although you have grown to accept it, her behaviour at times still makes you uncomfortable. Elizabeth seems to have no understanding that her closed manner is anti-social. She does not see herself as aggressive, in fact she sees herself as timid, but silence can be extremely aggressive in a social setting.

Containment remains a defensive red behaviour. Vanity is another expression of self-containment, admiring and grooming oneself continuously. Elizabeth is beautiful in her looks and she knows it. She does not use her appearance to manipulate but she has certain expectations. She likes to turn heads when she walks by, but unlike Alice she does not have the same sexual allure. Her life theme is not filled with infidelity or suspicion but with beauty and appearance.

> Elizabeth cannot wait to be moved up north. She wants to work and earn money to buy dresses and make-up. She is not rebellious like Campbell; instead she craves to emulate the finery and elegance of the families she worked for. On the farm she saw make-up, dresses, dances and romance, ladies with bonnets and graceful clothes, and Elizabeth would give the world to look as beautiful as them.
>
> Like Alice she is a romantic bonder but that part of her life has been more successful. Elizabeth has been with the same man since her early teens and he is good and loyal to her. She has had none of the aspersions cast upon her or the suspicion that Alice has had to bear. Both women are the same age. Elizabeth escaped thanks to her husband. Eight months ago he led a breakout while out in the fields away from her. Elizabeth worked in the house, so her chance of escape was small. Her husband took his chance but promised to return and get her out as well.
>
> Working in the house meant being watched. The right moment was difficult to find. Elizabeth's husband had been in contact with the network and on a shopping visit to town, the escape took place. Now, like you, she must be quiet for a while, lie low and keep her head down till the time is right to move north.
>
> She had news from her husband who has rented a house and is working and waiting for her to arrive. He has already bought her jewellery and a beautiful dress. She cannot wait to join him and is not coping well at all. Elizabeth is becoming more withdrawn and sullen,

moody, petulant, vain and closed. She needs her partner.

Elizabeth is not a princess nor is she a tantrum thrower. Elizabeth generally pitches in and helps and does not expect others to do her work. She is independent and talented but she is not a good communicator. She misses her husband terribly.

Circular motion makes it difficult for red to assess their impact on others. To those around them this closed red has no social skills and can appear disinterested. The force inside this type of red rarely moves off its axis. This makes it difficult for Elizabeth to comprehend any outside view. In essence Elizabeth's problem is that she cannot stop thinking about herself. She is frozen in the process of trying to work out what the other person is thinking about her. Her vain and egotistical attitude is a natural and central part of her outlook.

Elizabeth is in her survival instinct and her beauty and grace are her survival tools. Beauty is self-focused, it is not a skill or a talent; it does not involve others apart from their admiration. Being attractive is a valuable survival tool because people crave beauty.

Sitting opposite Elizabeth is Andrew, an older male who is tall and muscled but like Elizabeth, hardly says a word. Andrew is the strong silent type, reliable and confident but never bragging or pompous. Like Elizabeth, Andrew goes blank whenever someone asks him a question, so Andrew speaks through action. Andrew works as hard now he is free as he did when he was in slavery. He is highly skilled and has the ability to turn his hand to anything. He too is a strong red bonder and has a wife waiting for him on the farm.

They have a child and Andrew hated to leave. In fact at first he refused to go without them. However his wife convinced him he had to go, to set up a home they could all escape to. Without him going first the chances of all three escaping were slim. On top of this there was nowhere to go unless Andrew could arrange a new home for them all. Unlike Elizabeth, Andrew used circular motion as a way of concentrating and planning the future. Every detail was planned months in advance and Andrew already had contacts who would help him go back to retrieve his family.

Despite the fact that he rarely spoke, others liked Andrew because he was reliable and competent. He would always pitch in and help and he always tried as hard as he could with every task.

Next at the table was Dean, less competent than Andrew but far more social. Dean was brash and highly opinionated and used to working inside. In the past Dean was a butler, he polished shoes and brass and made the house clean. He dressed in a suit and served food for the main house. He brushed the family's clothes so they were free of lint and took the children on walks.

Dean was a house cat, used to luxury and only escaped because the family he worked for hit hard financial times and sold off their 'surplus' slaves. At this stage of life the family decided they could brush their own clothes so they sold Dean cheaply.

Refusing to go because he knew what would happen, Dean used his contacts to escape. He was an anxious person full of scattered energy, restless and suspicious when his survival instinct dominated. He found it difficult to sleep or to concentrate. He was the opposite of Campbell who rejected finery and everything it stood for. Dean craved money and comfort because they took him away from the labour of the farm. To him, life without money was too insecure and he would find himself digging and sweating in the field if he did not find ways of gaining a nest egg.

His survival instinct regarded work as enslavement and Dean had no problem letting other people toil. If they wanted to sweat and break their backs, that was their choice. To him, work was a symbol of servitude and he had no intention of going back. Luxury and ease was what he craved and he dreamt of a future full of comfort.

Cassie is sitting next to Dean and is the last of the runaway group. Cassie could not be more socially dissimilar to the others if she tried. If it were not for Dean and Cassie, every day at the table would be like a monastery, everyone eating in total silence. Dean is vivacious and so is Cassie, but unlike Dean she can never shut up. Cassie talks all the time, she talks over others and she is never wrong.

Cassie ran away for the usual reasons but many of the others wish she would run back. Cassie does not understand her impact, a common trait due to circular motion. Her social etiquette is also poor but at the other end of the scale. Instead of never opening her mouth, Cassie never closes it. Her constant loquacity means everyone else is aware of her opinions but she is not aware of theirs. No job is too menial or difficult for Cassie and she is loyal and dedicated to everyone in the group.

Red is often blessed with drive but Cassie's energy is scattered. Her survival instinct is in attack mode and she must win at all costs. Attack mode makes a person either highly competitive or never wrong; in Cassie's case she displays the latter.

Cassie never stops to take a breath because her survival instinct is in control. It is the same egocentric focus of vanity except the focus is on words and communication. Instead of capturing attention with beauty, Cassie captures and maintains attention by denying anyone else the chance to contribute to the conversation. Her continuous loquacity ensures she is the centre of attention.

## Effort and energy

Work and slavery belong together and red has survived by their capacity to work under the harshest of conditions. Under stress they constantly let those around them know how much they are doing by emphasising their effort and tiredness. Often the amount they do is no greater than what anyone else does and may sometimes be even less, but this will not stop them from highlighting their exertion or using work as a way of showing their value.

The farmer survives by working from dawn till dusk and the servant slave or convict labourer must make a point of showing how industrious and busy they are, otherwise food is replaced by a beating. As a result, red accentuate their productivity and effort by grumbling about tiredness and being overburdened or by genuinely making themselves so productive and busy that other people cannot help but notice. This type of red does not need to say anything, they just let the outcome speak for itself. Sweat and effort is red's way of out-competing others so it is the area they highlight when they feel stressed, tired or threatened.

The farmer needs muscle and the farmer needs endurance so a child who can work all day and not be tired is a valuable asset to the life of the family. In the past, not all the children of the farmer could stay. Fire, drought and poor growing seasons meant some on the farm were forced to leave because it could not support the needs of the entire group.

This meant that daughters were quickly married into families that could provide for them, while sons went into the town to look for work or worked on other farms. The children who could work all day were the last ones sent. The survival instinct of red is soaked in this memory and produces in some red people a surplus of physical energy to increase their chances of being needed and kept.

Today this surplus of physical energy is not required and is often diagnosed as ADHD. Physical restlessness and a constant desire to do something manual is a common and consistent product of being red, especially with males. Sitting in the classroom or in front of a computer is not the natural environment for the farmer. Medications are given to settle this type down, but careful management is also required. A surplus of energy is not only required by the farmer but by other traditional roles. ADHD is not exclusive to, but is commonly seen in red.

## Love and friendship
Central to the psyche of red are the life themes of attachment and bonding. In red this is exhibited as love and friendship and this is the central platform from which red gain their strength. Romantic attachment and intimacy is a strong driving force that presents itself at an early age.

Teenage years are a difficult time due to the competitive nature of school and the energy demands of puberty. As a result many red teenagers feel a strong desire to bond with another. In some, their attachment will be to a friend or a small but intimate group, while in others it will be to a partner. Often one is exclusive to the other, meaning the more red is attached to a partner, the less their need to bond with friends or the more red has attached to a friend the less they need a partner. As long as they are attached to someone, the survival instinct is calm.

When red uses bonding rather than bonding uses red, the soul is in balance with the survival instinct. This means red make decisions regarding love and intimacy with full conscious control rather than being swept up by emotion and adrenaline. They still feel the feelings that make life worthwhile but they are not addicted to these feelings nor does their life revolve around them. From the platform of a secure intimate relationship, they are ready to launch themselves into whatever their calling or desire may be. Their attributes of linear thinking and determination make red valuable and important contributors to the community.

## Facial features

Circular motion is designed to move in a circle on a continuous pathway. Red is represented by both circular shapes and due to its inability to go around obstacles, straight lines. Growth is another expression of red and is seen in large or ball shaped features.

## Circular motion

The following features express the circular motion of red:

## Ball shapes

- ball shaped nose
- ball shaped chin
- protruding eyeballs

## Straight lines
- straight hairline
- straight forehead
- straight or full bridge of nose
- single line between eyes
- cleft in nose or chin
- straight even teeth

## Growth (or fullness)
- large eyes
- wide nose
- full lips
- wide mouth
- wide or full smile

Chapter 15

# BLUE - INWARD MOTION

*Attraction*
*Withdrawal and hibernation*
*Etiquette*
*Collapse*
*Explosion*
*Basics*
*Winter*
*Focus*
*Simplicity*
*Conservation*
*Depression*
*The ice age*
*High energy*
*Inward*
*The sea*
*Yin and yang*
*Passive*
*Protection*
*Absorption*
*Group protection*
*The shepherd*
*Loner*

*Company*
*Night*
*Light sleep*
*Cold*
*Stability and calm*
*Routine*
*Focus on the small*
*Simplicity and peace*
*Nurture*
*Community*
*Authority*
*Management*
*Stubborn*
*Togetherness*
*Dependency*
*Yielding*
*Childish*
*Dogmatic*
*Cheerful*
*Emotion and communication*
*Lightness*
*Intimidating*

Inward motion is the final of the three primary forces and is expressed in the natural world as cold, contraction, withdrawal and gravity.

The larger the mass the more gravity an object has. The more inward motion grows in size, the stronger its force and influence becomes. Inward motion affects the survival instinct of blue in exactly the same manner. The greater the number of people around them the stronger and more secure they feel.

Inward motion creates a personality that feels secure in being part of a group. Like all people when they are in balance, blue can enjoy time on their own but nothing takes the place of being surrounded by the people they love. Whether their family is large or small, they are the centre of the blue universe.

Attraction is one of the tools used by inward motion. Opposite to the outward repulsive action of yellow, inward motion envelops and surrounds, drawing force and matter into itself, absorbing and merging them into one.

Blue is a group person who relies on and provides shelter and protection to family and friends. Human beings have always gathered together for protection and blue have specialised in this trait for their survival. Over time blue have become experts in communal living and these benefits, expectations, fears and responses still exist in their survival instinct.

When the survival instinct takes over, inward motion influences blue in four major ways.

1. Inward motion **attracts** and draws energy from its surrounding area
2. Inward motion **withdraws**
3. Inward motion **collapses** in on itself
4. Inward motion, once it has reached a point of critical mass **explodes** unpredictably

## Attraction

Inward motion is represented by the proton. The more protons that exist in the nucleus the heavier a substance becomes. Mass creates gravity which is an expression of inward motion. In human terms this is the equivalent of gaining strength from the safety of numbers.

Blue has a stable personality that puts others at ease. They are friendly and outgoing making them easy to be around. When in balance they are placid and adopt the principle of live and let live. Whatever others want is acceptable to blue, providing it doesn't affect their lives. This easygoing attitude is what attracts people to them. Other people gravitate to blue because they are accepting and impose few demands. Drawing support towards them is the strength of blue, a natural attribute because blue has lived in large communal families longer than any other colour group.

The shepherd is the traditional role that has evolved from inward motion. Herding communities travelled in large groups and often referred to themselves as a 'family'. In larger groups, individuals can share the labour and surround themselves with the safety of numbers. As a result, a code of conduct developed with the laws and etiquette necessary for communal living. Blue has these laws and manners imprinted into their survival instinct. Manners are important because they make others comfortable and put them at ease. In balance blue is sociable and polite, making them easy to be with and popular. Out of balance, manners and etiquette become excessively rigid and promote servility.

## Withdrawal and hibernation

Under continued stress, some blue people withdraw and make their world small. Interaction with others becomes limited and difficult and daily life hinges on a strict routine. Withdrawal blue will go into hibernation, shutting down in order to cope. How far they shut down is determined by genetics and stress. The immune system of blue withdraws to conserve, like bears in the winter they hibernate in an effort to reduce the impact of stress.

Out of balance, hibernation blue is the human equivalent of an ostrich with its head in the sand. They don't care what is happening and they don't want to know. The more stress they find around them, the more they shut off. If they find themselves in the middle of distress, hibernation blue will promise the world, any changes asked of them they will agree to. Any effort required, they assure it will be attended to – but often it won't. To the hibernation blue, a promise is a means to an end; a way to appease and to ward off strife, often with no intention of following it through.

All they want is to be left alone; hibernation is silence and peace from the world. Any request or expectation is a disturbance from their slumber. Like a hibernating bear they cannot be pushed, if responsibilities force them to wake, they grumble and roar like a gruff animal with a sore head.

If stress becomes great blue may go into hibernation in an effort to conserve energy. Stress makes them tired and the more stressed they become, the less this type of blue can keep their eyes open. Sometimes they will wake tired and ready to go to bed early that night. Their doctor may diagnose them as having chronic fatigue but more correctly they are suffering with chronic stress. There is not an antibiotic or a vitamin in the world that is going to make an ounce of difference.

## Etiquette

Politeness and manners are vital if a community is to be cohesive. Manners put everyone on the same level of importance. Opening the door or offering the last piece of cake, these small acts are the hallmarks of respect. From smiling at others when they walk into a room, standing up to say hello, getting out of the way of a faster driver or never leaving without saying goodbye; these are the bedrocks of civilised society and to polite blue these behaviours are as natural as breathing.

The intention of manners is misunderstood, especially in contemporary western society. Being rude has become the hallmark of independence but ill-mannered people are still judged harshly by others. The etiquette of smiling when someone walks into a room is not just a mindless act. It is for the benefit of those receiving the smile. Smiling in most cultures means friendliness and peace, and making friends quickly is one of blue's greatest talents. People want to be around blue, but out of balance they can also be taken advantage of.

## Collapse

When inward motion collapses on itself, pressure reduces it to virtually nothing. Blue mirrors this action when out of balance, by becoming increasingly reclusive or tired. The chronic fatigue they experience is extreme, their sleep comatose and generally un-refreshing. Shut off and locked away they become depressed and isolated, rarely venturing out of their home or even their bed. This instinctive shutting down leaves blue physically and mentally paralysed, sometimes sleeping up to twenty hours a day, only to wake up more tired than when they went to bed.

## Explosion

Inward motion is the only primal force that has at its core a contrary power for its own survival. This contrary force is a small amount of outward motion that lies within its centre. When inward motion contracts to its most dense point an explosion of energy occurs. Once the explosion has concluded, inward motion calms and settles to resume its natural inward flow.

This inner core of outward motion is like the small dot of yang inside a dominant and enveloping body of yin. It is the energy of the big bang needed to cluster all three forces together and explode them outward. In this way, the universe was able to begin. Many blue people are dominant in this same force and are just as explosive when stress limits are reached. Like the exploding force inside them, the volatile blue is capable of violent and extreme behaviour. It is within their nature to turn everything upside down, as they explode into a complete contradiction of their normal self.

## Basics

The cold is a display of inward motion. Cold contracts and makes matter shrink, sending animals into hibernation and making trees lose their leaves. Winter is a time for rest and sleep, life becomes Spartan, stripped to basic necessities. The frenzied work of summer is over and winter is the time to draw on reserves.

The forest is bare and life survives by stripping itself back to essential form. Life becomes Zen in its shedding of the unnecessary, in order for focus to be solely in the present. Blue exhibits this same total focus; nothing else exists when blue is engrossed in a task. Whether at work, sport or playing a game, focused blue concentrates with all their attention, making the present moment all there is.

## Winter

The cold of winter promotes the withdrawal of life and the blue survival instinct behaves in the same manner. Deciduous trees shed their leaves in the same way animals hibernate and blue people lie dormant through conserving energy. When stress becomes stronger than energy reserves, the survival instinct becomes dominant. If this state continues for too long a period, the body becomes drained of energy and chronic pathology begins.

In climates where the winters are harsh, animals struggle to find food. Mammals need extra energy to generate heat to keep them warm but with food being scarce, the distance travelled during winter for foraging and hunting is extended dramatically. This means winter requires more energy output but the energy intake is less. Animals must either have stored reserves or hibernate to conserve their energy. Blue under stress behaves in a similar way; one type having an energy reserve so bountiful they can withstand almost anything; while the second withdraws and sleeps through stress to conserve the reserves they already have.

## Focus

The benefits of total focus are as obvious as its failings. In balance blue are detailed and absorbed; attention of this kind is the basis of expertise allowing blue the potential to reach the top of their field. The negative aspects of total focus include obsession and addiction, often more to habit and routine rather than substances.

The line between obsession and engrossment is often indistinct. A person who is engrossed incorporates other aspects into their life, while maintaining focus on their passion. However when someone is obsessed, they maintain their passion to the exclusion and detriment of everything else. Blue are capable of both deep concentration as well as obsession, depending on their state of balance.

The sparseness of winter represents a blue that reduces life to fundamentals. Trimmings are pleasant because they make life enjoyable, but the fundamentals are the most important and blue never drops the basics to chase after the trimmings.

## Simplicity

Primary blue arranges their life around simplicity. Surrounded by choice and material wealth overwhelms and is not in harmony with their character. The simple life is what primary blue seeks; winter and inward motion represent simplicity and basic need. Primary blue rejects indulgence and is ill at ease with the contemporary western lifestyle of extravagance and pampering.

Primary blue is a minimalist having evolved from the traditional role of the shepherd. The fundamentals of life include food, shelter and family; everything else is inconsequential. Primary blue are lifestyle individuals not beguiled by money. They enjoy working and paying their way, as well as the little luxuries that make life rewarding. Indulgence in materialism for its own sake is not part of their personal ethic. This type of blue enjoys doing activities with their family or, if alone, making life as simple as possible.

While primary blue is as smart as anyone else, they often do not want to be the person in charge. To them, the demands of the office never supersede the needs of their family. Primary blue prefers less responsibility and money, to gain more time and a relaxed way of life.

## Conservation

When the survival instinct of the conserving blue takes over, sleep becomes an inescapable demand and they enter withdrawal as a defence against pressure. Like soldiers securing themselves inside a fort, conserving blue protect themselves saving their energy by slowing down.

Inward motion epitomises the cold and the survival instinct of blue is specifically suited to the challenges of these conditions. Human beings over the course of time have migrated to every region on earth. Strategies to survive harsh climates have been specifically adapted to give individuals a competitive edge.

Taking stress slowly and being patient and calm, is contrary to the way life is led in first world culture today. However for the conserving blue it is a way of existence that has kept them alive for thousands of generations. Suspending energy is the comfort zone to which conserving blue returns when times become hard and stress extreme. Conservation by withdrawal has been a successful trait employed by the survival instinct whenever energy reserves run chronically low.

Today, blue may live in a warm country and have plenty of food to eat, but if stress levels are high or energy levels low, their survival instinct still behaves as if they are in the mountains during winter. Blue's energy will drop and they start dragging their feet. They become increasingly more tired, wanting to withdraw from the world and to curl up in bed like a bear in winter. Sometimes at this stage they become sad, but more often they become frozen, feeling nothing at all. Under emotional pressure conserving blue can become numb, almost paralysed as their energy withdraws to the interior. Some will put themselves to bed for days or even weeks at a time. After sleep they are never refreshed because the problem is not tiredness, it is danger and stress.

## Depression

Depression is an outcome when inward motion meets stress. It may seem unusual to have depression as a defence, but the survival instinct doesn't consider happiness or enjoyment when it protects us. Its sole and only purpose is to keep us alive. When the survival instinct is dominant life becomes unpleasant, as the job of control and security is paramount. Depression is a form of human hibernation; thoughts, emotions and the body shut down, making the individual bedridden. Depression occurs because of energy exhaustion. The more energy depleted the individual the greater their depression. Although they are suffering emotionally, the survival instinct doesn't care because it has the memories of blizzards and storms. To be under a roof and in a bed is better than being outside in the elements. The depression of modern blue may have nothing to do with climate or famine, but the survival instinct still instinctually behaves as if this is the problem. For tens of thousands of years, the principal cause of energy loss was winter combined with famine. When blue becomes exhausted, regardless of cause, the survival instinct reacts as if there is famine and winter once again. Blue depression resembles a type of suspended animation, designed to help the physical body withstand the rigors of environmental hardship. That it may be caused by an employer, partner, financial position or too much junk food, is a situation the survival instinct has not had enough time to adapt to.

Thousand of years of living on snow capped mountains or frigid tundra has led the survival instinct to learn certain facts, in particular not to venture out into the elements when energy levels are depleted. Battling a blizzard is challenging for anyone but combined with low energy it can be a death sentence. The survival instinct of this type of blue will stay in the house, room or bed for extended periods of time, until energy levels begin to rise.

## The ice age

Inside the survival instinct of blue rest the experiences of thousands of harsh blizzards, bitter mountain winds and starvation. Surviving these conditions required endurance and strength and could only be achieved by working in groups. Frigid areas are sparse in animal life and vegetation, a climate where only the specifically adapted can live and multiply.

Human beings have lived in these frigid conditions for much of their existence. Ice ages and glacial periods were a major part of the climate during evolution. The survival instinct of blue does not exist only for the few who live in the worlds frozen areas, but exists for the many that lived through the ice age. Earth's climate has varied considerably since the time human beings took their first step. Sophisticated culture is a recent innovation only developing since the ending of the last ice age. Homo sapiens have existed for approximately 150,000 years and between 30,000 years ago to approximately 10,000 years ago a severe ice age enveloped the world.

During those twenty thousand years, the people who could best endure the cold, as well as survive on a bare minimum of food, patiently waited as storms raged outside, living harmoniously as part of a social group in tight crowded conditions. These were the people who survived with their physical and mental faculties intact. With the ending of the last ice age, human beings migrated around the globe to various locations and climates. Civilised culture began to flourish and as a result, the survival instinct also evolved and adapted to the new conditions. The survival instinct of blue has remained generally the same, utilising the strategies that helped them survive the ice age. A permanent winter of twenty thousand years has left an imprint in blue that still exists today.

The blue survival instinct remains primarily geared for the cold because in the mountains where the shepherd lives, the climate is similar to the ice age. The six other traditional roles moved away from the cold but the shepherd stayed in the mountains because it was the place best suited to their animals. The other traditional roles faced hardships and dangers at a frequency that replaced the memory of the ice age. But the shepherd remained in this harsh environment where the cold continued to be their greatest threat.

## High energy

Another adaptation of the blue survival instinct, specifically suited to endure long winters, is an indefatigable supply of energy ensuring that energy reserves always remain high. An abundance of energy gives an individual the ability to draw on existing reserves to last the winter through. Rather than conserving by hibernation, this type of high energy blue has a level of endurance and a physical stamina, which vastly exceeds the average person. In contemporary times the high energy blue enjoys physical training at a level that brings others to collapse.

Endurance is the key to survival in harsh climates and this type of blue has the energy to withstand the cold with a limited supply of food. Through hibernation or having excess energy human beings can sustain themselves through arctic conditions until spring. Most of us store energy through fat and this is why many of us put on weight so easily. Fat is nature's way of preparing for famine, storing energy to use when food becomes scarce. High energy blue does not need to store fat as they have enough energy reserves to last. Hibernation blue by contrast puts on weight just thinking about food.

Today high energy blue continues to train and enjoys pushing themselves to their physical limits. A gentle walk or a moderate swim is not enough to satisfy a survival instinct that flourishes on exertion and sweat. Their fitness routine is rigorous and demanding and they enjoy what other people would experience as pain, pushing their muscles and their heart to the utmost, many gaining energy to the degree they expend it. For this type of blue the more they exercise the more energy they attain.

## Inward
The survival instinct of defensive blue shields them from life like a coat of armour. As a protection against the extremes of stress, inward motion withdraws. Motion is force, it has no consciousness; inward motion draws inward because it is not designed for anything else. When people are in survival mode their instinct returns to the force that governs it. Consciousness and rational thought subside as the reactive response of instinct takes over. When the survival instinct is dominant, it can only return to what it knows. Whatever strategy helped it survive yesterday, will be the same strategy it employs tomorrow. In blue, defence rather than offence has been an effective protection for thousands of years.

By confining an individual to their house or bed the survival instinct limits the chances of harm. As with deciduous trees and hibernating animals, the survival instinct of blue shuts down both emotionally and physically, in an effort to conserve and protect. The less blue can cope with pressure, the more their survival instinct will close them down.

## The sea
The sea is a metaphor for blue. Colours are symbols rather than exact portrayals with true understanding coming from character and action rather than metaphors. Sometimes the sea can look more green than blue, while at other times depending on the weather, it can even look grey. For the majority of time the sea is blue reflecting the colour of the sky, and many of the qualities of the sea like that of winter are blue in character.

The sea is drawing and enveloping. We love its quality, all surrounding, cooling, comfortable and soft. House prices soar with just a glimpse of the sea, showing how much we value even a small view. The seaside is where we go to play. Families and lovers celebrate being together at the beach and use it as a place for fun, relaxation and romance. Its beautiful colour and healing properties make the sea a perfect place to repair the wounds life has inflicted. It is cooling on a hot day and home to a diversity of life that the land can barely imagine. It is where we go to rejuvenate and revitalise, to feel free and to re-connect with the organic.

The sea makes us feel relaxed and happy and it draws in people from all walks of life. Men and women both rich and poor are lured by the sea just as they have been since the dawn of time. Today, the oceans of the world still team with diversity. Coastal people from cave-times onwards, looked to the sea as a source of nourishment. Its currents influence the weather and its plant life furnishes oxygen. The sea provided the environment for the origins of life and from this starting place creatures came on to the land.

Many love the sea because it is tranquil, while others are enticed by its danger and unpredictability. Most of the time the sea is benevolent, gentle and easy, then out of nowhere it can erupt into a boiling turbulence capturing the unwary and unprepared. Blue in their nature resemble the sea. Depending on the degree of external stress, blue is generally a placid and stable person. However if stress becomes strong they can explode like a storm.

## Yin and yang

To fully appreciate the quality of blue, it's important to understand the principle of yin and yang. A tiny dot of yang lies deep inside yin, and vice versa to symbolise that nothing in nature is ever solely one dimensional. Life is a mutual correlation of opposite forces that make a unified cycle of existence. The three forces of the material universe comprise yang which is outward motion as well as yin which is inward motion, both held together inside a sphere of circular motion. Generally only yin and yang are spoken of and not the circular force that binds them together, but circular motion is equally important to the total symbolic representation.

Inside the enveloping and more dominant yin lies a tiny dot of yang dormant and waiting. Yang is too small to change the character of yin, yet without it the force of yin would cease. The white dot of yang is an explosive power that lies patiently inside the centre of blue; it is an opposite correlation that comes into effect when inward motion collapses in on itself. This is the normally placid person who is pushed too far and the 'storm at sea' that results.

## Passive

The sea, despite being a provider and a playground, is treated by some as a dumping ground. Whatever is not wanted, too difficult or dangerous, is thrown into the sea where the problem is 'solved'. Passive blue because of their nature are sometimes treated in the same undignified manner. Others may abuse or mistreat them, not because they deserve it, but because the perpetrators can get away with it. Passive blue children can be bullied at school because they are open and soft, making them a target. There is no use telling these yielding blue children to fight back, it simply is not in their nature to do so. The best they can do is to apply skills more appropriate to their character and make a new friend somewhere else. Passive blue is friendly and well liked, they make a friend wherever they go. Fighting back is not their style but making new friends comes easily.

## Protection

The sea never throws the waste that has been dumped back on the deck of the ship that dumped it, and passive blue rarely retaliates with force, but we love the sea and we rally to protect it. To the public, the vandals who dump waste in the sea are always the bad guys and held in contempt; the same is true for anyone who attacks passive blue.

People turn on bullies and judge them harshly. No one likes the aggressor who attacks passive blue and the anger it generates in others is palpable. The success of the blue survival instinct rests in the way it makes others feel distraught wanting to fight on their behalf. Through friendliness and caring, passive blue protect themselves. This does not mean that their friendship is disingenuous, their gentleness is real and so is their happiness but their survival instinct has learned to capitalise on this trait.

## Absorption

Despite centuries of abuse the sea still manages to store and purify everything thrown into it. It has a seemingly endless capacity to absorb and remain unscathed. This is not true of course but it seems that way on the surface. The same is true for blue. They can be treated with disrespect or talked to harshly and will often just smile in return.

Inward motion has the same qualities as the sea with a seemingly endless capacity to draw and absorb. This includes a gentleness of spirit and a tendency to be liked by a diverse range of people. A gentle, happy and consistent disposition puts others at ease and makes them relaxed.

Passive blue is non-threatening. Passive blue has no inclination to hurt or to harm anybody and those around blue feel the same; this is the blue survival instinct at work. With this type of blue there are no power plays or politics, the group surrounding them is friendly and protective.

## Group protection

Blue embodies safety in numbers. People think twice before attacking a large group, particularly one that is close knit. This type of blue may not be vicious but like everyone else they have their limits and they will attack if pushed too far. The small dot of yang inside the yin means inward motion cannot collapse on itself; it also means blue will hit back and explode if pushed in to a position where 'yang' takes over.

Being strong and calm as well as tolerant and helping has given blue a survival edge. Human beings can only survive in numbers, the larger the group the better the chances of survival. Security comes from helping other people and from allowing them to help us in return. The best way to exist in a group is to have the qualities that communal living requires. Like all traits and skills the best ones are innate, with an ease of naturalness giving a competitive edge. The qualities required for communal living are to be strong and calm as well as tolerant and helping. The natural passive blue character is perfectly suited to living in groups, which is why they have survived from the ice age till now.

## The shepherd

In the days of pre-history people lived one day at a time. The hunter-gatherer lifestyle which included scavenging, remained dominant, although specialisations gradually increased because of need and changing climate.

Grazing animals such as sheep, goats, buffalo, cattle, horses and pigs provided the basis from which civilisation began. Cultural development only occurs once people have time to develop their skills and passions. Social maturity can never take place in a group that spends all its time looking for food. As a result the shepherd has developed an intricate and specialised culture.

Although individual specialisations had already begun long before the thaw of the last ice age, they were limited in their scope and were underdeveloped until relatively recently. Ten to fifteen thousand years ago, when the farmer first started to turn the garden into a farm, and scavenging evolved into the traditional role of the trader, the shepherd stopped following the herd and started domesticating it. For tens of thousands of years, human beings followed the wandering herds rather than the other way around. Tribes and family groups trailed migrating herds of grazing animals mostly to hunt them. Then, at about this time, some groups started to live in a cooperative cohabitation with the animals they used to kill.

Many of the animals that congregate in large grazing groups were more docile than the other animals. These more docile species included some breeds of cattle, goats and sheep and although they would attack if threatened they tended to leave well enough alone unless they were disturbed. As a result, humans could begin to mix and blend with the animals provided they did nothing to make the herd feel threatened.

Following a herd rather than trying to kill it changed lifestyles dramatically. Life became easier in some respects but it also became more routine and Spartan. Hunter-gatherers were always on the move, shifting from place to place as the weather changed and food supplies dwindled, moving between summer and winter camps. The life of the herd follower became even more nomadic because the same herd of animals was trailed exclusively. Before this, herds of wandering animals were hunted as their migration paths brought them into contact with humans. Some grazing animals do not migrate and move only when they eat their food supply bare. These were the animals the shepherd began to follow being both non-migratory and often docile. Over time the shepherd began to walk and blend amongst these herds. Soon they realised and began to live by the saying, 'You can shear a sheep a number of times but you can only skin it once.'

The best protection for wild grazing animals was in habitats too difficult for their predators to survive. The steep and rocky slopes of the mountains were the perfect spot for these animals to flourish. The shepherd and the herd are a perfect match, both able to cope with the stress of extremes.

Not even wild mountain goats can survive when there is nothing but snow or rock to eat. The mountain tops are home for much of the year, but they must come down to greener pastures when winter freezes over. On the lower plains the herd is vulnerable because they are not protected by their environment. Hungry predators exploit this opportunity. The shepherd must be vigilant.

Over thousands of years a strong symbiotic relationship between the shepherd and the herd developed. The animals the shepherd used to follow became domesticated, as did dogs and horses. In exchange for giving milk and wool, the herd is given management and protection.

When an animal died every part was utilised, from the wool and skin for textiles to the meat, organs, brains and blood for food. Hunters of the past used herds such as these as meat for food, as well as bones and hide for weapons and fabric; they would creep up and run, killing as many as they could and scattering the rest. Sometimes they frightened whole herds to their death by running the terrified beasts over a cliff, but domestication changed this relationship and the new traditional role of the shepherd emerged.

Like the farmer, the shepherd utilises the cycle of the seasons. The blue survival instinct is geared for the winter, making every movement measured and deliberate. Unlike the hunter, the shepherd is not as reactive but careful and considered. Many blue people have these same qualities, in temperament or in thinking. For those who have this trait with their thinking, life becomes a process of precision and planning. They are patient, happy and kind, gentle souls who try hard not to upset anyone, doing whatever they can to keep life happy and trouble free.

In a world as savage as that of prehistoric man, it seems counter-productive for a survival instinct to develop a temperament that is gentle and nurturing. That was a time when only the strongest, smartest and quickest survived. Measured thinking and gentleness seem irrelevant and out of place. However, a new management strategy for group survival evolved, separate to hunter-gathering and the qualities it required.

A person who is smart and relaxed, calculating and calm is better suited to management and nurture than trade or farming; they exhibit the perfect personality for the traditional role of the shepherd.

Even docile animals will run when threatened. To the shepherd, being calm and non-threatening is an asset. Traditional roles evolved from need.

Different people with different temperaments had to find their place and contribute to the group. With a calm and gentle approach, the shepherd began to watch and mingle without making the herd scatter. Eventually the shepherd could move freely and domestication began.

Lifestyle and culture is based around climate and diet. From domestication came a consistent supply of meat, milk and cheese. The lifestyle that evolved stemmed from the gathering, making and protection of these foods and the animals that supplied them.

The life lessons imprinted into the survival instinct that stem from the traditional role of the shepherd include:

- cooperation
- patience
- gentleness
- endurance
- management

## Loner

Every colour group has its life themes. For blue their life theme often centres around people. One type is the loner shepherd who is solitary and private. This is a person who lives and works alone, spending weeks and even months in the high country of the mountains. The loner shepherd moves the herd from pasture to pasture, finding streams and safety and watching over their animals. The loner shepherd enjoys the peace and quiet of their own company. Like the shepherd of old, modern day blue can also be a loner. This type of blue works and contributes and pays their own way, but they are not social people even though they can communicate easily.

This type of blue prefers solitude to company, they are not misanthropic and they are not lonely. They enjoy being with company for short periods of time but are happy to return to the comfort of themselves. However, loner blue should not spend too much time on their own, they must remind themselves occasionally to get out and mix. Too much time leaves them lonely rather than alone, withdrawn rather than private and estranged rather than peaceful. In balance they make it a point to enjoy the company of friends, before returning to their lifestyle and the privacy they enjoy.

## Company

Another type of blue is exactly the opposite of the loner blue, taking pleasure in large social gatherings, parties or sporting clubs; preferring larger numbers to intimate one-on-ones. Intimacy makes up a smaller part of their lives and is usually reserved for their partner. To loner blue becoming rejuvenated means being at home alone or with their partner and family, locking the rest of the world away. Rejuvenation to company blue is about being social and mixing with groups. The more the merrier is their motto for life and while they have their special friends, they love nothing more than meeting new people.

These two extremes are an extension of the different roles performed by the shepherd. The loner shepherd living in the mountains is one aspect of the traditional role; the nomadic herdsman travelling in large communal families is the other. Both are two extremes of the one existence. The environment they endure and the role they perform is similar and forms part of the unconscious that exists in the survival instinct of blue, yet their way of living and interacting with others is completely different. Both contribute memories that exist in their survival instinct.

> You are a shepherd in the middle ages and your role is to tend to the village animals. Some of the animals belong to other people. Farmers who need to use their own land for different purposes hire your services to care for their animals, the rest of the flock you share with your family.
>
> You work in the mountains because the flat fertile soil of the plains is needed by the farmers to grow cereals and crops. More mouths can be fed by grain than by meat, but animal products are still highly regarded and add a valuable source of protein to the diet. The shepherd is needed to guide and protect the animals, leading them to graze on higher ground, land the farmer cannot plough.
>
> Mountain soil on the upper peaks is less productive than the soil on the plains. The weather conditions are also particularly harsh. Shrubs and grasses are short and hardy and generally less abundant so the

herd must be carefully managed. Sheep, goats and some cattle are perfectly suited to this mountainous terrain.

Watching over your herd carefully you make sure each animal is protected and nourished. Life in the mountains is arduous and lonely but it is also peaceful and allows you the time to think. On this trip there is one other shepherd, but because they are on the other side of the herd conversation is rare. Food is limited by the harshness of the terrain and the weather can change in the blink of an eye. A herd this size will eat sparse vegetation down to dust in a matter of days, so you need to gather the animals and move locations constantly. This is difficult and time consuming because the herd wanders in search of food. You need to keep a watchful eye at all times to know where each animal is.

Huts built for shepherds are dotted across the mountain ridge, providing shelter and warmth for a good night's sleep. Finally your day is over and you lie down to rest. Lighting the fire you take a slow deep breath and fall asleep to the crackle of burning wood. Suddenly in the middle of the night you are awakened by the animals. They are frightened and agitated. The slow dull metal clunk of the bells round their necks has changed to a loud rapid demanding clang. The herd is in a state of panic. Leaping out of bed you grab your club, wrap the far end in cloth and set it alight; now you have a torch. Outside is the growl of either wolves or wild dogs, you can't see which and it makes no difference. The goats and sheep are huddled together in a scared restless circle, so you and the other shepherd, who has also been awakened, run to the circumference and patrol. Shouting and waving the flaming torch, you yell and act as wildly as possible, trying to scare the attacking dogs away.

With a spear in one hand and a torch in the other you scream, yell and wave your arms, pulling faces and making insane gestures with your face, in an effort to confuse and shock. Every creature whether human or wolf is frightened by the crazy and erratic.

At first everything seemed as if it was under control, until one of the snarling dogs suddenly lunged forward to snap at a lamb. Drawing blood, it brazenly turned and decided to challenge you. As it snarled and began to attack, you pushed the flaming torch deep into its face, making the animal scream in pain. It retreated but only to circle and come at you again. Perhaps because it was injured or because your eyes had adjusted to the dark; whatever the reason the wolf seemed slower, and in the next attack, instead of the torch, you plunged a spear into its side. With a screaming yelp, it once again retreated but this time you took the offensive. Waving the weapon high above your head you let loose with a loud and blood curdling scream. You inhaled a deep breath and ran directly at the pack. The wolves stood their ground, snapping at the air, barking wildly, dripping saliva onto the ground. Each exposed their curled vicious teeth, until one broke free and ran forward to attack. Leaping high in the air to bite at your throat, you could smell its breath as you stabbed it in the chest. For a moment the wolf lay suspended in the air until it became too heavy to hold. You let it fall to the ground with a thump. Still struggling and growling you pushed the spear until you finally felt the resistance of its spine. The rest of the pack stood well back gnashing their teeth but not advancing. They looked threatening but not as fierce as you. You ran at them wildly but this time they took flight without any challenge. The herd was saved.

## Night

This experience was common to the shepherd and attacks of this nature would almost always occur at night. During the day most attacking animals watch from a distance because the shepherd is near, but the night gives them the cover they need to draw closer. At night the flock is unprotected and hungry carnivores can creep in silence, waiting for their chance to strike and feed. The senses of the shepherd must be ready and alert to hear any noise that might mean trouble.

The night can still be a difficult time for blue, a legacy of their traditional role. When in balance, sleep comes easily but out of balance the opposite occurs. At night, blue can remain wide awake while others around them are sound asleep. They can be tired and wanting to fall into sleep, but their mind will not let them, they must stay alert. Living in their survival instinct, their energy is out of balance and they have become the shepherd again.

For out of balance blue their physical aches and pains as well as their mind can be worse at night. The need to be semi-nocturnal has led to a survival instinct accustomed to drawing on energy during this time. When stressed, this trend to draw on energy in the evening continues because it is has helped keep the shepherd safe for centuries. Whatever reaction has worked the most to keep people secure in the past, is what the survival instinct employs as its first line of defence. The need to be alert during the night is primary to the shepherd. If the herd was wiped out, the shepherd would die. It was vital the animals remained safe and protected and for the shepherd, sleeping with one eye open was the best way of providing protection.

## Light sleep

Whenever blue becomes disturbed to the point where the survival instinct takes control, days or weeks of insomnia or light sleep can result because the protective streak of the shepherd has been triggered. Unless blue is the excessive energy type, the only way continuous light sleep can be managed without harm is for energy to be limited throughout the day. The typical image of the shepherd boy is of resting his back against a tree, taking it easy as the flock eats. Their traditional role is not a strenuous one by comparison to some of the other colour groups, and this is important because without rest light sleep would not be possible.

The farmer works and ploughs all day – a heavy workload full of effort and strain. If their traditional role required light sleep as well, life would be intolerable. The shepherd operates in an opposite way because they can offset their sleep loss by slowing their pace during the day. In contemporary times this energy mix is often unsuitable especially in high performance jobs but for centuries this balance worked well. The modern workplace does not take into account a thousand generations of evolution. When blue is out of balance they sleep poorly, with no opportunity to catch up during the day. The more tired they become, the more their survival instinct will keep them awake and without the chance to catch up during the day, blue in this state can find life excruciating.

With their system out of balance blue has shifted into a response designed historically to combat common dangers. Conserving energy during the day so it can be utilised at night can leave contemporary blue tired all day yet unable to sleep when they go to bed.

## Cold

The memory of the ice-age and the mountains resides in the blue survival instinct. Sometimes the need for cold is not consciously acknowledged and blue may even describe themselves as a person who prefers warmth. However, physical signs and symptoms express this heritage and many of these symptoms are relieved by the cold; a sore back that is relieved by putting ice on the area or a headache that is better for cold air or a compress, craving cold water or ice when they are sick, or keeping their skin cool so it does not itch. At night some need to uncover the blankets, they cannot sleep if they are too hot. They may have nightmares or wake up with a foggy head unless the window is open and cool fresh air fresh is coming into the room.

Rather than craving cool or cold things, some blue people manifest this trait as an aversion to heat. Not seeing themselves as preferring cold, their distaste for heat is more obvious. They sweat while eating hot food or drinks. On hot or humid days they find it difficult to think, they become cranky and irritable or get physical signs and symptoms. Blood noses on hot days, sneezing when the sun is bright, headaches, migraines, drained energy or a sinus infection that deteriorates rapidly whenever they are in a warm stuffy room; this type of blue suffers with the heat. Blue function better when the surrounding environment is cooler or cold, because that is the place their survival instinct calls home. The survival instinct governs the physical body and when it is out of its comfort zone, signs and symptoms begin.

> After nearly six months away you return to the village. The animals are safe and all are well fed. The farmers' reward you because so few animals were lost, while the older animals that belong to your family

are ready for sale. After spending the winter months at home, catching up with family and friends, it is time to depart once more. The farmers present another flock to care for, while the kids, lambs and recently matured animals, are growing fast and ready to breed.

Enjoying time with family and friends is an important aspect that fulfils your character. Being alone is part of your job but you love the company of others as well. Now it is time to move again and part of you is happy to be on your way. Family is important and you love them all, but at times you feel estranged. Being alone most of the year makes you feel like you never quite fit in with the group.

## Stability and calm

Inward motion creates stability. Without this force the universe would continue to expand at the expense of the space already formed. Inward motion allows what has been created to remain, while the outer reaches continue to move and grow.

Inward motion is represented by cold, contraction, gravity and looking backwards. In culture its influence is seen in a return to basics and the comfort of fundamentals. In the blue period of recent history (1500 – 1650 AD), not only was the little ice-age at its height, but Martin Luther revoked what he believed were the corrupt and superfluous additions to religion. To understand inward motion's influence on culture, it is important to view history by the ethics and ambitions that dominated its thinking. The major events of the blue historical time, at least in Europe, included the reformation and the renaissance which flourished in this time.

The reformation was a return to basics. This return to grass roots philosophy also formed the platform for the renaissance. Backward and inward are the same direction and whether it is back to basics or a return to the past, the energy of inward motion is the dominant force.

One type of blue needs stability and calm because their survival instinct is especially comfortable with routine. Individuals who are volatile and unpredictable are less stable because their personality is driven by swaying emotions. Consequently stability blue desires others less emotionally demanding for their survival instinct to be at peace. To an emotionally charged person, love includes the turmoil and extravagance that comes with emotional commitment. For the routine blue, love means comfort and care as well as stability and strength.

Enjoyment and happiness, together with effective communication is something that everyone, regardless of colour group desires. How happiness is achieved and who it is achieved with, differs markedly. Without stability happiness is impossible for the routine blue, in the same way that happiness is impossible for an emotional person to achieve in a flat and emotionless world.

One of the challenges of communal living is adapting to the behaviours and expectations of others. When the survival instinct is dominant, the laws of the material universe prevail, meaning that opposite forces attract. For routine blue the attraction to demonstrative emotion is strong, while the draw of stability and routine becomes equally as enticing to someone highly emotional. Both attract each other because the survival instinct is in control, and the survival instinct governs the material body.

## Routine

The traditional role of the shepherd was highly structured with the same routine day in, day out. Every traditional role has its repetitive aspects, otherwise it wouldn't become a role. Repetition is what etches experience into the unconscious of the survival instinct. However for the shepherd, the variety of daily life was more limited than for most. The rules imposed by communal living regulate spontaneity and restrict expression, while the nature of the traditional role is unvaried.

The shepherd's life was simple. Every day began with the same routine of caring for the animals, milking, moving and guarding the herd from predators. Simplicity underpins the shepherding lifestyle and it is what blue returns to when they are under stress. Blue are just as ambitious as anyone else and they can also be just as driven. However in balance, blue never lose sight of the fundamentals that make life worthwhile. Others may lose families and friendships chasing dreams of profit or prestige. The family is a fundamental aspect for blue; it is the cement that binds life together and without this focus all else is useless. With family, blue can accomplish anything, it is the platform from which they can launch themselves into any other aspect of life.

One of the reasons the survival instinct of blue still applies techniques from the cold, is due in part to the nature of the shepherd and a traditional role that is even and unspectacular. The shepherd's life is a constant routine with few peaks, troughs or risks. The herd is watched and the milking is done, wool is spun and cheese is made. When the pasture was eaten away, the tents were packed and the whole group moved on. Crossing the mountains was arduous but even that action was a routine because it was the same path that was taken every season. Even the diet was unvaried, because everything the shepherd ate came from the same source. Routine or sameness is a large part of blue. In balance it is consistency that can be utilised to excel. Out of balance it can become obsessive or ritualistic behaviour.

When the survival instinct is dominant in routine blue, life can be reduced to smaller repetitions. Checking light switches, taps or doors, making sure everything is safe. Their survival instinct is in control and the tribal life of the shepherd has returned.

The difference between organisation and routine becomes blurred when the survival instinct is the dominant force. Organisation is essential to the life of the shepherd. Moving the herd as well as the tribe, takes attention to detail and an organised routine. Without the consciousness of the soul, routine occurs for routines sake. It does not serve any purpose. The survival instinct embroils itself in routine, because the memory of the shepherd tells it to do so. The importance of routine or its purpose is lost on a survival instinct that does not think. Organised routine makes life efficient; routine without purpose is wasted energy.

## Focus on the small

It was important to prepare well for long trips such as the shepherd had to undertake, and management and organisational skills are vital to the process. Routine blue continues this trend and organises life with military precision. Everything down to the last slice of bread is counted and documented. This type of blue knows where everything is and feels upset when affairs are out of order.

Knowing precisely what is required so there are no surprises makes routine blue a proficient micro-manager. There are no loose ends and no broad concepts; to be alone in the mountains for months at a time demands careful planning and strict habits. The herd may eat and graze as they please but the shepherd cannot. Milk and meat adds to the supply but everything else must be catered for. Strict and detailed preparation is more than a way of life, for the shepherd it is what life depends upon and they must prepare for every circumstance they are likely to encounter. Getting details right is what the survival instinct of blue falls back on. The more routine blue is stressed the more attention to detail they project. This is inward motion in action; the bigger the stress the more attention to detail, and this can only be achieved by letting go of the big picture to focus on the small.

The shepherd looks after and plans for the little things in life. They must carry whatever they need, but looking after animals is generally an uncomplicated task. The needs of the shepherd as well as the herd are simple and straightforward. As a result, the survival instinct is accustomed to the small and detailed rather than the conceptual and grand. For routine blue the greater the stress, the more they focus on the intricate and small.

Out of balance they can be fastidious and nervous, unable to sleep because they feel as if 'There is something I have forgotten.' Overseeing every aspect, out of balance blue panic at the thought that they might be responsible for something going wrong.

> In the high valleys, your animals grow fat. The weather is warm and the feeling is lazy. Sitting under the shade of a tree, on higher ground to watch the herd, you rest your back against the trunk of the tree, close your eyes, and relax.

> This is one of the better parts of being a shepherd, free from the stress that town life imposes. Some could not cope with your kind of life, preferring instead to spend their time, pursuing the dream of riches and excitement. You are comfortable on days like this, the grass is green and the sky a cloudless blue. Keeping watch over the herd is more of a joy than a job. The chances of attack on days like this are low, allowing life to be relaxed and simple. Sometimes you daydream

about being more important and owning a business like the rich people in town, but you know deep down the pace would not suit you. On the occasions when you return to the village for the sale of the livestock, you often get caught in the throng of buyers, the haggling of traders and the arguments over money. In only a short time, the dream of being a big business man in town evaporates and you cannot wait to get away again.

## Simplicity and peace

Fantasies and day-dreams feed the imagination and depict the person we would like to be, but in reality know to be impossible. Dreams aside, peaceful blue likes life to be simple, without complications or demands. An undemanding life is comfortable for peaceful blue. They usually decide to leave the grand ambitions to others, preferring instead to be diligent but relaxed.

The survival instinct of blue tries to prevent trouble. The shepherd stands guard but they do not hunt. Their job is to prevent attack, not to execute violence and the more successful they are at preventing danger, the more food that is available and the easier they survive. The shepherd's survival instinct means putting in place the necessary requirements to ensure the peace and safety of themselves and their herd.

Two centuries have passed since your lone shepherd experience, and you are part of a large family tribe in the grasslands of north-eastern Asia. Genghis Khan is still a hundred years in the future, so life for the moment is tough but peaceful. This way of life is familiar to blue and within the group there are a variety of functions, each representing a different aspect of this colour group.

After rising at dawn, a young woman breast feeds her baby while her husband prepares breakfast. In your group there are more than a hundred people living together as a clan or 'family'. Wagons and tents create a nomadic village. The clan wanders from pasture to streams then on to the mountains, wherever there is food and water for the animals.

The herd consists of several hundred sheep, goats, cattle and horses, which provide nearly all the group's needs. The animals are domesticated and provide wool, milk, blood, hides, bone, sinew and meat. Some just graze while others are beasts of burden. Milk is both drunk on its own as well as turned into butter and cheese. Even fermented mare's milk is used by the group as an alcoholic drink which the adults enjoy immensely. Blood is also drunk or put into soups, while bones become weapons and sinew makes the string of the bow. Meat is mainly eaten only after an animal dies, or in times of crisis such as famine. However with such a large herd there is often an animal available and meat forms a part of the group's diet.

Each day is long but the pace is moderate. The men stand watch guarding the herd, leading the animals to food and water. The women stay behind preparing food and caring for children in between milking, churning, shearing and spinning wool. A teenage girl calmly walks amongst the animals, treading carefully and deliberately so as not to scare them. Looking for new born kids, calves, lambs and foals, spring is a dangerous and busy time for the group. In the herd, scores of mature females are about to give birth but some, mother and baby alike, will die. On top of these natural losses, more predatory animals are drawn to the herd by the noise and smell of birth and death. Already there are carnivorous birds circling and the howling of wolves comes closer each night. So a larger group stands watch all night long; everyone is protective and anxious.

During the teenage girl's patrol, she finds a struggling ewe exhausted from trying to give birth. The ewe is losing strength quickly and soon both mother and lamb will die, so the girl assists in pulling the lamb into the world. Once it is born the lamb begins to shake and open its mouth; the girl smiles and watches it stumble, its movements making her laugh. The lamb's mother didn't survive the birth and the girl wraps up the lamb and takes it back to her tent. Its chances of surviving are poor, but that does not stop her from trying. Every new animal is treated with care because the life of the group depends on them. The dead ewe will be skinned and eaten, while the lamb will be fed and nurtured.

## Nurture

Blue has a strong nurturing tendency that forms a deep aspect of their survival instinct. During times of stress when the survival instinct is in control, this type of nurturing blue will calm a troubled situation and try to remove distress. If a child, partner or friend is upset or angry, nurturing blue quickly involves themselves, offering comfort to smooth ruffled emotions and put others at ease. Out of balance, they can make themselves too caring for their own good, running around and waiting on others, leaving themselves open to being taken advantage of.

Nurturing blue enjoys a supportive role; it forms part of their ambition and desire in life. Wanting a partner and family to take care of, life is more than a career. It means family, children and giving love and protection. They will work to earn money for their family's needs, but to nurturing blue, especially if female, this is a necessary evil. Most would rather be at home with their children, serving and caring and watching them closely. They desire a family who needs them and a family to be devoted to, a family that wants and loves them in return.

Contemporary society downplays these ambitions and nurturing blue can feel embarrassed by their simple desires. Others may see their aspirations as not grand enough or where nurturing blue is female, they can be accused of throwing women's liberation back to a time before the suffragettes. The more nurturing blue is criticised, the more stressed they become and the greater their survival instinct strives to secure itself through nurturing.

For thousands of years nurturing blue have protected themselves by caring for their family and friends. Nurturing their spouse, children, siblings and parents, as well the animals they depend upon, has sheltered blue and kept them alive. This practice has been efficient and not something the survival instinct is about to relinquish just because another persons' values disagree. Large nomadic tribes often refer to themselves as a family. Making dinner or doing domestic duties is only demoralising to people whose internal politics reject these ways. With blue, whether female or male, the role of being a mother or family man is nothing to be embarrassed about.

The biggest challenge blue can face is convincing those around them that being family-driven is different to being subservient. Nurturing blue does not want to be a slave, but when their survival instinct is dominant they can behave like one. Others respond to the boundaries we create and it can be difficult for nurturing blue not to be taken advantage of. Their survival instinct is desperate to serve, but there are some who will capitalise on this. The more the blue survival instinct can nurture and care for others, the more it believes its place in the group is secured by contribution. Openness and nurturing would make some people feel vulnerable but to this type of blue it makes them feel strong.

## Community

Blue do not love their children any more than any other parent, nor do they love their parents or partner any deeper. They employ nurture as a form of protection when they are out of balance.

In our modern society many people put off having children in order to pursue their career. Others by choice will not have children at all. Nurturing blue has a strong urge for a partner and family. It is not the same as the ideal of romantic love craved by red, nor is it the desire for children without a bothersome partner sometimes seen in yellow. Blue are looking for the total package, a kind and loyal partner with healthy happy children. The picket fence fairy tale is a blue ideal of life.

They can be the typical mum or dad and once this base is established, their life takes on deeper meaning. Some may feel that until this point, life was biding time. From marriage and family comes the stability blue need; their unconscious instinct is filled with memories of clans and family groups moving through life, each supporting and protecting the other.

> The baby lamb was wrapped in a blanket and brought back to the girl's tent. The children of the group play close by, while the women gather by their huts to share the duties of the day. One group milks the animals, while other women take each type of milk and place it into large containers. Yet another group begins making the milk into

butter, cheese, yoghurt and alcohol.

With so many people moving and working it is crucial that everyone gets along. Not everyone has to like each other, but everyone must let the other person be. Each must respect the other's right to privacy and belief.

Intense communal living requires patience and manners, a relaxed easygoing attitude, and an adherence to the rules. Law and order is vital and so too is etiquette. Human beings easily misconstrue each other and this type of confusion can have serious consequences.

The shepherd has in their survival instinct thousands of years of communal existence. It is natural for blue to act in accordance to expected rules and etiquette. Blue instinctively understands the boundaries of personal behaviour. This type of communal blue knows how to communicate with people, what makes them happy and what behaviour does not appeal. In balance they treat people with decency and dignity, not to ingratiate in order to gain, but in a natural way. Out of balance, communal blue can be taken advantage of. They can be naïve and easily manipulated.

A stable manner and pleasant demeanour puts others at ease, making them feel safe. Communal blue is friendly and open but sometimes others can misinterpret incorrectly this friendliness as either inexperience or as a romantic invitation.

The young girl spent the morning laughing and feeding the baby lamb. Normally she was a hard worker, but she was smitten by the little lamb and did not want to be away from it. Forced by the other women to put the lamb aside, she joined in with the chores in an uncharacteristically lacklustre manner. Carrying only one container of milk instead of her usual two, one of the older women yelled at her, calling her lazy and good for nothing. Without thinking, and fuming with anger, the young girl rushed over to the woman and tipped the milk over her head. Both of them, the dripping old woman and the now trembling young girl, stared at each other not knowing what to do. It was uncertain who was the more surprised. The old woman sat stunned. The young girl displayed a mixture of fear, embarrassment and regret. It was the old woman who reacted first, breaking the silence with a scream so loud the birds in the trees took off in flight.

With a pot in each hand the old woman chased the girl, swinging the pots as weapons. The mother of the teenager was chasing the old woman, trying to calm her down and make her see reason. People came from everywhere to see what was happening; it was rare for such commotion to occur. The young girl easily ran away from the woman, but there was nowhere to go and she knew it. Later that night the council would visit.

The council comprised a collection of elders, whose task it was to make decisions on behalf of the group. With her parents they discussed the details of the day's events and their faces were very grave indeed.

The father looked at the daughter sternly; she in turn hung her head in shame. The council made its ruling. The young girl must apologise to the old woman and do her chores for a month. The girl could not believe such a harsh ruling, but she knew she would comply.

In modern times some will say, 'If I was that girl I would refuse to cooperate', but this is typical of nuclear family living and a tribal group such as a herding community can only function with the cooperation of individuals. Those who did not like communal living were always free to leave – but to go where? Occasionally the group would pass by a town and perhaps there were individuals who would leave to live there. However, for those who wished to stay with their clan, compliance with the rules was the only option.

Obeying rules and understanding etiquette is the bedrock of communal existence. Unlike red who can become tongue tied in company, or jump in too early putting their foot in their mouth, blue are adept at getting along, mixing with people and conversing on any topic.

Blue, especially in their teens may not be a part of the 'in crowd'. This is because the behaviour of the in crowd is too stressful to be around, being mostly driven by image and supposed independent behaviour. Friendly blue is open and sociable allowing themself the freedom to be who they are. The image-conscious by contrast are never free. They must always adhere to the fashion of the moment, dressing like the pack and thinking like the pack. The in crowd must constantly drag others down, otherwise outsiders would be equal. It is rare but not impossible for blue to behave like this. However, cynicism and disparagement goes against the spirit of community thinking and a peaceful attitude. The blue survival instinct dislikes this type of behaviour.

Unlike many other people who suddenly find themselves part of a group, blue can be a member without losing their individuality. Their survival instinct is used to communal living. Most people feel they must adopt a group ethic otherwise they will be ostracised and left on their own. For blue it is natural to be part of a team, they don't alter their character or adopt a persona. Others may dislike them, envious of their strength to withstand peer pressure and remain true to themselves. However this is not an issue of strength, it is a matter of naturalness.

## Authority

Blue does not like to break rules. Their survival instinct understands the need to comply with the expectations of the community. Following the rules and respect for authority is embedded into the survival instinct of communal blue. In balance they are stable contributors, doing what they can to help society run smoothly. They donate their time as well as their expertise to ensure the community benefits. From hospital volunteers to scouting or sporting groups, charity is one of the areas where blue believe they have something to offer.

Out of balance, this type of blue is a stickler for the rules and too frightened to think independently without approval. They check and double check to make sure they're right, then based on what they believe is required proceed to follow instructions. If anything goes wrong or the outcome is uncertain, this authority blue knows no one can blame them. They pursued every letter of the law and each instruction exactly as required. The fault for any negative outcome rests entirely with the rule maker, not the rule follower.

Out of balance, authority blue is petrified of doing anything wrong. Their survival instinct requires them to be compliant and respectful at all times. Today we are free to come and go between groups but for a thousand generations this was not the case. To leave or be expelled meant certain death, so obeying the rules and keeping the favour of authority figures was vital. The survival instinct has no concept of time and only changes in response to repeated experience.

Communal living means that tribal elders are the ultimate arbitrators of any dispute. Their word is law and there is no questioning their judgment. The blue respect for tribal elders is deeply ingrained. Parents, teachers, the boss or the police are all contemporary versions of tribal elders. Blue rarely take matters into their own hands; they follow procedure and refer to the appropriate authorities. This course of action is the only response the courts and police condone and the only way civilised society can continue to function. Without authority, family vendettas and anarchy result. Civilised society rests on this blue fundamental. The police dress in blue, so do the United Nations forces; both are designed to keep social order and peace.

## Management

Some blue people can also be the person in authority enjoying business and politics. They are drawn towards policy, management and administration, making excellent managers because as well as these ingrained skills they also communicate well with others.

One of the more difficult aspects of any high ranking position is not just the responsibility of the task but the management and organisation of people. Management is natural to this type of blue because they have generations of experience. Paradoxically, the shepherd has innate qualities making them suitable as both followers and leaders.

In historical times, when the herd had become domesticated, the shepherd's role changed from follower to leader. The job of the shepherd was to protect and manage, to take charge and be responsible for the welfare of the flock. The benefits of remaining calm were reinforced into the blue survival instinct, by the success that calmness produced. The more erratic and emotional the shepherd behaved, the more the herd ran away. The more calm and predictable the shepherd's behaviour, the more they were rewarded by a trusting herd.

The management blue survival instinct believes survival is based on:

- careful planning and thinking ahead
- attention to detail
- good management skills and good personal skills
- defining the objective
- interest in business and politics

Managing a community as well as a herd requires planning and skill, courage and perseverance, as well as good communication skills. In contemporary times these traits still exist, and many businesses and companies have a blue individual at the helm.

At the same time as the girl was bracing herself for a month of extra duties, the men in the group were faced with a dilemma. Whenever the herd needed to be moved, most of the men were required for the task. A few remained behind for security against attack, while the rest went off for the arduous task of shepherding the herd over the mountains. New pasture was needed, spring was coming to an end and it was time to move the flock to higher ground. In the mountains the streams and the cooler weather meant the herd could be fed and watered over the hot summer months. Moving back to the mountains was always difficult, because it meant crossing the territory of hostile clans. These people were not nomads like you. They looked on land as something to own, rather than the nomad's view of it as a temporary place to graze.

As the men crossed the hostile land, a number of warriors from the village rode out, waving their spears and bows and arrows, threatening to attack if the shepherds continued. However the shepherds had no intention of turning back and when the first wave of warriors began to attack, the shepherds were ready to strike back.

This was not the first time the shepherds had been bullied into moving and the village warriors didn't realise how highly skilled they were at defending themselves. The shepherds were excellent horsemen, riding was as natural as breathing and soon the first wave of village warriors lay dead on the ground, their horses and their weapons confiscated. The second wave of village warriors sat on their horses waiting for the signal to attack. When the signal came the warriors took off in whirl of dust and screams. The steel of their swords flashed in the sun, while the thunder of the hooves made the ground shake. Colourful banners and bellowing trumpets, boastful personalities looking for blood, all of them lasted no more than an hour, before the second wave lay as lifeless as the first.

Shepherds have a knowledge and skill gained by living with their animals. Genghis Khan would apply this knowledge and the nomadic tribes of the northern steppes would become the most feared conquering army the world has ever known. The shepherd and their animals live side by side, a symbiotic existence where each looks after the other. This relationship also extended to their dogs and horses and it is as cavalrymen that the shepherd excelled. Cooperation and management, nurturing and community are the foundation upon which their society depends.

The shepherd is a nomad, travelling in large community groups. As they travel they trespass on land claimed by others, and face the danger of attack. If the soft, nurturing, peace loving blue did not have a stronger more protective side to their nature, they would be pushed aside and the herd would be stolen. When the village warriors attacked, they were preventing blue from moving their herd. Their object was to remove the herders from their land, but to the shepherd, if the herd can't graze their family dies. Any attempt to remove the herd makes the shepherd fight for their very existence. In this situation the dot of yang explodes and an opposing force is overcome before it knows what hit it.

The shepherd is the human incarnation of inward motion and when pushed to extremes reacts in the same way. When a rival group tries to force the shepherd away, they push them past the point of no return. The shepherd must lead the community and herd to richer ground so all can survive.

## Stubborn

Thousands of years of friction and hostility have created a survival instinct that stands its ground. If blue was too easily pushed aside they would never have been able to survive. As a consequence the shepherd has developed a streak so stubborn, they are an immovable force. Historically this is what had to occur and it is a survival technique they still employ frequently.

Out of balance blue will argue that black is white even if they know it isn't. When blue is out of balance and the survival instinct is dominant, standing your ground becomes more important than the original disagreement. Right or wrong, black or white, it's all the same to a non-thinking survival instinct. All it knows is that it is under attack and the only defence is to stand your ground.

## Togetherness

The shepherd shares a symbiotic existence with the rest of their group and with their animals. Sheep and goats give meat, milk and wool, while dogs and horses provide security and labour. Dogs not only help herd the sheep, they provide an alarm when predators attack. Horses give strength and endurance and are used as a weapon against hostile forces.

Horse and rider are two soldiers not one, and the shepherd spends long hours of their life in the saddle. Their skill with horses and the animal's trust in their rider made the shepherd and horse an awesome duo. Contemporary blue continues this trait by forming relationships that are mutually beneficial. Family is the most common example of the symbiotic co-existence blue is comfortable with. The survival instinct of the shepherd is at home with community, relying on others for support and friendship, happy to give and receive.

The shepherd has survived the conditions that have caused the extinction of others, because they work together as a group. Each covers the other person's back, helping them out when trouble arises. This type of togetherness blue is an all-for-one-and-one-for-all person. They are the first to volunteer, no questions asked.

Even if they do not have the expertise required, they still offer their services in any capacity that may help. This is the natural outcome of inward motion, gathering strength by increasing its mass. The more energy inward motion pulls into itself, the denser and stronger the force becomes. This force relies on numbers, the same as the shepherd does. The bigger the herd and the larger the group, the stronger and more self sufficient the group becomes.

In balance, this type of blue is someone others like to have around. They are loyal and helping and always ready to support. Their survival instinct is accustomed to pitching in to help. Often during crisis, blue is first on the scene, giving moral support or practical help.

## Dependency

Out of balance, dependent blue relies on having stronger and more confident people around them. Afraid to take the slightest decision, this out of balance blue seeks reassurance before performing the simplest of tasks. The more they are stressed and out of balance, the more confirmation they need.

Dependent blue in an out of balance state clarifies everything to make sure they are right. The communal survival instinct of blue, believes that in order to protect itself, they must not upset anyone for any reason and should let others who they see as wiser than themselves, make decisions on their behalf.

## Yielding

Inward motion draws in energy to increase its mass and force. Blue increases the numbers around them with an attractive and warm personality. Gathering people around them is different to the mating desires of circular motion. Inward motion gains strength from numbers not romance. Blue is governed by the same instinctual pattern to collect and gather to increase strength. The more stressed they become the more this type of blue gathers people around them to secure their position. To blue the group represents security when they are out of balance and enjoyment when they are in balance.

If they have to choose between peace and truth, yielding blue takes peace every time. Unlike the more stubborn management type, yielding blue has no intention of digging in to make a point. Their survival instinct is communal and is only at home with peace. When trouble occurs it shocks their system. Large communities do everything in their power to make sure that trouble is stopped before it starts. Modern day cities have experienced trouble on a large scale. Should the power grid go out, crime and anarchy will result. Adherence to laws and to social etiquette distinguishes a community from a warring clan.

Arguments and violence are not only foreign to the survival instinct of blue, they are its enemy. If a partner, friend, sibling or co-worker needs to hear they are right – even if yielding blue does not believe they are – they will tell them anyway just to keep them happy.

Blue is at home when the climate is tranquil. Arguments and hostility are their enemy, their survival instinct recognises that success comes from being calm. Communal existence also requires a character that is patient and accommodating. Emotional hysteria is the opposite state to what made blue successful in their environment and in their past.

Yielding blue when out of balance will search to find a dominant partner. Without someone to ask them for support, yielding blue has no-one to take charge. When the survival instinct of yielding blue is dominant, they will be loyal to the point of subservience. They will attract a more demanding personality and they often fall in love with someone strong and authoritative. However, to think they are a pushover or incapable of looking after themselves is wrong too. They are strong but in their own unique way. Many families are held together because yielding blue absorbs the strain. To keep the peace and absorb the energy of conflict is more than what many other people could bear, but yielding blue in the wrong environment does it everyday.

## Childish

With their strong desire to nurture and protect, blue can seem the quintessential mum or dad. Dedicated to their children, blue delights in playing and spending time with their family. Sometimes the emphasis on play goes too far and they forget or ignore all the serious responsibilities. Cooking and cleaning often gets relegated to second place behind playing.

Inward motion draws everything backwards, including time. One type of blue can be an adult child. There is nothing delayed in their mental faculties, neither impaired nor retarded in any way and their looks and body match their biological age. They can hold down a job and look after a family but there is an essence about them that remains childlike. It may be a fondness for playing games or a naïvety generally found in the young and inexperienced. This naïvety or childishness is a quality; it has nothing to do with intelligence or responsibility. It is their expectation and approach to life that has a child-like innocence that seems out of context.

In old age, childish behaviour is not so pleasant. The passing of time has depleted their energy and the survival instinct is now dominant. Inward motion can revert blue back to an eighty-year-old child. Forgetting all responsibilities or even their entire adult life, this type of blue is diagnosed with old age dementia, brought on by a drain in energy from overwork or stress. Unable to cope because there is very little energy left, the survival instinct cannot support complicated and energy expensive strategies like the ones provided by its traditional role. Instead it regresses to its most primitive state and the aged blue either withdraws into hibernation or goes back in time to their childlike state. Dementia is not exclusive to blue.

## Dogmatic

Although it is uncommon, blue may be dictatorial by nature and this type is hard and cold. Dogmatic blue when out of balance is demanding and dictatorial and refuses to recant. They are used to laying down the law and making decisions for others. They are the elders of the group and their word is law. When in balance the memory of the elder survives and blue manages problems with eloquence and clarity. In balance they are never a dictator but a person who makes decisions in the best interests of all.

## Cheerful

The survival instinct of a lighter type of blue has learned to capitalise on happiness and use it as a defence and as a way of securing their position in the group.

When cheerful blue is out of balance, they become cheery and laughing in situations when it would be more appropriate to be upset or angry. In the shepherding society demonstrative expression was discouraged, because negative emotion might upset the group. The only emotions that were publically encouraged were happiness and contentment. When people expressed contentment whilst living amongst the group, it made others feel privileged to be there. Discontent, unhappiness or continual boredom resulted in upset and civil unrest. As a result some blue people have developed two different faces; one public and one private. Out of balance, cheerful blue keeps their public face on at all times, laughing off everything as if the most serious event were only a minor inconvenience that shouldn't interrupt the pleasantness of the day.

Avoiding any talk that is serious, cheerful blue laughs about everything but is not always sincere and others can find this habit tiring. Serious conversation is part of everyday life. Out of balance, cheerful blue with their survival instinct in control does not appreciate that seriousness and anger are two different states.

Keeping a happy face on regardless of whether you are a nervous wreck or in spite of the fact that it's draining your life force, is the behaviour of this type of blue. Communal cohesion rests on emotional suppression. For a group to stay functional the members cannot give immediate expression to their feelings. 'I will say what I want, when I want to say it', is an ethic promoted in modern times, but it is detrimental to community health.

## Emotion and communication

All situations and behaviours are best expressed in the middle ground. It is inappropriate to suppress every emotion but it is also unconstructive to express them continuously. The survival instinct cannot tell the difference between expressing an emotion *to* someone, from expressing an emotion *at* someone. If a person is angry the people around them will unconsciously respond as if they are being threatened. Consciously the other person realises that this is not the case, but the survival instinct reacts as if it is. The person who is angry may have no negative emotion toward the others in the room, but the survival instinct does not think and cannot know this.

Being around someone who displays their emotions openly can be difficult for the survival instinct of others, as it makes them unconsciously respond as if they are the cause of that emotion. Constant anger makes others defensive, while continuous sadness makes others feel guilt. The one who is expressing the feelings may not intend this outcome but the people they love will feel the outpouring regardless of intention. Healthy relationships cannot flourish in an environment where emotions consistently over-rule courtesy.

People who are angry, blunt or indiscreet have a survival instinct that believes this behaviour will get them what they want. It is appropriate jungle behaviour, provided we never want to be loved or respected. The human soul wants to lift itself from the jungle to explore happiness, contentment and learning.

In balance, blue is successful at social interaction because they speak to others in a manner that is appropriate. This skill represents more than pleasantness and politeness, it is about knowing how to speaking in a language that others understand. Not a cultural language, such as English, German, Japanese or Hindi but a *survival instinct language* such as yellow, red or blue. Knowing how to speak 'survival instinct' is deeper and more effective than any other way of communicating. Generations of communal living gives blue a natural ability to communicate by putting others at ease. A pleasant demeanour and an open smile transcend linguistic boundaries making the survival instinct calm so the soul can listen to the words.

Speaking to anyone from a different colour group means understanding what they want to hear, how they need to be spoken to, and what makes them secure. Speaking to others in an appropriate manner heightens our chances of getting our own message across. Effective communication by recognising the survival instinct in others means we can speak in a way that gets heard by them. Some people say they need to get angry because others ignore them until they do, but if we are constantly getting angry, then the anger isn't working. Speaking to others, including blue, in a hostile tone may get us what we want in the short term, but it will destroy whatever relationship we have.

Anger and hostility are emotions to be suppressed except in extreme situations. People cannot become over-wrought or take the law into their own hands; if they do the group falls apart. Speaking in an angry tone forces blue to jump to attention, their survival instinct instantly alerted to danger. No one can be their best while they feel threatened.

## Lightness

Avoiding serious conversation can make blue seem light and some blue individuals can become disillusioned or upset by how others see them as stupid, but this is often a result of their own making. The blue inability to keep their light-heartedness in context makes their unnecessary laughter inappropriate and childlike. They want to be treated as mature, but their behaviour is not an appropriate adult response. When the survival instinct is in this mode, blue find it difficult to focus on anything serious. Their survival instinct only lets them behave in a manner that is giggly and superficial.

Blue do not like to think of themselves as naïve or childish, but others can only take their character the way that it is presented. Inside them, blue's soul is craving acceptance, yearning to be taken seriously and treated like an adult. However their light and giggly manner may deny this desire and slowly but surely their energy drains under the suffocating weight of 'happiness'.

## Intimidating

Sometimes the face of blue is far more fierce in presentation than their personality. This is a survival tool that stems from their traditional role and although not all blue people exhibit this, it is commonly seen. This type of blue is a gentle soul wrapped with a fierce facial exterior. For some it occurs only when they are upset but for others it can be a lasting facial expression. The permanence comes from a prominent bone structure that can make blue look fiercely competitive and aggressive although their personality may be much milder and more gentle. In their traditional role of the shepherd, scaring away predators was a necessity. Whether poachers, wild animals, or villagers were trying to scare them away, the shepherd had to yell and scream at the top of their voice, and look as hostile and as forbidding as possible so that animals and adversaries were frightened away. With their upturned eyes and prominent cheekbones, pointed chin, sharp teeth and deep set eyes, especially when combined with the loudest voice nature can provide, this type of blue is enough to make anyone run. Underneath all this bluff, bluster and volatile countenance beats the heart of the shepherd whose traditional role is to manage and nurture. Protection for the flock was accomplished by looking and sounding intimidating.

As the world's population increases the need for appropriate social communication grows. Blue with their instinct for putting others at ease and communicating calmly and effectively are the example we need to draw from. Blue supplies stability and structure, nurture and support. They are the bedrock of successful communal living and a model we can follow.

## Facial features

Inward motion is designed to draw inwards. Blue is represented by both inward features, sharp features and pointed features. Pointed features symbolise energy being drawn to a single point. The sharp or jagged teeth of blue result from their meat and protein based diet. Blue has a curvature of the bones caused by the constant exposure to cold. As heat and energy withdraws into the interior of the body, the exterior is weakened considerably. The bones are slightly curved and the skin can be dry, parched and fissured. Asymmetry of facial features is another sign of blue. Symmetry represents strength because every part is even. Asymmetry is a weakness caused by a contraction of energy due to conservation.

## Inward motion

The following features express the inward motion of blue:

## Inward features

- dimples
- recessed lids of the eyes
- indented bridge of the nose
- inward direction of the teeth

## Pointed features

- pointed chin
- pointed teeth

## Curved and prominent bone structure
- curved forehead
- prominent cheekbones
- defined chin

## Asymmetry
- asymmetrical features
- crooked hairline
- crooked teeth

## Chapter 16

# ORANGE - OUTWARD MOTION AND CIRCULAR MOTION – RESISTANCE

*Competition*  
*The warrior*  
*Everyone for themselves*  
*Resourceful*  
*Measurements against others*  
*Preparation and planning*  
*Struggle and ambition*  
*Fire, protection and security*  
*Change*  
*Power and endurance*  
*Emotions*  
*Protection of assets*  
*Loyalty*  

*Crisis*  
*Memory of pain*  
*Guilt*  
*Depth of suffering*  
*Blame*  
*Righteousness*  
*Endurance*  
*Core values*  
*Rescue*  
*Martyrdom*  
*Drama and hysteria*  
*Denial*  
*Wounded*  

What makes orange, and the other combination colour groups green, purple and brown, different from the three primary groups, is that their driving influence comes from the *interaction* of the motions rather than the motions themselves. The drive behind red comes from circular motion while the drive behind yellow comes from outward motion, but the drive behind orange does not come from a combination of yellow and red but from the *interaction* of yellow and red. This is why people from complex colour groups are never half yellow and half red in their behaviour but have their own unique drive.

In order to produce orange, outward motion and circular motion must be of equal strength otherwise the stronger force will suppress and dominate the weaker, to the point where the weaker force will not produce any noticeable effect. The result of these two dissimilar or opposing forces interacting is a new force that is distinct and separate from the two from which it originated. The outward motion of yellow and the circular motion of red interact to define the new and unique character of orange.

## Competition

Orange is a person who projects the sense of competition that comes from outward and circular motion struggling against each other. Orange projects this internal conflict onto the external world and as a result can see life as a competitive struggle to acquire the resources necessary to survive.

Outward motion relentlessly pushes itself onto the circular motion of red which in turn tries to capture yellow. In a confined space these two forces create an environment where it is yellow *versus* red creating resistance and competition.

Yellow manage excessive stress by distancing themselves from its cause – that is the nature of outward motion. Red go over and over a problem until a solution is found because that is the character of circular motion, while orange will meet a problem head on because that is the expression of two continually competing energies.

Natural law states that energy or force must compete or cooperate. This can be a real pitfall and one of life's great challenges for orange because cooperation is not their natural strong point. This does not mean they are not team players because they can be. In fact orange work well in a team, but functioning as part of a partnership or team and being competitive can create difficulties.

Orange are deeply committed people who like most people, long for an intimate relationship and a good social network but their internal force gives them a nature that makes deep connection difficult when they are out of balance.

When the survival instinct is holding sway and in charge of the decision making no relationship is in a healthy state but for orange, relationships can be their most difficult and cumbersome challenge.

The reason for this is the black and white nature of their internal force. Each motion hangs on precariously knowing that if the other gets the upper hand, it will be overpowered. Each strives and competes in an endless life or death struggle that shapes the orange survival instinct and makes it react in the same way whether threatened or exhausted.

## The warrior
With the internal resistance between yellow and red continuing without end, struggle, endurance and competition are just some of the outcomes that can be a way of life for orange. In the same way as the expanding outward motion of yellow creates the perfect foundation for the personality of the trader, the constant struggle for domination and control makes the perfect backdrop for the warrior.

## Everyone for themselves
The continuing contest between yellow and red can make orange see the world as a hostile and competitive place if they are out of balance. Competition is a way of life that only supports winners and promotes the ethic of everyone for themselves. Orange in this out of balance state can come across as a hard and blunt person who seems battle weary and wary of everyone. They behave as if they have been bitten one too many times and now they are not quite sure of who they can trust. Life has often proven this to be true.

## Resourceful
Having a survival instinct which sees the world and everyone in it as competition has some advantages. For a start it makes orange a resourceful and competitive pragmatist. Continual competition also serves to create an outlook where somebody wins and somebody loses. Someone gets things and someone misses out. Somebody survives and somebody doesn't. A survival instinct that has this blueprint as its driving force is a survival instinct determined to stay one step ahead of the competition.

Life is about survival of the fittest, both physically and socially. As a result we are all competing against each other, trying to highlight our strengths and other people's weaknesses. Orange is not unique in their competitive spirit but their intensity during competition is fierce. Orange is the resistance that results from outward motion and circular motion, a relentless pressure and struggle for supremacy that infuses the orange survival instinct. Their projection is that life is a continuous battle requiring effort and resilience. Out of balance, every day is a struggle to hang on to life, making orange a tactical and resourceful survivor.

## Measurement against others

Orange measures themselves against the performance of others. It is not enough to beat their own personal best, it is also important to surpass everyone else around them. We are all competitive and we all strive to secure ourselves. However, it is orange who is continually attempting to measure themselves against other people's skills. The reason for this comes from the traditional role of the warrior who exemplifies the internal competitive orange force. For the warrior it is not about doing your personal best it is about beating your opposition. The circumstances of battle require winning not just doing well.

Orange is under no illusions about life. The world can be a hard place where bad times are not exclusively reserved for others. Having this nature, orange are also people who understand the necessity of making things happen, and they are prepared to put in the effort needed to protect themselves and their family. They never leave anything to chance.

## Preparation and planning

Orange have thoughts about giving up under extreme pressure like everybody else, but generally these thoughts are fleeting, as their competitive spirit never allows them to succumb for too long. Orange has learned to buffer themselves against an uncertain future by preparation and planning.

The constant competition between yellow and red makes orange familiar with effort and struggle before they even enter the world. Before birth the embryo has the energy that will shape their survival instinct and outlook already locked in place. This force shapes the survival instinct, not the soul. It does not affect our ability to use free will. Our soul has free will but our survival instinct does not. It is a program designed to be reactive and responsive and to keep us alive, nothing more. It has nothing to do with freewill because the survival instinct does not think or plan; its sole purpose is to protect the individual. It has no concept of altruism and it certainly cannot grasp abstract concepts such as time.

The warrior is regimented and drilled because they know that life depends on precision. The warrior is the only traditional role designed around battle. Soldiers train for hours each day in readiness for that one moment when they are pitted against their adversary. To be sub-standard or lacking at this point in time means losing your life. Whether the final day of battle ever actually happens is up to fate but the warrior must be ready. Orange bring this attitude into daily life through meticulous precision and planning. Under stress they revert to the drill and procedure that has kept them alive in the past. Others around them may question why they are pushing themselves so hard but they are not the warrior.

## Struggle and ambition

Struggle is one of the key words that describes orange. Not all life is a struggle and for many orange people, life can be an avoidance of struggle. However, out of balance orange can make a struggle out of nothing. Emotions are the fuel of response. Anger and fear are the primary drives for attack and running away. These two reactions are basic emotions for orange because anger and fear is what the warrior experienced most during battle.

In an out of balance state orange can turn quiet, peaceful moments into tempests of hysteria and rage. Their survival instinct, used to fighting and struggle, sees peace as a foreign concept. As a result, the survival instinct of out of balance orange can turn a peaceful environment upside down within a moment's notice by their quick temper or changing emotions.

Struggle creates the ability to strive. Many orange people are ambitious and have enormous capacity for effort and endurance. However, orange have a natural tendency to take over and assume command and many can end up doing too many tasks. It is not unusual to find an orange person managing a high level business as well as running a household single-handed. Some will complain bitterly about their workload without recognising they are victims of their own out of balance state

When orange is out of balance, they have an energy of effort and struggle. Some around them may take advantage of this. The more orange is in a state of struggle the more they will attract around them a person or an event that makes them struggle. Looking for a cause or someone to defend, orange may befriend the helpless and lost. Protecting or managing the needy is something the orange survival instinct looks for because it gives purpose by repeating the traditional role of defending those who cannot help themselves. Being a better defender and fighter is what secured the warrior's position. If a person can stand up for themselves they have no need for the warrior, so orange out of balance searches for those who are down trodden and defenceless.

Orange can over emphasise the significance of any emotional decision or disagreement because their survival instinct interprets competition as a life or death struggle. Out of balance orange does not recognise the middle ground of compromise and this can create turmoil.

The need to struggle can also be seen in the high expectations of orange. Accomplishing a task that is easy is the opposite of struggle and drive. Setting their sights on the difficult to attain is perceived by others as ambition. To those around them, ambitious orange's drive to reach the top and willingness to take on responsibility and difficulty is viewed as an insatiable ambition for success. For ambitious orange it is immersing themselves in the familiarity of struggle.

## Fire, protection and security

Fire is one of the best examples of orange in the natural world. To understand the colours of nature is to understand the energy behind that natural state.

Fire moulds, shapes and purifies, but above all fire like orange itself, gives protection, comfort and security. Anyone who has spent time alone in the dark knows how quickly our mind begins to play tricks, when the darkness of night envelopes our senses.

Parents know how easily a child's excitement when the power fails on a stormy night, can be replaced by fear if the power does not return quickly. Even candlelight makes a twilight glow that casts shadows and throws the mind back to the primeval world. Prehistoric nights were filled with dread. Predatory mammals and snakes, insects and rats, bats, spiders and centipedes, all crawling, scuttling and ready to bite – and that was only the known world. The night was filled with howls and cries, growls and screams, wild animals as well as demons and ghosts all lurking and ready to strike.

The modern world has replaced fire with electric light. Towns are kept alight all night, not only to allow work to continue but to sooth our natural and long held fears of the dark. The night is unpredictable and unknown and our survival instinct hates the unknown.

We fool ourselves when we pride ourselves on how much we have matured. Walk down a country trail with no lights and no torch and see how long it takes for a contemporary urban sophisticate to revert to the nervous superstitious cave dweller. Not long! We still need light and fire.

Fire protects us from danger. It cuts through the night and lights up the surroundings. A fire defines our space and turns a cave into a home. It reduces the element of surprise, because an animal must come into the light to attack. Fire also means we can retaliate quickly to fend off an attacker because fire is one of the most effective weapons we have ever had.

Nothing organic can withstand the effect of fire. It is stronger than the strongest creature. Whoever controls fire wins.

Fire also offers protection from the elements. Human beings do not have fur coats nor can they maintain internal body temperature without help. With the one tool of fire we can protect ourselves against the dark, the cold and anything hostile. In time, fire would also be used as power to drive engines as well as to transform one substance to another and give rise to both alchemy and chemistry.

Fire was so important that people were assigned the specific task of caring for it, and this became their full time job. Because it could not be easily produced, it was carried around and nurtured like a baby. Wherever a group went, so too did the small burning ember and enough people to ensure that it stayed alight. This highlights how much we protect fire, as well as how much it protects us. <u>Protection and security is the fundamental drive of orange.</u>

The role of fire is to protect, to change and to power, and orange people exhibit all these functions as part of their survival instinct. Emotions will often be involved in these traits.

Orange has an inbuilt need to protect and to nurture. When they are in balance, orange is protective but still open to letting others express themselves and make mistakes. Out of balance, orange can be smothering and overbearing. Sometimes neurotic while at other times dictatorial, an out of balance orange person sees danger and calamity everywhere and some will become hysterical when even the smallest thing goes wrong.

## Change

Fire is used to transform substances because it forces matter to release energy through heat. Fire changes ice into water and wood into charcoal, it changes solids into liquids and liquids into gas. Some people who are dominated by orange energy live in a constant state of change. Building businesses, buying homes or studying new topics are all part of the orange expression to change and alter.

This desire to change is sometimes expressed on a personal level by what is called the 'saviour' complex. This is the driving need for a person to find, protect and help those who are vulnerable and needy. A 'saviour' could be a woman befriending and giving herself to a man who is addicted, violent or down on his luck, in the belief that he can be changed with the aid of a 'good woman'. This is a story that is common and rarely successful but it does typify the orange need to protect and offer security. Just like fire itself. Many of these relationships have an unfortunate ending that also typifies another orange energy, that of suffering.

## Power and endurance

Heat from fire has been a primary source of power and energy throughout history whether from wood, steam or electricity. Many orange people have this same endurance and high energy output and can accomplish long and difficult tasks, completing what many others would find too arduous and gruelling. Even today many orange people find competitive sports or activities such as running, swimming or surfing a necessary part of their routine.

## Emotions

Orange under stress views life as a shifting balance of power and influence. Emotions are needed by the warrior in the same way the hunter needs adrenaline. They are a motivating force that dominate many orange people. Love, loyalty, kindness and friendship were the positive experiences of the warrior and helped to fuel the orange survival instinct. They rely on these emotions to recharge themselves.

When they are out of balance, orange use emotions as leverage to gain the upper hand. Emotions are used by some orange people as a way to maintain dominance. Through anger and sadness, fear or guilt, out of balance orange upset their competitor in an attempt to put them off guard. Emotional turmoil is a weapon used by orange to ensure they get what they want. In the past this reaction was beneficial to the warrior as they faced their enemy in battle but for out of balance orange people today, the enemy of their survival instinct may also be their partner, children or parents. This interaction can cause long term damage to close relationships. Whatever form it may take, emotion is the language of orange and it is specifically used to keep them protected or to keep others they feel need their protection close at hand.

## Protection of assets

Throughout history, tribal groups have wandered incessantly because of the shifting fortunes of nature. Heat waves came and went leaving fertile lands dry, cracked and barren. Rising tides, melting snows and changing conditions made migration for many early humans a necessary way of life. These wandering groups settled wherever conditions were favourable and food supplies were plentiful. Weather was a less important factor than a regular food supply, which is why there are people living in harsh arctic or desert environments. Wherever a regular supply of food could be found, human beings settled in numbers proportional to that supply.

Comfortable fertile environments were premium sites and highly sought after. Early humans relied entirely on the productivity of the land on which they dwelt and they protected it because their lives depended on it. This need to protect fertile land was the beginning of the warrior.

Imagine that you are taking part in an experiment like 'the greatest experiment in history', except you are allowed to choose the type of environment in which to settle. What sort of place would you choose? Would it be a tropical oasis with oceans of fish, waterfalls and pleasant weather? Or would it be undulating hills with a freshwater stream, pastures, grazing cows and a nearby wood? Perhaps you would choose a desert with heat so relentless there is barely enough water to drink, let alone ever allowing you to bathe. Or would you ask for a frozen wasteland so cold it freezes the tears in your eyes. Maybe you would request a crawling impenetrable jungle full of stinging or biting insects or a rocky barren mountainside that slices your face with its icy wind?

Naturally you are going to ask for either the oasis or the gentle pasture land because they are fertile and welcoming places. Life is comfortable and won't be spent turning rocks or melting in the sun. In the oasis or the pasture, life can be enjoyed instead of being dominated by a constant struggle. Environments like these are fertile places that provide food and housing so life can be relaxing as well as prosperous but remember that in this game you are not the only bidder. When the oasis or gentle pasture is chosen there will be others who will want to live there too. However much of the earth's surface is not oasis or gentle pasture but ice, desert, jungle and mountainside. These areas of paradise and fertility are rare and everyone wants to live there, so those who do must also be prepared to defend their land.

In the 'the greatest experiment in history', life was relatively tranquil until an early and harsh winter hit the mountain group forcing them down the mountain to graze their animals on the pasture land of the farming group. Left with no other choice, the farmers retaliated against the shepherds by assigning some of their group to the specific task of protecting the borders of their land. Forced off the plains, the mountain shepherds had no alternative but to herd their animals into the forest, which caused the forest group to react and a ripple effect occurred.

Life is linked to fertility. The more fertile the land, the fewer environmental struggles there are. Conversely, the less fertile the environment, the more precarious the hold to life will be. Harsh climates and infertile soils mean food sources are scarce and one bad season can be disastrous because such small food supplies means no backup. Like the mountain group, people without food are left with no other choice but to move elsewhere. The biggest problem for refugees is that the land they are searching for is always occupied by someone else, and that means a fight is imminent.

Fertile lands with rich soil means food can grow with such abundance it can be stored. Occupations beyond subsistence farming can occur and markets appear full of food followed by arts and crafts. These newly developed trading towns were irresistible targets for those who were struggling and hungry.

With the starving and homeless pouring over the border, traditional land owners are faced with only three possibilities.

- They can supply those in trouble with aid
- They can open their borders and allow those in need, free access to their resources
- They can defend their resources and ensure they are not overrun and/or lose their land

Human beings nearly always choose the third option.

Option number two is the least preferable but sometimes the numbers are so overwhelming it is not possible to defend traditional lands and a takeover takes place. In modern times first world nations can afford foreign aid which in turn ensures their position remains secure and the mechanisms exist to send supplies, but in the past this was not the case.

If you were lucky enough to be part of a group that lived on fertile soil threats from raiders, thieves and invaders was constant. If your group was too easily pushed and did not put up resistance, a takeover was inevitable and you would be forced off your land. Sometimes you were not even this lucky and instead of being forced off the land, you and the entire group would be slaughtered outright.

The only protection against raiding forces was the warrior. Part-time warriors from farming or other trades were no match for trained soldiers. To ensure wealth was protected full time armies solely devoted to protection began.

> One minute you are planting in the fields, minding your own business and going about the duties of the day. The next minute there is a screaming horde running over the hill and down into your village. Stunned, you stop and stare. Suddenly you regain control of your senses and run sounding the alarm. Everyone, male and female alike,

grabs a weapon and runs to counter the attack. Some of the older women collect the children and hide inside the huts ready to defend themselves with spears and axes, while the men and the younger women clash against the invaders in a fight to the death.

Nerves tremble and muscles shake as these foreign raiders with their screams and blood-curdling cries wave their weapons in the air. With every minute that passes these murderers draw nearer and some of your group starts to run and scurry for cover. Others flee back to collect their families and escape into the woods.

The elders bark orders to stay and fight but it is too late, many have already run and your defences are severely weakened. Those who remain raise their spears and axes in readiness for the charging human wave that is now only moments away. With a bone shuddering crunch the opposing force crashes into the remaining villagers making bodies fly and scatter.

You are a fit woman in your early thirties and it is your job in times of crisis to supply the men with weapons. The older women are in the main hut guarding the children but you are not convinced this is a good hiding place under the circumstances. It is also the place where the spare weapons are kept so you make your way to the hut as quickly as possible. Inside you go to the wall where the weapons are hanging and grab as many axes as you can carry. While gathering the weapons an invader charges into the hut and begins screaming at the huddled group of women and children on the opposite side of the room.

Amidst tears, cries and wails of fear, the invader reaches down and grabs one of the women by the hair forcing her to drop her child. The infant, no more than two years old, screams for its mother, holding out its hands and crying, but the invader has a firm grip on the mother and laughs as he draws his sword. It is at this point that you plunge your axe into the back of his skull.

When the invader entered the room he did not see you behind him and now he has paid the price of not being cautious. Soon another man comes charging into the hut but this time all the women are armed and the screaming man finds himself alone, surrounded by a group of quiet, hate filled and slowly advancing women. The room is charged with a deadly silence and nobody is quite sure what to do next. Despite the commotion going on outside, inside the hut you can hear a pin drop. Suddenly the man raises his axe high into the air and shrieks at the top of his voice. In return the women also scream as they raise their weapons and charge. The man is outnumbered at least forty to one and despite the bravado he is hacked to death.

The older women then gather the children and escape to the nearby woods while you and every other able-bodied woman from teenage girl upwards return to the fight. With the majority of men away hunting, the women have no other choice; if the tribe loses they will all be killed. The men who remain in the village are craftsmen, gardeners and the group's priest. Today they, along with the women, are all warriors.

You see a man from your tribe struggling because a stronger invader has him by the neck. Both men are choking each other but the foreigner is winning until you stab him from behind with your knife. Other women join the fight by attacking the invaders from the rear; there is no chivalry here. Soon the tide of the battle begins to turn as the raiders fall to the ground and become outnumbered.

The invaders were driven by shortages of food. They had been spying on your village for a while and the fertile soil your group lives from made you all an irresistible target. This time you managed to retain possession of the land but next time you may not be so lucky; everyone must be prepared.

Abundance is a beacon to the less fortunate, their needs drawing them like a moth to the flame. 'Why doesn't everyone just share what they have, then everyone will have enough' is a question often asked but life is not this generous. Environmental change makes sharing a dangerous exercise because no-one knows what tomorrow will bring. Perhaps there is no valid excuse for modern first world nations not to share food, but in times gone by, abundance could turn to famine with one failed season.

What the invaders did not account for was the spirit of the tribe. Convinced that everyone would cower and capitulate, the invaders were over confident so lacked caution. Now they lie dead or injured. Human beings have an enormous capacity for kindness and compassion but not when they are attacked.

The women who hacked the invader to death were neither nasty nor cruel. They were just human beings who were unbearably afraid and acting on instinct. Instinct turns human beings into human animals and the survival instinct will ruin the happiness of life if it remains in control. Understanding survival instinct triggers is vital.

When the hunting party returned and found their village almost destroyed, they were overcome by two separate emotions. Firstly they were enraged and wanted to hunt down the remaining members of the invading tribe to ensure they never attacked again. Secondly, they were filled with awe and reverence for the people who had struggled so hard to defend the families and possessions of everyone in the group, and made promises of eternal gratitude.

By standing your ground and defending what was yours, you and the other women secured your place on the fertile land you call home. At a personal level the bravery of being a warrior will protect you against famine and expulsion should it occur in the future. During famine those most important to the group are the last to be expelled. By providing protection and security the warrior has earned their right to stay.

## Loyalty

The survival instinct of the warrior has a number of important survival tools in its memory, the first of which is *loyalty*. When the invaders came storming over the hill every nerve in your body told you to run but you ignored these impulses to stay and fight. People in dangerous situations bond quickly because there is safety in numbers, so when danger is as extreme as it was when the invaders attacked, those who were left became closer than tribesmen, they became family. They became people who could be relied on for support through the toughest of circumstances.

Protecting and defending what belongs to the group including the children is rewarding for the tribe as well as for you. The survival instinct of orange embraces protection and a willingness to defend because without it all would have been lost. At a personal level, defending the helpless and protecting what is rightfully yours, has led to security and social esteem. You no longer have to be the best trader, farmer or shepherd to stay in the tribe because you are now a warrior and that makes others need you.

Your survival instinct is now the survival instinct of the warrior and to the warrior loyalty is everything. It was loyalty that saved your village and it was loyalty that saved your life. Under pressure some of the others ran away and that is the same as condemning those who stayed to death.

In the heat of battle the warrior relies on the fact that others are watching out for them. Soldiers who run leave those who stay in an extremely vulnerable position. As the warrior you gave your loyalty and you were given loyalty in return. Reward for action imprints response into the survival instinct. The survival instinct of the warrior regards loyalty as its most valuable commodity. The deserters who ran were either expelled or looked down on, proving and etching even deeper into the survival instinct of the warrior, that disloyalty is something dangerous and intolerable.

To the warrior someone who cannot be trusted or relied on is someone not worth having around. This can cause difficulty for loyalty orange today whose instincts still demand the same undivided devotion and faithfulness as the historic warrior. Their excessive demand for loyalty places a heavy expectation on those who share their life with orange. Warriors have a code; never leave your partner and always do whatever is necessary to get the job done. The end justifies the means. Tie up all loose ends and never be caught unprepared. For modern day orange, these warrior expectations can be isolating because they forget that six sevenths of the world do not have warrior instincts and do not share these values.

Loyalty is something that must be proved. It cannot remain in the spoken word or as theory, so when loyalty orange is out of balance, many will force partners and friends into situations that make them prove their weapon. Like the stereotypical Jewish mother in the send up, this type of orange person will remind you of what they have done for you. Emphasising how much their effort took out of them or the endurance that was needed to accomplish a task. Crisis orange stays in the moment, never letting the memory go. While the satirical send up is amusing, this type of behaviour can have emotionally devastating consequences for those who must live with it.

Why do orange need to remind themselves and others of the suffering and pain they have endured? Simply because the warrior is not at war very often; when a warrior is not in battle their traditional role may be forgotten. The warrior is not the best craftsman, priest, farmer or trader – they are the best warrior, but without a battle they are either second best or unemployed. For the village woman in the story to stay a legend rather than just another mouth to feed, she must constantly remind those around her of her past achievements and sacrifice. People have very short memories once a critical moment is over.

How many times will an invading tribe attack your group in the future? Maybe there will be more attacks, but maybe there won't. Even if there are more attacks it could be years before the next one, so what does the warrior do in the meantime and how do they stay important?

Thankfully, battles are few and far between, but this causes real difficulty for crisis orange. Their survival instinct has to remind others of how much they owe to the warrior's efforts and of the sacrifices made by the warrior on their behalf. This instinctive tendency can have negative consequences. It is the role of the survival instinct to make us indispensable.

## Guilt

Remembering suffering serves a two-fold purpose. Firstly it highlights to others the importance of keeping the warrior around by emphasising their value. Secondly, highlighting suffering creates a sense of guilt in the conscience of others which can be useful if anyone is thinking about expelling them during a famine.

The negative consequence of staying in or constantly remembering the past is the pain for the orange person themselves. Orange does not want to loyalty. Loyalty orange when out of balance wants to test those around them, to find out whether they are truly worthy, or whether they are all talk. And the best test of loyalty and reliability is crisis.

## Crisis

Loyalty orange measures the loyalty and commitment of those around them by creating circumstances of high emotion. Making mountains out of mole hills and divorce out of disagreement, an out of balance orange person is constantly testing the trustworthiness and dependability of their partner or friends. The more out of balance the orange person, the more hysterical and emotionally devastating each event becomes. Ultimately this behaviour will reach a point where even the slightest disturbance is met with a barrage of anger, tears and upset. Loyalty orange does not have minor upsets, they have calamities. They expect the full and total support of those around them, otherwise they will feel bitterly let down.

Crisis works well for the orange survival instinct, even though it does not work well for the orange soul. The warrior is at home with crisis because they have the competitive energy suited to the role. To the warrior, crisis serves a two fold purpose. Firstly it makes them important. After the battle the woman was no longer 'just another woman', she was a heroine – a warrior. To the orange survival instinct crisis is important because it is the warrior's chance to shine. In crisis, orange becomes important again. The second way crisis benefits orange, is as a test of loyalty and commitment.

## Memory of pain

There is a send up many Jewish comedians make of their stereotypical mothers: 'What do you mean you want to go out with friends? What kind of child leaves their own mother alone and defenceless in the city? Is this what it's come to? All the pain I endured giving birth to you is all for nothing? I don't know what I have done for you to hate me so much. Go on, go out with your friends, go out and run with the pack if that's all your good for. Go and be happy at my expense and don't give another thought to my suffering and loneliness.'

Remembrance is vital to the warrior and this type of orange will not hesitate to use the memory of pain or crisis as a strong and persuasive live in the pain of the past anymore than anyone else. They, like everybody else, prefer to move away from what is causing pain but if the orange survival instinct is out of balance, it must emphasize to others the suffering it has endured.

The result of this memory for hardship is a person who remains locked in the painful experience, unable to break free no matter how hard they try. Orange is desperate to laugh and enjoy life and their soul cries out to connect to others as friends, rather than as sounding boards for their pain. They long to go out and see a movie, enjoy a wine and to talk about nothing in particular rather than reminisce about the past. But an out of balance survival instinct does not allow this; it does what it believes is in your best interests.

Out of balance, either the message to say that danger has passed is not being sent, or the message is being sent but it is not being received. The person reacts as if danger is still present regardless of whether this is true or not.

## Depth of suffering

Suffering hits orange hard, and while the causes may vary, the suffering is always deep. Orange can grieve for a loved one who has died, or for an unrequited love for years. Grieving orange will suffer and mourn as if the experience occurred yesterday and it can take others by surprise when they learn that their tears are over an event that occurred a long time ago. Time does not diminish the pain of the event for grieving orange. It can be difficult for others to understand how they can still be so totally enveloped in the pain of many years before.

All of us experience death and most people experience emotional break up and hardship. Regardless of our colour we all suffer with grief and loss at some point. Most of us over time distance ourselves from these painful experiences so we can continue to function. We do our best to put painful times behind us because we do not want pain to be the centre of our lives.

Not all orange people dwell on past painful memories but for those who do life can be an endless blend of one aching day after another. Dwelling-on-the-past orange demands that others recognise their suffering, but those around them will eventually turn away, finding the focus on painful times a continuous ordeal. As their closest friends move away from them, orange feels betrayed by their disloyalty.

Trauma throws the survival instinct into a state of tension but for the warrior, trauma means recognition so they stay in the moment as long as possible. Loyalty and commitment are the warrior's code and orange feel disdain for anyone who does not share these traits. Others cannot give such loyalty. It is not their natural state to dwell in pain and eventually they will remove themselves from their relationship with the orange person. This reminds loyalty orange that the world is indeed a two-tiered existence, the loyal remaining and the disloyal leaving.

## Blame

Guilt and blame are techniques that people from all colour groups use to their advantage but it is orange who has turned these behaviours into an art form. It is the weapon of guilt that orange uses more often and more effectively than most.

Blame is a common human trait because it is the outcome of the struggle between the survival instinct and the soul. Blame is what we do when we are doing the wrong thing but have every intention of doing it anyway. Laying blame is how we have our cake and eat it too. It is an excuse to do what we want while making another person take responsibility for our actions.

The internal state of yellow versus red creates a two-tiered view of the world. Out of balance this two-tiered approach means life and death, black and white as well as right and wrong. When wrong decisions are made or wrong actions taken, out of balance orange needs someone to be wrong for them to be right. In a stressed state 'and' replaces 'or' turning right and wrong into right or wrong, meaning someone else is to blame.

## Righteousness

The essence of orange is represented in the art of chivalry – the knight in shining armour who is courteous and well mannered, prepared to defend the righteous, the underdog and to stand up and fight for a due and just cause. They are a David willing to challenge any Goliath provided the motive is righteous. The focus may be a corporation or an influential person, or somebody who has done them wrong or who is not up to scratch and not pulling their weight. Whatever the reason, orange embroil themselves into the philosophy, ethics and fight for 'righteousness'. They are a constant thorn in the side of anyone hoping to have an easy ride and escape unnoticed from any wrongdoing. Orange of course decide what is right and what is wrong.

Like the knights of old, righteous orange is a fight looking for a cause. The force inside them makes orange view life as right or wrong. Individuals or businesses are either acting honourably or not and if not then righteous orange will make them accountable.

Over time many orange people soften and begin to see areas of grey but for some life remains a clear cut choice of one way or the other. In balance orange relax with the moral principles of right *and* wrong and become more forgiving of the actions of others and their differing points of view.

Seeing life in black or white makes this type of orange someone who is firm, strong and committed to doing the right and honourable thing. However it can also make them a person who is too holy and self-righteous for others to relate to, much less confide in. Righteous orange is easily disillusioned by the actions of others because they are trying hard to uphold the principles of honour and decency. To them these principles should be the first and natural choice for others to choose in times of trouble and confusion.

If orange is flexible, their combination of good judgment based on firm and fixed principles of what is right and what is wrong, together with their ability to understand and relate to the suffering of others, makes them an ideal person to go to for advice and help. However if orange does not have this attribute, their manner may be too bombastic or severe for other people to warm to or trust. Their advice may be sound, but their cut and dried delivery can make orange too blunt and too dominating to connect with. Their black or white, right or wrong base is too judgmental and limiting for others to confide in, and as a result righteous orange can feel unappreciated and hard done by. They want to help but their offers keep being rejected. From the other person's point of view, out of balance orange advice is more like a directive than a recommendation.

It is 1190 AD and you are a knight of the realm. Medieval England represents all that is holy and good – at least on the surface. You are a member of an elite class born into a privileged family, one of the few of the noble warriors. Most soldiers are conscripts, people who work at their trade and are only called upon by the king for war if the need arises. Shoeing horses one week and conscripted to fight in the front line the next with a minimum of training. It is a requirement that all men of a certain age undergo some kind of military training or service and they must agree to serve for a period of forty days in the king's army should they be required to. But you are already a knight, a full-time warrior. You train constantly and you are clothed and fed by the people who you serve, all paid for by taxes.

The life of a knight from birth is to live and serve with honour. You have sworn to be a servant of your baron, your king and God, and it is a pledge you take seriously.

Three months ago you said farewell to family and friends and soon will be arriving at the Holy Land to rescue it from non-Christian hands. From the Arabs' perspective your army is both invader and intruder and you have no right to call a place you have never even seen yours, but through your eyes you are a warrior of God on a sacred and holy mission. You have trained all your life to be this warrior. You have prayed earnestly to be allowed to give yourself to a just cause and now the time to fight for that ideal has arrived.

Close to the shore you leave the ship, not by the gangway but by jumping overboard. The water is deeper than it looks and because of this you nearly meet your end before you even begin. The water you jumped into is over your head. Not only can't you swim but the chain mail armour you are wearing is so heavy it has made you sink like a stone. Luckily one of your companions is there to grab you and pull you to shore.

Gasping and eternally grateful you glance at your friend but he looks back at you sternly. Rather than asking if you are alright he berates you in front of the other men so severely that your gratitude turns to anger. Your humiliation is heavier than the armour on your back, then you realise it was because he was frightened. Fear turns quickly into anger and is often released as an explosion, but you are grateful to be alive so you hold your tongue and let him have his say.

On the shore all the knights gather into groups and are led toward the town. As you near the town you hear a thunderous roar but it is a difficult sound to comprehend because you have never heard it before. It is a sound you will never forget. It is the sound of war.

Arriving at the town's outskirts, the siege is well underway as heavy equipment and rocks crash into the town's walls. Battering rams, catapults, arrows and fireballs all fly beyond the barricades and into the town's centre. The only sounds louder than the thunder of the siege machines are the screams of the people being injured on the inside.

With a thunder as loud as an earthquake, the walls of the town can stand the onslaught no more and sections crumble to the ground. This is the moment you have trained for. You draw your sword and raise your shield as the commander of your group, your lord and baron, gives the order to prepare for attack. The archers step back and make way for the knights.

On horse back, you are ready to charge. The commander raises his flag, and lowering your visor the outside world condenses into a narrow window. The flag is dropped and the charge begins.

Jumping the barricade of rubble and rock you ride into the wailing, smoke and the screams. Swords clash and arrows fly as you hack and slice your way through the crowd. Unsure of the difference between civilian and soldier because you are unfamiliar with the custom of dress, you swipe your sword at everyone within reach severing heads and limbs.

Hour after hour your endurance is tested but by the end of the day, although exhausted, you are still alive. Dismounting, you turn and make your way on foot to the raging battle taking place behind you, and once again begin to swing and slash your sword. Many times you wish you could stop. Your arms ache to such an extent that you can barely raise your sword, and you are not sure you can take the bone shattering jar of an axe striking your shield even one more time. Never in your whole life have you been so exhausted. This is fatigue that seems unendurable, beyond exhaustion and yet still you continue.

Hand to hand fighting is the most frightening and vicious form of combat. Currently you are engaged in a struggle with a warrior just as tired and just as bloodied as you. Every strike he makes, you must block and counter then strike back at him.

Now, so exhausted that you are both virtually leaning on each other to keep yourselves upright, the Saracen you are fighting drops to the ground unable to continue and struggling to breathe. On his knees he looks up at you and for a moment you feel pity, he is beaten and he knows it. If you were anywhere else but in full view of your fellow knights, you might let him survive. But you cannot do that because you are under explicit instructions, there will be no prisoners.

Regretfully you raise your sword and turn your head so as not to look into his eyes, then exhaling a breath you strike and take off his head.

## Endurance

Life is full of unpleasant duties but they are necessities that must be accomplished. The survival instinct of the warrior is unlike any other, for it relies on impossible endurance. Every traditional role has its hardships but the warrior walks a particularly difficult path. The hand to hand fight with the Saracen soldier is an example of the memory that resides within the survival instinct of orange.

Orange can have enormous reserves of energy. They can also have a relentless drive to put this vigour to use. Many orange people describe themselves as workaholics, restless and always on the go. High energy levels make endurance orange a person who enjoys throwing themselves into projects and difficult tasks. Endurance orange enjoys being challenged

This type of orange person often attaches themselves to people who need looking after. They enjoy at least at first, the idea of being needed, important and skilled by comparison. Later in their relationship when hard times arise, the novelty of being indispensable wears off. Then endurance orange can begin to feel exploited rather than essential.

Endurance orange needs to expend large quantities of energy. When they are stressed there is nothing better for them than to exert themselves in an energetic activity such as running, swimming or surfing. This is a legacy that comes from the endurance required by the warrior to see the battle through. The more stress endurance orange is under, the greater their need for physical exertion as a release from the pressures of the moment.

When the Saracen soldier fell to his knees, his life was over and the warrior's survival instinct absorbed the experience as well as the reaction. What the orange survival instinct absorbed was the knowledge that to give up is to die. Only by pushing through to the bitter end is life guaranteed to continue.

Endurance orange strives hard to accomplish their goals, and when in balance it seems like nothing can stand in their way. Out of balance endurance orange can become an overwhelming personality that is difficult to be around.

Everyone projects their values on to the people and circumstances around them. We judge others by how closely they meet these expectations. Expectations are based in the experiences instilled by the survival instinct.

## Core values

The beliefs that the survival instinct holds as truth, are based on past experience. These truths manifest as core values. Orange people assess others by the criteria of loyalty and commitment. These are traits the warrior relied on because they continually proved their worth. These qualities are valued highly by orange and anyone who has them is well regarded. Conversely, anyone who does not have these core values is poorly regarded and respect for this person is low. Everyone sees life differently and we all have separate values based on the diverse experiences of the past. The farmer has a different set of core values to the warrior because their survival depended on different traits.

The material universe is governed by the law of opposites and this can make relationships difficult. The law of opposites is like a proton attracting an electron, a quiet person attracting a lively person or an ambitious person attracting someone laid back. This is a law that regulates matter as well as the survival instinct. The soul is not bound to material substance so it is exempt from the law of opposites. The more the survival instinct is dominant, the more we attract opposite personalities and the greater the chances of a person, opposite in nature and character to ourselves, being attracted to us and us toward them.

When times are good and both partners are in balance, opposites add diversity and growth but when partners are stressed, being opposite means speaking different languages and desiring different contributions of character.

## Rescue

Orange is drawn to people who need their help because the survival instinct of the warrior survives by defending others. Like the medieval knight, orange look for a damsel in distress in need of a rescuer. However it is important to point out that the knight does not have to be male. Many orange females fall into this category by instinctively searching out a partner who needs rescuing, in the hope that the rescued in return will be eternally appreciative.

Gratitude is the currency of orange, because it is what the warrior relies on to maintain their importance when battles are not being fought. This makes the orange survival instinct, when out of balance, driven to find someone grateful for their efforts. Obviously someone who is confident and self-secure is not in need of saving, so the orange survival instinct attracts towards them those who are vulnerable. Beyond conscious interpretation because it is not a conscious action, orange are drawn toward people who need them because they are looking for appreciation and someone who will look up to them. Confident and highly skilled people do not need anybody to assist them, so orange attracts and is attracted to, the helpless and the needy and this is where their long-term relationship troubles can begin.

In search of gratitude, orange are attracted towards those who cannot help themselves. However those who cannot help themselves are also people who often do not have the qualities of endurance, sacrifice and perseverance; the very attributes the warrior values so highly. Without these qualities rescuing orange condemns themselves to romantic disappointment.

Of course this only occurs when orange is out of balance, otherwise they would not need to satisfy their survival instinct. It is also important to point out that despite the desire to blame the partner for their inabilities, it was orange who chose their partner.

Most orange people however choose and make good partners because they are committed and willing to take the good times with the bad. Having a survival instinct that is used to trials and tribulations also has its positive side, and when it comes to relationships, fortitude is seen in the endurance and loyalty that orange have.

With many relationships tough times can mean the end but rescue orange is different. Their survival instinct is ready for hardship and as a consequence can endure what many others cannot. This makes their relationships strong and enduring especially when tensions ease. This strength of character finally helps orange achieve what their survival instinct has craved for so long – gratitude. Except this time it is all for the right reasons and so the response is genuine rather than strained by guilt.

## Martyrdom

In balance orange know the difference between loyalty and suffering, out of balance they do not. Willing to put up with anything to satisfy their survival instinct's need for suffering, out of balance orange can become a dutiful and selfless martyr, running the risk of being abused and disregarded.

'War is hell' and the warrior knows only too well the pain that is involved. It is etched into their survival instinct. If this type of orange person is out of balance for too long, suffering becomes an unbreakable addiction because pain and hardship together with endurance is the orange survival instinct's strength.

When they are in balance, orange does not confuse love with suffering. The trouble with an out of balance survival instinct is that its drive can be so strong that our whole being is disturbed until the angry beast is pacified. Once the survival instinct is calmed the feeling of release can be so enjoyable it can be mistaken for love. Needing to be needed, the orange survival instinct searches desperately for someone they can serve. When they find this individual, the sense of elation from the survival instinct when it believes it is safe and has purpose can easily be misinterpreted. Believing it to be love, orange is prepared to do anything to regain that feeling of elation and release by making themselves irreplaceable.

When an agitated survival instinct is finally secure, the release is intense but if orange misinterpret this release as love, they may find themselves in a position where the relationship will fall apart, if their partner becomes balanced but they do not. The orange martyr chose someone needy who has now gained strength and confidence thanks to their support. If orange is still out of balance after their partner becomes strong, they can feel distressed and agitated because their survival instinct believes there is no-one who needs them. If the soul of the orange person also is in balance, they are happy their partner is independent and their relationship gains in love and strength.

The out of balance martyr gravitates toward the philosophy that regardless of what happens or what is done to me, my reaction and feeling towards you will remain the same. But this is a philosophy of sacrifice and martyrdom and always means trouble.

Unconditional arrangements bring out the worst in us because it is the nature of the survival instinct to take advantage of others. We are part soul and part human animal and nothing brings the animal side of our nature out more easily than another person's weakness.

It is now eighteenth century Japan and you are a samurai. Feudal Japan is where the warrior has reached their peak both in skill and technique. You belong to your lord just like the warrior in the crusades but this time there is no religion involved. You do not fight because God wants you to; you fight because it is noble and because it is the way of the warrior, nothing more. To be a warrior is to live with honour and individual life has no higher purpose.

Your role is to protect your lord. You are not a mercenary like those bandit assassins, the Ninja. You have principles and you have been rewarded with position and status because of them. Ninja are for hire. They might be highly skilled, but they fight for money so they are ignoble and ugly. Other warlords employ them as assassins to kill any opposition, so your lord is in danger because he is popular and powerful.

There are rumours that an assassination attempt is going to happen soon so everyone is ready and vigilant. Tonight you are relaxing while the other guards patrol the village. You are in charge of all the lord's samurai and you have left nothing to chance. You have doubled the guard because it is a dark night and the moon does not come up until late. This means assassins have a better chance to sneak around unnoticed. Monkeys have been tied to posts as alarms against intruders and samurai dressed in your lord's clothing are in each building as a diversion.

You make your last check before retiring and go through the usual preparatory routine. You will not be able to sleep tonight and you know it. Your wife and children are in another room and they too are under guard – just in case.

Missing them and wanting to kiss them goodnight you tip toe to their room and slide the bedroom door open as quietly as possible. Finally, when your eyes have adjusted to the darkness, you take in what is happening and see that an assassin is about to attack them. Quickly you draw your blade and scream at the top of your voice. Startled the assassin turns to face you and your wife and child wake up and also begin to scream.

Just as you are about to strike, you feel a cord around your neck and you are pulled backwards – there are two of them. One of your own rushes to your aid, alerted by the noise, but is cut down as soon as they enter. Part of the roof opens and a rope falls down as another assassin comes into the room. The palace is crawling with Ninja.

Drawing a small blade from a hidden pocket you stab the man choking you in the groin. Screaming in unendurable agony he releases his grip and you throw the blade into the face of the other attacker who is rushing toward you. As the assassin sliding down the rope turns to face you, you swipe with your sword and now he is dead.

Racing to the porch after telling your family to stay where they are, you ring the alarm bell frantically and samurai come from everywhere. Torches are lit, screaming monkeys run every which way, while soldiers and civilians alike rush around creating as much confusion as possible by yelling and setting off fireworks. Totally confused, the remaining assassins search wildly for their target but everyone is dressed in the same clothing, making one person indistinguishable from the other.

Completely panicked the assassins rush about without thinking and this makes them easy targets. One by one the murderers are cut and slashed until they have either escaped or they are dead.

The group that was hired is well known and they are organised and generally highly efficient, but this time it has ended in total disaster for them because you had organised the defence campaign well.

Your samurai were outnumbered and the element of surprise was on the side of the assassins. Everything was in their favour but still they lost and now the lord you serve has the upper hand. This has occurred because you used the often underplayed trick of *organised chaos*.

Nobody can function properly when they are stressed and confused, and chaos is one of the most effective weapons the warrior has.

## Drama and hysteria

A warrior who is disoriented is a warrior who is dead. It is just a matter of time and the orange survival instinct is well of aware of it. Under stress it is not unusual for an orange person to instinctively return to this confusion and chaos as a way of gaining the upper hand. When out of balance, orange can walk into a perfectly sedate room and within minutes leave it in total disarray with everyone arguing, and nobody really sure of how or why it occurred.

When orange is stressed or anxious everyone around them knows about it and is disturbed and upset. Their survival instinct creates this confusion and disorientation because it is a valuable weapon that rarely ever fails. When they are stressed it is one of the first things their survival instinct does to gain an advantage.

Others accuse orange of being addicted to drama and of doing anything to make a scene. This type of orange is accused of being hysterical and emotionally demanding, of making mountains out of molehills. Sometimes they are considered aggressive and the type of person who bites the hand that feeds them, which can all be true but it is because their survival instinct believes they are in danger.

> It is 1944 and the world is at war. Your husband is away fighting and you are left alone to fend for your young family. Both your parents as well as your parents-in-law have all been killed by the fearsome air raids that occur each night. Some nights the city looks like hell itself as it burns endlessly and furiously.

> This is not like the romantic tales you were told of as a child. In the stories war was away from the city and full of dashing heroes and beautiful maidens waiting for their triumphant return. This war is vile. There is no honour in this war, only suffering and tears. The real truth is that all wars are vile and the fairytales of the knights and the maidens are exactly that, fairytales. Lines have become blurred

between good and evil, and all you want is for the war to be over regardless of who wins, but you cannot say that because that is unpatriotic and you can be arrested for seditious talk.

'Loose lips sink ships' and spies are everywhere. Your job is to keep the home fires burning and to smile and pretend that nothing out of the ordinary is happening. At home there is no display of anguish and you are not allowed to miss your husband or fret. In fact you are expected to act as if there is no war, just carrying on as if nothing is happening, smiling as usual.

Everything will be fine and the country is in good hands because our leaders are honourable and know exactly what they are doing, at least that is what they say. Propaganda plays such an important part because spirit and morale is everything. At its most basic level it is not guns that win wars, it is the will of the people.

## Denial

Denial is part of the orange survival instinct because morale must remain high. Ignoring the troublesome and pretending things are fine is the only way some orange people can cope when life becomes too difficult to endure. When problems cannot be changed denial orange acts as if nothing is happening. Suffering for this type of orange is not allowed to be expressed and is suppressed as deeply as possible. In this way life fulfils its two-tiered beginnings by creating an outward life and an inward life with one bearing little resemblance to the other. The outward life keeps up appearances, while the inward life crumbles due to lack of attention.

Denial orange deliberately narrows their thinking and refuses to be diverted. They know what must be done to survive and they fully intend to see that it happens. However living in denial means censoring what is said or done, and it limits what others can do while they are in your presence. This makes denial orange domineering and very controlling.

Denial orange will limit discussion and censor thought. They are only prepared to involve themselves in activities and lines of thought that do not challenge existing beliefs. They are people who are just hanging on, and too much shaking will make them fall.

## Wounded

One type of orange is a wounded animal caught in a trap and unable to get loose. Frantically searching for an end to their pain, an animal in a trap must be subdued before being approached even by those wishing to help, otherwise the helper will be attacked.

Under stress, wounded orange behaves in the same manner as the animal caught in the trap. Requiring support and guidance, this type of orange seeks help from professionals and friends but soon becomes disillusioned. Too untrusting to open up, their efforts to find help end badly and achieve nothing more than yet another bitten therapist. In balance orange is communicative and friendly and other people are happy to offer their friendship and support, but to this very out of balance wounded orange, help remains elusive because of their manner.

In this state, orange will confront and challenge the very help they have sought, finding the advice ridiculous or damaging because of the stupid questions being asked. But this is because their survival instinct is dominant. Wounded orange must suppress the past as well as the present if they are to have any hope of a future. They are like a wartime nation singing only patriotic songs and thinking only patriotic thoughts. They must not hear or think about anything that does not contain a glorious future. When a therapist or practitioner dismantles this defence by asking them to think about the past they are trying to forget, the practitioner or therapist must be ready for the counter attack that is heading their way.

> Slowly you make your way home with some meagre groceries that must be dressed up somehow to be presented as a meal. For the children it is yet another night of hot water with some onion and garlic, celery stalks and a few beans with stale bread. For you it is just the bread. Your neighbour looks after your children each day while you work at the munitions factory so you can buy food and help the war effort. As payment she gets to share in the food you have, as well as the offering of a small wage from what you have left over, but she never takes it.

## SOUL & SURVIVAL

Your young daughter is tired and both she and her older brother are bored and moan constantly about their empty, rumbling stomachs. It is cold but there is no fuel for a fire. With dinner over it is time to relax and spend time with your family. Soon the inevitable questions begin about daddy and the war, and your son excitedly begins to tell you how they said at school that the war will soon end in victory for our side. The enemy cannot hold out for much longer they said, because every one of our soldiers is worth ten of theirs.

You're not sure whether you really believe any of this talk. The only thing you do know is that life is hard and you have not heard from your husband for almost a year. The government postman is the most feared person in the country and he is the last person you want to hear from, but not knowing whether he is dead or alive is also killing you.

Your husband is not a soldier and secretly he did not want to go, but life is what it is, and now he is somewhere and you are here, so you cry. Your son comforts you and tells you that daddy will be fine and that the war will soon be over. Your daughter also begins to cry, but she is crying because her mummy is sad.

Exhausted you put them both to bed and collapse onto the mattress on the floor. Your head aches with its now familiar throb from behind your eyes so you rub them for relief before drifting to sleep. Soon you hear a trumpet being played and become confused as to why the musician persists in playing the same single note over and over again. You tell yourself this must be some sort of new music because it seems so strange.

You try to leave because not only is this music unpleasant, it gives you a frightening and sinking feeling that makes you feel trapped and breathless, but you cannot find the door. You begin to beat at the walls with your fists screaming in panic as claustrophobia weighs down on you. You feel like you are under water in a game to see who can hold their breath the longest and you are struggling because you have reached your limit.

Consciousness finally awakens you in panic. You are dreaming, and the trumpet is not music, it's the air raid siren. Quickly you get up and race into the children, gathering the blankets that you had prearranged earlier. Sleepy and rubbing their eyes they are reluctant to move and tell you that they don't want to go, but you scoop them up and shake them into wakefulness because you need help to carrying everything.

Last night it was the east end of the city that bore the brunt of the bombs so who knows where it will be tonight. The night is clear which is why the sirens are sounding without the sound of bombs, they have spotted the planes early.

As you gather what you need the thunder of the anti-aircraft guns begin and adrenalin surges as your fear grows. Without warning you are knocked off your feet as the left wall of the house is blown in by a massive explosion. You rise to your feet but you feel strange and everything is muffled as if you have cotton wool jammed into your ears. You know where you are and what is happening but you have no fear. It's as if you are a spectator to the event rather than a participant.

The blast has sent you into shock and you watch with indifferent detachment as a little girl screams and holds her bleeding face. Suddenly you remember that this is your daughter, and by a sheer act of will you overcome your disorientation and snatch her up in your arms, then begin to look for your son. You find him unconscious under the rubble and drag him out and throw him over your shoulder.

Holding your daughter's hand you grab the two bags you prepared earlier, make your way along what is left of the hall and leave the house. In frenzy you bang on your neighbour's door and shout at her to open it, but the door is locked and no one is answering. You kick at the door with the heel of your foot but it doesn't budge and you drop everything as another bomb explodes and the roof collapses around you. Crawling to your children you find them both alive and breathing although your son is still not conscious. Telling your daughter to stay where she is you put both your hands on the door knob and shake it as hard as you can, in the hope it will open.

Reluctantly you give up and gather your children and bags and run. The city is in agony as it burns and groans and falls and explodes. As you enter the street some people are perplexed because they are dazed with concussion, they cannot see the point of hurrying. Others are immobilised by fear and one woman is in a corner jumping up and down on the spot screaming hysterically and holding her ears. Some are holding their wounds, struggling to move while others are composed. You are one of the composed.

Continuing on you make it into the underground shelter where you sigh and cry and shake and curse. You open one of the bags and pull out some cloth and some iodine and begin to wipe the blood off your daughter's face. She screams in pain and it is then that you understand that there is still glass in her wounds, so you get the tweezers from your medical kit and set to work, stopping constantly to monitor your son who is only now beginning to stir.

In the morning you make your way back to the pile of rubbish that used to be your home. Your neighbour is in there somewhere but there is no hurry now because she could not be alive. She was old and her hearing was not good but she was friendly and kind and you liked her. You shared what you could and welcomed her as family. When you can you will find her possessions and send them to her family who live in the country.

There is no point staying anymore so you take your children and make your way toward the charity house. This was set up about a year ago for the sole purpose of storing and preparing food for those left homeless. You have worked here since it opened and enjoy the sense of contribution. In these times of brutality and savagery, you thought it a noble and charitable act that reminded you of being human. Luckily the charity house has escaped the bombing and the people there are happy to share what they have with you.

Settling your children by giving them food, pencils and paper, you join the other volunteers dispensing food and dressing wounds. This is an act of kindness and the compassion you have for the suffering of others is obvious but you are also doing it for yourself.

To have nothing to do in times of crisis just adds to the torture. In times of stress the warrior is compelled by their survival instinct to do something active because a warrior who is stationary is a warrior about to be killed. The survival instinct of orange makes them spring into action during times of stress and chaos because crisis is familiar. What is foreign is not doing anything and this above all things makes orange agitated and restless.

Many orange people have a natural instinct for composure in a crisis. It is true that orange when out of balance can create chaos as a way of taking charge by unsettling their enemy, but it is just as true that they can be very calm and cool in chaotic circumstances that are not of their own making. The warrior creates pandemonium when there is none, because their survival instinct needs it, but when chaos already exists they are calm because they are at home with it.

Orange has the ability to be practical during stress, a trait that is perfect for the warrior but not so good for contemporary orange, because it can make them seem emotionless and clinical. Some can even interpret this behaviour as blunt, cold and hard.

The recent air raids have killed people by the thousands, perhaps even tens of thousands, but you and your children are alive. In the street while the bombing was taking place people were bewildered, dazed, panic stricken and hysterical, but you were composed. Apart from a momentary lapse when the first bomb exploded and knocked you off your feet, you remained in control of your senses and this enabled you to successfully escort your family to safety.

Due to a breakdown in services, hygiene and medical care is absent and even bandages are difficult to obtain. As a result many of the injured developed septic conditions in their wounds as well as the constitutional fevers and ill-health that result from it. When you reached the safety of the shelter you opened your medical kit and dressed and treated your daughter's injuries. Her wounds will not turn septic because you had planned and catered for this moment. At the front door of your home two bags had been packed months in advance. One contained spare clothing and blankets, as well as soap and some amusements for the children, along with some basic food. The other contained torn linen to use as bandages as well as scissors, tweezers and iodine.

There is a saying that battles are won or lost on the drawing board before the battle even takes place. How well prepared one side is compared to the other, is the difference between victory and defeat. If an army does not prepare and supply their lines, that army will lose. At the same time the warrior is also aware that once the battle begins, anything is possible, so while they are meticulous, they are also responsive to change.

Intense planning has saved the warrior countless times and the need to be calculating and meticulous is something the orange survival instinct still carries. What it also harbours is a strong sense of charity and community spirit.

War is expensive and often it takes every available resource to win. The warrior has all the repercussions of battle in their unconscious survival instinct. The fight is only one aspect. There is also the preparation, immediate rallying and response, building and manufacturing, together with intense and constant training. But there is also another side to war and that is the human side.

The human consequences are just as etched into the orange survival instinct as the battle itself, because they are consistent and inevitable outcomes. The warrior has every aspect of warfare burned into their survival instinct because they are the repeating patterns of their traditional role.

The consequences, results and outcomes of war include death, suspicion, pacifism, charity, generosity and bravery. For every negative there is a positive. Paranoia is offset by commitment while emotional frenzy is mixed with extraordinary courage. For many, courage meant facing overwhelming odds and standing up for what is honourable. Sometimes it meant risking your life for nothing more than the ineffable reason that it was the right thing to do. This is the good side of the internal competition between yellow and red. Black and white make right or wrong and in the orange mind a person can only be one or the other. They are highly moral when in balance but self-righteous when out of balance.

Caring for the sick and injured together with the rebuilding of morale, homes and lives resides in the survival instinct of orange. Orange is driven by a need to contribute above and beyond the call of duty. Instead of a fighting army they are the Peace Corps and Salvation Army rolled into one.

Suffering is not only part of the warrior's experience; help for those who are suffering is part of it also. The warrior is not an attacker as much as they are a defender. The warrior's role is about defending life, liberty and property. It is about stopping and defending the helpless against the exploitation and aggressive acts of others. In this way the warrior's reputation and esteem is respected as valuable and worthy amongst the whole community, and they become admired and rewarded members of the group. With this comes all the fringe benefits such as partner, children, friends and comfort.

The warrior defends the helpless and protects the land and lifestyle of the people who support them but they also care for the sick and under-privileged. The knights of the Middle Ages with all their courtly romance, chivalry and dedication to the common folk are a perfect symbolic representation of the ethical drive of the survival instinct in orange. Castles were not only filled with knights ready to fight for king and country, many were filled with knights trying to be holy and ready to defend concepts more noble and heavenly than earthly possessions. Soldiers of God were commonplace and earned their salvation by good works and deeds to the sick and unfortunate. The templar's and the knights of St John are two examples of this orange ideal.

Out of balance, the warrior's drive to seek out the dispossessed and unfortunate, can lead orange into romantically linking themselves to lost causes or committing themselves to hard work. But it can also provide a tireless worker for the family or community. The warrior's ethic to do what they can and then a bit more, makes them indispensable workers and highly sought after by employers. Orange consistently do more than their job description requires. However they must also be careful not to leave themselves open to exploitation.

Like all traditional roles the warrior is vital to the development of the community. Some may question the need to have the warrior as part of our social structure. After all, if nobody stole there would be no need for the warrior, but this is fantasy, not history. The resources of the earth are not evenly distributed. Regions vary in their fertility and in the ease with which life can be lived within them. The idealistic fantasy of everybody living in harmony and sharing what they have, may be a dream to the soul, but it is a nightmare to a survival instinct compelled to acquire more than what is needed. History is full of incidents that prove that individuals as well as whole countries undergo extensive periods of stress, and that makes the warrior necessary.

Orange defends the rights of those who cannot defend themselves. Whether a parent, a partner, an employer or a friend, in balance orange approaches life and relationships with a sense of equality and justice for all.

## Facial features

Orange features are a combination of equal or near equal amounts of yellow and red. One colour group, either the yellow or the red, can have *one* more facial feature than the other but that is all. Anymore and the face would no longer be orange. Blue must be at least two or more facial features *less* than the dominant colour group, otherwise the person will be brown. Only one extra facial feature is allowed between yellow and red.

## Chapter 17

# PURPLE - INWARD AND CIRCULAR MOTION – SPACE

*Separation*
*Duality*
*Drugs*
*Royalty and religion*
*Expectation and responsibility*
*Suspicion*
*Assurance and faith*
*The Church*
*Religion*
*Medicine and magic*
*Paranoid*
*Purity*
*Nothingness*
*Refuge and shame*
*Separated*
*Internal division*
*Intuition*
*Haughty*

*Spirituality and sprits*
*Ungrounded*
*Art and music*
*After death*
*Peace and insight*
*The divine*
*The supernatural*
*Angel and devil*
*Self-importance and devotion*
*Expecting to receive*
*Power*
*Attention*
*Charisma*
*Sickness*
*Jealousy*
*Sex and fidelity*
*Morality and judgment*
*The confessional*
*Charity and benevolence*

Purple is the existence of both circular motion (red) and inward motion (blue). Inward motion pulls weaker forces into its centre to absorb and grow. Circular motion is fixed and its role is to join together weaker forces. Circular motion co-habits the purple body but is immune to the pull and absorption of blue because it is *equal* in strength. At the same time blue inward motion is too strong to be captured by red. This creates a distinct separation between the two forces. This emptiness, nothingness or space is unique and purple is the only colour group where two dominant forces never meet. As a result, their primal drive stems from a *lack* of contact.

## Separation

The nature of circular and inward motion causes a separation and division between the two forces. Purple is founded on a *lack of* interaction and not *because of* an interaction.

Blue is at one end and red at the other, the space in between is the essence of purple. It is the place they return to when their survival instinct is under stress. Because separateness and nothingness is due to the forces inside them, it is nothingness that purple returns to when their survival instinct becomes dominant due to danger or exhaustion.

If purple becomes overwhelmingly stressed, links with the material world begin to weaken as their survival instinct returns to the safety of the nothingness it calls home. However this separation from the material world can also cause enormous concern and fear, which in some cases serves to separate them even further.

Separation can mean removal of the stress but it can also mean separation from others, or separation from themselves. In some cases separation means pretending the problem does not exist, while at other times it is understanding the problem is there, but refusing to do anything about it. If stress is great, purple can separate themself from life by spending time alone hiding in their house or bed. They can also separate from themselves by detaching from their physical body and moving into the astral world, or just shutting down into a catatonic nothingness. Both are extreme responses and generally do not form a part of the everyday life of purple. However, if stress is extreme, it is a common purple response.

The problem with dissociation is that the survival instinct is our link to the physical world. Our soul is non-material and does not need matter to function. The survival instinct is what joins us to our body and earthly life. When it ceases, our bond with the physical world is severed. Individuals, who experience this break even momentarily, feel disconnected, strange, dreamlike and ethereal. Jesus fasted for forty days in the desert while Buddha sat in a state of meditation without food or water. During this time both faced their demons and both received enlightenment and grace. This does not imply that either Buddha or Jesus were purple, just that they pushed their physical body into an extreme state. When the bonds with matter break, the ethereal is all that is left and it is this state that purple returns to in times of extreme stress.

The ability of the survival instinct to disconnect from the external world in order to remain focused on its internal needs is natural to everyone, but for purple this can cause problems. For them the disconnection is easy and complete. Natural withdrawal from the external world generally only occurs due to necessity or sleep, but purple also has a natural disconnection due to the emptiness and space caused by their internal forces. This combination means that for some, the desire to go into nothingness can occur far too easily and out of proportion to the stress they experience.

Under intense conditions such as violence, sexual abuse or loss, the purple survival instinct returns to the refuge of space and nothingness. In its need to escape stress, the survival instinct creates the desire for any substance or activity that will help it achieve the state it is searching for.

Drug taking, comatose sleep, sleeping pills, collapse, fainting, dreamlike states, mental confusion, disorientation, astral travel, possession by spirits, out of body experiences and visions both good and evil, are all part of the purple experience under stress. Like every colour group purple must exercise restraint and strengthen their willpower, otherwise they will spend more time out of this world than in it.

## Duality

The space between red and blue means purple often live in two distinctly separate worlds. For many people the contrast would be too great, but for purple there is naturalness to separation so they can cope quite easily. Being one thing as well as another is not a problem for purple and many exist as two people in the one body. Orange see the world in an 'either or' way. This means orange is either 'this *or* that', but purple is an 'and' person and sees no difficulty being both 'this *and* that'. Sometimes duality is contrary rather than complementary but somehow purple manages. An orange person is either in business *or* in art, but purple don't see life this way and have no difficulty being in business *and* in art.

When existence depends on practical contribution, how can 'nothing' be of any benefit? The answer is that 'nothing' gives purple an ethereal link that most other people do not have. Their bond to the supernatural is strong and this bond gives them a decisive and competitive edge.

## Drugs

Drugs, both legal and illegal, are a common way purple calm their survival instinct because drugs, particularly sleep inducers and depressants, create the nothingness their survival instinct demands, even if it is a false nothingness. Unfortunately the drugs themselves can increase stress, as drugs destroy life energy. The more energy that is used, the more the survival instinct needs to return to its primal state. It is nothingness that the survival instinct is craving, not the drug. Drugs are an impermanent and false way of mimicking this primal state and because they are not real, the survival instinct remains stressed and in a permanent state of alarm. Unless a real and constructive way of managing stress – in an acceptable purple manner – is found, the suffering will continue.

Withdrawal into the primal space has both positive and negative consequences. The primal state is the most basic instinctual level a human being can operate in. It is where the survival instinct returns when other coping strategies fail and the greater or more extensive the stress the greater the chance of reverting to this primal point. The primal state is the survival instinct's foetal position; its deepest level where consciousness is almost entirely lost and instinct is all that remains.

For purple, returning to the primal state creates two separate and contrasting emotional responses. The first is the emotional response of comfort and security. This is created because the survival instinct has returned to the safety of home. The second emotional response is the terror that arises from withdrawing from the material world by breaking the bonds of physical existence.

## Royalty and religion

Purple is one of the most difficult colours for human beings to artificially make. Due to its rarity, it has only been worn by royalty and high ranking religious officials, because they were the only people who could afford it. As a result, purple is the colour associated with wealth and position. Purple stands above other colours and is a symbol of prosperity and importance. Regal purple is no ordinary person; they are respected, esteemed, admired and adored.

Today purple is the chosen colour of many new-age and spiritual movements. Spirit guides painted against purple backdrops adorn the walls of new-age festivals, while purple books covered with silver writing tell the buyer of the mysteries and secrets that wait within.

Purple is exclusive and stands alone. It is apart and above everything else. Every colour has a symbolic environmental representation. Every colour that is, except for purple. Yellow is represented by the sun while green is the jungle, red is the desert and brown is the earth, but purple has no earthly equivalent. Only ultra-violet light comes close but even this is a non-material example. This lack of terrestrial embodiment is not surprising considering the space and nothingness of purple's primal state.

Disconnection from the physical world seems odd for a survival instinct designed to keep its host alive. It is just as difficult to understand how 'emptiness and nothing' can be of value to the rest of the group. How can something non-material be of any material use?

Despite this anomaly, purple fulfils one of the most important and most primal of all human desires. Along with orange, purple offers protection and security, not for the body but for the soul.

Religious history is filled with accounts of visions and angelic encounters. Mohammed, Jesus and Buddha all received messages from the world beyond and each communicated with 'higher' beings. These and other prophets bring their revelations back to earth usually in the form of holy law or higher knowledge.

The traditional role of purple is the priest – a counsellor, healer, spiritual advisor and comforter.

Everything in life changes – the seasons, the hunt, even the dynamics within the tribe itself. It was not that long ago that rainfall was good and animals and plants were abundant. Times were easy then because everyone had full bellies and that meant the tribe was content and stable. There were always tiffs and struggles but by and large life was peaceful. Then the land started drying and the animals moved away. The plants did not produce as much fruit and the stream you lived by began to run dry. Soon it became murky and stagnant. The water in those early days was good. It was cool and clear and tasted clean, but then the stream became shallow and the water brown and muddy.

The land has been in drought for a long time and it is tired and thirsty and refuses to nurture any growth. Some years earlier a larger, more savage tribe forced you away and took over the land that used to be yours.

It was hard for everyone to be forced away from what they believed was theirs by right but there was no other choice. At first there was resistance but the men who fought back were killed, while the rest of the group was lucky to escape at all. Everyone thought it was a miracle to find the land the tribe now lives on, because it was both uninhabited and out of view. It was less than what the group had before but better than nothing. The fact that it was isolated was perfect and the tribe thanked the spirits involved with dances and prayers for a whole month.

Where you live now is at the base of a canyon, almost invisible because the land above is flat. Without warning the ground opens up and a large canyon appears. Most of it looks dry but right down the bottom are a number of water holes and caves as well as a small flowing stream. It is as close to perfect as a second home can be. Your friend, the woman who found this place was congratulated and thanked so profusely that her chest nearly exploded with pride; but it was you who found this place and that is a secret you will take to your grave.

Your mother found the tribe's first home all those years ago. She was a shaman, a wise woman who had 'the gift'. Your mother was revered because she could move between worlds and communicate with spirits. She saw visions and made prophesies. She was a holy woman who told the tribe what the gods had in store; she even had bones that could tell the future.

A generation ago the tribe had also been forced to move, again because of bandits and murderers. Lost and wandering, the group suffered terribly because the hunting was poor and water was scarce. Then one night in a dream, your mother was visited by a dead ancestor who told her of a place where the whole group could live in security and comfort. This was a place that had water, plants, birds and animals. Ignoring these images at first she began hearing voices, not just in her dreams, but during the day as well, as if her own thoughts were being controlled by some outside force. The voices were not audible and nobody else could hear them. It was more like a thought from inside her own head, yet at the same time knowing that the thought came from someone else. Soon she began having conversations with her thoughts and started to believe that, even though it was her own mind and voice, it was someone else she was talking to. The voice started teaching her things. It started telling her about abstract concepts such as meaning and death and what happens beyond.

Over time she began to trust the voice implicitly and soon it began to tell her to move the tribe to a new place. She met with the tribal leaders and told them of her visions. Many were sceptical of her at first and some were even hostile, but in the end the tribe had no choice, it had to believe her because it was dying, and some hope is better than no hope. The next day she led the group from their desperation like a mother duck guiding her ducklings.

The journey was arduous and tiring and the further the group walked the more angry and disenchanted it became. Some began to threaten her and to convince others that she was mad. They may not have understood the mechanics of mental illness ten thousand years ago, but they knew it existed and purple intuition runs close to that boundary.

What is the difference between clairvoyance and fantasy, and what is the difference between a vision and a delusion? The difference rests in the accuracy of the outcome. In your mothers case she was told exactly where to go and how to get there. She was told of the perils along the way. She was also given an insight into exactly what the land would look like. When the tribe finally arrived, everything was exactly the way she had been told. Delusions and fantasies never come to pass but visions work out exactly as predicted. There can be no excuses and many have justified delusion as vision. When things do not work out as they should, the seer makes a justification like 'the universe changed its mind' or 'the timing wasn't right', but these are all excuses. God doesn't need excuses. Your mother was right, not once or even twice, but for the whole journey, and the tribe was safe because of her knowledge.

For a time, life went well in the tribe's new homeland and everything turned out just the way your mother had said. Some tried to make her the tribal leader but she did not want that position and knew it would cause friction. She was a woman and that alone would put a few noses out of joint, not the least, the nose of the tribal leader already in power. Secondly she was not a planner; her talent came from her instinct, not her intellect or her experience. As a result she turned the offer down but that did not stop others from seeking her counsel in all manner of problems. The tribal leader may have been in charge of the tribe's direction and delegation but your mother had just as much control and power, and that split in the power base is frequently seen in organised society.

The priest is a traditional role that has had many avenues of expression; the shaman, the wise woman, the witch, the witchdoctor, the medicine man, the monk and the prophet. All belong to the traditional role of the priest.

The priest is the person who drifts between worlds, who relies as much on their intuition as they do on any material talent. They are the person who uses 'the space' and as a result, they are the individuals others turn to when ordinary help is insufficient.

The priest is there to help and to serve. From shaman times to the recent past, the priest has been there to help with problems of the mind, body and spirit. Mental health and demonic possession, cures for physical ailments as well as contact and guidance from the world beyond, are all the realm of the priest.

The relationship between church and state has always been a difficult one and even in modern times many countries grapple to come to terms with who should be in charge of what. In earlier times the problem was no less difficult.

The tribal leader believed that he and he alone should be the one to control the hearts, minds and affairs of the group, but the tribe had different ideas. To them it was just as important to stay on the good side of the gods, because it was they who controlled destiny. To make them angry or upset was an unwise thing to do. The spirits had favoured your mother. They liked her and wanted to protect her, why else would they speak to her the way they did. It was her willingness to involve and guide the rest of the tribe that saved everyone from misery and death. The tribal leader was an important man, he was a great warrior, hunter and leader but he did not have the friendship of the gods and without them all is lost.

No matter how hard he tried, the tribal leader could not shake the devotion the people had towards your mother. They turned to her when they were sick and she gave them herbs and other remedies to help ease the pain. She gave relief and comfort to those who had lost loved ones by contacting the deceased during her dreams. Then on waking, she would tell family members intimate details to confirm that their loved one was alive and safe in the next world. This placed your mother in a protected position, but the tribal chief hated her with the crippling abhorrence that only envy can create.

The tribe was deadlocked in its loyalties and as a consequence each had to tolerate the other. This tightrope of power has played itself out thousands of times over thousands of years. In the Russian revolution churches and monasteries were sacked, looted and left to rot. Monks were expelled and some were killed. The Church lost all its power because the state made religion too dangerous to support. Loyalty cannot be divided and religion separates according to politics. Belief must be put in its place. Now communism is gone and the Church is once again a force to be reckoned with. Whatever the ebbs and flows, the survival instinct absorbs the memory of anything that is threatening. If a threatening or emotional event is repeated enough, especially to a large number, it becomes part of the survival instinct's 'knowledge'. An unconscious memory that is never consciously understood even though it dominates conscious thought.

The purple survival instinct absorbed this valuable lesson and it remains there to this day. This is the lesson of expectation and responsibility.

> During their arduous journey to their new home, some of the tribe became disgruntled. Some were ready to turn on your mother and kill her, but rather than panic, she stood firm. She knew what the voice was telling her and she knew that the future of the tribe depended upon them accepting her information. However that doesn't ease the task because when everyone is turning on you, holding firm is extremely difficult and most people fail. All she had was blind faith. She knew the health and security of the tribe rested upon her shoulders whether they acknowledged that truth or not, and this sense of overwhelming responsibility continues to nag at purple even today.

## Expectation and responsibility

For purple, responsibility is a life theme because of its significance. The purple sense of responsibility can develop at a very early age. Expectation goes hand in hand with responsibility and both form part of the human condition. For many purple people, expectation is a feature they struggle with constantly. In reality they have no more responsibility than anyone else, nor are they actually expected to do any more than anyone else. As always it is the survival instinct that is putting pressure and emphasis on the trait.

Purple can feel this responsibility as a sense of destiny, even if they do not know how or why. They have an innate feeling that others are looking to them to perform or fulfil some task that is required of them. Sometimes it is a sense of responsibility to be a certain type of person or to achieve something grand. At other times responsibility is treated as an evil to be avoided. As soon as any pressure or expectation is placed on to this type of purple they collapse, as if carrying a weight too heavy to bear.

Expectation purple when out of balance cannot manage tasks continuously. They start out with good intentions but the more commitment that is required the less inclined to fulfil the job they become. As soon as a partner, parent, teacher or employer asks for any sort of commitment, expectation purple collapses into a bundle of nerves and aggression, before withdrawing back into the safety of nothingness. They will lock themselves in their room, run to someone or something more frivolous and undemanding. Some will even become physically ill, developing all manner of timely complaints.

This is not a delusion nor is it hypochondria. The physical complaints are real but the cause is mental. Too often there is the accusation, 'It's all in your head'. Just because a complaint does not have an observable organic cause does not mean the consequences are any less for the sufferer. Anxiety can cause heart palpitations, pressure can cause headaches, fear can cause sleeplessness and anger can cause high blood pressure. All of these outcomes are physical but their origins are not.

Purple's sense of expectation, when they are out of balance, creates an acute state of stress and anxiety which burns vast amounts of energy in the form of panic. As a result, signs and symptoms return as predictably as spring follows winter. This type of purple will get diarrhoea, headaches, nausea or dizziness every time the pressure to perform is placed on them.

Others however will thrive in pressure cooker environments because the more difficult a task is to accomplish, the more responsibility and expectation is lived out. The innate feeling that others are looking to them to show them the way, drives expectation purple *toward* the hierarchy of management and responsibility rather than away from it.

## Suspicion
Suspicion is one of the unconscious memories embedded into the purple survival instinct and ranges from general wariness to complete paranoia. To suspicious purple, people are feared and they can never relax around them because their survival instinct is never quite sure what they are going to do next. The cellular memory of the priest is of betrayal and turning loyalties. One minute everyone loves you, the next minute those same people are out for your blood.

Throughout the course of history many have turned to the wise woman, the conjurer, the witchdoctor or priest, to be saved from disease or calamity. Some of these special people completed this task and did so in good faith and belief in what they were doing but many did not. The perspective of the priest differed from those around them because they could see things that others could not. Their concept of reality was unusual and strange and as we are not comfortable with the extraordinary, there is a tendency to distrust and attack anything regarded as out of the normal.

The priest offers a service, not a product. The warrior is the only other traditional role to rely on a service as their offering rather than a product, but the warrior still offers a tangible service. Their role is both worldly and practical, while the priest offers a service that is difficult to measure. If the tribe is on productive land but they are not defended, sooner or later they will be attacked. The role of the warrior is substantial and physical. The role of the priest is intangible and spiritual.

## Assurance and faith
The priest provides some tangible services in the form of medicine and care but some of their contribution is intangible. The world and everything in it changes constantly and change brings uncertainty. The survival instinct hates change and it will fight it wherever it can. The priest offers stability in an otherwise unstable world. Priests, through their links to God and the afterlife, divine the future and pave a way for happiness and prosperity and avoidance of hardship. Taking the unpredictability out of life and replacing it with God's assurance and faith is what each of us desires. The priest exists to help lead the tribe to fertile ground, or to save an individual from making a serious mistake. The priest is called upon to find omens, to make

charms and divine how to make sure the king's army cannot lose. The priest who can perform these tasks successfully will become one of the most important assets a person, tribe or country can have. The priest who is more often wrong than right is soon for the chopping block or the bonfire.

For many purple people, life is a tightrope, a delicate balance between this world and the next. This inner tightrope replicates itself externally – as it must. All life is projection. Separation and the difficulty of making two worlds meet is the burden purple bears. Like every other colour group, the more out of balance they are due to pressure, worry or exhaustion, the more difficult it is to maintain balance.

> Your mother found herself in the difficult position so constantly experienced by the priest. However, she did not heed the warning signs and paid dearly for it. You on the other hand have learned from her mistakes.
>
> After the drought ravaged your previous home, it was your friend who stumbled across the tribe's new home; or so they thought. In truth, it was you who led your friend to the spot where the tribe's new home would be found. Convincing her to come with you on a long foraging expedition, you led her to the right location and sent her down one path while you pretended to look for food on another. At first it seemed as if she would never 'stumble' on to the opening of the canyon, but eventually she found it. Suddenly she screamed as she found herself looking over a rich and fertile land. It was hidden from all around save for one small opening. Once you both arrived home she told her story to the tribal chief. Later around the fire she recounted how she had found what could be the tribe's new home, adding that she had a feeling that something important might be there. The next month the whole group went to investigate and decided that a new home had been found.
>
> You had dreamt of the place months before your friend 'found' it. You had even gone there first to make sure that it was real and found that it was. You debated in your head whether to tell the tribal chief or not

but eventually you decided against it. Not long after the first dream you began to hear voices, as if other people were using your thoughts to talk to you. They told you of the importance of moving the tribe to the new place. They also said the rainfall would continue to get less and less and life would be even harder if you stayed. It was important to go to the canyon because it had a stream. Birds and other wildlife would come to the stream to drink so there would be enough food, water and shelter for everybody.

In your mother's time food was also plentiful and life was good, until thieves came and stole the land. That was the beginning of the hard times and you watched as your mother became the scapegoat for the tribe's misery. Your mother had led the tribe to a fertile place but she had not foreseen the attack. Murmurings began amongst the group, fuelled by the tribal chief and spread by personal pain and hunger. The tribe believed it was being punished, what other explanation could there be? The spirits had favoured them before but now everyone was suffering. It was not long before your mother was held personally accountable for the distress of the tribe. Not because she failed to see the suffering coming but because she must have done something to upset God. Now everyone is paying for her mistake. No one knew what she had done but that she had done something was obvious, otherwise the bad times would not have come. The tribe held a council meeting and decided that the situation must be righted. They must once again find favour with the Gods in order to be blessed. The next morning your mother was murdered, her organs were taken out and burnt as an offer of forgiveness.

This brutal sacrifice didn't change anything; the drought didn't change and the tired land remained just as weary. When you started receiving visions in your dreams it was history repeating itself and you panicked. Once again the burden of responsibility became heavy and you became confused and uncertain of what to do. Responsibility or the avoidance of responsibility once more became etched into the purple survival instinct because of the emotion you had endured.

You did not confide in anyone even though you wanted to do so, not even your husband because you knew he would worry. He was a trembling mess after the murder of your mother and he was terrified that you would be next. As a result you made a personal decision never to let others know that you were experiencing visions or voices. You gained a reputation with your husband and family for being highly intelligent because of the decisions you made. They couldn't tell that intuition played just as big a role as intellect.

You agonised over what you should do. Being a kind and giving person you knew it was not right to make others suffer because of your fear. At the same time you were self-protective and saw what happened to your own mother. There was no way you were going to open yourself up to that kind of attack. As a compromise you led your friend to where she could make her chance discovery.

For months after coming to the new home your nerves were on edge. You could tell the tribal chief was suspicious; the chance find was just a bit too convenient. You were the daughter of your mother, and it was you that 'just happened' to be out walking with your friend on the day that she discovered the opening to the canyon. He could not accuse or say anything because the tribe was content. When people are happy no-one cares about suspicion or anger, it is only when they are demoralised and hungry that they become ripe for exploitation. The tribal chief did not want another power play like he experienced with your mother; he wanted total authority and that made you scared. Your fear was not to last, as his death came the year after the tribe was settled.

Life is full of peaks and valleys and when one of your children became seriously ill you returned to the herbs and chants your mother had taught you. It was an epidemic illness and many of the children in the tribe were dying or going blind. When your son recovered and returned to health more quickly than most, other mothers turned to you for help. Some children were aided while others were not, but people appreciated the help you gave. The group was glad to have you around and rewarded you for your efforts.

## The Church
The role of the priest has always been a delicate blend of material necessity together with spiritual expectation. Too much emphasis on self-sacrifice and self-denial makes spirituality lose its appeal, and only the fanatical remain interested. At the same time, if too much attention is placed on business and materialism, spiritual guidance ceases to be of use.

## Religion
Every society has someone who fulfils the traditional role of the priest. From ancient times to the present, the priest not only formed part of the social structure, but in many cases they controlled it. The modern western world has only recently separated church and state, but politics and business are still cautious in what they say regarding faith. The west may regard itself as secular but the pull of religion is a force that can never be underestimated. People need to believe in something that is strong, wise and protective. Some claim that humans invented God out of our own neurotic need to feel safe, but this perspective does not account for personal experience. Religious and spiritual experiences are divided deliberately into two separate groups because the two experiences are not always interchangeable. However they occur regularly to those who search for meaning, as well as to those who do not.

Too often a spiritual experience is demoted by sceptics as something crazy or inexplicable, but this is hardly an answer. The fact is, too many people have too many spiritual experiences far too often, for the phenomenon to be swept under the carpet with meaningless replies such as 'no they don't', or 'they're all deluded'. These experiences range from clairvoyant dreams to intuition and feelings that turn out to be accurate. Inner voices that tell an answer or hearing someone calling your name, knowing someone has died before you have been told, or thinking about someone you have not seen for years only to find that they ring you the next day. There are very few people who have not experienced, even if only once, a phenomenon of this type. Even if every second person has experienced something 'mysterious' once in their life, it still means over three billion spiritual experiences have occurred in this lifetime alone. To say they are rare or not happening is absurd. An occurrence once or twice is coincidence; three billion episodes is part of life.

What if the spiritual masters are right? What if everyone who experiences one of these happenings is not deluded? What if life does not end at the grave and what if God is real? Most people believe in something even if they don't know how to define what it is they believe in. The priest is not a meaningless traditional role, it is alive and important and vital to the healthy functioning of life and society.

The difficulty with spirituality is sorting fact from fiction or even spirituality from religion. Sometimes the last two go hand in hand but at others times they are worlds apart – which of course is typically purple. The spirituality of the Church and the business of the Church are not one and the same thing. It is true that the Church has manipulated and exploited. The Church has used people as pawns for their own very temporal ends, but the Church has also sheltered, fed and educated people. It has given sanctuary to the persecuted and provided hospitals for the sick. It provides company for the lonely and compassion for the broken hearted. The priest's role, like every traditional role, is able to be perverted by some for their own gain.

The Church and religion in general is an accurate metaphor for the energy and character of purple, just as the jungle is a metaphor for green and the desert is for red. Not every purple person is spiritual and some may be anti-religious. A person can have the same traits without sharing the same beliefs.

There has never been a moment in the history of humankind when spirituality and religious practice did not play a part in the ethics and culture of the time. Even moving beyond Homo sapiens and back to Neanderthal times, we see reminders that religious burials and practices took place. As far back as humans have existed a belief in the afterlife has been present. Visions, visitations, out of body experiences and clairvoyant and inspirational dreams all form part of the human experience.

Understanding the difference between soul and survival is the same as understanding the difference between consciousness and instinct.

Indulgence in instinct can never open the channels of consciousness; what is fed the most grows the most. Religion is right to teach discipline and temperance but it is wrong when it divides us into sinners or saints. Denial of the survival instinct does not make us pious or enlightened, but it can make us tired and upset and at war with ourselves.

Without understanding the division between soul and instinct, human beings are doomed to struggle and fight against demons who can never be beaten. It is not the devil that is making us selfish, it is our survival instinct struggling under stress and trying to help us survive and prosper. The survival instinct is there for our benefit, so both the soul *and* the survival instinct are positive aspects of being human. It is only when stress becomes extreme or continuous that the positive survival instinct turns negative and begins to act as if no-one else exists. Balancing our soul with our survival instinct, makes the temperance of instinct and the development of the soul each person's life mission. How we apply both temperance and development is by the use of our free will.

Self-punishment and self-flagellation, either physical, verbal or emotional, for transgressions committed by the survival instinct does nothing to improve the strength of the soul. On the contrary, it ensures that energy stays focused in the survival instinct because energy flows to the area of focus. Thought creates energy and energy brings things to life. Like Frankenstein's monster, everything needs energy to bring it to life. Whatever we focus on most, regardless of whether the focus is positive or negative, receives the greatest amount of energy and strength.

Religion teaches us respect, not just for ourselves but for other people and the planet. It is true that religion is littered with evangelists dressed in Italian suits and gurus driving Rolls Royces, but religion is also a priest sitting alone with a dying patient in hospital, a minister giving shelter to people without homes, monks who pray for the salvation of the world and nuns who devote themselves to caring for the sick.

Religion refers to itself as a calling; not a talent, fascination or a drive. A summons by God to devote your life to the work he has decided you must do. A calling carries an expectation of belief. It carries with it a code of conduct and an expectation to behave in a certain way because you have been chosen specifically. God is watching and God knows all your thoughts, all your weaknesses and all your desires. God is inescapable and you cannot hide. It is this belief, repeated over and over that forms the basis of the purple feeling that 'something' is expected of them.

As a fourteenth century healer you recognise that sometimes illness is made of this world and sometimes it is not. The physicians in town think they know it all but they don't. What everyone does know, is that people are beginning to die and that everyone is running for safety. All their leeches and potions, their bleeding and fumes, everything that forms the basis of 'rational' medicine has become a useless waste of time. You can't really criticise them though, because nothing you have done has been of any help either.

In times gone by you were praised for keeping the village healthy. Now you are powerless and must stand and watch as the people you once helped waste away and perish. Through the use of herbs, rest, prayers and touch, you eased the suffering of many and won their gratitude and respect. Now you live in different times; dark times where fear and suspicion are within all.

You live on the outskirts of the village, in your early thirties and a widow. Your husband died in a farming accident a year ago and since then you have been on your own and life is difficult.

This sickness is the plague, and people are dying in the streets. Some say it is disease while others say it is sin. They declare the world is being punished because of all the wickedness. The first death in your village was only recently, a young child who fell ill in the morning and was dead by nightfall. He was the son of the widow nearby. She was poor and had taken in a boarder willing to pay for a night's accommodation. He had left the next morning on his way to relatives in the country. His body was found by the roadside, black and pus filled. The next day the widow's son had a fever and started developing lumps under his arms. He was coughing and sneezing and in a panic the widow swept up her son and ran as fast as she could

## SOUL & SURVIVAL

bringing the lifeless bundle to you, begging for you to do something.

Placing the boy on the table, you lifted his blanket and were shocked by the blackish discolouration of his body. At first you wanted to run for protection, but instead you stayed and comforted the mother. You told her you would do your best, but first you make him comfortable.

You told the mother to care for the boy while you went into the garden to prepare the medicine. You picked herbs, brought them inside and mixed them with butter to form a paste. Then you placed the paste over the swellings and let it sit. You also made a tea but the boy was impossible to rouse so he did not take it. By the late afternoon you knew the boy was going to die, the blackness of his body had spread and his poor little chest was heaving under the strain of lungs filling with fluid. The mother also knew he was dying but she couldn't bring herself to believe it. There were other signs, ones you could not mention, like the shrinking and fading of the boy's aura. There was also a golden light that had begun to fill the room, only gently at first but definitely there. As the child's life force faded, so in proportion did the intensity of the light grow; but how could you tell the mother.

Over and over again the boy's mother looked to you, 'He will be alright won't he; you can save him can't you?' You avoided a direct answer for as long as you could but eventually decided to say what had to be said. 'I don't think there is anything I can do for your son, all we can do is to make him comfortable and pray.' There was disbelief in the mother's eyes but as reason returned she knew you were right.

'I can tell you what I see around him, if it is of any help,' you said. The mother replied that she would like that very much.

A faint but definite fragrance entered the room. You knew this smell because you had experienced it before. It was the smell of the people coming for the ones about to die. In order to fully grasp what was occurring, you placed yourself into a half conscious state, achieved by constant and continuous prayer repeated over and over again. After about twenty minutes your mind began to loosen its grip on your body and your surroundings faded. The constant chanting put you into the familiar altered state that you need to see the next stage of events clearly. You had performed this ritual many times and you warned the mother of what was going to happen, but that was not enough to keep her from being scared out of her wits as your eyes became blank and your lids half closed. An emptiness came over your face and your body became limp as you entered into the space.

Going into a trance-like state was as common for healers as it is was for monks. Whether it was achieved by meditation, chanting, prayer or drugs the result was the same. The trance is a state where the bonds of life are consciously subdued so the mind is released from the body. The space is where divine communion takes place.

You began to describe what you saw to the mother. In the room the fragrance was sharp, like the perfume of flowers, subtle yet strong. You watched and explained as the boy's survival instinct released its struggle to keep him alive, and began its transformation of returning to its collective.

The golden light in the room intensified and began to swirl like mist in a breeze. Slowly these swirls of gold became dense as human shapes materialised. These were guides waiting by the child to comfort him and care for him.

The little boy's body began to jerk and jump in its struggle to take in air. Even in this time of grief you could not help but compare him to a fish taken out of the water and left to struggle on the land. His mother began to cry as you continued to explain what was happening in front of your eyes. She cried as she lost her son and she cried because she believed her son would continue to live after his death and be safe.

## SOUL & SURVIVAL

As the golden light took on a human form, some of the figures became observable. One of them reached over and held the boy's hand. Reaching down with his other hand he placed it on the boy's forehead and bent down to whisper in his ear. The mother let out a short cry as you explained what was happening, then stifled any more by covering her mouth with her hand. At the exact moment you described the man whispering to the boy, the mother saw him open his eyes and smile before collapsing back into a stupor. A sudden noise nearby almost brought you out of your trance. The mother had collapsed, but you were not aware of it at that time.

Other golden figures gathered around the child and you knew it was time. The figure that whispered to the child turned and stood in front of the mother and you saw him smile. Then he turned to you, recognising that you could see him, acknowledging you with a short nod of his head. You returned the gesture and described the man you were talking to.
As the boy took his last earthly breaths the aura that surrounded him swirled away like the smoke from an extinguished candle. This was his survival instinct leaving. Then his body began to glow the same subtle gold as the guides that were around him.

Reaching down, the man who had whispered took the boy's hand in his and lifted his spiritual body out of his now dead physical one. You looked on in amazement. You had seen this incredible happening before but that didn't matter, its impact only increased each time. You tried to describe it to the mother but you were unable because it was an ineffable moment.

One by one the figures changed form and returned to their original quality, each fading ever so slowly back into the mist from which they came. Finally the mist, the figures and the fragrance were gone.

Slowly you regained earthly awareness and began to feel heavy and extremely tired. Blinking slowly in an attempt to regain perspective, you breathed deeply to reawaken to who and where you were.

You turned to the mother and were shocked when you saw her collapsed on the floor. You could not lift her so you put a blanket over her and a pillow under her head. Her fainting was the noise that stirred you during your trance. She had lost consciousness at the shock of your description of the man at her son's bedside. The man was the boy's father, her dead husband.

Both the son and his father visited you so you could let the mother know that everything was fine and that they were both happy. She was glad to hear this even though the pain of separation continued. Over time you and the boy's mother became friends and each visited the other when time allowed.

Over the next few years your quiet and gentle life was disrupted by people needing your services in numbers you could never have imagined. You didn't even know so many people lived in the area until people started coming from all around the province just to see you.

The plague and its consequences were beyond comprehension. All you had at your disposal was your garden and your small house. The garden became a dispensary and your house became a hospital. Occasionally your herbs and prayers seemed to help and not every patient brought to you died, but most did. You lived each day knowing you could catch the disease yourself, but so far you had been protected.

Every day was the same, another morning, another patient. Some survived but many more did not. You always did your best but your knowledge of what to do was limited. But then again so was everyone else's. It was not long before the huge number of deaths caused panic in the land. At first people were afraid and tried to protect themselves by escaping to the country or locking themselves away, but that was to no avail. For some, fear was dealt with by searching for a solution, but no cure could be found. There were always rumours that someone knew someone else who knew a doctor who was getting miraculous results, but these elusive physicians could never actually be found.

## Medicine and magic

Medicine and magic have always gone hand in hand and the two have a love-hate relationship – it is sibling rivalry. In fact they are more than siblings, they are identical twins. People were just as fearful of physicians as they were fearful of the Church, because both were powerful and both could turn on you. Life in purple times was full of stress due to fear; fear of witches, fear of the devil, fear of poverty and fear of being alone but most of all fear of the plague.

Public dread turned to public hysteria and all sorts of reasons and treatments emerged. As the dead piled high, it seemed for a while as if the disease was going to kill everyone. In some villages there were more dead than living. Charms were worn and refugees scattered. Jews were burned because preachers shouted that God was angry for letting Christ killers into their town. Irrational solutions have their basis in a survival instinct that does not think.

Wandering groups of flagellants began to roam the streets and highways, whipping themselves continuously in an attempt to save the world by taking the burden of penance upon themselves. The flagellants whipped their backs until their flesh hung in strings and finally fell to the ground.

## Paranoid

This is another side of purple, a side that is not dutiful or caring nor one of responsibility or a sense of importance, but one where the survival instinct is manipulating consciousness. Paranoid purple is suspicious and frightened of their own shadow. They have the aggression, blame and rage that only the frightened and dependent can have. They are superstitious because of the embedded memory of the priest and the devils that tormented them. They see or feel the presence of evil everywhere, in the form of violence, murder, demons, witches or even the devil himself.

## Purity

Making yourself worthy and acceptable to God is the basis of religion. Purity as a concept is central to the priest. Keeping their chastity and refraining from impure thoughts is expected and demanded. Purity continues to exist in purple and presents itself in a variety of ways. It can be a rejection of human beings in preference to animals because the spirit of the animal is pure and uncompromised. It can also present as chastity and an ingrained avoidance or fear of intercourse for no conscious reason other than the feeling of vulgarity. Purity can also take the form of vegetarianism or veganism. Trying to keep all impurities from the system and be as natural as possible for the purity of the body and the planet.

Worthiness to God means acknowledging unworthiness in yourself and seeing yourself as flawed, imperfect and unacceptable. Knowing you must work hard to salvage some goodness and redeem yourself, so God will be pleased and not look upon you as the failed disgrace you once were. This sense of utter unworthiness is common to the purple colour group because it belongs to the history of the priest. None of us feel we are as good as we could be or as talented as we should be, but that should not be confused with a conviction of unworthiness. The first means, 'I can do better', the second is a belief of lowliness that if not restrained can lead to deep self-loathing. Fears of evil and sin run deep, making purple feel tormented and tortured, a sense that all is lost and hell is the only future.

> It took years of practice to be able to put yourself in the trance that enables you to see beyond this world. You used to slip into it naturally sometimes before you fell asleep, that's how you knew you had this ability. However, you stopped for a long while because you were not in control and the events that happened made you too scared to continue.

> The first time you left your body you were young and on your own, unsure of the place you had come to and why you were there.

Suddenly you felt a presence around you and noticed a person standing beside you. You instinctively recognised him as your grandfather although you had never met. No words were exchanged, just a look and a peaceful feeling. When you woke the next day you were uncertain at first as to whether it was a dream or real, but you sensed it was different from a dream as there was an essence of reality so acute that you knew it must be true.

Excited you couldn't wait to go there again the next night, almost staying up the whole night as you nervously waited to drift into that half sleep where the parting from the body took place. Finally, only when you accepted defeat and surrendered did you drift off enough for the separation to happen again. This time it was not so pleasant. Wherever it was you went to was shrouded in fog and difficult to see. There was a sense, a presence, just like the previous night but this time it was menacing. There was no-one to smile or hold your hand and let you know you were safe. This was not your grandfather. This presence was cold and threatening and wished you harm for no other reason than because it was its nature to do so. It was malevolent and the more frightened you became the more it laughed and mocked you with childish exaggeration.

Frightened beyond belief, you awoke shaking and feeling as if your body was full of ice. Barely able to talk, let alone move, you stumbled into your parents' bed in an attempt to find security and warmth. The sky was beginning to become lighter so you knew that dawn could not be far away. Relaxing as the room became lighter, you settled with the warmth and peaceful sounds of your parents' breathing. You looked at your mother's sleeping face with relief until you heard the cold malicious hiss in your ear, 'She can't help you'. It had followed you.

Night after night, week after week, sometimes for months at a time, you would dread the night. Coming into your dreams was bad enough but sometimes even before going to sleep, while the candle was still lit in your room and you were dressing for bed, it would begin again. 'Nearly bedtime,' it would say and then laugh. For a while you thought you would go insane because you lost so much sleep but there was still work to be done at home and you were too humiliated and much too scared to say anything. You were thoroughly exhausted.

Your mother grew concerned and fretful and served you extra at dinner in case you weren't getting enough food but to no avail. Every night you prayed until finally a voice came, not like the evil one but kind and calming. This voice was audible; the bad voice was inside your head, like your own thoughts but saying things you did not want to hear. This kind voice came from outside you. It was a real voice from a real person, separate to yourself and all it said was, 'You are safe now, go to sleep.' And you did.

It was many years before you would begin to experience anything that tormenting again. This time you were older and you remembered to ask for help. You prayed and you searched in your mind for memories and people that were happy and comforting. When 'the bad' did return, you were ready and with your guide you dealt with each difficult moment.

## Nothingness

Nothing is empty and the moment it is filled, it is no longer nothing. Many purple fear emptiness and are driven to do anything to avoid the space. They will work like maniacs never giving themselves a moment's rest, always anxious if there is 'nothing' to do.

Too much to do means 'nothingness' is filled; an unnatural state the survival instinct resists. 'Too much' can mean a lot of different things to a lot of different people. It can mean too much work, too much responsibility or it can mean too much effort, fear or anxiety. Whichever is the case, purple are meant to have internal space and the more stressed they become the greater will be their need for nothingness. Some will suddenly pack up and leave, quit their job, leave their partner or go on a holiday at a moment's notice.

If they are in balance, they will manage their commitments appropriately but if they are out of balance, purple can collapse under the strain of everyday life. The more out of balance they become, the more space they need. If this problem is not addressed purple will moan and groan their way through life, waiting and expecting help from everyone around them. If their survival instinct gets too out of balance, purple can spend their life as a full-time patient, unable to cope with the slightest of tasks without falling into bed with a migraine or panic attack.

## Refuge and shame

Some out of balance purple people will seek refuge in the nothingness that only drugs, alcohol or pills can provide. Prescribed or otherwise, drugs are alluring to purple when they are out of balance. Cutting themselves and tearing at their skin can also be common especially if their survival instinct feels ashamed or unworthy. Like the flagellants of the past, purple can feel sinful and dirty, worthless and disgusting, because that is the experience of the memory that lies within the survival instinct of the priest.

Pain, reward, emotion and danger ensure experience adheres to the survival instinct like glue. Repeated experience becomes instinct and is impossible to remove. The survival instinct of the priest includes collective experiences both good and bad that were emotionally charged, painful or dangerous. The survival instinct also absorbs what was rewarding, profitable and what endeared it to others.

In the purple survival instinct lie the experiences of the shaman and the monk, the healer and the medium, the doctor and the witch, the prophet and the flagellant, the inquisitor and the saviour. Which one is brought to the surface depends on what happens to the individual throughout their lifetime. The same is true for every colour group.

## Separated

Every colour group is unique but it is purple, when they are highly stressed, who are the most difficult for others to understand because their actions are so foreign. When other colour groups return to their primal state they generally return to a state solid and perceivable. What they crave is identifiable and understandable to others even if it isn't what they would desire themselves.

Outward motion, circular motion and inward motion have the physical outcomes of progress, growth and stability. The primal states of orange, green and brown include resistance, reactivity and unity. All are tangible and recognisable. Separation and nothingness is not tangible. Every other primal state has something, only purple has nothing.

## Internal division

As a result of this different stress response, purple's actions under pressure can seem strange, wrong or self-destructive by comparison. Their actions are foreign and frightening because 'nothing' is contrary to 'something'. Taking strong painkillers or sleeping tablets, binging on illicit drugs or alcohol, collapsing and fainting, cutting or tearing or 'unconsciousness and spaced reactions' are too different for others to understand, let alone to cope with. The purple response only serves to separate and divide them from the rest of the group, making their internal division apparent to all.

The dual nature of purple makes perception and conscious control difficult under continued or extreme stress. The more extreme or continuous the stress, the greater our survival instinct reacts to it and the less stress is needed to illicit the same response.

Consciousness is one of the main areas of pathology for purple because focus is the basis of consciousness. If someone cannot focus then they cannot plan or control their life. Duality and all the consequences that come from it, is a strong purple outcome because their internal forces remain active but separate. From mood swings to schizophrenia and everything in between, duality is the cause of all these complaints. With their mind swinging everywhere, their ability to rationalise is limited. Duality means limited focus and limited control. One type of purple depends on the willpower of others to do what they cannot. Dependent purple rebel against other people when they take charge of purple's life. At the same time they do not take control of their own life themselves. Out of balance, they beg for help then bite the hand that feeds them.

For purple, returning to emptiness may be a natural instinct but it has serious consequences because 'nothing' is contrary to healthy physical functioning. Breaking the bonds that tie us to organic life in an attempt to return to space can mean immediate or long-term harm to the physical body. Whether drugs are legally prescribed or illicit makes no difference to the liver, kidneys or heart. When purple is in turmoil, the chance of misusing and abusing substances is high and they must come to terms with a constructive coping strategy before they do irreparable harm. Like every colour group, acceptance of negative behaviour is not the answer. Effective management by bringing the soul in balance with the survival instinct is paramount and anything less is an excuse.

## Intuition

By far the most constructive way in which purple can manage their need for separation and emptiness is intuition, because intuition resides in the realm of inspiration and creativity. Ideas, songs, paintings and insight have all been gained during the emptiness of sleep. In this space scientists have come up with ideas and musicians with masterpieces. Art, meditation, spiritual development, prayer, contemplation and even exercise are all activities that can get purple into their emptiness without the destructive effects of self-harm or drugs.

> At the height of the plague the village was visited by a local priest. This priest is not humble or helpful. He is a zealot, a fundamentalist, who is fanatical about the Church and the task of saving it and the world from the grasp of the devil.

> He had come to check on what you were doing, spurred on by stories of Satan worship and witchcraft. The priest was not concerned with how many people you had helped or comforted, all he was concerned about was who was performing these miracles; God or the devil.

> From your perspective you have been blessed because you see and know things that others do not. There is a special feeling in what you know; a feeling that you have been chosen, selected as someone to whom the cosmic can impart knowledge and you are thankful for this awareness. You have always been an open person and that is a trait that purple carries in their survival instinct even today.

Open purple is willing to bare their soul, to show themselves 'warts and all', because baring the soul is part of forming a connection with God. Generosity and support are other positive and valuable traits handed down by the priest, so too is cooperation. Purple in balance have these traits as natural attributes. In balance, purple is more than willing to roll up their sleeves and to get in and help. Someone in need is not to be avoided and the priest will do all they can to supply support and comfort. In balance, purple have an open and communicative personality that other people warm to, and without thinking, others can find themselves telling purple their deepest thoughts and feelings.

An individual does not have to be totally committed to be a farmer or a shepherd. Most traditional roles are tasks designed for the physical survival of the individual and the continuance of the group. There is no need to adopt an ethic to be a hunter or a trader but you need an ethic to be a priest. The priest is a traditional role based on belief. To believe, an individual must be prepared to commit heart, body and soul.

> Commitment in itself is neither honourable nor dishonourable. It depends on what you are committed to. The God you are committed to is not the same as the priest's version. You believe in compassion and forgiveness and leave the role of judgment to God because only God sees and knows all. This priest does not think that way. His God is the old time jealous God who has no equal and who will burn and destroy anyone that chooses not to obey. This cleric believes in vengeance, in separating the wheat from the chaff and throwing the souls of sinners into the eternal fire of hell.

> One day when you were nursing a seriously ill woman, her husband, who had already passed away six months before, came from the afterlife to her bedside. The woman was going to survive and both you and the dead husband knew it, so you were confused as to why he appeared. Suddenly he stopped looking at her and turned to you, 'When she wakes tell her I am sorry for all the pain and all the anger.'

When the woman had recovered enough, you told her of what her husband had said, but she was incredulous and disbelieving. That was far too soft to come from the mouth of the husband she remembered. Her husband was a hard, disbelieving tyrant. He hated the Church and all its finery. He thought the Church and everyone involved were money sucking leeches that lived off the blood, sweat and tears of common people and used the fear of hell as blackmail. He was an aggressive man who had beaten her and their children more than once. When he died, the family had been thankful to be rid of him. However it was this man who had returned whether the wife was willing to believe it or not, and it was this man who convinced you that earthly life was not a test of faith but a continuous learning cycle, unlike the visiting priest. You were not sure how big and mysterious the afterlife was, but it was too big for you to understand so you let it be.

The priest did not believe that what you were doing was 'Christian'. Witches and Satan worshippers were being burned and hanged by the dozen and you knew you were under suspicion, otherwise he wouldn't be here. Only the Church had the right to decide who is good and who is evil. Anyone who differed from its teachings was punished for heresy.

## Haughty

The arrogance of such punishment is extraordinary and beyond the ability of most people to grasp, let alone accept but accept it they must, otherwise the afterlife will come sooner than they think. Setting yourself up as judge and jury requires a haughtiness and self-conviction that is beyond the normal. This type of priest not only represents arrogance, he exudes it from his pores. He has the air of pompous self-importance and the total conviction that everyone else must submit to his judgment.

You try to talk and reason with this man but he is not to be reasoned with. He is your better and any attempt at equality is dismissed with contempt. You are playing a very risky game because you are stepping on the toes of two fragile egos. The Church is dictatorial and jealous in its demand for devotion and attention, but so too is medicine. Both ridicule and destroy any intruder into their territory. The Church's territory includes ownership over the minds and souls of all who live on earth, while the physician's territory is disease and the body. In this period of history, both demand exclusivity and throw temper tantrums when they do not get what they want. These temper tantrums include legal action, excommunication, imprisonment and death. There are serious consequences for anyone who does not toe the line.

After the priest had spent a week with you, watching your actions and questioning those who used your services, he told you that he would be returning to the abbey to submit his report. It would not be favourable because the stories of spirits and healings are too satanic and numerous for his liking. When he asked the woman whose bad tempered husband had visited her why she believed you were so popular with the sick, she stated it was because you gave comfort. He then asked her,

'Do you think it's because she is entrancing people towards the devil?'

'No,' she answered.

'Why then has this woman not fallen sick with plague?'

'I don't know.'

'Is it because she is protected from death because she is doing Satan's work?'

'I don't think so,' the woman replied.

'Are you an expert on the works of the devil?' he questioned.

'No,' she replied.

'So you don't know for certain that she is not a witch or working for the devil himself?'

'No.'

'Are you saying that it's possible she is a witch?'

'Perhaps – yes – maybe.'

'You even saw her talking to your dead husband?'

'Yes.'

'Was he a Godly soul?'

'No, he was an evil and spiteful man.'

'A man more connected to God or the devil?'

'The devil.'

'And she was talking to him?'

'Yes.'

'Is she Satan's friend?'

'Yes, I think she is.'

'Will you testify to this?'

'Yes.'

The priest was convinced that unholy acts were going on under your roof. He believed you were luring unsuspecting Christian folk into the clasp of the devil because you were his servant. The devil lived in your house and the devil lived in you. If you were not stopped you would keep bringing innocents to Satan because you did not care about their souls. You were a slave to Satan and they must burn you so others could be saved.

Armed with first hand information of communicating with spirits and demons, together with people who were willing to testify regarding ungodly conduct, the priest set off to make his report. For the next few days you feared for your life. You were in real trouble. Fortunately, providence stepped in and the priest was found dead by the side of the road, his body disfigured with black buboes. He had contracted the plague while staying at your house. No report was ever made.

The positive side of the purple primal state includes a highly developed sense of intuition and an ability to create and to draw on inspiration for art, business and science. Purple use their intuition for events as well as people. When they are in balance purple have a strong ability to sense danger and they can accurately interpret the thoughts and actions of others. This makes an in balance purple perfect for judging responses and attitudes as they have an inbuilt ability to know and understand the feelings of others.

## Spirituality and spirits

Not all purple people see or hear spirits, some never do at all. Spirituality can take many forms, from an interest in religion or spiritual development to a study of the supernatural and astral travel.

Often their interest can be quite conventional, choosing to participate in the congregation of an organised religion or support group, to a personal spiritual quest through books and documentaries. Purple can be an office manager, nurse, tradesman or soldier and still experience the space and division characteristic of this group.

Many purple people choose to keep spirituality intellectual, while others involve themselves in practices designed for experience rather than knowledge. Regardless of what form it takes, the need for purple to know about the non-material world is strong, because by doing so they learn to understand themselves. When a large part of you is void, finding out about what happens in the void becomes important.

When purple is out of balance the sanctuary of empty space can become a nightmare. In balance it is a place to rejuvenate and to re-energise, a place to become calm so the outside world can be faced with confidence. Out of balance it ranges from frightening to mind altering and sometimes to the dangerous.

## Ungrounded

Out of balance emptiness leaves purple ungrounded and this is a precarious position if continued for too long. Being ungrounded makes decision making difficult and long-term planning almost impossible. Losing touch with reality is a possibility for anyone if stress is extreme, but for purple the chances are higher because losing the connection is part of their primal state. The allure and release that is gained by 'nothing' can be dangerous if succumbed to continuously or if mismanaged. Rejuvenation, creativity and contemplation are helpful and productive outcomes, but drugs, isolation and paranoia are not.

## Art and music

Many artists and musicians belong to this colour group because of the creative inspiration that comes from the space. The priest as a traditional role would have died out long ago if it were not one of the fundamental pillars needed to form society. Artists, healers, guides and priests all form the body of what is purple energy, but it was the priest, in all its variants and forms that did so most successfully. Success means staying alive. It means being accepted and rewarded and the priest was the most rewarded of all the purple roles. The artist may use purple creativity but when times turn hard and famine returns, the artist is expendable, the priest is not. No matter how much others appreciate their work the artist is in a precarious position. Priests and healers are primary to life. They form part of the tapestry of civilisation and as a consequence it is the experiences of this role that dominate the purple survival instinct.

## After death

The survival instinct holds on to life with all the energy it has been provided. It has no other function and this means people will hang on to life for as long as they are able. A fear of death and what may or may not lie beyond is natural. What happens after we die has occupied the thoughts of humankind since we first began to think. Now time moves so quickly that we can fill every waking moment, so spare time left to ponder is limited. In the past this was not the case. Death was all around and the knowledge that it could occur at any moment was understood and accepted. People didn't like it nor were they blasé about it but it did give a sense of reality. Life was something to be treasured rather than something to fill. The constant presence of death and fewer time-filling distractions made people question, and the search for meaning began. The more distracted we are the less we focus on meaning. The less distracted we are the more we turn to meaning naturally, without being prompted.

It is no accident that prophets and sages, monks and nuns sought solitude in caves and monasteries away from the hustle and bustle of life. Contemplation and communion needs an emptiness of mind that cannot be achieved when the mind is active and distracted.

The priest has survived as a traditional role because people need and want this specialty. People need comfort and they need the security that only the priest can provide. Thinkers may speculate about what lies beyond but the priest has either been there or can communicate with someone who has.

## Peace and insight

Monks, nuns and other holy people search for peace and a place to escape the distractions of life because peace is another expression of nothingness. This does not mean that every nun, priest or monk is purple, but what they are trying to achieve is. Religion represents purple and cultivates peace in order to connect with God and the afterlife. To attain this state of bliss they must go into the nothingness and disconnect with earthly life through meditation or prayer. It is here that insight and revelation takes place.

Modern day purple must have some peace and nothingness in their lives. Without this quiet space the survival instinct can feel overburdened because it is where purple recharge. Quietness and insight can be achieved through art, music, meditation, exercise, silence or prayer.

For some purple people, 'nothing' is a dangerous place because their survival instinct associates this place with fear or death. As soon as they are quiet, all sorts of disturbing thoughts begin but this is generally because they are out of balance. Taking time to examine, contemplate, assess and re-think is vital to all healthy functioning individuals but it is particularly important for purple.

## The divine

The role of the priest is to communicate with God and the spirits in the afterlife. It is to devote oneself entirely to an ideal, to serve with humility and to help those in need. Whether physical or spiritual the priest gives comfort and solace. The priest and the healer are two sides of the same coin.

The difference between a priest and a story teller rests in their commitment and the accuracy of their vision. Whether Mohammed or Buddha, Jesus or St Francis, divine vision and revelation lie at the heart of religion and determine the difference between insanity and insight.

As soon as proof becomes obvious, the messages ascend from ramblings to revelations and status ascends from fool to prophet. The ability to communicate with God and the afterlife is the key to the social acceptance and survival of the priest. The more effectively they can converse the more highly they are regarded and the more accepted and rewarded they become. The priest's acceptance depends on how skilfully they can perform their function. The more their skill is cultivated the more successful for both soul and survival it becomes.

## The supernatural

Whether as a shaman, healer or religious prophet, the priest relies on the ability to communicate, so their visions and revelations must be accurate. As with all traditional roles only the skilful survive while the ineffective are expelled. The skills of the purple survival instinct have been cultivated by the process of elimination so only the best remain. Modern day purple continues this trend to a point where clairvoyance and supernatural occurrences are common.

Hearing voices is all very well for a person who has trained for this experience and who is balanced. These people connect with the supernatural world in a positive and meaningful way. However voices from beyond are not so agreeable when they appear against someone's will, without permission. It is also not pleasing if they occur after using drugs or if they harass by making vile and negative statements.

In periods of extreme danger and stress purple may begin to hallucinate and hear voices. Ghosts that come into their room can be benevolent or they can torture with their haunting voices. The same supernatural occurrences can take place with drugs and alcohol and some purple people don't need much to make this happen. For others, visitations and voices occur without warning, just walking down the hall or doing the dishes when suddenly there is someone next to them. For most others this would be a frightening experience and for many purple people it is too, but for supernatural purple, visions are a part of life and have been happening since childhood.

Hearing voices is often associated with a dysfunction of the brain, such as occurs in certain types of mental illness, but whether the voices are a self-made delusion or real is impossible to say. Certain medications help relieve the torment by blocking pathways of transmission but that does not mean the voices have gone away, just the ability to hear them.

People receive instincts, messages, visions and voices all the time, but because they are generally positive or deal with daily life they are not regarded as mental illness. This does not imply that hearing voices or receiving messages is not a mental illness but it does mean that channels for supernatural contact exist and have been cultivated by the experiences of the priest, regardless of whether the outcome is positive or negative.

## Angel and devil
The nothingness caused by the lack of interaction of circular and inward motion can leave an out of balance purple feeling divided. The more

duality purple becomes stressed, the more they will retreat into the survival instinct and the more divided and separated they will feel. Some feel the need to escape into emptiness while for others the sense of separation or division will be dominant. The same energy exists in all but presents differently in different purple people.

Those who manifest this internal purple nothingness as division feel torn in two when they are stressed. Many feel as if they are two people in the one body with two different thought processes and two different desires. Sometimes the difference is compatible and sometimes it is not. Sometimes the desires and motivations of one are diametrically opposed to the desires and motivations of the other. There is a saying, 'united we stand, divided we fall', and a divided purple can collapse and shut themselves away, exhausted by the continuous competition of self versus self.

One part of them wants something while the other part hates them for wanting it. One part of them behaves in a particular manner while the other part curses them for behaving that way. In this state, their moods are changeable and their mind refuses to stay focused. Most manage to come to terms with this part of their character and learn to manage it comfortably. As always, the best strategy is to stop stress before it reaches this point. However even when not stressed, the duality of division can still be seen in their art and music because creativity and intuition comes from the 'space' that creates division.

Many parents describe their purple child as both an angel and a devil. The duality of their personality is highlighted during change. Inside the home, the out of balance purple child can be a destructive devil, but those who only see the child outside the home refuse to believe this because they only see the angel in public. The same can occur in purple children who are sick. Normally well mannered and gentle, they can become furious and badly behaved, especially during a fever.

Fevers are an immune reaction that creates the space. Purple children during a fever can often be delirious. Many will talk rapid gibberish while others will see frightening spectres. Purple children are also prone to night terrors. Different from nightmares, night terrors are a state where the dreamer is so engrossed in the reality of their dream that it continues even after waking. During their sleep they will thrash, strike and hit in an effort to escape what is chasing them. They can also experience visitations, clairvoyant dreams and visit other realms.

The music of purple is often multi-dimensional, as if two separate pieces are being played at the same time. In their art, the shadow often lurks somewhere in the background. It may be the subject looking in the mirror or the main character with their shadow on the ground. Sometimes it is a person sitting in a room with a spectre behind them or someone being watched from the other side of the window. Their art may display the good side and bad side of human nature or greed and its consequences, power and the downtrodden or the benevolence and fury of nature.

## Self-importance and devotion

Being able to connect with God, angels and spirits elevates the priest to a position of authority rarely achieved by anyone else. The priest is God's mouthpiece, his representative on earth. To defy the priest is to defy God himself. Heaven and the afterlife has always been thought of as better and above anything that exists on lowly earth, and this makes the priest the highest amongst the low.

No other traditional role had the same perks and privileges as the priest. They did not build their own monasteries nor did they work in the traditional sense. Some grew their own food while others walked with bowls expecting food or money. For the world, prayer is invaluable, and the small bands of people who spend their time praying for the souls of others perform an extraordinary and important task. To the survival instinct however, this task is irrelevant. An out of balance survival instinct sees anyone with their hand out begging as just another moocher so when times turn hard, it is the priest they will turn on.

There is a saying that you get the politician you deserve. A person peddling easy answers and radical solutions can only get into office because the constituency wants it that way. The priest is lavished with praise and gifts because people want someone to be higher, better and more revered than they. In response, they are given offerings such as devotion, time and goods. The flock is prepared to work hard for little or no pay because to work for the Church is noble and charitable. To expect payment would be vulgar. God's work is centred on devotion and charity. To do more than what's asked for, and asking for nothing in return, is holy.

Socially it is the priest who is invited to dinner, not the warrior or the farmer. It is the priests who lives in a monastery or house built and maintained by the congregation around them. People indulge the priest and give them things, as if it would bring them luck to do so. The priest does God's work while the rest toil in the earth. The pampered priest refuses to toil and never does any work that will dirty their hands. Earthly work is for others to do. The priest is the person you give to because to honour the priest is to honour God.

Devotion and commitment are part of the purple survival instinct and devotion purple is ready to commit themselves mind, body and soul, to any purpose they align themselves to. It could be a task, person, family or a role. Devotion and affection come naturally to purple and they display their care through many different avenues.

Purple is demonstrative when they are in balance and the need to form a close bond can be as strong as found in red, but often purple can be even more grateful. Purple, being the priest, need to believe and to devote themselves. Like the nuns who marry themselves to God, purple want to give themselves in fidelity, forsaking all others.

When devotion purple is in balance they are admired for all the right reasons. Living by the ethic of the priest, they respect both service and care and there is nothing that devotion purple won't do in their support of others. This type of purple is gentle and lenient, forgiving and open. They share themselves and what they have freely and naturally. However, some of these good Samaritans turn the other cheek more often than is good for their own wellbeing, and their charitable nature and inability to say no leaves them open to manipulation.

## Expecting to receive

The automatic expectation to receive is common in purple, especially when in their teens and early twenties. 'Others will do what I want, otherwise I will treat them terribly.' Even if this type of purple does manage to extort the 'devotion' they demand, they will treat the giver badly regardless. Expectant purple has people picking up after them, providing for them, running around for them and waiting on them hand and foot. Others must be available for whenever they need them and they must let them have their way. This is not learned behaviour, this is an ingrained expectation and will occur despite parents or partners attempting to prevent it. As a result, an air of arrogance and expectation surrounds them which in turn can make them horribly dissatisfied. They have a regal glide rather than a walk and expectant purple believes with certainty that they are above other people.

Not all purple people have this self-important attitude but enough do for it to be a strong purple trait. The unconscious memory of being important continues to exist, as does the expectation of the rewards of importance. As a result this type of purple walks around full of airs and graces and expects the rewards without doing anything to deserve them.

## Power

Historically, religion required that people be generous and subservient and expectant purple can struggle with power and its management. The soul of religion requires humility, but the survival instinct of religion says that as God's chosen representative the priest should dominate and be above. This split is typical of the nature of purple and characterises the division and duality experienced by many in this colour group. Power and influence are life themes for many purple people whether it is the pursuit of power, the basking in it or being dominated by authority.

Internal drive is expressed externally as ambition and expectation. Every action we perform is an expression of who we are because action is the will at work. We can only put into action what we have already thought of. We might whitewash and justify our actions with words but it is our actions that display what and how we think. Actions are how we project our inner world onto the outer world and if words contradict action, it is words that are incorrect. Power and influence are centrepieces in the lives of influential purple because it is essential for their self-management and balance.

## Attention

In some purple people, an out of proportion need for attention comes from the separation and division caused by circular and inward motion. This creates a sense of isolation, separation and a search for fulfilment. The more they try to fill this space either artificially with drugs or trinkets, the greater their lack of fulfilment becomes. Space, whether outer space or inner space provides a place for creation to begin. An out of proportion craving for attention is the human manifestation of the unfulfilled impulse that is happening within. By craving attention purple is unconsciously trying to fill the emptiness of space and turn off the beacon that drives their two forces. Each force is trying to attract the other because they are opposite motions, but they cannot interact because they cannot reach each other. 'Notice me', says each force to the other. 'Notice me', says purple to the outside world.

It can be difficult to fulfil the craving an internal force like this creates, but the drive for fulfilment in purple is often strong and relentless because of the two forces, circular and inward. Some try adventures to make this gnawing sense of 'attention' disappear. For others family, a passionate commitment to a project or ethic, and spirituality are amongst a small selection of pursuits that offer the completeness and wholeness purple are searching for. Many will enter the performing arts where attention is guaranteed.

## Charisma

In contrast to the good Samaritan and humble servant is the priest who is captivating and fascinating. Devotion is linked to prestige and charismatic purple has presence and prestige radiating from within. The more charming a person is, the easier it is for others to submit themselves. The more charismatic the individual, the more devotion a group is willing to give. For the survival instinct this means reward and security and it embraces this trait wholeheartedly.

Charismatic purple has inherited a survival instinct that captures and charms. They don't know why or how but they do know that people like to give to them, share with them, protect them and supply them with their needs. They may not ask for these gifts but they are given anyway. Some charismatic purple recognise this trait early and fight to keep their instinct in perspective so as not to abuse other people's kindness, but many charismatic purple fail at this task.

The purpose of charisma is to draw and hold the attention of others. The more charismatic purple is in the spotlight, the better they feel. Gurus, both legitimate and conniving, understand that the more devotees they have, the stronger their community and the more good or bad they can do.

Attention is how the priest secures numbers which in turn secures their social position. In balance purple is content with the right amount of attention from the right number of people. If they are out of balance, purple can take the demand for attention to new levels. In this state purple will crave attention in any form from anyone. To them, attention is about numbers and the type of attention becomes irrelevant.

## Sickness

Attention purple will dress, talk and behave in any way necessary to ensure the focus stays on them. Sickness is another way purple capture the concentration and emotion of others. Being sick requires a nurse and it is not beyond an out of balance purple to magnify the severity of their symptoms, or to develop an illness every time their need for attention is not satisfied. The symptoms are real and quite physical but it is the survival instinct that is the cause not a virus.

Some refuse to eat and develop anorexia, not because they consciously want this state but because their survival instinct demands around the clock attention. Their survival instinct is out of balance. Drug addiction is another possibility, due to both the emptiness of space and the whole family becoming embroiled in a race to save them from themselves. This doesn't diminish the seriousness of the situation but can be impossible to correct unless purple learn to manage their own need for attention. The first step is to identify the problem.

## Jealousy

With a demand for attention as strong as this, it is not surprising that jealousy plays a large part in this type of purple's life. Their language will describe how everyone else is jealous of them. They are more skilled than others, prettier or more successful. They explain how the husbands of friends desire them more than they do their wives. As a result all the wives are jealous and refuse to talk to them. It may be that it is they who are jealous and so cannot bear to see anyone else happy or successful. Jealousy means they turn the topic of every conversation back to themselves, or deliberately sit in the line of vision of two people talking to each other. It is embarrassing and juvenile behaviour and their soul hates it but the survival instinct can be an embarrassing and childish creature.

## Sex and fidelity

Some purple people have a strong sexual charisma. Consider the reputation Rasputin earned himself. Sex and spirituality have always gone hand in hand either in the indulgence, the abandonment, or the fidelity of both. Generally fidelity is the stronger. In religion itself, abandonment of sex plays a far stronger role than the indulgence of sex. Most monks and nuns regardless of religion stay 'pure' in their fidelity to God.

Having an attention seeking personality combined with a survival instinct that has learned to manipulate charisma and desire, means attention purple can have a strong sexual presence. Desire is an expression of attention and an out of balance purple will use sex to achieve attention. If they are very out of balance their need for attention is exponential, and drawing attention with sex becomes more about numbers than meaning. Others can be drawn to this type of purple because their attention craving survival instinct demands being included, but the attention they receive is neither deep nor lasting. To the survival instinct, desire means numbers and numbers means safety.

For purple in balance, sex is expression, not currency. Promiscuity however is not the only outcome of an out of balance attention purple. In even more cases it is celibacy. The code and conduct of most religions is abstinence; rather than being promiscuous, purple can be prudish and inhibited as their out of balance survival instinct returns back to the priest, generating feelings of vulgarity and disgust about sex. The embedded memory of the priest is a belief that sex is either sinful or wrong. If it must be entered into, it should be done for procreative reasons and no other. To religion, each sexual act is a lowering of the human soul to the base act of an animal. The 'sins of the flesh' are a strong and active memory for purple and it affects them more than any other colour group, because the priest has been the only traditional role to agonise and focus on it.

## Morality and judgment
Morality and judgment are strong purple traits that create a genuine and unshakable code of conduct when they in balance, and a moral crusading disapproving critic when they are not. In balance they give an impressive strength of character that others admire. Out of balance they make a disapproving, bitter and hard authoritarian, who judges, sentences and executes anyone who falls below their measurement of righteousness.

## The confessional
The combination of priest and doctor is the only traditional role where it was historically expected for others to reveal their inner thoughts. Troubles of the mind or troubles of the body require an openness and honesty that purple continue to elicit. Whether at a party or social gathering, talking with people they know well, or sometimes even barely know, one type of purple has an energy about them that makes others tell them their life stories. Individuals who under normal circumstances would remain private and keep their problems to themselves, find they are telling confessional purple their deepest secrets and seeking advice. It will often cross the mind of confessional purple whether they should do a course in counselling as so many people seem to come out of nowhere asking them for answers.

## Charity and benevolence
The importance of the traditional role of the priest rests in the significance others attach to their role. The hunter and the farmer offer a commodity in return for position and security but the priest does not. The priest offers a service in the form of charity and care for the sick and the downtrodden.

Benevolent purple gives to others and enjoys helping where they can. They are dependable and eager to involve themselves in tasks they ethically believe in. They love good causes because they are honourable and worthwhile and many are happy to donate their time to charity or community service. Like orange, they will champion noble ideas spurred on like the missionaries they represent. Benevolent purple loves to share their beliefs and involve others in projects they are committed to.

Benevolent purple is a people person who revels in company. Their aim is to help in any way they can from simple tasks to saving souls. Not all benevolent purple people feel the need to save, most just want to pitch in and help doing the little things that count. Their home is open to everyone and can sometimes seem more like a drop-in centre than a private house. This type of purple is open and friendly. 'My house is your house', 'What is mine is yours' and 'We don't have much but we are happy to share what little we have' are their mottoes. As a consequence they are surrounded by people who respect and love being with them.

## Facial features

Purple features are a combination of equal or near equal amounts of red and blue. One colour group, either the red or the blue, can have *one* more facial feature than the other but that is all. Any more and the face would no longer be purple. Yellow must be at least two or more facial features *less* than the dominant colour group otherwise the person will be brown. Only one extra facial feature is allowed between red and blue.

## Chapter 18

# GREEN - OUTWARD AND INWARD MOTION – REACTIVITY

*Reactive*
*Sudden reaction*
*Over-reaction*
*Alert*
*Energy and the adrenals*
*Stimulation*
*Learning*
*War and disease*
*The jungle*
*Camouflage*
*Benevolence*
*Quick thinking*
*Vibrancy and exhilaration*
*Refined*
*The hunter*
*Communication*
*Memory*

*Verbal communication*
*Skill*
*Alcohol*
*Happy go lucky*
*Unsupervised*
*Free*
*Defiant and contrary*
*The kill*
*Taking command*
*Lateral thinking*
*Trapped*
*Reserved*
*Nerves*
*Determination*
*Conceptual*
*Thinking*
*Living for the moment*
*Detail and quality*

Green is the existence of both outward motion (yellow) and inward motion (blue). Green is a consequence of the interaction of these two forces; it is not a combination of them. Inward and outward motion interact constantly, creating an endless cycle of action and reaction. The result for green is a driving force of reactivity. The green system is reactive and in a constant state of balance and counter-balance, a continuous flux of shifting energy from one periphery to the other.

Blue has a reactive force embedded in its design to keep the momentum of inward motion going. Like the big bang, inward motion draws other forces into one small dense spot, which causes inward motion to explode. The more energy blue draws in, the more frequently it explodes. Yellow outward motion continuously pushes into blue. Blue absorbs the energy of yellow until it reaches its critical mass and reacts by exploding outwards. Under normal circumstances this reaction occurs infrequently in nature but in the green person because they are a confined space this action occurs continuously.

Both forces become highly sensitised because each exerts effort to counter the other. This makes green extremely reactive as their system struggles to find balance. Highly sensitised forces make a highly sensitive system, and the defence system of green is the most reactive of all the colour groups.

## Reactive

Green is extremely reactive as their system struggles to find balance. Reactivity caused by interacting forces creates a reactive defence system, reactive senses, reactive thinking and reactive emotions. Green can search for topics, people and situations to cause stimulation to create reaction. If they cannot find it they often initiate stimulation, causing others to respond and react.

A reactive defence system exhibits itself in two main ways:

- sudden reaction
- over-reaction

## Sudden reaction

Sudden reaction is common in green, creating quick and unexpected responses. One minute, green is feeling physically okay, the next they have a fever. At five o'clock they felt good but making their way from work to the train they get soaked due to a sudden down-pour. Arriving home they change out of their wet clothes, have a shower to warm up and get on with the rest of their evening. However even before they get to bed, they have a fever and are shaking with chills.

## Over-reaction
Over-reaction is an excessive response and can occur mentally, emotionally or physically. Continuing the scenario of the man who has just caught a chill, it is now night-time and he is in bed. He feels internally so frozen, that he goes to bed with a heavy jumper and pants, but still shakes and shivers. His partner can't sleep as she lies awake next to him. If he was anyone else she would be starting to panic but she has seen this cycle before and knows that such an extreme reaction is not unusual for him. She asks if there is anything she can do, but 'no' is his only reply. While she is concerned she knows this reaction looks worse than it actually is. His teeth chatter so much they sound like Morse code, while his body shivers and shakes. An unfamiliar outsider would swear that he is coming down with the plague, but it is nothing of the sort. It is only a chill that will turn into a cold by tomorrow or the next day.

Extreme and violent reactions with excessive counter measures are part of the green make-up, especially for their defence system. Their survival instinct is used to acting with excess because of the reaction between yellow and blue. Green can continue this trend of excessive reaction in everything they do. Over-reaction and over sensitivity is the green calling card.

## Alert
The outcome of yellow and blue is an alert and highly responsive defence system. The senses are used by the brain to gather information from the outside world. Through the senses, the survival instinct gains knowledge of what is happening around it. The green survival instinct is so highly reactive that their senses must work overtime just to keep pace. Sight and hearing, touch and smell must accumulate vast amounts of information because the green brain processes at such a fast rate, it requires more input than normal. As a result the green nervous system is primed and ready for action. If green is out of balance, their high state of alertness continues twenty-four hours a day.

The body's defence system consists of separate parts all working for the whole. In orange the emotions are the dominant force but in green the nervous system is dominant. Their hearing is acute, so too is their vision, touch and smell. Out of balance green has trouble getting to sleep or staying asleep. The slightest noise wakes them up and their mind immediately begins its process of rapid and relentless thinking.

With all their senses as well as their brain operating on high alert, energy is burned up quickly, which is why sugar and green have such an ongoing affair. Stimulating foods such as sugar, alcohol, coffee, dark chocolate or spices satisfy green taste buds because the defence system controls the type of food we crave. Out of balance, the green nervous system runs at full speed, and needs sugar as fuel to maintain adrenalin.

## Energy and the adrenals

In traditional Chinese medicine, the kidneys are the organs that help supply life energy. The adrenal glands sit on top of the kidneys. The adrenals draw from the kidneys the extra energy they need to maintain adrenalin during a long-term fight or flight response. The adrenals under normal circumstances have more than enough reserves to cope with the demands of running away, or fighting an attacking animal. If stress or danger continues beyond what is naturally expected, energy is taken by the adrenal glands from the life force that resides in the kidneys. As a result the nervous system and the kidneys are prime areas for chronic pathology in an out of balance green.

## Stimulation

Green has a well developed fight or flight response because of the constant push and shove between yellow and blue. This interaction makes the whole green system over-reactive and alert. As a result, green is ready for action at a moment's notice. The greater the stress the better some green people will perform. Others may not like stress, but they think more clearly with it. Some green people are adrenalin addicts, jumping off cliffs, sky diving or putting their lives in danger in other ways. However, there is another type of green who avoids any stimulation or emotion. Their nervous system cannot handle any extra stress, and they shy away from situations that raise blood pressure.

Quiet green is born overloaded with a survival instinct that equates stimulation to danger. The combination of adrenalin, acute senses and quick reaction makes green naturally gifted for the traditional role of the hunter. Adrenalin and stimulation are vital to the hunter. They are the fuel their reflexes need for a sharp and decisive attack. Hunting was a dangerous business, and many hunters were crippled or died in the process. The survival instinct of quiet green equates stimulation and adrenalin to danger.

During the hunt adrenalin surges, thoughts are rapid and senses acute. The green survival instinct is used to this state and it is what has made them successful. Stimulation green becomes bored, restless and depressed without excitement in their life. For some, stimulation means speed or a death defying activity to get the survival instinct active and ready. For other types of stimulation green excitement is not linked to danger, but to inspiration, freedom or fun.

The hunter's mind is active. Without a culture of reading or writing information was committed to memory. The hunter has the capacity to absorb enormous amounts of information. Their mind exploding with ideas, stimulation green searches for knowledge that inspires and keeps them awe struck. Many become involved in art or literature because creativity has infinite possibilities. Stimulation green is very easily bored and ritual has them climbing the walls. Many can be big picture people who have big dreams and ambitions, and they love nothing better than to immerse themselves in a subject that is complicated and difficult. The harder, more intricate and elaborate, the more stimulation green is drawn to that topic.

Boredom is the enemy of stimulation green and its influence is so strong it can throw them out of balance. Without anything to inspire their mind, stimulation green can search for excitement in all the wrong places. This type of green when they are bored can become either depressed or hedonistic, depending on their nature. Some will give up and collapse into melancholy, while others will manufacture excitement anyway they can.

## Learning

The green survival instinct rebels against anything that is not inspiring. Parties, travel and physical activity are common ways green finds stimulation. School or work that is regular or routine is the enemy of green and has them biting their nails with agitation. Many greens get their stimulation from doing the things they love; dancing, acting, music, fast cars, travel or high pressure work, can make their survival instinct excited returning them back to the role of the hunter.

Everyone enjoys doing what they like but green can refuse or be literally incapable of learning anything they don't like. We all absorb what we are taught, but in order to learn both teacher and pupil must be speaking the same language. The hunter has a million years of learning by example and of performing activities linked to adrenalin. To other colour groups green can seem belligerent or living in a dream world. Looking indolent as they struggle to learn, or refusing to cooperate with what is being taught, usually because the delivery is dull and the teacher is speaking a foreign non-green language.

Memory is retained when it's attached to energy and the best adjuncts to memory are adrenalin and exhaustion. The more a moment is charged with adrenalin the more that event is remembered. The hunter's role is high in adrenalin which explains why their memory can be excellent.

Green like every colour group has a survival instinct that ranks memory in degrees of importance. The more emotionally charged a memory, the more important the survival instinct believes that memory to be. For the hunter, their existence relied on adrenalin because without it they cannot hunt. To the survival instinct, the traditional role of the hunter is all that matters. Hunting is the chase and the kill which means hunting must include adrenalin. For green any knowledge that is not linked to adrenalin is knowledge the hunter does not need to know. In contemporary times this can cause a problem because the modern classroom is one of the least adrenalin charged environments on earth. Adrenalin green can be a late developer, only coming into maturity when they finally work in their area of interest. They are often self-taught.

The hunter is not smarter or less intelligent than anyone else, but they learn in their own way. If the delivery of information is dull and unstimulating that is the end of their association with the topic. There is nothing unique in this, everyone learns more when they are inspired, but for this type of green learning cannot take place unless it is inspirational. It is the way their survival instinct learns. Others can push through to the end regardless of how flat the topic, but stimulation green cannot do this because their survival instinct becomes dominant when they are bored, which in turn ends their ability to learn.

When the survival instinct becomes dominant, we become more instinct than intellect. The survival instinct of green becomes dominant when they are bored because boredom is a foreign state. To the survival instinct the foreign is interpreted as hostile and something to avoid. As a result the survival instinct makes the stimulation green mind drift to anything that carries an element of excitement. Green begins to remember activities that were fun, while others create imaginary scenarios or drift into topics more interesting.

The purpose of the traditional role is to offer something of value. The hunter was valuable because they were an important contributor but only the best hunters survived. The best hunters were the ones who could think on their feet and had sharp senses. When there is no adrenalin, stimulation green is out of their element, so the survival instinct begins to panic.

## War and disease

During the green time (1800–1950 AD) two significant events occurred that imprinted onto the survival instinct. The first was World War One and the second, World War Two. Fear, adrenalin, sorrow and exhaustion formed such a part of everyday life that even though the two wars only lasted a total of ten years, their impact was unlike any seen before in history. In World War One there were between fifteen and twenty million dead, while for World War Two, figures vary but fifty million is the average. Added to this are the twenty million dead from famine and disease as a direct result of battle and the total for World War Two is seventy million dead, in only six years of fighting. Then after World War One in 1918, an influenza epidemic occurred killing twenty to forty million people worldwide.

On the surface, the war and the flu seem separate but there is a relationship. Green was the prevailing cycle of the time. For an individual to get sick after a period of stress or exhaustion is expected and hardly surprising. For the planet to do exactly the same is not surprising either. It is also no coincidence that the 1918 flu was the first and only disease in history more deadly to people between the ages of twenty and forty than to the very young and very old. Fifteen to thirty-four year olds had the highest risk of all. The recruitment age for the armed forces was eighteen to thirty-five.

These factors make the death toll for both wars extraordinary. Added to this are the people who were injured and families that were traumatised. Tension, pain and misery on such an enormous scale entered directly into the collective survival instinct of green.

Quiet green wants a life free from emotional upsets and disturbance. Loud noise and boisterous behaviour is enough to put their survival instinct on edge. This type of green is the polar opposite of the type of green who needs stimulation to function. Quiet green is refined and calm, genteel and easily disturbed. They want no ups and downs or any disruption to their quiet relaxing day.

The defence system is divided into four distinct parts, each playing its role against different types of stress. The immune system is specifically designed to defend us against biological invaders, while the nervous system provides protection against the environment. The nervous system reacts spontaneously to heat, cold and pain, while the senses alert us to the sights and smells in the world around us. The job of the nervous system is to gather information so we stay one step ahead of our environment. It warns us of inclement weather or a predator coming our way. The emotions are the fuel for action, telling the body what is happening via hormones. Hormones make the body experience what the emotions are feeling. Our face is for social protection, externalising to others the emotion we feel.

Disease was not as prevalent in hunter-gatherer communities as it was for communities living closely together or for those who tended to animals. The hunter lived off animals but the hunter did not nurture them like the farmer or the shepherd. The nervous system was the hunter's strongest defence, because of the dangers that lurked in the jungle. The immune system of the trader, the farmer and the shepherd were central to their protection, because of the diseases around them. The trader travelled to foreign ports while the shepherd lived with animals in large human groups. The farmer also lived in collectives with animals by their side, so their immune system became their primary protection. The hunter was naturally protected because their villages were smaller and more open. People scattered throughout the day to perform their various tasks. Their nervous system was suited to living in the open and not suited to intense communal living, and explains why they were so affected by disease when Europeans arrived into hunter-gatherer societies. This does not mean that the immune system of the trader, farmer or shepherd is biologically different from that of the hunter, but each has adapted to different circumstances.

## The jungle

The jungle and forest, tropical or temperate, typifies green energy. As the lungs of the world, rainforest jungles contain more diversity than any other land area on earth. Every surface is covered, while every tree is draped with vines and creepers that provide a home to numerous species. Abundant varieties of plants and animals can be found living and breeding in the jungle.

For many, the jungle is a daunting place full of unknown and unseen eyes, but more terrestrial life calls the jungle home than anywhere else on the planet. The jungle is full of wealth and abundance. In many other regions life pushes and struggles to eke out an existence. The desert strains under harsh conditions while the mountains are cold and changeable. The jungle by contrast is plentiful. Fruits fall to the ground and new life flourishes. Hunting is easy and so too is gathering. Food is everywhere.

The plains are open so animals congregate for protection through safety in numbers, but the jungle is a different world full of shadows and watching eyes. The jungle is a mind game, a place where tactics and camouflage play more of a role than size and speed. Senses are ready and always alert because in the jungle sometimes the only skill preventing you from being eaten is controlling an out of place movement or the rustle of a tree at an inappropriate time. A shuffle of leaves or a snap of a twig can be all that separates you from breathing and breakfast.

The senses of the hunter have adapted to this environment. All their senses are alert because the nervous system is the primary defence in the jungle. Biological invasion through microbes and germs is not as big a threat as a lurking tiger or a snake about to strike. In the jungle, visibility is limited and yet it must be highly acute to differentiate food from the backdrop of vines.

## Camouflage

Camouflage is the main strategy for both hunter and hunted alike. Concealment is a mind game designed to confuse and outsmart, with the best defence to not be attacked. The jungle is a world where the nervous system is on constant alert. Nothing looks as it should and nothing is as it seems, always on alert and expecting the unexpected. There are carnivorous plants that smell like rotting meat so rats and other small animals enter the plant, hoping to find food but finding death instead. There are insects that look like sticks or innocuous bugs that look like dangerous ones. Some creatures have spinning tails that deflect attack away from the head, while others seduce with perfume or colour entrancing their victims. Some animals and plants are the real deal when it comes to potency and danger. They have numbing poison and spiky thorns, razor sharp teeth and excruciating stings, while other creatures that look exactly the same aren't dangerous at all. Some have skins of brilliant red, warning other creatures of their highly toxic venom yet another creature with brilliant red skin has no venom to back up the warning. The question is does the hunter risk being wrong?

The jungle is a place of espionage; where maybe it is, but maybe it isn't. Some of the senses say yes, but the other senses are not so sure. Do I risk it or do I leave it alone?

What about life for the herbivorous animals, grazing and foraging in peace? Unaware that they are being watched, between mouthfuls they look up and sniff, searching carefully for any movement, turning their ears like radar, while slowly and without a sound, the hunter inches forward.

The grazing animal is not sure whether everything is right or not. Its nose picks up an alarming scent but it's confused as to where it comes from. It strains its eyes but cannot see, nor can it hear anything potentially dangerous. It decides to put its head down for just one more munch and like lightning, life is over.

## Benevolence

As well as a place of tension, the jungle is also a benevolent provider. It is a place of security and abundance for millions of different creatures; an environment where there is always somewhere to hide, to build a home and a source of food. Jungle animals do not store food for the winter months and they do not have to hibernate to escape the harsh conditions. The jungle is the most fertile place on the planet, with a consistent warm climate and water for all. It is beautiful, benevolent and giving. Creatures do not make the rainforest fertile; animals are drawn because it is fertile already. Jungle living and the traditional role of the hunter, together form the basis of the green survival instinct.

## Quick thinking

Camouflage and quick thinking are the hallmarks of green. Their senses are already reactive because of the interplay between outward and inward motion. Combined with their reactivity is the jungle environment that relies on senses and perception. Filtered light flows through the jungle canopy making twilight its constant state, while the combination of mist and heat turns the jungle into a steam room.

Green under stress has the instincts of the jungle; braced, ready and alert. Their system is used to life in these conditions and many still sweat like they have sprung a leak on exertion or on becoming embarrassed. Twilight in the early evening makes some green people nervous. Physically many of their signs and symptoms can become worse at this time. The signs and symptoms they suffer from can be varied, such as headaches that come on at the end of the day but lessen through the night. Energy can drop in the late afternoon only rising after the evening meal and once twilight gives over to the night.

The jungle never plays favourites. Every creature knows what it is like to be predator or prey. Creeping up unnoticed, the hunter had to make sure that no other animal was creeping up on them. This was part of everyday life and the environment where the green survival instinct evolved.

Tourists visit the rainforest and jungles to experience the vitality of green. In the same way the beach offers the carefree family setting that encapsulates the energy of blue, the rainforest provides a sense of enthrallment and life giving that is green. In television, the green room is a place where people relax and settle their nerves before going on camera. Rainforests are the same. When people think of a Garden of Eden they usually create an image of a modified rainforest with a stable climate, waterfalls, fruit and flowering plants. It is a modified Eden specifically designed for human beings and very little else. In the vision there are no predatory animals such as jaguars or tigers, no wild boar and no snakes. Nonetheless the vision of paradise remains, theoretically, the rainforest.

Forests and jungles burst with life and vitality filling the senses with fragrances, colours, vibrancy and sound. People immerse themselves in the forest to feel alive, rejuvenate and regain their energy. Eyes clear and senses come to life because the forest pulses with spirit.

## Vibrancy and exhilaration

The difference between a pleasant forest and a jungle is the difference between in balance and out of balance green. It is also the difference between vitality and adrenalin. Vitality is passion and an enthusiasm for life. Adrenalin is animal fear. Out of balance green confuses the two as if passion and fear are the same. Vibrant green is in balance while exhilaration green is out of balance.

Vibrant green is alive with energy when they are doing something they love. They live for the surge of power they receive and others are attracted to them because of this vibrancy. Out of balance, green is looking for exhilaration, an argument or a death defying sport, which lets them know they're alive. The feeling they emanate to other people is confusion and unpredictability. Those around them can feel edgy and nervous, not quite sure of what exhilaration green will do next. Exhilaration green in an out of balance state has moved from vibrancy to adrenalin. Their need for adrenalin manifests in their actions or unconscious body language.

When we are out of balance, we behave in a way that makes others feel about us the same way that we feel about ourselves. The need for adrenalin puts green on edge, anxious and ready to go. Others pick up on green's adrenalin but they interpret it as something different. To exhilaration green adrenalin is the spice of life but to everyone else it means wariness and fear, as adrenalin is always related to trouble and danger. Exhilaration green is adrenalin looking for an outlet. Others sensing the presence of adrenalin usually become defensive or alarmed. The jungle is a place to be on guard because attack can come out of nowhere. This type of green when out of balance gives others the sense of being in a jungle.

In balance, vibrancy is kept in check and utilised by the soul. Instead of apprehension and fear, adrenalin becomes passion. In balance, green do what they love and are so alive with enthusiasm that others want to be around them just to soak their eagerness in. When they talk their eyes shine and their face lights up with animation, their whole body becoming a communication tool as they convey their thoughts and opinions.

People are drawn to vibrant green because they are a life-giving forest. No longer a jungle of shadows and tension, they are temperate and inviting. The air and mood of the temperate forest is crisp, lively and clear. This is green at their best, a person full of life and passion with dreams and clear objectives. They enthral others and sweep them up with their enthusiasm and drive. In balance green has clarity and this clarity is reflected in their dialogue as well as in their thinking.

## Refined

Green is endowed with a refined artistic sense. Refined green is attracted to the beautiful either in colour, shape or design. This type of green brings finesse to everything they do, beautiful lines and soft colours or the bold and brassy when in context. All form part of the eclectic tastes that green enjoy. Their refinement doesn't represent a particular type of art or a specific sort of music, green can even be attracted to the ugly provided it's enchanting. Green is enthralled by the exquisite, the exotic and the historical.

This refinement was epitomised in Victorian times. Less grand and ornate than the preceding red time, Victorian architecture, dress and art were more elegant than opulent. The jungle is not a dazzling array of colours and yet its beauty can be breathtaking. Refined green likes to immerse themselves in the subtle, smooth and stylish, specifically designed to sooth the senses.

## SOUL & SURVIVAL

# The hunter
Since the dawn of time green has been performing the task of the hunter.

> You are awakened early by the sound of a crowing rooster, and by the look of the light it is dawn. You get out of bed and leave your hut to stretch in the cool morning air. Some of the other members of your tribe are also beginning to stir, and soon you are joined by other men to talk about the coming day.
>
> Most of the chickens are wild but many stay around the huts because the tribe feeds them, so eggs, left over meat and fruit make today's breakfast. As a group you eat, relax, talk and joke. You talk with your wife and children. Then you join the rest of the men to discuss the day's hunting. Sometimes you hunt alone while at other times you travel in small, mobile parties. Often the group starts out together only to separate when an animal is spotted.
>
> The key to hunting is communication and planning. Everyone must know their role and how to adapt quickly to the changing fortunes of the hunt. Each hunter must be dependable and able to act independently. Conversation will suddenly turn serious as the hunting group focuses and begins to spread out, slowly advancing in all directions.

# Communication
Without skilled verbal communication, hunting could not take place. In prehistoric times when animals were massive, the ability to yell instructions in the heat of the moment, loudly, decisively and clearly is what made the human hunter so deadly. Verbal communication is central to many green people who love nothing better than to have a social drink telling stories and anecdotes. Planning was also a priority and another type of green continues to be skilled at preparation, making sure there are no surprises and that every possible event has been catered for.

> Today it has been decided that you will join a small hunting party heading down to the river. This region is dense jungle, highly

productive but very difficult to move in. You have to be careful in this part of the jungle as the vines are so thick they can be easily taken as solid ground, until you slip and fall through. Sometimes the fall is only short but you have known other hunters to drop so far they were seriously hurt. The river bank is a favourite place for predators, as all the jungle animals go there to drink and to bathe. Big cats lurk on the jungle floor while snakes slither in the trees. As for the river, it is vital that no-one goes to the same spot twice within a short space of time because, as night follows day, a crocodile will be waiting.

The jungle near the river is far too thick to hunt as a group, so the party only stays together for the walk there. On arriving you and the other hunters spread out. One of your friends may be only a short distance away but in the density of this jungle, it is impossible to tell. Sound is the only way to communicate because everyone is invisible. The foliage is virtually impenetrable.

You walk the walk of the hunter, making as little sound as possible by slowly planting your heel in the earth, then flattening the rest of your foot onto the soil beneath you. Stealth is the key and that means slow and steady, being patient and waiting for the right moment. On the outside your movements are slow and deliberate, hardly making a sound. On the inside however you are surging with adrenalin and your heartbeat is like thunder in your ears. Every sense is working overtime, listening, looking and waiting for the slightest indication of the presence of an animal.

A bird call screeches through the air and you stop dead in your tracks. The call is another hunter, alerting you and your friends that an animal worth hunting has just been spotted. Is it coming your way or should you move toward the call? Slowly you lower yourself into the surrounding foliage and completely disappear. Remaining perfectly still, you reduce your breathing so as not to make a sound. The eye of all animals including human beings is attracted to the slightest movement. You must remain still to lessen the chance of being seen.

Move and all will be lost.

Suddenly you hear a shuffle and sounds that are consistent with an animal rummaging on the forest floor. The leaves and ground cover are being disturbed in the animal's quest for food. At first you think it is a bush turkey or some other sort of bird, scratching and turning over the leaves, but it is far too loud for that. This is a heavier sound, and most likely the sound of a boar. A large boar is both good and bad. Good because its meat is fine and the animal is large enough to feed many. Bad because wild boars have thick hides that are hard to pierce with arrows, large tusks that tear the flesh and very bad tempers.

You search the forest for any sign of the other hunters, but the jungle is impenetrable; you are on your own. Stomach down lying on the ground, not making a single move, you scarcely even breathe. Very slowly you get yourself into the crouching position. You must be on your feet because you need to be ready to run.

Out of the jungle and into a small clearing just ahead, comes the foraging boar. It is a large male with sharp tusks. As it turns over the ground with its flattened snout, it suddenly stops to look around and sniff. Satisfied that everything is safe, the boar returns to its search for food. You raise yourself slowly and silently and begin to draw your bow. The wood groans slightly as you pull back the arrow and the boar stops and looks up with a start. You stop also, and wait. Refusing to even blink in case you need to act in the next few seconds, each moment seems like a week. Your legs begin to ache from remaining in the squatting position while sweat runs down your forehead and into your eyes, making them sting.

The boar looks in your direction and takes a few quick steps as if to charge. If it attacks you are in trouble because there is no place to run. Any escape attempt will be hampered because jungle this dense makes speed impossible. With its tail is in the air and its back hackles raised, the boar knows something is out there. It is not trying to run so this one will fight. Your mind races wildly as you assess your options. Adrenalin is pouring into your body as your heartbeat pounds and your sweat glands open. Internal heat caused by adrenalin makes your skin itch and crawl, while every muscle twitches with a desire to run. Remaining motionless while this internal storm rages takes a strength of will that seems impossible to maintain. Self-control in a crisis and the ability to think during outside confusion is still a strong point of green.

A noise unexpectedly comes out of nowhere; the screech of a monkey high up in the canopy and the suddenness makes the boar jump. It aggressively turns and faces the noise, grunting and ready to charge, but it has made a mistake by turning and you fire two rapid arrows deep into its back. Screaming with pain it turns around and around, like a dog chasing its own tail, in an attempt to remove the arrows. You run out from your hiding position with your spear raised in the air. The boar sees you and charges in retaliation. As it tries to attack you, you lunge at it with your spear, driving its point deep into the boar's body just under its neck. Wild with fury the boar continues in its effort to try and slash you, while you use the spear as a way of keeping it from getting too close. Blood flows from the wound and its face is on fire with rage. Some people say animals cannot show their feelings because their faces are always the same. This must be a particularly evolved and expressive boar because you can see and feel its hate.

Holding the boar at bay it tries again to charge, when two more arrows come from nowhere sinking into its back. Another hunter emerges from the jungle and the boar starts lashing even more wildly as you struggle to keep it attached to the spear. If the boar breaks loose all the effort will be undone and you will be seriously hurt. The second hunter also sinks his spear into the boar's side and finally the furious beast falls with a piercing squeal. It lies on the ground panting heavily but you still must be cautious. The other hunters pin the boar to the ground while you place your knee on its neck, quickly you draw your knife and cut its throat from ear to ear. The hunt is over.

Exhausted you collapse to the ground, take a deep breath and start laughing with your friend. Whether your humour is just stress release is difficult to tell and it doesn't matter anyway, the hunt was successful and nobody got hurt. After a moment to catch your breath, you and the other hunters set about the task of bleeding, gutting and skinning the boar. Once that is finished, its legs are tied to a pole of bamboo so the animal can be carried. With one end of the pole on your shoulder and the other on the shoulder of your friend behind you, and the boar dangling in the middle, you make your way back home.

Later that night as the tribe sits around the fire you recount the events of the day. With each new telling the hunt gets more dangerous and the hunters even braver. Everyone in the village communicates verbally. There is no reading or writing and no counting. There are no agreements and no contracts to sign because there are no stockpiles. For the hunter, when food is scarce, they go out and get some more. If you want a fish you go to the river. If you want a bird you catch one. Fruit dangles from the trees, and roots are dug from the ground but it is not all a Garden of Eden.

The hunt with the boar was adventurous and made for a great story, but the reality is in two more days all the food it gave will be gone, and another hunt must take place. In modern times an adventure like this is a once in a lifetime event. For the hunter however it was no such thing. The danger of the hunt was part of everyday life. The meat from the boar would keep stomachs full for a while and then the hunter must go out again. There was no such thing as a supermarket and farming was out of the question. Every time the tribe was hungry, the hunter had to reach for his arrows and spear.

Because the hunter comes from a tradition of going out and getting more, there is no need to stockpile and there is no mass exchange. Trade takes place both inside the tribe as well as with neighbouring villages, but compared to the life of the trader, trade in the jungle is small. A pig for some chickens and some fish for spears, simple trade goods that are bartered and exchanged on the spot, not accumulated or stored for profit. The farmer stockpiles for the purpose of exchange but the hunter does not come from this culture. The hunter has no need to count, check, list, or contract. As a result, reading and writing failed to establish itself as a way of life. Instead an oral tradition of story telling, legends, art and song became the communication medium, which places a much greater reliance on recall.

## Memory

The hunter had no maps and no written directions. Everything in life was committed to memory and taught to others by demonstration. Young hunters were apprenticed by older ones as knowledge was passed from one generation to the next. On the job training rather than classrooms and books was how the hunter learned. Many green people today must still learn in their own way and only be guided when absolutely necessary. The hunter had to teach themselves after being shown the basics. Much of the hunter's future time would be spent hunting alone. Trusting their own judgment and acting by reflex, the hunter must be independent.

Many green people are self-governing and find it difficult to learn in a classroom. The hunter started small. They joined adult hunting parties to learn the basics, before being sent out to hunt small game on their own. As confidence grew and the hunter matured, small game became large game and the hunter left the other boys behind to take their place with the men. Being mentored at the beginning then left alone to practise their skill is still the best way some green people learn.

## Verbal communication

The oral tradition of the hunter is strong and many green people are good communicators. Communication green can often explain the heart of an issue clearly and succinctly. Verbally they can connect with other people easily and freely regardless of whether the conversation is social or serious. Communication green thrives in company and for some, the more the merrier. Talking to a variety of people is what communication green does best. They are the perfect host or hostess, mingling freely and talking to all. They move up and down the conversation scale from light humour to political debate, without skipping so much as a beat.

The hunter's background, like all traditional roles has its good points and those not so good. Because modern society has changed so quickly, many legacies of the traditional roles are more a hindrance than a help. There is a saying that inside the chest of every dog beats the heart of a wolf. Inside the modern day man and woman beats the heart of their traditional role. Nature runs to its own time and refuses to keep pace with cultural change.

One of the main disadvantages green experiences from this quick cultural change is schooling. Because of their strong oral tradition together with their link to adrenalin, stimulation green can do poorly academically, finding school boring and difficult. Stimulation green can feel left out and fall behind by comparison to others who pick up the written processes of school more easily and naturally.

## Skill

It is the skill of the hunter that is most admired, not the labour of the hunter. To turn the earth by horse and plough requires strength and endurance, but to outwit an animal, especially one that is stronger, quicker and more dangerous, the traits of communication and skill are required. It is skill that green falls back on when they need to defend or impress.

Colour group traits are what people use to highlight their importance. Red often highlights effort and many readers will believe they are red because their life is snowed under with work. In truth red does not work any harder or longer than anyone else. To impress others of our worth, we highlight the difficulty of the skills we have, to make those skills seem more valuable. Red deliberately takes the fun out of work and moans about all their effort. Making work look easy, as if anyone could do it, defeats their attempt to seem irreplaceable which the survival instinct is trying to uphold. Red does not work harder; they just moan about it more. The same is true for green with skill. The more they can convince others of the difficulty of their task, the more impressed others will be and convinced that only green can do it. Out of balance green will play down the ability of others, to highlight how skilled or smart they are in comparison. They are no smarter than anyone else but they try to convince you they are; that is their survival theme.

The Rocky Mountains are a difficult environment in which to survive. Summers can be blazing hot while the winters are cruel. You are a hunter who works trapping furs, and have always lived on the outskirts of civilisation. The more an area is developed, the more the natural environment is destroyed and the deeper into the forest you must venture. But this suits your personality.

It is the nineteenth century and towns are developing as fast as the railroad can lay down tracks. You could have stayed back east where you were born, but then you would be working in a factory and that is not the life for you. You like your time free and easy, a life where you call the shots, nobody telling you what to do and no clocks to live by. As a trapper you get up when you want and you stop when you are tired. You live, eat and work by your own hand and that suits you fine.

Throughout the year you spend many months away from your family living in the woods in search of furs. Once laden with pelts you return to the trading station and trade the pelts for money. Then you head back home. It takes a few months before your provisions and equipment are ready for the next journey and that gives you long stretches of time to relax and be with your family.

Like the hunters of old, time is broken into stretches of work and relaxation and like them, you try to keep work and play as separate as you can. Trapping requires intense concentration and long continuous hours. However when you are at home it is time to relax and enjoy the people you love.

The mountains are precarious and they change at a moment's notice. You make your living out of trapping for furs and that means hunting animals that are rarely cute and cuddly. Trapping beavers and squirrels for hats is easy, but trapping bears and wolves is dangerous but this is where the real money is. The distance required to trap enough beaver for a long expensive coat can mean weeks and sometimes months away, while one or two bears means instant profit.

Wolves, foxes, mountain lions, bear and coyotes all have sought after skins because they are harder to kill. Being larger animals makes them ideal for garments but they are predatory animals and catching them is risky. Furs from these types of animals come with a high price tag, because predatory animals do not always run away but often turn and attack. If buyers want hunters to kill animals like this, they must be prepared to pay.

In the past, hides of softer animals such as sheep, goats and cattle were just as valuable but since the emergence of the shepherd these animals no longer need to be hunted because they are numerous and domesticated. What the shepherd cannot supply is fur from wild animals.

Your task today differs from the hunters of the past and the hunters of the rainforest, because you are hunting for trade, not food, meaning you are specific in what you are hunting. Rabbits and other smaller animals remain valuable but they are not what you are looking for. This type of hunting is dangerous and you are at a distinct disadvantage. Every beast you are trying to kill is bigger and more vicious than you and these predators do not always run away, especially when they cornered. Instead, they can turn and attack as quick as lightning. Trapping in the mountains is a very dangerous business where one slip can mean death, and not only the animals but the environment is unforgiving. Careful planning and attention to detail is required before each trip. The successful hunter is not the one who is willing to face danger; the most successful hunter is the one who makes it home. Like all hunters you must outsmart, not out fight.

Times have been hard and success elusive. You have been in the mountains setting traps for almost a month and despite a few minor catches, it has been unfruitful.

Tracking means being observant. The slightest anomaly or the weakest imprint in the earth can be all that stands between success and failure, and sometimes between life and death. Fur dangling from a small branch, droppings or bones on the ground, nothing ever slips by. The trapper is different to the jungle hunter. The trapper is an observer, who relies on study, patience, inspection and endurance. The trapping hunter is meticulous with detail, calculating and able to withstand all that nature can throw at them.

To be skilled at hunting there is a need for natural talent and a suitable personality. The skills of the hunter include:

- alert senses to spot animals
- quick reactions to charge or escape
- accuracy to shoot
- strength and speed in explosive short bursts

The mental and personality traits include:
- **Attention to detail**. Needed for both hunting and tracking, the hunter must be able to follow a lead across grass, rock, through sun and rain. The trail left by an animal can be almost impossible to follow. The hunter's mind is trained to observe the slightest trace.
- **Patience**. As well as adrenalin, patience is also required. If a hunter does not have calculated patience they may attack before the time is right and the hunt will be lost. The ability to remain calm, even motionless, during times of tension is vital to being effective. Many green individuals have vast reserves of patience.
- **Acceptance**. Linked to patience is the trait of acceptance. For others the idea of waiting hours or days before a fish comes out of the weeds or a fox is caught in a trap, is too much for their character to cope with. They do not have the temperament for that degree of patience and are naturally suited to other more profitable avenues.

Acceptance of failure is also important in the make-up of the hunter. This does not mean they want to fail but they can accept failure when it occurs. It is common in other colour groups to find the thought of failure unbearable, but patience green accepts the lack of success as just another part of life. Animals often escape their arrows and traps stay open for days. Accepting that effort does not always bring outcome makes green a realist.

- **Flexible thinking**. In the middle of the hunt anything is possible and nothing is predetermined. In the lead up to the hunt green can be methodical but once it begins, the outcome is unknown until the hunt is over. Tracking involves a degree of detail and concentration, rarely needed by other traditional roles. Every hunt has various possibilities and the hunter must be ready to react to them all. Adjusting to the changing actions of the animal requires a highly reactive system, and this makes green with their internal yellow and blue interaction perfect for the task. With each move the animal makes, the hunter must readjust and counter, often while on the run.

Early in the morning you awaken with the sun. It is bitterly cold and the snow is deep. Last summer you built a cabin knowing you would be back this winter. The cabin is small and it lets in the drafts but at least it provides shelter and is better than the tent you used last year. Now you have an indoor fireplace. This week you have been a little worse for wear because you recently spent your earnings at the bar in town. Alcohol does not agree with you and makes you feel awful afterwards, but drink draws you strongly.

## Alcohol

Alcohol makes green feel energised. Another attraction of alcohol is its social appeal. The hunter has a strong oral tradition, so verbal communication comes easily. Green enjoys communicating and story telling and many have an ability to speak effectively and clearly. Alcohol and stories go hand in hand.

Unfortunately you communicated a little too effectively at the bar and now you are paying the price. You should not have spent that money because most of it was for your family, but you had one more than you should have. Besides, you told yourself, if you can get a few good pelts, no-one will be any the wiser. This is not the first time you have got drunk and spent most of your money and it probably won't be the last, despite promises to yourself to the contrary.

## Happy-go-lucky

The happy-go-lucky green attitude stems from their hunting background and being able to go out into the jungle at any time and get whatever they want. The farmer and the trader have learned the necessity of stockpiling against a future rainy day, but the hunter comes from a culture of plenty where everything is there for the taking. As a result investment and planning for happy go lucky green can be lax by comparison to other people leaving them unprepared.

This 'happy-go-lucky', 'plenty more where that came from', 'live for the moment' attitude can also cause deep relationship problems when green is out of balance. When out of balance, happy-go-lucky green becomes easily tired of the everyday financial limitations most people have to endure. In the same way green rebels against boredom, their survival instinct also rebels against restraint, because restraint is not in the hunter's culture. It is not long before happy-go-lucky green accuses their partner of dictatorial miserliness and of treating them like a child. To the partner, green should not spend the family's food money on expensive clothing or luxuries, when they are battling to make ends meet. To the happy-go-lucky green however, their partner has turned into a parent, refusing to let them have any fun at all.

> The wind is howling outside and its sound is made worse by the gaps in the walls. Some scoff at this type of life but for you it is fine because it suits your personality. You always found it difficult to conform to regulations and you are easily bored with anything that does not stimulate you. It is true that wealth remains elusive but you measure wealth in a number of ways. To you, the good life means enough to get by, the freedom to make your own choices, few

restrictions and an absence of authority.

Making your way through the snow you come to the first trap, but it is empty. So is the second. Failure is difficult to endure but a part of life you must accept. Things do not always go your way and while you have learned to live with failure, your wife finds it difficult to come to terms with. To her you are too happy-go-lucky, unwilling to put in the extra effort, but to you it is about accepting the ebbs and flows of life. You have learned to roll with the punches and to accept things as they are. Some people are optimists while others are pessimists, but you are a realist. Sometimes there is food in the traps while at other times there isn't. Life is as simple as that.

The hunter has evolved to think quickly and act independently. As a result, many green people require a lifestyle or occupation that allows them that independence. Their personal and work life is best arranged with this in mind. For some people, rules and hierarchy are an important feature of life and their traditional role reinforces the value of these structures. Sometimes this causes problems for green. Hunting requires that life is undertaken in a free flowing way. Trapping means being slow and steady and working at your own pace; the hunter does not work to a timetable and many greens live and work in this way.

In the workplace and the home green expects everyone to behave appropriately, knowing what to do without being asked. To be self-starting is the nature of the hunting party and a way of life that green is at home with.

## Unsupervised

Hunting parties or individual hunters were trusted to go off on their own and many would be gone for days before returning with their catch. The rest of the tribe trusted the hunter to perform their task unsupervised. The hunter in return expected the group to give them the freedom and leeway they needed to perform their role effectively. Any modern day fisherman knows that fish are not always biting. The hunter must be patient until the fish bite again, while the group must be patient with the hunter.

This type of green works better unsupervised and left alone to get on with their task. Having someone watch over their shoulder makes their survival instinct nervous. To get the best out of anyone, the survival instinct must be in balance but this can only be achieved in an environment that is familiar. Familiar means balance, unfamiliar means threat. 'Let me do it in my own way and at my own pace,' is the only way the green hunter can be effective. Independence and group cooperation is the bedrock of the hunter-gatherer culture. Being trusted to do the right thing in a manner they feel is best, without supervision but with help when asked, is how the successful hunter worked.

Green can find themselves exploited by this sense of cooperation. Others misinterpret their independent trust as an easygoing personality that hardly seems to care. The person willing to take advantage of green is often taken aback, when independent green suddenly explodes like a human Vesuvius at their exploitative behaviour. Freedom and independence are not the same as laziness and anyone who confuses the two will soon find out why green is the hunter.

## Free

Being easygoing, accepting and free is a natural trait because a trapped and cornered animal is capable of anything. The hunter must be ready to respond, and the reactivity caused by yellow and blue gives green a natural edge. A mind too rigid or structured is a liability in hunting, even though it's a valuable asset for other traditional roles. Structure is only successful when everything runs according to plan, but in hunting events rarely run according to plan. The hunter must have the willingness and ability to change at a moment's notice. Without this trait the hunter could never be successful. The hunter who can think quickly and independently is the hunter who is successful. They are the hunter who is never expelled and the one who adds to the collective of the survival instinct.

To get the best from the hunter, green must be free to work according to their pace and nature. Green in the modern workplace is the same. What they need is to know the goal, then to be left alone to work out how best to achieve it. However this utopian business arrangement only works when green is in balance. Out of balance, green may be found exercising their freedom with a four hour lunch.

The hunter must be accurate and methodical but not obsessively so. Out of balance green may go to extremes and become excessively meticulous. The hunter's broad objective is to track and make a kill. The actual detail of how this takes place is impossible to predetermine. Flexibility and freedom are key issues because without these qualities the hunter cannot hunt. The hunter must be ready to react as soon as required. If the animal runs left, the hunter must run left. If the animal attacks, the hunter defends. Being caught is the worst place on earth for the hunter because they must be free to move. The hunter was never more vulnerable than when they were cornered.

## Defiant and contrary

Out of balance, green can turn freedom into defiance and become recalcitrant just for the sake of it. Defiant green will say black when it's white and day when it's night. Blue can also behave in this manner but their purpose is to stand their ground, while for green it is to start a fight to get their adrenalin and thoughts racing.

The green survival instinct rebels against anything rigid or too constraining. To the hunter predictability is dangerous; it is a weakness and a trap. Only by remaining unpredictable can the hunter avoid being prey. Out of balance green can go out of their way and deliberately stir the pot. In the midst of turmoil anything can happen and the hunter is now at home. In balance, routine is an accepted part of life but out of balance green can be unpredictable. Stable for long periods of time they suddenly do something upsetting or confusing and even they do not know why.

Defiant green when out of balance may refuse to cooperate with anyone. They refuse to join in or perform the simplest task asked of them. To say no is their immediate reaction and some reach a point where they refuse to do anything for anyone but themselves. Green at this point is no longer defiant, they are just plain selfish.

## The kill

The hunter often has to over-power much stronger or faster animals, using nothing but skill and the ability to think as their decisive weapons. The reason human beings make successful hunters despite physical limitations, is because animals are generally predictable and their routine makes them vulnerable. Animal routine is the hunter's greatest weapon and the animal's weakest link. The hunter can think quickly and clearly but most importantly of all, the hunter has a good memory. This means the hunter can memorise the actions and behaviour of their prey. The hunter knows what they want and remembers where to find it, its character and how it can be killed.

This gives green the ability to uncover weaknesses quickly. In the modern day this is used against humans instead of animals. Stressed or out of balance the green brain is designed to find an opponent's Achilles heel. Like the hunter, green will zero in and exploit the other's frailty. They have found this person's weak underbelly and now they are going in for the kill. In present times green uses words instead of arrows, but the technique and skill with which they are applied remains the same.

As you arrive at the third trap, you stand perfectly still and stop breathing in order to get a better grasp of the sound you are hearing. It is a groaning, wailing, deep sound, mingled with angry growling and the rattling of chains. An animal is attempting to escape from your trap. You know that sound because you have heard it before. It is a bear.

Cautiously you creep to a better vantage point where you see a cub struggling to free itself. It is in pain and howling for help. In modern times we recoil from such scenes but this is not modern times. A bear in a trap means food on the table and a good price for the fur.

You fight the instinct to run in and kill it because the bear in the trap cannot be more than a year old and that means its mother may still be in the vicinity. Although you are a good distance away, you can see two sets of footprints in the ground, one set larger than the other. The mother is nearby somewhere.

Slowly and as quietly as you can, you draw back the hammer of your rifle and take aim. With a single shot the young bear falls motionless to the ground. 'Wait,' you whisper to yourself, 'do not come out into the open too quickly.' For more than half an hour you sit quietly, watching and waiting.

Finally you make your move. Rising slowly you make your way down to the dead cub. Although young it is still too large and heavy to carry back to your cabin, you will need to skin it before you leave. Releasing the trap you set about your work while keeping your senses at the ready, in case the mother returns. Quickly you throw the cub's smelly intestines into the river a short distance away, and begin the task of skinning it. You also cut large slabs of meat for yourself. It is not the best tasting meat in the world but it beats eating snow.

Suddenly there is a thundering roar as the mother comes smashing through the forest, her teeth gnashing and full of rage. Taken by surprise your mouth opens as you stop and stare. Quickly you return to your senses, grab your pack and rifle and run as fast as you can. Heading for the river, the bear is gaining ground, and you are surprised how quickly a beast of this size can move. The bear is to your right, parallel to your path and that is a lucky break. You run into the shallows but the bear has run into deep water and must swim.

The shallow water gives you a distinct advantage as you make it across the river to the other side a long way ahead of the bear. It is a calculated risk but you decide to eat into your valuable running time, by turning to shoot. Quickly you pull back the hammer of the rifle and take aim; the shot must be good because there is only the one chance. It is a difficult shot because the bear is swimming so you only have its head in view. The bear has no idea what is about to happen and continues swimming to get to you. You take aim and exhale. In between breaths is the best time to shoot because your body is not moving. The animal's large head is in the middle of the sight and the hammer is drawn. You pull the trigger but all you hear is a low sickening click. The rifle did not fire. Once more you quickly pull back the hammer take aim and once more there is only a click.

Panic stricken you run because the bear is too close to risk another shot. Running as fast as you can you search frantically for somewhere to hide. The bear is gaining ground quickly and in a short space of time it will be on you.

The bear is now so close you can hear the pounding of its feet. A large tall pine is just ahead and reaching the trunk you scamper up its branches, like a monkey up a tree. The bear tries to follow but it is having trouble, and the further you climb the more distance you place between you. Suddenly the branch the bear is on snaps from its weight, and the animal falls down to the ground where it decides to wait. Patrolling around the base of the tree, you sit while it growls. It has no intention of leaving. Your ability to endure and be patient is vital because you must out wait the bear.

It took nearly eighteen hours but the bear finally gave up. Early next morning the coast is clear so you climb down the tree and make your way back to the trap and the cub you left behind. When you arrive you make certain that the mother is nowhere around. You come out of the forest with your weapon loaded, collect the pelt and reset the trap. Now you go back to the cabin.

Freedom, reaction and the ability to think quickly has saved you once again, just the same as it saved the lives of countless hunters before you. Attack is a common experience for the hunter so nature adds that experience to the collective. Future hunters will have at their disposal heightened senses, free thinking and quick reactions, because of events such as these.

Every day the hunter lives and works in an environment where nearly every creature is stronger, swifter or better camouflaged than themselves. The main quality the human hunter has going for them is their brain and skill. The hunter survived by skill and intelligence and this is what they accentuate when stressed. Whether academic, creative or technical, green competes in the skills arena because it is where they excel. Group competition is not a game; it is a life and death struggle. Every colour group tries to bring competition into the arena where they have the greatest advantage. Green uses intelligence and skill as their measuring stick of importance. They highlight other's lack of skill in an effort to highlight their own. Out of balance green make fun of other people's intelligence, or scoff at how they cannot build or create. Highlighting weakness brings others into a field where green has the advantage. Every colour group makes a weapon of their specific traits.

The traits that come from a traditional role generally emphasise need. The more others need us around, the safer we feel as part of the group. Traits are also what we are most sensitive about because they are what we rely on to survive. When they are down played or ridiculed, people are left feeling vulnerable and defenceless because they have nothing of worth to contribute.

> As everyone sings happy birthday, you can't help but wonder at the twists and turns of fate. When you were a young girl your dream was to marry a nice man, have children and build a house. Who would have thought that in 1917, you would be celebrating your twenty-first birthday as a nurse serving at the front?

> Growing up in rural France there was plenty of room to play. Your two older brothers would search for hours playing hide and seek, but they could never find you. No one was better at hiding than you because you could make yourself motionless and invisible. One of your brothers, the eldest, has been dead for over a year. He died of shrapnel wounds that cut through his abdomen, causing him to bleed to death. Your younger brother is still alive, at least as far as you know, but no-one knows where he is. There have been no letters coming through from the front because all the communication lines have been cut, and the heavy rain has caused the ground to become so muddy it's impassable. The tension this situation causes is so unbearable all you can do is read as much as you can, in an effort to take your mind off the death of your brother and the war.

The mind of green is designed to know, it cannot be any other way. The hunter's greatest asset is logic, skill and memory; without their brain the hunter is helpless. Not knowing is as stressful a state as the feeling of being cornered. Both create an internal pressure that can have green pacing the floor. For many, this sense of anticipatory anxiety catches them in a trap, which only serves to make things worse because green hates being trapped. When green is in a situation where they do not know the outcome, they feel weak and vulnerable because their survival instinct demands they learn all there is to know. While this response to an uncertain outcome is part of the human condition it is exemplified even further in out of balance green.

> In the moments when you allow yourself to reminisce on happier times, you remember your eldest brother rushing excitedly to sign on for the army. He was in a hurry because he was convinced the war would be over before he had a chance to fight. All his school friends had signed up, and he wanted to be the same. Your eldest brother joined the army in 1914, and was dead in just over a year.
>
> As most of the young men left to go off to war, the town became empty of life and the community lost its soul. In 1916 you decided to join and volunteered to help as a nurse. You had never put on a bandage before and you were not sure how you would react to blood. Now you can pull shrapnel out of a screaming man's leg.
>
> You volunteered to go to the front and work in a makeshift hospital. You work in tents instead of operating rooms and use benches instead of beds, patching up wounds for the critically injured before moving them to hospitals for recuperation and care. Sometimes when there is a staff shortage you help in the field ambulance. At the start of the war the administration would never allow a woman to go to the front, much less ride in an ambulance. But that was 1914. Now it is 1917, and any social conventions about who goes to the front were abandoned long ago.
>
> Another big push is scheduled for tomorrow to create a new front.

Supposedly this new front will disrupt and confuse the enemy, bringing the war to an early end. How many times have you heard that before? 'Big push' is military code for making a fruitless charge at the enemy; men leaving their trenches to run headlong at waiting machine guns. The men don't employ this tactic because it is effective; they do it because they are ordered to, by generals who have run out of ideas. You hate big pushes, they break your heart. A big push just means more amputated limbs, men with shellshock and a pile of dead bodies in the mud; stupid generals with stupid ideas, making stupid mistakes.

As a nurse you have written hundreds of letters to mothers and sweethearts at home. The soldiers lie in bed, dictating their thoughts and feelings, while you write their letters and try not to cry. The letters are all the same, telling loved ones they are injured but that everything is fine. They dictate their feelings instead of writing it themselves because they have no arms, or no eyes. 'Everything will be fine' is a lie, and sometimes you wonder if anything in their life will ever be fine again.

Lately you have been working on the 'nerves' ward. One of the new young officers christened it the coward's ward, but he is an ignorant fool. These are men who suffer from a new complaint the doctors call shell shock. It comes from years of being in the trenches, cornered, with nowhere to run. Artillery shells pound the ground trying to blow the troops to hell. When the shell-shocked soldiers first came in, they were dazed and their bodies shaking like leaves in the breeze. At first you were scared by the sight of these men and you thought they were insane. Now you show more compassion, and your feelings are a mixture of pity and rage. You waited for the nerves of these men to calm down, thinking because they were away from the front they would soon settle and relax. But they never did and most just stayed in the foetal position, doing nothing but tremble.

Many soldiers are no longer alive, but are still regarded as heroes.

Some have been given a medal of honour posthumously. These men could no longer stand the constant barrage and fear. Out of desperation they attacked the enemy's trenches and became instant heroes. A year ago, like everyone else, you admired the bravery of these men. Now after all you have seen; you wonder if hero is just a word that describes a person too scared to care?

In spite of all you have seen and heard you have not become disillusioned. The spirit and humanity that lives inside the average person is awe inspiring and humbling. There are men who bring in their comrades carried across their shoulders. For miles these men have endured the fear of being shot and the agonising ache of their limbs begging them to put down the weight. These friends never gave up and they pushed through all the pain, delivering their companion to the door of the hospital, before collapsing from exhaustion themselves.

## Taking command

There were also soldiers who step to the fore and assumed great responsibility, by taking command and making decisions that could mean life or death. These were some of the positive traits that came from the experiences of war. Green in balance makes use of these traits as tools for ambition and command. This type of green is not afraid to take charge and do what must be done. They accept responsibility for their own actions and decisions. 'The buck stops here' is an ethic this type of green is willing to accept. In order to achieve this they must take in their stride, the consequences and criticisms that come with making decisions.

Decision green is aware but not afraid of taking charge of the moment. Their survival instinct has learned by example that taking control is beneficial. It has seen people make silly mistakes that others have to wear. Instead of standing helplessly by, wondering what will happen next, decision green decides that something must be done. And if no-one else will do it, then the someone must be them.

This does not mean green are controlling, just willing to take control. Trusting their own judgment and willing to back themselves is what has kept the hunter alive. In balance green are open to the decisions and opinions of others, then they put in place their own judgment. Out of balance green cannot take the slightest criticism or opinion. They feel they already know what is best and to disagree only demonstrates another person's stupidity. All thinking people would naturally agree with them. When in balance, this arrogance is not present and they recognise differences of opinion. Decision green has learned to trust their judgment, and they will always follow their instinct. A contrary opinion may be a valuable adjunct and perhaps they will employ another person's idea if their own decision should fail, but decision green will always go with their own instinct first.

## Lateral thinking

When in balance, green are often more right than wrong because the green brain belongs to the hunter. This allows them to link ideas quickly, and they have senses that take in information from the widest area possible. In balance, the brain of the hunter evaluates the possibilities around them. Not only what is in front of their vision, but also what lies in the periphery. Green can be excellent lateral thinkers.

## Trapped

For green, trench warfare was worse than hell itself. The soldier in the trenches faced the worst green horror; being constantly attacked with nowhere to run. There is no worse situation for green, than to be stuck in a trench while bullets fly and shells explode all around. It is a cause of fear so desperate that it burns itself into the survival instinct's core.

When emotion and reaction is as horrific as it was in the First World War, the survival instinct prevailing at the time was compelled by nature to absorb the events and carry them on as instinct. Not the memory of the event itself but the emotion that surrounded it. The actual memory of trench warfare thankfully belongs to the past, but the emotions that type of warfare evoked and the feeling of being trapped and cornered, continues as unconscious reaction. Nature devised this system so the survival instinct ensures that individuals of the future are protected from the dangers of the past. So many people were maimed and killed because of the two world wars. The survival instinct does everything it can to make sure green is protected in the future.

## Reserved

In war you learn to keep your head down and avoid coming out in the open. It is these traits the survival instinct absorbs and passes on for green to share. Green can be quiet and unassuming. They can be low profile people who keep their head down and rarely make a fuss. Rather than standing out, reserved green is shy and timid by nature. Reserved green is the type of person who is at home being at home. They like a place where they can relax, avoiding loud and confrontational behaviour. Wild parties or any environment where people get carried away have the potential to make others drink too much and possibly become abusive. This upsets the reserved green survival instinct that is already nervous of danger.

Some reserved greens go out of their way to suppress all highs and lows. They earn a reputation for being prim and proper, mimicking nineteenth century deportment. They are well mannered and highly refined, enjoying all that is suave, smooth and sophisticated. Well dressed and debonair, they enjoy a spot of tennis before tea.

> There is no use talking to the shell-shocked soldiers, because there is no soul left in their body to speak to. It's as if their soul could take the stress no longer and simply went back home, leaving a lifeless body shaking in a heap on the floor. As days turned to weeks and weeks into months, you realise these men have been ruined.

## Nerves

Out of balance, nervous green cannot take continuous pressure. For the hunter, adrenalin was a vital part of life but shellshock is the other side of too much adrenalin. The old-fashioned term of a nervous breakdown is a potential for nervous green. Their senses and nervous system are so highly reactive they cannot take the slightest upset without becoming overwhelmed. Their nervous system has extreme reactions to a minimum of stress. They panic instead of displaying caution, and show terror instead of concern. Loud noise sends adrenalin surging like a soldier who has been worn down; not one more shell, not one more order; not one more patrol and not one more big push, is the way the nervous green survival instinct behaves.

Since their nerves are frayed, this type of green avoids pressure and stress because they are linked to danger. Life is kept quiet and their day in routine. Home is their sanctuary away from the world where they allow select visitors. Some are content with a small quiet family while others just want to be alone. Anything more than the calm and relaxed sends their defence system into alarm. They have inherited the nervous system of the trenches, and are desperate to find peace and quiet.

Next morning you went with one of the trucks taking you and your colleagues to the front. No sooner had you arrived and put up the tents, when fighting started again. You have been chosen because you speak both French and English. In this battle the soldiers come from the British Commonwealth as well as from France. There are English and Canadians, Australians, Indians and New Zealanders. For most of your life you didn't even know these countries existed.

The rough and ready hospital only works two shifts; day and night. The staff say that is appropriate because they only have two states; work and collapse.

These two states come from the hunter. Once the hunter is on the trail they must continue until the end. If the weather changes and begins to rain or the wind begins to blow, the trail is easily lost and the hunter returns empty handed. The hunter has been gone working for days, and now they have nothing to show for their efforts.

## Determination

The hunter learned early not to give up once the hunt began. Determined green applies strength and willpower to make sure the job gets done. Regardless of how difficult it is and how long it takes, the hunter must push through till the end. Many determined green people may fall sick or collapse after the task is finished, because they push themselves hard and never stop until the job is complete. In the past, if the trail went cold during the hunt the animal got away, and the hunter's efforts turned into a waste of time. Determined green wants the job finished, and they want it done all in one go. Only at the end when the job is complete can this type of green relax. Many green people still get a great sense of satisfaction whenever a project concludes. Some people hate endings. They make them feel lost, sad or unsettled because the project created stability through routine. Determined green enjoys endings, because they are an unconscious symbol of a successful hunt.

## Conceptual

The nerves and senses of a scout crawling through the mud to observe the enemy's trenches are the nerves and senses that continue in green when they are out of balance. Like hunters before him, the crawling scout employed all his senses. As he crawled on his stomach he strained his ears to hear the slightest noise; perhaps the shuffling sound of other men crawling, or whispers coming from a trench. Peripheral input is taken in by the scout at a level not normally needed. The hunter is aware of everything around them in a three hundred and sixty degree circle. The scout in no man's land is exactly the same, because like the hunter life depended on it.

Conceptual green takes in information from a variety of different sources. Out of balance they are on alert; a scout in no man's land, taking sight and sound from every direction. This type of green can be engaged in two conversations at once. Talking to one person yet listening to another, without losing the thread of either.

Conceptual green has a brain that links information. Their brain makes patterns that join independent pieces into a holistic picture. In this way the hunter can turn the obscure into the tangible. A snapping twig means nothing by itself nor do squawking birds, but put together with a rustling bush the brain of the hunter becomes alerted. If the scout hears a click as their eyes pick up a glint, the two come together and the scout is alerted to the presence of an enemy soldier.

Conceptual green has an abstract way of thinking because their brain is designed not only to concentrate on the indistinct, but to turn each piece of information into something comprehensible. When this trait is strong and the survival instinct is dominant, green can be highly abstract. They live in a world that is different from others, seeing and knowing what others do not. Out of balance, they link ambiguous signs, each more obscure than the last. This type of green is a conspiracy theorist, eccentric or even mad, but to them others are ignorant and too dull to understand. If the soul is in balance green uses the trait of linking information to observe, design and explore, making innovative and original creations.

Out of balance, conceptual green lives in a world of ideas. Science, art and religion are their favourite realms because they are boundless. Without the balance provided by the soul, conceptual green remains in the obscure without turning their thoughts into tangible form. In balance they have a gift for understanding the ambiguous and sometimes even the unfathomable. Their skill is to turn the incomprehensible into simple terms.

> It is one week into the push, and the fighting is worse than ever. In one night alone over five thousand men were killed or injured in battle. You are in the operating theatre helping as best you can. The lights dim and flicker as the bombs explode near the camp. Early next morning as you sleep in bed, collapsed because you have pushed yourself to exhaustion once again, you are awakened by a friend who tells you that your other brother is dead.
>
> As your friend watches, you get out of bed, get dressed and begin to work. Your friend is waiting for you to burst into tears but shock takes many forms. You are in survival mode and now you are the hunter. Your mind races wildly with a thousand different thoughts because this is how the hunter survived. A hunter who is not alert and thinking is a hunter who would soon be killed. Under stress when the survival instinct becomes dominant the green brain comes alive. All the senses come alive also, because the senses are an extension of the brain. Thinking is what kept the hunter alive and thinking is where the survival instinct returns.

## Thinking

The world of thought is where green is at home. In balance they enjoy grounding their ideas and giving them practical value. Out of balance, thinking green is a perpetual student or an intellectual snob. This type of green constantly learns but never puts learning into action. They are highly academic and want to stay that way, without compromising their ideas by the tainted influences of business and money.

The war has been over for a year. After the armistice you went home to your village, but only your mother was there. Your father had died shortly after hearing his second son had been killed. Doctor's say illness is only physical, but you know that's not the truth. The death certificate said your father died of a heart attack, but the real cause of death was heartbreak, too deep to bear.

In February of 1920 you suffered a nervous breakdown due to exhaustion and grief. Friends knew there was something wrong because you were no longer carefree like before. You needed consolation so you turned to the Church but found nothing of any comfort. Others had their faith renewed, finding strength through the Church to cope with their grief. You turned your attention to spiritualism. Mediums had been popular years before and now after the destruction and slaughter of the Great War, they were in demand again. The Catholic Church to which you belonged said mediums are the spawn of the devil but you didn't care and disregarded their warnings. You are a green in crisis, so faith is not for you. Green, like the hunter, must know for themselves, their brain linking missing pieces together. To you belief comes from knowing; faith has no place.

In time you return to your former self but this time with a difference. Now you rarely take anything seriously unless it is a life or death situation. No more heartache and no more tears, life is there to have fun. After getting married you had a child and settled into normal life. All you wanted was a relaxed simple life, leaving the ambitious to go their way.

## Living for the moment

'Live for the moment' came from the jungle and was accentuated by war. The roaring twenties were an expression of the endless youth found in green. Many behaved in typical party green fashion; as if life would never change. Soon Hitler would invade Poland showing the green time was not over yet.

Inside the green survival instinct is the torment of war and the emotions it caused. So too is the attitude of 'live for today', and 'celebrate while you can'. Party green believes in Saturday night, regardless of their age. For out of balance party green, Saturday night can occur three times a week. Party green drinks, socialises and laughs as if their teenage years never ended. Many in their forties and fifties still talk as if all their life is ahead of them. This type of green never stops talking of what they are planning to do. They start courses they never finish and they have half-finished projects everywhere. Some live off the reputation of their past deeds, which never seems to match their life in the present. When young, party green was probably fun and flamboyant, but when older they are a Peter Pan who needs to grow up. For out of balance party green the mature world has passed them by. They remain adult teenagers.

## Detail and quality

Green is enthusiastic and passionate and no-one is more committed to detail and quality. From prints in the ground the hunter could tell the size and direction of their quarry, they could also tell how long ago the animal passed by. Green's attention to detail is only surpassed by their commitment to quality.

Green has the talent to become an authority in whatever topic they are passionate about, because they approach their passion with skill and commitment. Some cannot ever be good at any other tasks, but will be an expert in their field. They have all the necessary attributes to specialise, because of the legacy of the hunter.

The best hunters were able to make quick and accurate decisions. The window of opportunity was often very small, so the hunter must have good instincts and an ingrained knack of making accurate decisions quickly. Some green people make brilliant decisions on the spot, others believe they have inspired intuition. The hunter has accurate instincts and green has learned to trust them. Those around this type of green have learned to trust them also.

Green has contributed not only through providing food but by the way they can think. By linking information unnoticed by others, green can create new and exciting concepts, as well as works of art. Their eye for detail makes them connoisseurs of the intricate, subtle and refined. Some employ their talent in art, craft or trade. They all display the same skill, quality and attention to detail.

The modern day hunter is not afraid of going out on their own. Green is used to making their own decisions, possessing a sense of independence many others do not have. They back their own judgment and trust their own skills; they know what is right for them and the best way to achieve it.

## Facial features

Green features are a combination of equal or near equal amounts of yellow and blue. One colour group, either the yellow or the blue, can have *one* more facial feature than the other but that is all. Anymore and the face would no longer be green. Red must be at least two or more facial features *less* than the dominant colour group otherwise the person will be brown. Only one extra facial feature is allowed between yellow and blue.

# Chapter 19

# BROWN - OUTWARD, CIRCULAR AND INWARD MOTION - UNITY

*Vulnerable*
*Balance and harmony*
*Natural dangers, artificial solutions*
*Fear*
*The soil*
*The cycle of life*
*Nurture*
*Unity and perfection*
*Confrontational*
*Replication*
*Development*
*Precision*
*Rebuilding*
*Synthesising*
*Problem solving*

*The craftsman*
*Looking to the external*
*Isolated and lost*
*Fear of nature*
*Embracing nature*
*Fastidious*
*Diversity*
*Protection*
*Confrontation*
*Need for change*
*Having it all*
*Equality*
*Strength*
*Pleasing everyone*
*The peacemaker*
*Breakdown*
*Abundance*

The laws that make the universe work are simple but far reaching. Not only do opposite forces attract, they are fused together by attraction when all the forces are of equal strength, because each can neither absorb nor pull away from the others. As a result all become locked together. When all three forces become locked and bound by the laws of attraction, the combination they make is brown.

Brown was created when matter began. The three sub-atomic particles

– proton, neutron and electron – represent inward, circular and outward motion respectively. Only when all three forces come together does matter and brown begin. Outward motion gives life progression, while circular motion provides growth and inward motion provides stability. Brown and matter are synonymous and interchangeable. Red provides the medium for matter to begin but brown is the matter that is created.

Facial features highlight the precision and balance of the three forces. When the number of facial features of the leading colour group exceeds the others by a figure of two or more features, that particular colour group becomes *dominant*. When the number of facial features is *equal or separated by a single feature,* the result is brown.

In brown all the internal forces are in equilibrium and are united. Like all colour groups, brown has absorbed the memory of the past. Brown has both unity and disunity. Unity holds its structure together, while disunity and breakdown allows it to dissolve so it can be used to recreate new forms of matter. Unity and breakdown exist in the brown survival instinct and the drive for both is expressed in brown's behaviour, expectations and desires.

## Vulnerable

While stability is important to every colour group it is even more important to brown because their task of maintaining unity is more difficult. In brown the three internal forces are locked together unable to move. It is an environment where one cannot dominate any other but instead all three forces are embroiled in a balancing act of equal strength that creates internal unity.

Yellow pushes against red and blue, but is not strong enough to move them. Red is strong enough to stand its ground but not strong enough to capture. Blue is strong enough to withstand the pressures of yellow and red but not strong enough to draw them in. Each is locked against the other. With each force exerting its strength but unable to gain the upper hand the slightest external pressure can upset this internal balance.

The best analogy is the electron, proton and neutron coming together to form matter. Independently they are particles but together they form substance. These particles continue to accumulate through attraction until life begins to form. Brown is represented by physical form or matter.

Heat, cold, gravity and wind all affect matter but don't affect non-material energy. A force like outward, circular or inward motion *whether alone or in a duo*, has no physical body to break down and as a consequence is not susceptible to the ravages of time or the elements. But when they all come *together* they form matter. Physical matter always breaks down. As a result, brown is more vulnerable to change and destruction, and this vulnerability has many far reaching consequences when it comes to understanding brown people.

## Balance and harmony

The balancing act of three opposing forces is unique to brown and forms its primal drive of unity. Perfect balance and harmony is the tightrope walked by brown. In order to achieve this balance, brown must remain in control of their internal environment and resist the array of external pressures that are sure to come their way. Disunity leads to breakdown and the saying, 'United we stand, divided we fall,' sums up brown's position in life perfectly.

In balance, brown is a person who includes everybody and it is not unusual to find them at the centre of a social gathering. Sometimes the gathering can be a number of unrelated people whose only link is their friendship with brown. When life is good brown are in total control of themselves and their environment. They have the right mix of work and play, together with an innate knowledge of when to take charge and when to let go.

Brown is matter in a universe of energy. They are the speck of something floating in a sea of nothing. The bonds that unite the forces inside brown are solid but not unbreakable. One difficulty for brown is the knowledge that external pressure can place dangerous levels of stress upon the bonds that bind their internal forces together. If that external pressure becomes excessive, their internal unity can break.

## Natural dangers, artificial solutions

The outside world is the natural enemy of brown because it has the pressure to force internal change. This fear resides in the brown survival instinct and manifests as a desire to seek refuge in the synthetic and artificial as an escape from the dangers of the natural world.

## Fear

Fear of disease, fear of danger, fear of crime and an out of proportion need to control the events and circumstances of life, are the predictable outcomes based on the material vulnerability deep in the survival instinct of brown.

When out of balance, brown secure their life by shielding it from the outside world. Security alarms, constant visits to doctors and specialists as well as an incessant demand for tests and opinions, form just part of the fear of disunity and breakdown that is embedded within their unconscious. Vulnerability is part of life but no-one feels more vulnerable and open than an out of balance brown.

## The soil

Soil is the platform of life. Brown is represented by the soil, not only being the same colour, but because soil is the result of breakdown. Inorganic matter such as rock begins the first layer of soil as it weathers and disintegrates into finer forms. Organic matter in the form of leaves, dead plants and dead animals add to the mix that becomes soil. Soil is brown because it comes from the process of generation and degeneration, building and breakdown, life and death.

Brown is the foundation of life because brown is physical form. As such, brown is also the cycle of life and death as well as birth and rebirth. This does not mean reincarnation but the disintegration of physical matter after death into its simplest molecular and energetic form, so it can be synthesised into new life. When a person dies they are put into the ground and slowly over time their body breaks down and is taken into the soil. Plants grow from the nutrients in the soil and the cycle continues.

Soil is where life is built. It is a factory that swarms with activity whose sole purpose is to dismantle and rebuild. This is brown unity and disunity at work. The essence of brown is development; that is the manufacturing and production of life. While the blueprint to life is imprinted into every survival instinct, it is the soil that brings terrestrial life together and acts as both an assembly plant as well as a breakdown and storage area.

## The cycle of life

From the moment of conception, each individual begins a new cycle. Conception leads to birth then growth and maturity, which in turn gives way to disintegration. This is the cycle of life and death and everything in the material universe is subject to this cycle, which is why the universe is in a state of constant change. Force cannot break down because it is not material, but brown is and the cycle of life is strong in its memory.

Every life form is built from and maintained by the same chemical building blocks. Various compounds including proteins and sugars make life possible and the soil not only stores and provides these essential ingredients, it also arranges, assembles and distributes them. The soil is a nurturer and also a cleanser, uniting by providing the nutrients of life. Plants and animals all rely on the soil to provide what is needed for healthy nutrition and sustenance. The soil itself must also be nurtured as many farmers have found, otherwise it becomes tired and infertile.

## Nurture

Brown people, like the soil, can be the foundation of the family providing nurture and sustenance for everyone. However brown can have a tendency to give unconditionally. Like the soil, brown need to be nurtured in return so their own fertility can be replenished. The cycle of life means nutrients go back into the soil for redistribution to the life that remains. The soil is compelled to give everything it can but plants and animals do not give anything back, apart from waste, until after death. Nurturing brown must be careful that they do not provide a platform of giving without receiving.

Nurture without expectation means love without discipline and generosity without responsibility. The end product is often a child who takes their parents for granted or an adult who expects everything for nothing. Nurture without limits means there is no restraint on attention or indulgence. The most obvious relationship where this can occur is the parent-child relationship but it can also take place within a marriage.

This is not to suggest that children need to be harshly disciplined. It just means we should not confuse being exploited with giving love. Too often nurture brown allows themself to become a role rather than a person and the results can be emotionally and physically disastrous.

## Unity and perfection

Brown must maintain the forces inside them in perfect harmony and two traits result from this need - unity and perfection. When perfection and nurture come together in brown the temptation to give, give and keep giving is strong. Even blue, in whom nurture has become a life theme is generally not this giving. As soft as they are, blue recognise that loving a child does not mean giving them everything they want but brown sometimes fail in this area and are prepared to still be making their child's bed even though their child is now twenty-four.

The desire to nurture and to be perfect in their role is an intrinsic part of being brown, but so too is breakdown and disintegration. Being perfect is one of the most stressful demands any human being can make upon themselves, because the energy it takes to maintain is vast. Perfect brown can make themselves servile but this can be perceived by others as weakness. Sometimes very little energy is returned in the way of love, fun or respect because it is a natural instinct of all human beings to dominate and discount the weak.

Sometimes this behaviour has less to do with nurture and more to do with avoiding confrontation. Perfect brown often has trouble dealing with confrontation and will do anything to avoid it. Most people avoid conflict but some, including perfect brown are petrified of it. Conflict means coming into contact with a strong external force and the survival instinct of brown is wary of external pressure. Pressure wears matter down causing it to disintegrate. As a result perfect brown let their teenage children learn how to 'drink responsibly from a young age' rather than say, 'No!' They will let themselves be spoken to in an appalling manner rather than doing what they really want to do and that is saying, 'That's enough!' Perfect brown knows that sugar should not be given to children just because they ask for it, but under stress they will do it anyway. Their excuse is to keep the peace; the reality is to avoid conflict.

The fear of meeting a strong external force head on is too much for perfect brown to cope with and many prefer to bury their head in the sand in the hope everything will turn out peacefully. Perfect brown can try to be a friend instead of a parent, someone with whom their child can discuss all manner of problems. And perhaps they, as a parent, can share some of their own problems in return. To be a friendly parent is valuable but to be a friend *instead* of a parent is not, and the survival instinct of the child will capitalise on this weakness.

Brown suffers the same consequences as anyone else if more of their energy is going out than coming in. However, for some the consequences will be dire. When the body is depleted of energy for an extended period of time, chronic pathology begins. The predicament for brown is that disintegration is part of their make-up. If energy is too low for too long there may be real and irreparable consequences. Some auto-immune disorders are common to this colour group because they represent internal destruction.

## Confrontational

The opposite of perfect brown is a type who is aggressive and challenging. Eager to prove that they are beyond the influence of the outside world, confrontational brown is defiant and deliberately difficult and brazen, as they seek to show the world that nothing can harm them. Instead of running from confrontation this out of balance brown is often the cause of it. They enjoy being hard and they enjoy putting other people on edge. It is the type of bullying behaviour that can only come from a survival instinct desperate with fear, and living in the dread that life may not always be safe. Confrontational brown pride themselves as the type of person who says whatever they want, to whoever they want and if others don't like it, that just too bad.

There is a contemporary catch-cry of 'deal with it'. It refers to the fact that if you don't like who I am or what I do, that's your problem, not mine. The sole purpose of this behaviour is to make others conform so the survival instinct of confrontational brown can relax in the knowledge that the outside world is not strong enough to attack and dissolve their internal unity. Eventually the opposite can happen because an individual cannot possibly go through life confronting others without a stronger force hitting back and when that occurs, the brown survival instinct can be shattered because their greatest fear has come true.

## Replication

The moment conception takes place, whether plant, animal or human, the cell begins to divide, with each daughter cell a replica, or as near as possible to the mother cell. Replication is vital for successful growth and development. Each species must replicate itself as closely as it can because the survival instinct it inherits is specifically designed for that particular physiology. A change in physiology can make certain survival strategies redundant.

Life reproduces itself to a tried and tested formula. Deviation can occur but generally as a mishap because it is in life's best interest to reproduce itself as completely and as effectively as possible. It is important to reproduce the traits that helped the previous generation of plants, animals or humans. Replicating what was successful is in nature's best interest. The cycles that control organic life are the cycles that control brown.

Replication and perfection are two traits of the brown survival instinct that together make brown suited to the traditional role of the craftsman.

## Development

Brown continues the trend to replicate with a survival instinct designed to develop and construct. This type of brown is always on the look out for how they can make things better. To development brown it doesn't matter how well something is running, it could always use a little bit of help to make it go even better.

Development brown loves to improve products, systems and people. Others cannot see the sense of pulling a perfectly good machine or system apart based on some problem that may or may not appear in the future. This type of brown will nod in agreement, pretend to take their opinion into consideration, and then proceed to pull the whole thing apart anyway.

## Precision

Reproduction is a meticulous process because nature must be precise. One change in a gene can sometimes mean disaster. Precision brown has this same trait for meticulous accuracy. This type of brown often find themselves in charge because they are the ones who are prepared to spend the extra time dotting each 'i' and crossing each 't'. Precision brown will spend hours on a detail even if what they are working on is not important, just to get it right. The more out of balance precision brown become, the more they revert to this exacting instinct.

When they are in balance, brown are dedicated workers whose patience and eye for detail is far beyond most people. Building and replication is how nature uses brown and it is also how brown people survive. The human representation of this replicating energy is the traditional role of the craftsman. The craftsman is not a gender specific role.

Being brown does not mean being skilled at building any more than being in the army means someone is orange. Brown is the desire to improve, to make things harmonious and to do your best at all times. To be brown is to be supportive and to fix whatever problems need to be solved. It is the desire to be perfect either in personality or in performance and often in both. To be brown is to be demanding, either on themselves or on others. To be brown is to coordinate because brown in balance can mix with anyone. Brown can be smart but not aloof, skilled but not showy, friendly but not easy, in control but not controlling.

## Rebuilding

Decay and rebuilding is the cycle of life. Decay of life releases nutrients back into the soil so the soil can support and grow even more than before. To produce in abundance is the purpose of life and brown is an integral part. As soon as an animal or plant dies, nature gets to work breaking down what used to exist and to rebuild it into something else. Human beings are made out of everyday materials such as proteins and inorganic compounds like salt, sulphur and iron. New life requires all these products if it is to be successful and strong. Brown is decay and breakdown as well as building and development.

## Synthesising

When the soul leaves the body the survival instinct does the same and the body begins to decay or be eaten by other animals because the nutrients the dead body contains can be utilised by the life that remains. Inside the body, the brown force is hard at work synthesising one substance into another. In this way the body turns what is available into a supply of what is not.

Brown people have this same quality. Under stress, brown try to be of help in any way they can and the most common method is to reorganise life, so outside pressures are no longer capable of causing havoc. In this state brown throws themselves into the work of restructuring and reorganising. Their entire focus becomes external, looking at how they can remake the outside world to better suit their needs. Less emphasis is given to working with the environment as most is given to changing the environment.

## Problem solving

Many people from other colour groups, facing a problem that is difficult and draining, choose to change the problem but if they cannot, will leave it behind. Responses range from ignoring the problem altogether, changing tack and moving in a different direction or moving around the problem, but controlling brown likes to tackle a problem head on. This type of brown does not by-pass stress instinctively and this is both their greatest asset as well as their greatest liability.

Brown are reliable and consistent problem solvers, forging ahead against opposition and obstacles to create solutions and improvement. This type of personality is vital for the prosperity and evolution of society. However, brown are prone to focus obsessively on stress. The belief that everything can be improved and changed, makes problem solving brown difficult for others to be around, because their focus on issues can be manic. When brown refuses to let go of a problem, they are simply acting in accordance with their out of balance nature, but when brown's pedantic personality forces others to see problems everywhere, difficulties arise.

## The craftsman

The craftsman is the traditional role of brown. Internal forces create the natural attributes which human beings use to survive and contribute. Because these traits are part of our make-up, they are a natural way of looking at life and a routine response to problems and stress.

Brown energy holds the blueprint for the reproduction of life and this makes many brown people both conscientious and determined. This eye for detail combined with a personality to develop, makes brown the perfect craftsman because building and development relies on reproduction.

In the tribe in which you live, life continues in the manner it has for generations. You live in the frozen wastelands of what is now called northern Canada but that name is still centuries away. It is winter and the ice is thick. Snow falls almost constantly and life is hard. Food is scarce but there is nothing that can be done. When spring turns to summer and the ice shelves thaw, the hunters will return to the sea and the catch will be good once more. In the meantime the entire group must batten down the hatches, band together and make the best of what is available.

Winter is a time to catch up on energy. In the other seasons fishing, salting and drying must be done during the long daylight hours, but in winter, life slows down as the days become shorter. The hunters have worked hard for months securing the group's food supply; fish, walrus, whale and bear. In the forest there are berries in summer as well as many edible roots. In the winter, there is only fish.

You take part in the hunts of summer along with everyone else. Many of the group are specialist hunters and do little else. When you were younger you went out with the other men and were taught how to stalk and catch. You enjoyed hunting but your mind was always elsewhere. Some of the tribe would craft and make tools and implements and you were fascinated by the skills they had. You would watch them for hours as they turned bone into hooks and weapons. Some made kayaks while others made warm clothes and beds out of the skin and hides of bears, foxes, elk and moose.

Over the winter you and many of the other craftsmen worked on the leftover dried bones of whales and walrus and fashioned them into spears, jewellery, fishing hooks and tools.

Even during the winter some of the hunters will still venture out in the elements in the hope of bringing back more food. Every winter the group loses some valuable hunters to animal attack, breaking ice, blizzards and starvation. Being a craftsman means you work inside and don't have to head outside during wild weather.

Most traditional roles bear the brunt of the elements but the craftsman is protected in their working environment. Brown has an instinctive wariness of the elements because of the way the external environment both breaks and wears down matter.

The life of the craftsman is more synthetic than other traditional roles. Brown doesn't work in nature but utilises nature. Their three forces direct them to unite and to synthesise. Every time they turn the wood from a tree into a boat or bones into a weapon, they use an organic substance to create a synthetic one.

Humankind needs the craftsman because the craftsman makes life easier and more comfortable. There is not a tribe anywhere on the planet in any period of time that has not sought shelter from the elements. Regardless of whether it was in the form of a cave, wigwam, hut or castle, human beings tried to avoid the relentless pounding that nature inflicts upon our bodies. Like the structure of brown itself our physical bodies suffer and begin to breakdown if environmental pressure is too great to bear. Infection, starvation, exposure and hypothermia are all consequences of being left unprotected and brown has this memory embedded in their survival instinct.

> Being one of the craftsmen in the tribe keeps you insulated from the battering of the elements, and that helps your chances of survival even more because shelter provides a buffer between you and the life draining elements of excessive cold, wind and rain.

> You are also a favourite of the trader. There are a few in your group who trade with neighbouring tribes, heading out every few months to bring back goods that are hard to get where you live. Last year the traders were all that saved the group from oblivion as the worst blizzard anyone could remember hit the village out of nowhere and destroyed many of the stores the group had prepared for winter. The

traders were invaluable because they brought back food and the majority of the group survived because of their actions. What is also true is the traders could not have been the heroes of the story without you and the other craftsmen.

While the hunters were out hunting and the gatherers and food preparers were smoking and salting the fish, the craftsmen were busy making all manner of tools and weapons. When the food supplies were destroyed in the blizzard all that was left were the things made by the craftsmen, and it was these that the traders used in exchange for food.

Building igloos and shelters, watercraft for travel and spears for hunting gives comfort and ease to others. The job of each traditional role is made smoother by the tools of trade that the craftsman produces.

Brown is comfortable surrounded by material objects. They are skilled in craft and manufacturing and their survival instinct has learned that the more they produce the safer they are.

The craftsman has learned to place value on the products that screen the elements from daily life. The resulting lack of connection to the organic environment creates an array of problems. Focus on the material exclusively can mean a loss of meaning in regard to the naturalness of life.

Modern society is sanitised and divorced from the earth it lives upon because brown is the dominant energy of the time. When human beings separate themselves from nature, two outcomes occur. The first is that life becomes less hostile and protected from the ravages of the environment. The second is that human beings begin to lose their perspective and become divorced from the organic, the important and the real.

When life is synthetic it is safe and comfortable. The storm is outside and the dying are in hospital. Food is something you buy in a supermarket and children stay children until well into their twenties. Life in the past was hard.

The craftsman has helped take us all a long way. The biggest inconvenience in a storm today is when the power goes out or the roof leaks but without the craftsman a storm may have meant death, as a baby becomes chilled or stores are destroyed. No one is suggesting that life was better in the past, nor was the lifestyle of the average person happier, but people must also be careful that the synthetic does not cut them off from meaning and purpose.

## Looking to the external
When the survival instinct becomes dominant due to stress or energy drain, brown often look to find the cause outside themselves. The craftsman has survived by changing their external world. This stems back to the primal state of resistance to the external so they can protect the internal. Brown's focus on the problem being 'out there' can leave them lost and bewildered when they make all the necessary external changes but still feel the same internally.

## Isolated and lost
Feeling isolated without direction or meaning, lost brown does what their survival instinct tells them, 'find an external solution to an internal problem'. As a result they will improve their environment, changing furniture, carpets and sometimes even the people in the house but all to no avail. Lost brown may indulge themselves in all manner of hedonistic behaviour and many are especially prone to drugs. Like purple, brown can find chemicals an easy solution and are more than prepared to stay on a daily dose of a mood altering drug, than to try and change how they feel inside.

Brown can be introspective, but lost brown generally reaches the conclusion that when they are upset, there is an outside reason and that means there must be an outside solution. The more out of balance they become the more their survival instinct blames the environment for their problems. Over time this outlook can create enormous difficulties as lost brown searches and moves from one place to another and one person to another. In the end, lost brown for all their searching can end up alone feeling more isolated than when they started.

Some lost brown individuals go overboard and attribute everything that happens to mean something about them, and this is not true either. In balance lost brown has learned to search for meaning inside, as well as outside.

When the winter passed there were fewer people than before. Some had died of starvation and illness, while others got lost during a storm and were never heard of again. When your cousin didn't return you were shaken to the point of panic. You lost your breath and your heart pounded wildly, you cried and screamed and thought you were dying. You kept asking your wife to say you were fine, but when she did you yelled at her for being disingenuous. Nobody knew what to do or what to say. Everyone in the tribe knew of death in one form or another and your wife on hearing the news that your cousin was gone, knew you would grieve but this behaviour was a complete surprise.

You had seen your share of death in the past. Your parents had both died but were elderly. One of your sisters had a child that 'wasn't right', so the women took him and left him outside. The death of your cousin however was a shock. He was your age and he was a hunter. The weather was threatening but a small party of hunters went out anyway. The traders should have been back with more supplies but the weather had delayed them. Near the shore the hunters had spotted a herd of seals and silently crept up to attack by surprise. They spread out so the party would have a better chance and then the blizzard hit. Separated from each other, the hunters could not see their own hands, let alone find each other. Struggling to his feet, your cousin fell backward into the frigid water; his death would have only taken minutes.

The situations that our survival instinct fears most are the ones that reinforce our personal vulnerability. When the outside world turns on us, our survival instinct panics, because our helplessness is highlighted. The brown survival instinct fears the outside world as it is both dangerous and unpredictable. It does not recognise that nature is not out to get everyone.

## Fear of nature

Brown can greatly misjudge nature because it is at war with the elements. Fearful brown lives in a constant state of anxiety because they are never sure what calamity may be just around the corner. A survival instinct that relies on total balance, yet at the same time has the inbuilt understanding of the natural disintegration of matter, is challenged constantly.

Because fearful brown views the natural world as an enemy, it can also lead the survival instinct into a misunderstanding of what nature actually is, and one of the biggest misconceptions is the personalisation of the environment. This is an anthropomorphic projection – giving human qualities to something that is not human.

Nature is a system. It is perfect and it is in place for the benefit of all life but 'Mother Nature' is not conscious. Some cultures talk of the spirit of 'Gaia', a life force surrounding the growth and harmony of earth, personalising it like a mother looking after her child, but nature is a programmed survival instinct designed for the benefit of all. It governs in a uniform and dispassionate manner because it operates to a set of laws. The survival instinct is a set of laws for the individual while nature is a set of laws for the planet. 'Mother Nature' lets cute and cuddly animals like baby deer and seals become the lunch of larger predators because 'Mother Nature' is not a carer looking after the weakest, but a system designed to develop the strongest.

## Embracing nature

Some people go off to explore the wilderness, searching to find their own personal meaning. Not all of these people will be brown but it is a brown way of approaching nature. Believing that the truth lies in communing one on one with nature can be dangerous. Challenging nature head on is lost brown's way of trying to prove to themselves that they are stronger than the force they fear most.

Human beings survive by living in groups. Regardless of culture or time in history, families, groups, tribes and communities have always existed in balance with nature. It is common for human beings to use natural resources as their base for establishing a community, while also using nature as a way of finding meaning and spiritual expression.

However, existing in balance within the relative safety of a group is not the same as an individual challenging nature on their own.

Many contemporary brown people feel the call of the wild and the need to find themselves by challenging nature. Only a few will ever take up this challenge but many will feel its pull. The drive behind this urge is two-fold. Firstly brown is a speck of matter in a universe of force and motion and it is easy for them to feel lost and separate from the environment in which they live. Secondly there is no better way of reinforcing the belief of internal strength than to challenge the external forces that threaten its existence.

Becoming 'lost' is common to brown because of their natural tendency towards feeling different and isolated. This lost sensation is also accentuated as the brown world becomes more synthetic and withdraws from nature. Human beings have survived by taming nature, not by throwing themselves into its fury. Our task is not to see whether we can be stripped naked and withstand the storm but to be smart enough to build shelter to escape it. Harmony is co-existence and a balancing act between the needs of society and an acceptance of our place in the natural world.

Humankind has secured itself, at least in the developed world, against the ravages of climate, competition and shortage. We have houses that are heated, plumbed and air-conditioned. Animals and other predators cannot enter and threaten this artificial world and developed cultures no longer suffer from the pain of famine, but instead the destructive consequences of abundance and over indulgence. At the same time anti-depressants, spiritual searching and the hunt for meaningful personal philosophy is as strong as ever.

Brown may feel as if they are separate from the natural world but this is a misinterpretation. Every colour group suffers from a fundamental misunderstanding and the same is true for brown in its belief in its separateness. Matter is not separate from the other forces of the universe but is a *consequence* of those forces. Brown is neither separate nor subject to nature but an integral part of it.

Out of balance brown can be challenging and confrontational to every force, including other human beings within his or her vicinity. In balance brown is in harmony with their environment and is an integral link between people and nature. Rather than alarmed by the natural world they are understanding and awestruck by its magnificence.

> When the hunting party returned with the news that your cousin had drowned during the storm, your survival instinct was pushed into a state of alarm, creating fear and anxiety, which was then channelled into perfection. As a result you began to work harder than ever at your traditional role making each tool and weapon more refined and perfect than the last.

This internal need for order and structure comes from a sense of vulnerability to the external strength and unpredictability of the outside world. The more unpredictable the external appears to be, the more predictable the immediate world must be, to compensate. Many contemporary brown people experience this state of high alarm and anxiety and try to make their work and family life perfect.

## Fastidious

Fastidious brown will colour code their pantry, measure out portions of food by weight and size, make sure the towels are perfectly aligned and their house clean to the point of gleaming sanitation. The slightest external pressure or the slightest change in routine leaves this type of brown panic stricken and neurotic, desperate to return to their cleaning, polishing, straightening and arranging. This is brown returning to the nature of the craftsman. The craftsman survives by making tools and weapons. The more perfect their creation the more in demand they will become. When fastidious brown is under stress, they will refine, order and perfect because it is the nature of the craftsman to do so.

> Finally the winter was over and spring gave way to summer. This is the busiest time of all. In summer every creature, including human beings, are making the most of their time and energy. Every plant and animal is active and moving and each is taking what they can in preparation for next winter. For the group in which you live, there is a need for boats, clothing, weapons and utensils.

As the craftsman, you must be all things to all people. You must understand the needs of the hunter yet at the same time know how to build smokehouses and huts. New skins and fur must be sewn into clothes whilst baskets are woven to gather the berries and fruits.

Every traditional role needs the craftsman as support because without the craftsman no other traditional role can be performed effectively. Whether it is baskets for the farmer to gather food, weapons for the hunter to trap and kill, spears for the warrior, jewellery for the trader, dog pens for the shepherd or talismans and charms so the shaman can protect the tribe, the craftsman underpins and provides for all. The ability to communicate and comprehend is vital for the craftsman to do their work. They must be organised and practical as well as inventive and imaginative. The craftsman is the foundation upon which material growth depends.

You have had many demands by the hunters of the tribe to work exclusively on their behalf because your work is the most prized. A number of years ago when a winter was particularly long and harsh and seemed to extend through spring and half the summer, food supplies dropped to critical levels. Many became ill and food was only allocated to those most useful. While it was heartbreaking for the group to take the stand that they did, there was no option but to leave the sick, elderly and dying to perish by denying them food. As always, a hierarchy of importance was formed with the most useful being at the top and the unskilled, lazy or sick at the bottom. When rations grew scarce, the skilled received food at the expense of those who were not. For the tribe to survive it could be no other way.

You and your family were protected because of your skill. With this bargaining chip you ensured the survival of your wife and children. Your wife is also part of the craftsman clan and is skilled at making clothes, baskets and blankets. She probably would be protected in her own right but because both you and she are so valuable to the group, you received more than the normal rations. Your three children were fed and kept healthier than the majority of those around them.

Some of the craftsmen chose to specialise in the making of particular items for a single clan or group but you and your wife chose deliberately not to follow this path and this choice has kept you both alive.

The craftsman survives by generalisation and being all things to all people. Even though their task is a specialised role, it is in their best interest to diversify what they make to supply the entire group. A craftsman who specialises in one item limits what they can offer.

## Diversity

When food is at a premium it is more valuable for the group to supply to the person who can make weapons and baskets rather than to supply food to one person who can make weapons and to another person who can make baskets. The craftsman who can achieve the most is the craftsman who is given the most in return and the craftsman who will survive.

This trait continues in diversity brown and is seen commonly in the high achiever. Diversity brown is driven to be the best they can be in as many areas as required. It is not in their nature to accept being average.

In contemporary society many parents try to encourage their children to strive harder and to take life and school more seriously. For the parents of diversity brown such encouragement is unnecessary. In fact many parents are concerned with the pressure this type of brown places upon themselves, and their inability to relax and accept any outcome even mildly below the best. Diversity brown is an accomplished musician, head of the football team, well liked by all and has friends from all backgrounds. They are smart yet practical, driven but compassionate, successful but at the same time understanding of others who are not.

You can't help but think what an odd array of feelings are being generated as you look around the room seeing your friends and family mix, laugh, drink and eat. Your children play with their cousins as your sister wipes the food from around her baby's mouth; her husband jokes that there is more food around the baby's mouth than in it.

## SOUL & SURVIVAL

It is 2007 and your fortieth birthday. Everybody is here to celebrate your special day. You take another sip of your wine and look over the room spotting your husband talking and laughing with your boss. Feeling that someone is watching him, he turns and your eyes make contact and you return his smile. Your two children are healthy and your home is a showpiece. The barbeque is roaring as your father burns yet more steak, and the teenagers relax in the bubbles of the spa.

Your house is in a nice suburb near the water. From your balcony you can see the ocean and life is about as good as it gets, yet there is background unease that prevents the contentment another part of you believes you should feel.

You grew up the middle child of three girls. Your parents provided a stable home and gave you the best they could afford. By and large your upbringing was sound and safe. It wasn't perfect and like everybody else you have known your fair share of trial and heartache, the worst when your eldest sister died of a drug overdose fourteen years ago. She was always the rebel and you were always the good girl.

Born two years after your eldest sister, you can always remember being described by your parents as their 'perfect little angel'. Your eldest sister was not always self-destructive. It was true that she was independent or as your father used to say, 'A bit too independent for my liking', but she was never a trouble maker or dangerous to herself, until she became involved with drugs in her late teens.

At university she became involved with a confrontational group that did nothing but talk about the meaninglessness of society and life. Her boyfriend at the time was a mouthpiece for this group and your sister would often spout word for word his ideas as if they were her own. Both you and your eldest sister are brown.

As time went on, your sister and her small group became increasingly disenchanted as their focus on what was wrong with the world made them more and more pessimistic. You knew she was drinking too much and you also knew that she was a heavy smoker. The prissy and more logical part of you wanted to tell her that it was bad for her health, but you knew that this would sound too conservative, not that it would have made an ounce of difference anyway. So you kept your mouth shut and watched as she fed more and more chemicals into her system and became increasingly separated from the rest of the family and society. You were good friends when you were young but by your twenties you were distant. You gave her the loyalty and support that blood and memory demands, and now even at forty you curse yourself for giving her so much money and for not suspecting that she was spending it on harder, more dangerous drugs.

Of course you didn't contribute to her death. How she spent the money was her business and her responsibility, the counsellor told you. But that didn't stop the gnawing in your soul. Many times even now you lose a night's sleep in both your anger and your sorrow for your dead sister. The sorrow comes because you lost a part of your family; you were good friends and played and laughed your way through childhood. Your sorrow is understandable but you are also angry and it is this emotion that is causing your dilemma.

You are angry at her because she should have known better and you are angry at her for the pain she caused. You are angry at her for letting your relationship die and you are angry at her because she was selfish.

Craftsmanship is the remodelling or rebuilding to make a simple substance into something better. It also can mean the synthetic manufacturing of natural resources into products that buffer and defend against the outside world.

The desire to create a man-made world to improve on nature and to secure from the elements, when out of balance, leads to rejection of the organic at the expense of health and vitality. Currently we live in a brown time. This means that culture is influenced by the values of the brown survival instinct. It does not mean that everyone is brown but just that culture is dominated by brown values. It is not surprising that junk food and synthetic chemicals both illicit and prescribed, are the sanctuary that a stressed society such as ours runs to for comfort.

> As you stand chatting to one of your oldest friends, you are annoyed at yourself for the thoughts that flicker through your mind. For all the anger and pain that your sister caused through her discontent and destructive behaviour, you are reminded that despite being surrounded by everything and everyone that you have always longed for, you still have moments of feeling lost.
>
> You had said this once to your best friend over coffee – the one you are talking to now and that is a subject you will not bring up again.
>
> 'Lost! What does lost mean?' she exclaimed.
>
> 'I am not sure how to define it. I suppose, just a sense of not knowing who you are,' you had replied.
>
> 'Not knowing who you are? What sort of psycho-rubbish have you been listening to? How can you not know who you are? You are the person who is standing in the mirror and the person who does what she does. Who are you? You are the sum total of your actions, nothing more, nothing less. What you do is who you are.'
>
> Your friend is a practical person and this was practical advice but she is not brown and neither is her philosophy.

Stating that you are what you choose to do in your life is useful for the other six colour groups. Many people feel a lack of direction in their lives and a need to reprioritise what is important, but not everyone loses who they are, what they are doing and where they belong, like brown can do.

After your sister died you became the perfect mother, wife and employee. You took more work home than necessary and did it in the hours that remained after providing for the needs of your husband and family. You were burning the candle at both ends and you felt its consequences. When you were in your last year at high school you had glandular fever and chronic fatigue as a result of burnout caused by your obsession to achieve high marks. The feelings in your body and the lack of energy then, are the same as you are experiencing now, and you know if you were to go to the doctor she would diagnose you with chronic fatigue.

It has been a long time since your last check-up and that is worrying you too. As a teenager your mother would tell you to relax, she even sent you to meditation classes thinking it would be beneficial, but all you did was sit cross-legged with your eyes closed revising your homework. Your mind and nervous system were too restless for meditation and still are now. You have learned to channel this energy rather than try and quell it.

Busy, busy, busy is how your friends describe you and your husband calls you the nickname 'bee'. Everyone sees you as competent, energetic and highly motivated and you survive on as little sleep as you can manage, but anxiety and motivation are not the same stimulus. When you stop you become fearful and edgy, your feet tap watching television and your mind flitters for something to do. Your nervous energy stops you from relaxing and you have learned by experience if you do not use it constructively on some sort of project, then it will turn its attention into an unmanageable fear. These fears are varied and until recently have no basis. The fear of health and protection for your family are the areas that worry you most.

When your children were young, you moved into their room and they were monitored with alarms in case they stopped breathing. There was no history of cot death anywhere in your family but that did not allay your fears. 'You have already got the kids miked up and alarmed,' your husband would say. 'Why do you have to move into their bedroom as well?' 'They are just little kids and are completely defenceless,' you would reply. 'I don't understand how a father can be so cold towards the health and safety of his own children.'

At this point the conversation would stop because there was no defence to such an accusation, even though you knew the accusation was harsh and unreasonable. This made you feel guilty because there was an underlying anxiety that you did not share with anyone else. This was the fear that your children would be kidnapped or attacked during the night. So overpowering was this fear that you were prepared to sacrifice your marital life. You knew the fear was baseless but that didn't matter, you were compelled to act on it anyway.

Childbirth had drained you of what energy you had and your survival instinct was placed into a state of alarm because your energy was down. Once again your survival instinct reverted to the primal state it calls home, which included in this instance a morbid fear of the external world and a securing of the internal by battering down the hatches.

## Protection

For this out of balance brown, children become beings to protect and defend rather than family to nurture and enjoy. If protective brown becomes very out of balance they can forget to find enjoyment in their children as enjoyment comes through relaxation and acceptance. Protective brown moulds and secures every moment of their children's lives by involving themselves as a caretaker for their every waking minute.

> You are aware of where your children are throughout the day and you take seriously your role of maternal supervisor and protector. Sometimes however, particularly when you are tired or stressed you are too wary.

> An example occurred the other day when your son started telling you

a story of how he told his teacher a joke and the teacher laughed and patted him on the back saying what a good story teller he was. At that precise moment while one part of you – the more rational part – was happy at your son's enjoyment, the survival instinct with its overprotective streak, forced you to begin asking questions about the way the teacher patted him, how long the pat took and in what fashion was the touch directed. Your instinct screamed at you to get the police involved and to tell the school what had occurred but you realised you were being over protective.

You also feel you need to protect your children from their grandmother, your mother-in-law. The more tired you are the less you can tolerate her interfering with your children or family matters. From your mother-in-law's perspective she is simply being their grandmother; picking them up and giving grandchildren toys and sweets is part of what a loving grandmother does. There is part of you that understands this, but your tired, weary body is low in energy. When you are tired your mother-in-law is no longer a giving, loving but slightly interfering woman, but someone who is defying the laws you have created for your own household, someone who oversteps the mark on too many occasions, devaluing your authority.

The reason you don't go back to the doctor, even though you are worn out and tired is because of the anxiety you feel. She has given you medication for your depression and occasional panic attacks.

Two years ago the mother of one of your son's friends died of breast cancer. You attended her funeral as you had been good friends. It was a horrible and depressing affair that drained the emotion from everyone who was present. The woman who died was everyone's friend. She was sweet and giving and three years younger than you when she died.

Just as life began to settle, your fear of fears occurred when a routine mammogram discovered the lump. Today on your fortieth birthday you are thankful to be alive and you believe you owe it all to the reprioritisation of your life. It is easy to go off track and to lose perspective about what is real and important. The mother who died was a superwoman like you, always pleasant on the outside, busy for everyone else and the person who could be relied on to complete a task perfectly no matter what that task was. The mother who died was Penny and her nickname at the school was 'Penny Perfect'.

The problem with Penny Perfect was that she was all things to all people, just like you. Penny Perfect and Dad's 'perfect little angel' may have ended the same way without changes being made but you decided to make those changes. You had treatment and also decided that not everything had to be done when others asked for it. It was not your responsibility to make everybody happy. You decided that you had a greater responsibility to the people you loved than for the people you worked for. Or even your friends. You decided it was not your role to keep the peace for everyone else and if other people became embroiled in a quarrel or fight, it was their business and their responsibility to deal with it or learn from it. You decided it was not your role to control and manage every minute of your loved ones' lives and you found by allowing them to be, that your relationship with them grew closer.

Now you are forty and everyone is celebrating. The feeling of being lost still occasionally arises just as it has at the party but now you know what you need to do. The sense of being lost comes when you are working too hard, or your detachment from the natural world has continued for too long. Sometimes you need counselling to get another person's opinion for the problems you feel, but this is becoming less frequent as you take control and know your own life.

When the party is over and you have slept as long as you need you will wake up tomorrow and you will dig in the garden or ride on your bike. Touching the plants and turning the soil, scraping the mulch and watering the trees are all you need to begin to return to the person you like to be. The bike ride gives you the freedom you love, with the wind in your hair and your children smiling and laughing beside you. Tomorrow night you will make a family dinner and sit down and enjoy the people you love and by the end of the day, you will know who you are and where you are going.

Outside on the balcony, your younger sister is talking with some friends. You have no idea what it is she is talking about but the chances of it being about business or equality are high. Your younger sister became a liberated feminist by choice when she was in her early teens. Your parents believe she was indoctrinated by the rebellious streak of your older sister but you are not so sure. Both your father and mother clashed with your older and younger sisters and often turn to you to be the peacemaker and mediator between the two warring parties. Sometimes you got sick of the role of family peacemaker but you still performed it anyway. It was like all things you do, the right thing.

As you walk out onto the balcony your sister is talking with a number of friends and you decide to join in the conversation.

'What's everybody talking about?' you ask.

'Nothing much, your sister is just telling me how I should approach this job situation,' her friend Jenny replies.

'I was just explaining,' your sister says, 'that there are avenues open for Jenny here, to appeal against her unfair dismissal.'

'Have you found another job yet?' you ask.

'I don't think that's the point,' your sister interjects, 'the fact that she was treated unfairly and dismissed without cause is the topic, not whether she has accepted being tossed out like a trained dog.'

'I am not implying she is a trained dog, all I am asking is whether or not she has found another job,' you reply in your own defence.

'How can you be so misdirected? To get another job and forget what has happened is to allow bastards like this to get away with treating woman as second class employees,' she retorts.

'As a matter of fact, there were more men laid off than women,' Jenny responds.

'That doesn't make your old boss less of a bastard, just because he sacked a few token males as well.'

'Is everything all right at home, Jenny?' you ask. 'The financial pressure is bearable I hope.'

'For goodness sake!' your sister cries. 'There you go again, diverting the conversation from its real objective.'

Your younger sister is not rebellious in the same anti-social, 'tear down the walls of the establishment' way your elder sister was, but she is challenging and confrontational in her demand to be accepted as unique and independent. She enjoys and continues to enjoy shocking people out of their apathy and making others conform to her beliefs and opinions, at least that is the way you see it. You know her perspective well because she has preached it to you on countless occasions but only rarely does she let you voice your own 'incorrect and misguided views'. When you told her that you believed liberation and confrontation to be two separate issues, and that you can be strong without being challenging, she replied, 'It's not my fault that others can't handle my own inner strength or they have troubling dealing with a woman with a brain.'

When your sister was young, she challenged all conventions. It was not just the influence of your older sister, because she wasn't living at home at the time and the two rarely got together due to their age difference. She was not influenced down this avenue; she was destined for this avenue. In her late teens and early twenties, she had her hair cut short and wore very low and revealing tops for a girl so well endowed. As a result she drew her fair share of male attention which always made her angry and she would verbally attack anyone she saw ogling her.

'If you don't want to be ogled why do you show so much?' you used to ask.

'It's my right to wear whatever I want. I am not going to be forced into wearing what other people want me to wear, just because others can't control what's in their pants.'

'But don't you think you are inviting it just a little?' you had responded.

'I wear these clothes because they're comfortable not because they're sexual, if others can't control themselves that's not my problem. But if they come into my space they soon will have a problem.'

Personally you thought, this was naïve and aggressive, although you could never openly tell her that, because again you would be put down and not listened to. You had two ways of looking at the world, the two of you, and each world was remote from the other. You hate confrontation and you want everything to be harmonious and as perfect as life can be, while she enjoys confrontation and seems to go out of her way to create it. She believes she is exercising her rights and that she has the right to say and behave in any manner that she sees fit, but that others do not. She has the right to wear revealing clothes but others do not have the right to look. She has the right to voice her opinion but others do not have the right to question that opinion.

'If she doesn't want guys to look at her then why does she dress in a provocative manner?' your husband used to say.

'She believes that others should turn away and use their willpower not to look at her and that it is their fault and their failure if they do,' you had replied.

'So millions of years of biological attraction is expected to disappear just because she says so,' he had commented.

'It seems that way.'

He would always end this conversation in exactly the same way. 'Well that's just stupid!'

Your husband and your sister do not see eye to eye. They are cordial and friendly and provided both stay off any topic of ideology they get along fine. In the early days they were better friends. However, since having children they have gone separate ways. The final straw was when she chastised your husband for referring to your daughter by her gender.

It was a family gathering and your daughter drew a picture and presented it to her father as a gift.

'What a fantastic drawing. Did you do this all by yourself?'

'Yes,' she replied. 'I did it all by myself.'

'Well you must be the cleverest little girl in the whole wide world so that must make me the luckiest Dad ever.'

Your daughter had laughed and went off to draw some more.

'Well that was demoralising,' your sister exclaimed to your husband.

'What!' he said in disbelief.

'How is equality of the sexes ever going to be achieved when we keep dividing and talking as if gender was a primary issue?' she replied.

'So what should I say? That's a great drawing. What a clever little camel you are?'

'Be facetious then. It's only your children's lives you're wrecking. I feel sorry for you that you can only see life in terms of gender but it would be more appropriate to congratulate your daughter by her name and not her gender,' she bristled.

'Look, I know I was being smart with the quip about the camel, but I honestly don't feel calling my daughter a clever little girl is harmful to her self esteem,' he replied.

'You are making her a girl first and clever second.'

'Well as a matter of fact, I called her a clever girl and clever came first'.

'So what you really mean is that she is clever for a girl – is that right?'

'This is just ridiculous and such a stupid topic that I am not going to continue with it. My daughter gave me a picture, it was an innocent comment.'

'Mistakes done with all good intent are still mistakes. Research shows that children flourish better when they are not confined by gender,' she smugly replied.

Furious your husband turned on her, 'I bet your researcher is childless too.'

At that moment whatever friendship that existed between them dissolved. Your sister had made a conscious decision not to have children deciding instead to focus on her career, and she took this comment as a deliberate attempt to be spiteful and cutting.

## Need for change

When confrontational brown is out of balance the world is a place that needs to be changed. Everyone has to become more understanding, evolved, compassionate and patient. Education becomes the key to all change. This outlook is coming from a belief that these values are automatically the right ones but when they are out of balance, confrontational brown has no such concerns. Their values are right, emancipating and beneficial to all. Anyone who disagrees with these values by definition must be wrong. Confrontational brown is out to change the world.

In balance this type of brown uses their determination to change situations where people or environments are being abused. Through confrontation they secure positive changes for all.

## Having it all

Brown balances all three forces within their natural primary state. They are the people most adapted to successfully juggling the demands of work, family and relationships. When their three internal forces are in balance, these three external priorities will also fall into line. If they are internally out of balance one or two of these external areas can suffer. Many people from other colour groups are happy to drop one of these three aspects of life in exchange for achievement in either one or just two areas. For some this means stopping work to concentrate on their family and partner while for others it can mean foregoing a family to concentrate on a partner and career. The more brown is in balance the more they can successfully incorporate all three aspects of life harmoniously.

The time we live in (1950–2100 AD) is dominated by brown. This means culture is infused with the brown ethic of unity. The demand to juggle family, relationship and work is more dominant at present because brown demands all aspects be accounted for. This is the external projection of brown's internal drive. When this drive is out of balance it is demanding and intolerant of anyone who opposes these values.

There are many women and men at present who feel pressured and put down by the brown demand to balance all three areas of life without question. However it needs to be remembered that people from other colour groups, especially women, do not share this same internal drive or external projection and are happy to forego either partner, family or career. However many struggle to keep up with the ethic they believe they must follow. To reject this contemporary ethic, is to sound like an archaic dinosaur. So they push, work, struggle and fight to perform the tasks that contemporary culture demands. Men and women alike are becoming disenchanted and burned out.

## Equality

Strength through unity is the essence of brown and they will blend cultures and break down any stereotypes or cultural hurdles that impede, demote or demoralise a particular gender, sub-culture or class.

With family they will ensure that each member gets an equal share and an equal proportion including an equal say in all family matters, regardless of whether every member wants this input or not. Many people are quite happy to be followers rather than decision makers and many children in particular are happy to let parents lead the way, but brown are seeking equality. The family, company or culture must all be united and moving in the one direction.

Women in western society until relatively recently have been a servile underclass, that has been exploited and prevented from reaching any personal potential. Brown cannot have a weak link within its system. Strength through unity means energy must flow to the area of least resistance. When brown is in balance they will bolster and fortify the weaker areas of themselves and of their culture. Unity brown is a firm believer in nurture dominating nature. They must believe that this is the hierarchy, because nurture can be changed, nature cannot. This is why such emphasis on education and retraining forms part of unity brown's psyche.

In balance, unity brown is helpful and willing to nurture and strengthen those people or cultures most in need. They protect the underdog and they feed the downtrodden because their primal drive demands they support the weakest. This does not diminish the altruistic benevolence of their actions, nor does it downplay the sustenance and support needed by those who they help. For many in the world or those lost in the cracks of the city, unity brown can be their only link to salvation or survival.

Out of balance however, unity brown can focus too much on the underdog giving them an over-represented voice in the community at large. This type of brown can push so hard for underdog issues that minority groups representing only one or two percent of the community can get attention and funding far beyond their numbers. This doesn't mean that their cause is less valid, but it is representative of brown's need to send extra energy and resources to the weakest social links, in an attempt to maintain stability and strength.

In modern times there are many benefits from living under the influence of unity. Safety nets exist in First World cultures where none existed before. In previous times the rich had everything, while the poor barely got by, their existence routine, bleak and hungry. The brown desire to supplement and elevate the weakest areas has meant that the average person in the first world has had their standard of living raised beyond the wildest expectations of anyone who lived before. The serfs and peasants of the past could never have dreamed of a life where they could put their feet up at the end of the day and drink coffee and eat chocolate. Never could they imagine going to bed under a roof that didn't leak, surrounded by walls that didn't let in the wind. The benevolence of brown to support the weak, which in social terms means the majority of the population, cannot be overvalued nor can their kindness be underestimated.

## Strength

Strength through unity is a driving force of confrontational brown. By confronting the larger external world, they replicate the struggle of matter in the universe. Desperate to prove they can withstand and compete with the outside world, confrontational brown challenge the conventions of culture, tackling head on anyone or anything they believe to be repressive.

Strength is the key to maintaining individuality and like everyone else they will cling to existence with every breath they have.

Out of balance this type of brown can be misguided in identifying who is an enemy and who is not. They become confrontational for confrontation's sake and are seen by others as rude, blunt and arrogant. Confrontational brown can isolate themselves from others, leading to separation and the sense of being alone in the world.

Individuality becomes a life theme for this type of brown in both their demand and rejection of uniqueness. Out of balance they demand the right to be heard and to challenge. They demand the right to change what they see fit and to talk and dress in any manner they please. At the same time they shun the rights of others to not accept their values.

In balance brown knows who to fight and how to undertake the process. They fight for the right reasons, not just to prove their internal strength. When brown is in balance their rational soul is using the natural strengths given by the survival instinct to look after themselves and others.

The survival instinct, supplies everyone with natural attributes and talents that can be creatively used for the benefit of all when the soul is in balance. In balance brown protects the weak and the lost, and nurtures those who are unable to help themselves.

## Pleasing everyone

Some brown people try so hard to be everybody's friend they never speak up for themselves. To pleasing brown, challenge is something to be avoided rather than relished and they will give any token of appeasement to delay or avoid a clash of wills. Giving everything they can, in effort and time to ensure others are happy and never have a problem, they expend enormous amounts of energy so the transition through life is smooth and easy for those who they love.

Taking on all the burdens, responsibility and hardship so those around them do not have to do the same, can send this type of brown out of balance very quickly.

Giving a labyrinth of options only creates confusion and out of this confusion discontent results. Brown, in trying to please everyone, offers endless variety in an attempt to satisfy. It is not unusual for a pleasing brown mother to ask her child, 'What would you like to do today? Would you like to go to the movies or the zoo, or perhaps to the park, or would you like to go on some rides? What about the museum? Or maybe we could go bowling? Or would you prefer to go to the beach or stay at home? And what about for lunch – would you prefer hamburgers or hotdogs? Or perhaps something healthy or perhaps …'

In balance brown has learned not to succumb to this ingrained trait to try to please everybody. Too many options make people overwhelmed. Brown out of balance believes children are adults and that they are capable of adult decisions and behaviour. In balance they realise this is not true at all. They realise that the best type of mother is the mother who insists that her child eats their broccoli, goes to bed early when asked, is forced to use their own imagination when they are bored and is punished appropriately when they do something wrong. Instead of feeling they are responsible for the wellbeing and harmony of everyone around them, releasing themselves from the pressure of perfection, allows them to enjoy their family and themselves.

## The peacemaker

When personalities become aggressive, dominating or excessively influential our survival instinct becomes dominant. Peacemaker brown when surrounded by strength or hostility reverts to their primal state of unity and do all they can to pacify or satiate the tempers and needs of those around them. When they are out of balance, they can become a full-time service provider ensuring that every need no matter how small of the people around them is met, so others do not have to lift a finger or suffer a minute's inconvenience which may disturb the harmony of the home.

The consequences of this imbalance are expensive and dire. At a personal level peacemaker brown runs themselves ragged and drives their energy levels way below the level where self-replenishment can take place. Within the family the consequences are no less serious by creating spouses and children who are disrespectful, demanding and lazy. Peacemaker brown believes they are doing the right thing for others when in fact it is their own survival instinct that is needy.

Whenever the survival instinct of one person is active and on alert, the survival instincts of all are soon involved. When somebody is competing for their own survival that competition forces others to compete in return. The natural question is how can support and service, switch on the survival instincts of their spouse and children? The answer is simple. Peacemaker brown is doing too much for their family, and their spouse and children do not develop the skills they need to feel competent. Vulnerability makes the survival instinct dominant. Balance can only occur when the survival instinct is secure which happens when we are competent, able to look after ourselves and able to contribute.

By providing everything brown has inadvertently switched on the survival instincts of everyone around them by creating people who are dependent and lack self-assuredness. They have set the scene for disintegration rather than unity.

Brown in balance is not afraid to do what is necessary to create confident and competent children and partners. They understand that giving all their time is too much of a good thing and never achieves what they were hoping for. Balance is the key, and balance embraces the concept of unity. Supporting rather than taking over keeps brown's energy in check.

## Energy exhaustion

When energy levels plummet to the point where reserves are drawn upon for healthy functioning, changes in lifestyle must be put into place to ensure that the amount drawn is kept to a minimum. Everyone comes into the world with a limited amount of energy. In some, levels are high and they can live off a small amount of sleep and continue to work and play hard, with very few consequences. For most, this is not the case. Most people have an average reserve which means it must be managed appropriately.

The more energy we use beyond our capacity in the present, the less that will be available for daily life in the future. There are very few people who can damage their health and draw on their reserves of energy for an extended period of time, who do not pay the price later in life. Perhaps only five percent have energy supplies far beyond the normal range. The problem is that ninety-five percent of us believe or hope that we belong in that five percent range, but the odds are vastly stacked against us.

Worry, drugs, overwork, stress and continued exertion use more energy than normal daily input can provide and as a result energy needed for the future is burned. When the future finally arrives the extra energy that is required is no longer available and pathology begins.

Life requires movement, and stagnancy is the biggest killer of all. The primal forces inside all matter and life are all associated with movement. Outward motion, circular motion and inward motion all have one thing in common; they are all motion. To not aspire, create or make is one of the most dangerous and destructive outcomes for our health and wellbeing, but motion also comes at a physical cost. Our joints, ligaments, muscles and bones all bear the stress of physical motion and it is a fine line between too little and too much. Too little motion and our body becomes weak and eventually breaks down. Too much motion and it becomes tired and worn down before its time.

As we age we require more energy to maintain efficiency. Millions of heartbeats have occurred and hundreds of tonnes of food have been processed in the intestines. Tens of thousands of kilometres have been travelled and all manner of potentially dangerous chemicals have been neutralised by the time we reach middle age. The general wear and tear of life demands that energy must remain high if we are to avoid physical disease and decay.

Women are generally given more life force than men due to the demands of childbirth and feeding. As a result, women often outlive men.

Very few people escape the ravages of time or inheritance, and suffer some sort of problem as they age. These problems do not have to be serious and many people go through their lives putting up with symptoms that in the grand scheme are only minor inconveniences. But if energy reserves have been exhausted to dangerous levels before middle age or senior years arrive, pathology can turn from minor to major and even to life threatening, at an alarming rate.

## Breakdown

Physical breakdown occurs in every colour group because it is part of the cycle of life. Inherited strengths and weaknesses combined with energy loss and wear and tear means pathology and organic dysfunction result. In out of balance brown health and illness becomes even more complicated because organic breakdown is part of their natural drive.

Matter is designed to breakdown and rebuild. When outside forces become too strong for internal unity to be maintained brown decomposes so it can reform and restructure into a new and stronger arrangement.

Rather than resisting overwhelming odds, the forces in brown break down and disband so new life can begin. Nature has instilled into brown the instinct to build rather than to endure. This can be seen in contemporary society where products are made to be replaced rather than to be fixed and certainly not to last a lifetime. When a product breaks down, we throw it away and get another one. This is the energy of brown because it is what their forces are designed to do.

If life becomes too difficult and energy levels drop below the point of no return for an extensive period of time, the brown survival instinct immediately returns to its nature of breakdown and replacement. This time however, the breakdown is to a person not a product, but motion doesn't care, because motion doesn't know.

The natural brown cycle means that once unity is fractured, systemic breakdown begins. In human beings this is most commonly experienced as an auto immune disorder like diabetes or rheumatoid arthritis, or as an organic degenerative disease such as cancer. This does not mean that all brown people will get cancer, nor does it mean that everyone who gets cancer is brown. There is no such thing as pathological inevitability and in balance, brown have no greater chance of getting cancer than anyone else. At the same time, it is also true that systemic breakdown plays a natural part in their make-up once the survival instinct believes it is no longer capable of withstanding any further external pressure.

Not all breakdowns are physical. Emotional and nervous energy also plays its part when external stress becomes too strong to cope. What used to be called a nervous breakdown is common to this colour group if they are subjected to excessive or continuous stress. A complete emotional collapse can take place to such a degree that conscious rationality is replaced by blind panic. In this instance, energy levels have been pushed beyond endurance and the survival instinct has taken complete control, suppressing almost entirely the reasoning of the soul. Each colour group has its own version of a 'breakdown' but the classic nervous type is most common in brown and green.

These examples are extreme and thankfully do not occur unless stress is great. However the one illness that is common in brown is chronic fatigue. This is a mild version of systemic shut down where due to the poor management or severity of stress, breakdown is more functional and energetic rather than nervous or organic.

In balance, unity, perfection and strength play a much greater role than the breakdown process. Everyone can avoid the physical ramifications of stress induced pathology through self-management and awareness. By knowing themselves and focusing on what is important people accept who they are rather than the often mistaken image of who they would like to be. Once self-recognition is achieved, people organise their life around their personality and ambition and finally begin to live the life they were designed to live.

## Abundance

Remodelling the natural environment into a more conducive setting to human needs is the role of the craftsman. Making furniture from wood and fireplaces from stone means human beings can live in greater comfort and security. Protection from the harshness of the elements has given longevity to the entire human race. Deep in the recesses of the survival instinct of brown is the knowledge that removal from the harshness of nature is beneficial.

Out of balance this instinct drives brown under stress to search for bigger and better ways of answering their problems through synthetic means. Synthetic abundance is the answer to stress when the craftsman is out of balance. The survival instinct always reverts to what it knows. In times of stress and energy depletion, the survival instinct becomes dominant and the drive to fight in our own unique way supersedes everything else.

Historically the more comfortable and happy the craftsman could make others, the higher their social status and the greater their chances of survival and breeding became. By providing to others tools, weapons, utensils and clothing, the craftsman made themselves indispensable to the group. Under stress the brown survival instinct returns to its past, safe in the knowledge that the more it can reshape and remould nature the happier and more accepted it will become.

Regardless of stress the result is the same. The craftsman returns to a synthetic solution. In contemporary times this can take a number of different forms, the most common of which includes shopping, drugs and excessive amounts of artificial food.

Surrounding themselves and indulging in masses of clothes, shoes, cars, drugs or growing fat on chocolate and soft drink is a predictable outcome of brown under stress. Making one product of supreme value does not keep the craftsman safe when famine returns. One product makes one purchaser content, but the craftsman like every other traditional role is attempting to make as many people within their group as happy with them as possible.

Only by numbers can personal security be assured in times of extreme hardship and rationing. As a result the craftsman makes an abundance of goods rather than spending their life perfecting one. To reproduce as faithfully and as quickly as possible is what keeps the craftsman alive. In contemporary society the essence of the craftsman dominates every aspect of our social structure. Producing more than enough is the ethic of the time. The same recipe gives the same result, and the drive to franchise the same stores with the same products, in the same way with the same outcome, is the craftsman at work. The fact that this is the basis of our culture also highlights that we are a society under stress. Turning to synthetic abundance and indulgence in synthetic drugs and food is the hallmarks of a tired, lost and stressed society.

In balance, the craftsman understands that while we have synthetic needs we are also natural creatures. Separating ourselves from nature is not the solution. Rather, it is finding how we can live the lives we want *within* nature. The importance of walking in nature or digging in the earth cannot be underestimated.

The challenge in contemporary times is how we can balance the needs of our internal nature to be both synthetic *and* natural. How do we take from nature, create from nature but not exploit nature. Many brown people in an attempt to rebalance themselves and the earth have become staunch defenders of environmental issues. Current times are a manifestation of the personal battle that brown face, and everyone on the planet regardless of colour group is dominated and influenced by these issues, because of the brown time in which we live.

To understand society in these current times is to understand the nature of brown. How can everyone be given shelter while allowing the natural environment to survive? How can human beings flourish but space be put aside for other animals to do the same? The earth was never intended to be a monoculture and forests and biodiversity provide the raw materials the craftsman synthesises in order to survive. In this way the craftsman is linked to the survival of these raw resources in a deeper way than their survival instinct can imagine. It is not surprising that the crisis point between man and nature is occurring in these brown times, but if anyone has the capacity to solve the problem it will be brown.

## Facial features

Brown features are a combination of *equal or near equal* amounts of yellow, red and blue. One or two colour groups can have *one* more facial feature than the others but that is all. Anymore or less and the face would no longer be brown. Sometimes there is *the same* number of yellow, red and blue features but more frequently there is one feature of difference between one group to the other two.

Chapter 20

# HISTORY

The forces that lie inside time are the same as the material universe. Time is part of the physical world because it depends on space and matter. The forces in time maintain their character but time does not have any physical boundaries.

Throughout history the colour groups move in cycles rather than compete for dominance. Time is not physical so dominance and interaction does not come into effect. Each colour period lasts approximately one hundred and fifty years before changing into the next colour period. Colour periods influence time, space and matter according to their nature. From weather to culture, the earth is shaped by the influence of the colour group that presides over that period.

The cycle of the colour periods is as follows.

| **Colour period** | **Time period (AD)** |
| --- | --- |
| Orange | 0 to 150 |
| Yellow | 150 to 300 |
| Purple | 300 to 450 |
| Blue | 450 to 600 |
| Red | 600 to 750 |
| Green | 750 to 900 |
| Brown | 900 to 1050 |
| Orange | 1050 to 1200 |
| Yellow | 1200 to 1350 |
| Purple | 1350 to 1500 |
| Blue | 1500 to 1650 |
| Red | 1650 to 1800 |
| Green | 1800 to 1950 |
| Brown | 1950 to 2100 |

The influence of a colour during a particular period is subtle rather than forceful. Its influence does not change the character of human nature but it does inspire and leave its mark on the culture and ethics of the time. The effect of a presiding colour can be likened to the influence of climate on culture. Human beings are the same whether they live in the ice or the desert. There is no internal anatomical difference between an Eskimo and a Bedouin. The social structure of each is similar with marriage and children existing in both. Each has their gods, history and music. However, Eskimo culture is different from Bedouin in diet, beliefs and cultural stories that result from the influence of terrain and climate.

The effect of colour on human existence is similar to the effect of climate; subtle yet all-pervasive. People are a product of their time, and time is a product of motion. During the yellow period, yellow people were not more common than people from other colour groups, and not every event that occurred during that period was a representation of yellow. The Bedouin are not a different species of human; the Bedouin are a different culture. During a colour period human nature remains the same but ethics, ambitions and social stress changes. While disease affected every age, society's reaction to disease varied enormously. During the Black Death which occurred during the last purple period, heretics were burned as human sacrifice. A century later when the plague re-appeared burning heretics no longer occurred because the influence of the colour group had changed. The priest was the only traditional role to practice human sacrifice as part of their professional function. Aztec priests sacrificed virgins while early Christians sacrificed themselves. Sacrifice and the priest were synonymous, which is why it occurred during the stress of the Black Death but not during other epidemics.

What was enlightened a century ago is no longer considered acceptable. In the 19th century it was brazen for a woman to sit in a skirt that revealed her ankles, yet a century earlier wealthy women wore dresses that exposed every inch of their cleavage.

Cultural change cannot be explained solely as social evolution. Opinion also changes because of the shifting periods of the colour groups that reside within time. What is learned can never be undone because knowledge cannot be unlearned. However knowledge is constantly reapplied to suit the changing beliefs of the periods.

In the 16th century absolutism of the king was accepted and even revered. Royal absolutism was accepted by commoners freely and without reservation. In the 13th century the Magna Carta was put into place to curb the excess of the same absolutism the 16th century admired. Freedom and personal liberty did not come from an evolving process because the Magna Carta was signed three hundred years before this absolutism began.

The 16th century was also a time when Europe was at war over religion. Galileo was placed under house arrest by the Church for saying the earth revolved around the sun. However fifty years after Galileo's death, intellectuals of the enlightenment ignored papal threats and the church was powerless to stop them. The enlightenment believed the natural world was better understood through measurement than mystery.

This chapter looks in detail at the last thousand years beginning with orange in 1050 AD. Cultural history becomes difficult to examine the further we move back in time. Each step back means less documentation to tell us about that period's beliefs. The last thousand years is easier to examine than the thousand years that preceded it. Focus in this chapter also centres on Europe because European culture is documented in greater detail than most others.

Often there is a five-year or ten-year period when a crossover of events occurs, due to the influence of changing colours. At other times a specific event heralds the end of one colour period and the beginning of the next. One hundred and fifty years is the average span of a time period although a few years variation is common.

# The orange period 1050 to 1200 AD

## Outward and circular motion – resistance
Life themes during the orange period were:

- duty
- death
- grief

- loyalty
- honour
- suffering
- righteousness
- moral crusade
- hysteria
- compassion
- discipline

During the orange period the frequency of famine reduced, and a new age of prosperity began. Land reclamation meant more ground for farming, while merchants and travellers needed safe accommodation which led to the development of new roads and towns. Thoroughfares were built to join villages normally separated by forests and pasture. With prosperity came bigger churches and more imposing town cathedrals.

Merchants formed trade guilds to regulate and protect their industry while the military class reached its peak in various parts of the world. By 1180 the samurai in Japan were stronger than the aristocracy, while in Europe the nobles evolved into a knighted cavalry. They became professional soldiers born to lead the king's army. The legend of King Arthur was written around 1130 AD, epitomising the ideals of the warrior.

The orange time period was the time of chivalry and knighthood, the crusades and courtly love. Religious fervour swept across Europe and the cross became the new emblem of holy war. With a cross on their chest and a sword in their hand, priests and knights urged all righteous men to join them in a holy crusade. Before the orange period the cross was a sign of humility and peace, but in these times it was a call to arms. Crusaders were willing to sacrifice everything just as Jesus had sacrificed himself on the cross. The fact that Jesus was a man of peace did not deter the knights. To them the holy land was under attack and Christian soldiers were ready to kill and dismember anyone threatening the sanctity of the lord.

Priests were employed to recruit enough peasants to create an entire army. They joined knights practiced in the art of war, all drunk on the promise of salvation and plunder.

War and crusades have been a regular part of history because fighting is part of human nature. During the orange time fighting became the crusades – a fight for a principled cause. To anyone not Arabic, the knight was a hero who upheld the sanctity of religion. Knights were courteous and chivalrous, steadfast and strong, but to the Arabs they were arrogant invaders, merciless and domineering. They were infidels who stole and governed without permission. Out of balance, orange can still be seen this way.

The crusades were more than blood for the cross. The knights of St John and the Hospitallers were legendary for their compassion and care. These holy knights did everything within their power to protect and nurture the sick and injured. This trait of defending the helpless and vulnerable continues in the orange survival instinct.

To the knight the crusades were a fight for principles. They were an earthly test of courage and devotion, a trial of hell in defence of heaven to see who was worthy of everlasting life. The knight was prepared to place God and the cause above their personal security. The orange survival instinct sees dignity as sacrifice and honour. Orange believes in noble causes and they never give up the fight.

At home maidens waited while their knights went to war. The orange period was a time when troubadours serenaded lonely hearts with songs of eternal yet unrequited love. Knights fought for the love of their maiden, while their maiden pledged chastity and devotion. Orange embodies the ideals and essence of fidelity and adoration.

During the orange time period, William the Conqueror took military control over England. Every pound, shilling and pence was counted and recorded with typical orange precision. Professional judges were first appointed during this time to ensure the quality of justice.

The crusades became part of the survival instinct of orange not only because it was the prevailing force of the time, but because the crusades influenced the hearts and culture of the Arabic and Christian worlds. While vast numbers were killed in battle, even more were emotionally embroiled in its fervour. Stories told of city streets that flowed shin high with blood.

While the knights had a number of victories, the peasant armies recruited by the priests were generally no match for the Arabic warriors who massacred them like lambs to the slaughter. The knights may have put up a noble fight, but the average peasant received their heavenly reward sooner than most expected.

The orange survival instinct carries the reactions of death, suffering, honour, caring for the sick, protection, idealism, sacrifice and devotion. Orange is the unrequited love of the lady in waiting and the pedestal of adoration for those they admire.

In the previous orange period, 0–150 AD, the ideals of sacrifice, righteousness and devotion were repeated in the life of Jesus and the crucifixion. The crucifixion of Jesus, his betrayal by the disciples, the death of St Paul and the martyrdom of the early Christians, all epitomise orange. Average people who converted to Jesus were willing to risk death rather than betray their faith. The events surrounding the early Christians resemble the knights of the crusades, because orange was the influence in both. The orange survival instinct believes that sacrifice is love, and that devotion is measured by endurance. Honour, commitment and caring for others, defending the vulnerable and giving comfort to the suffering are the foundations of the Christian soldier.

## The yellow period 1200 to 1350 AD

### Outward motion – progress
Life themes during the yellow period were:

- money
- blood family
- charity
- law
- education
- business
- independence
- new ideas
- authority
- outcast

The universal function of outward motion is to progress and expand borders. In the yellow period universal rule became as close a reality as it ever would in history.

Christendom became universal in Europe and a pontifical theocracy was a reality. During the yellow time period the pope was regarded as not only a spiritual leader, but someone who was invested by God to lead the government of the world.

In Asia outward motion was seen in the actions of Genghis Khan. Within the space of twenty years the Mongols became the largest empire that would ever exist on Earth. Genghis Khan was their one supreme leader. The Mongols were never content by conquest alone and had no desire to settle. The Mongol armies moved from place to place killing and plundering as they pleased. Genghis Khan and his armies only stopped long enough to gather stores, before returning to their outward expansion.

Born Temujin in either 1154 or 1155 during the orange time period, he received the title Genghis Khan in exactly 1200, and began his first war against the Tartars. Genghis Khan exterminated the Tartars in only two years. By 1213 he had reached the Great Wall and was able to invade China. When he died in 1227, the empire he had conquered took two years to cross and was the largest the world had ever known.

Outward motion did not stop after Genghis Khan's death, because yellow had not finished its period. His descendants continued their yellow expansion until their conquests included China, Russia and Eastern Europe.

Under his grandson Kublai Khan, all of China was conquered and Kublai Khan became the first 'king of the world'. His empire stretched from the Danube in the west to the East China Sea. During the yellow time Marco Polo became the first European to travel with his family of traders into China. Under Kublai Khan economic growth flourished and paper money was introduced, although later this led to financial collapse.

In Europe St Francis of Assisi founded an evangelical order based on Christ's teachings of poverty and charity. Money is one of the major life themes of yellow and St Francis continued this trend. During the yellow time instead of the acquisition of money the Franciscans devoted their lives to the distribution of wealth, giving clothing and food to the poor. The rejection of wealth in the yellow time went further than financial poverty.

Many monks made themselves physically impoverished by eating only a minimum of food. Some refused to bathe or even change their clothes, they became the 'great unwashed'. Poverty replaced endurance and pain as the ultimate expression of devotion, because the yellow time had replaced orange and was now the prevalent force. Some of the monks were so deliberately unclean they were riddled with scabies, mites and worms.

Filth became a badge of honour because it symbolised disregard for vanity and pleasure. While lepers were being expelled as unclean, monks did their best to exemplify it. Treating their bodies with contempt, monks during the yellow time rejected earthly comfort because 'it was easier for a camel to pass through the eye of a needle than it was for a rich man to enter into heaven.' Poverty was holy. Stories circulated about monks and saints with so many worms crawling out of their skin, bystanders grew sick just looking at them.

In 1215 the Magna Carta was signed to limit the power of the king. Nobles and barons refused to let anyone, even the king, restrict their independence. While the Magna Carta is connected to justice, it was mainly about the right of nobles to control their own property. The Magna Carta was the beginning of the idea that no-one should be above the law. No person at any time would agree to relinquish control over their property and assets. Attempting to control goods and chattels during a yellow time was not a well thought out plan as King John found out.

In England trial by jury began in 1285. Law was vital to the trader because the law gave freedom and security. If nobody is above the law, including the head of state, no one can interfere with anyone else's business or take what is not rightfully theirs. Free trade is more than a word, it's a statement of intent that requires both freedom and trade to make the combination work. Trade creates personal wealth that buys freedom of choice, but trade can only be successful when it is completed without interference.

The fear created by the Mongol armies still exists in the survival instinct of yellow. War continued during the yellow time because fighting is an unfortunate part of human nature. However in the yellow period, the previous orange emotional fervour, moral righteousness and sense of purpose was replaced by a fear of foreign invaders and the dread of being slaughtered. There were no titanic struggles between adversaries like Richard and Saladin; instead there was only the simple terror instilled by Genghis Khan. The Mongols slaughtered their way across the world and the panic that went before them alarmed communities to such an extent that many gave in without a fight. Some decided they would challenge Genghis Khan and died a torturous death.

In an earlier yellow period 150 to 300 AD, Rome was at its peak. While the Mongols had conquered an empire that took two years to cross, history's other dominant empire was Rome which was at the height of its power also during a yellow period.

# The purple period 1350 to 1500 AD

## Circular and inward motion – separation
Life themes during the purple period were:

- spirituality
- space
- division
- paranoia
- supernatural
- charisma
- expectation
- betrayal
- attention
- generosity
- death

In the fourteenth century hopes for a universal Christian empire faded because it was an ideal that no longer applied to the new purple world. During the purple time not only did the idea of a united Christendom vanish but, true to the separating nature of purple, a situation evolved where three people would claim to be the 'true' pope. This situation became known as the Great Western Schism.

France went to war with England and Joan of Arc became France's heroine for her victories and visionary prophesies. Despite her military success, Joan of Arc was betrayed to the English who burnt her at the stake for witchcraft. Five hundred years later she was exonerated by the church and canonised.

Witchcraft, suspicion, magic and fear were a tone set by purple that culminated in the Spanish inquisition. Inquisitors were religious police sanctioned by the crown and church to torture and gain confessions of heresy. Fear of the supernatural was everywhere because this time belonged to the priest.

Despite these trials the greatest cataclysmic event to occur during the purple period was the Black Death. By the mid 1300s leprosy had run its natural course because the yellow time was coming to an end. Thousands of leper houses normally full became empty as the purple time took over. As leprosy vanished, the Black Death created misery on a massive scale. The Black Death terrorised the world while doctors and priests looked helplessly on as up to 75 million people died. As the disease gained strength attention turned from finding a cure to finding a cause.

The priest believes in supernatural answers and the obvious conclusion for all the pain was that God was angry and cursing the world. Many deduced that God was angry because the Jews had killed Jesus. Actually it was the Romans who killed Jesus but this never seems to count. Jew burnings began as a way of saving the world from God's punishment

Others also believed the plague was God's wrath but were less specific about who to blame. One group took on the sins of the world and punished themselves for atonement. The flagellants walked the countryside whipping themselves and taking on the sins of the world. Later, perhaps because their actions failed, they also turned on the Jews.

The priest walks a fine line between life and death as well as religion and medicine. These purple fundamentals came into play because of the impact of the plague. Life and death were a daily routine as a third of the European population died within a span of two years.

During the purple time the population decreased dramatically and emphasis switched from the group to the individual. Wages soared because of the shortage of labour and luxuries became affordable. The purple period highlighted the precarious nature of life. One minute everything was fine, the next a third of the population was dead. Priests were hit especially hard because they were the ones who cared for the sick. While disease was the curse of God, the priest who was doing God's work theoretically should have been spared, but they were not. Deep in the purple survival instinct is the unnerving thought that perhaps God cannot be trusted either.

In the previous purple period 300 to 450 AD, Constantine divided the Roman Empire in two, while Roman persecution of the Christians began by burning the churches and imprisoning the clergy. History repeats.

# The blue period 1500 to 1650 AD

## Inward motion – stability
Life themes during the blue period were:

- management
- simplicity
- cooperation
- social etiquette
- easy going
- happiness
- withdrawal
- routine

As the blue time was about to begin, Columbus brought syphilis back from America (1494). Syphilis starts on the periphery of the body before working its way to the nerves and brain, where it causes most of its damage. This is the opposite of leprosy where most of the damage is peripheral. Yellow pushes out while blue draws in.

During the blue time absolute power was returned to the king in many European nations. In some places this led to decadence amongst those in authority that continued until the red period took over. Red would remove the power of the king by removing his royal head. Until this time, blue was happy to have their national ideals and pride symbolised in their monarch.

When the world moved from the purple time to blue, superstitious hysteria returned to traditional faith. While the Black Death reappeared the burnings did not, nor did the magic that previously surrounded it. The Black Death no longer created supernatural panic because the world was no longer purple.

Martin Luther was the biggest influence in religion as the reformation changed the Christian world. Luther wanted to bring the church back to what he believed were its basic values. To him only what was written in the Bible should be accepted as God's word. Making saints out of men, idols out of relics and selling indulgences to get out of purgatory was not, according to Luther, appropriate behaviour for the Church. His formula for salvation was based in belief, not in deeds, faith could not be bought. Back to basics is blue.

Luther's nailing of his ninety-five theses to the church door of Wittenberg, as well as being revolutionary was a naïve blue moment. An individual cannot expect to challenge the same ruthless power that sanctioned the Spanish Inquisition, yet seem surprised when it retaliates. However that is exactly what happened. Luther showed genuine surprise upon receiving his summons to Rome, but he must have been the only one who was surprised. The religious war that followed Luther's comments was a release of repression that turned Europe into a blood bath. Luther once again acted surprised. Later he rallied and managed the situation well. Many blue people have this ability to withstand the pressures and taunts of others, to continue what they believe is in the best interests of all. Violence and bloodshed is not exclusively blue because it is part of human nature, but the puritan movement that came from the reformation was a result of blue beliefs.

The puritans tried to follow the Bible down to its most minute detail. Their aim was to be humble and obedient. Puritans rejected worldly pleasures to live simple and austere lives. God placed blessings on those he was happy with, so prosperity became a measurement of God's reward. This was the origin of the protestant work ethic. It was pure to make money but impure to spend it. Puritans believed in the plain and simple. The more complicated and indulgent life became the further away from God it was.

The nuclear family and community was the foundation of puritan life. It was the glue that held together their doctrine of simplicity, authority and obedience. Disobedience was the puritan's worst enemy for reasons that belong more to blue than to God. Disobedience meant a breakdown in the fabric of the community. Love was discipline because discipline was respect for God's natural order. The puritans were unknowingly repeating the role of the shepherd.

In a much earlier blue period (600 to 450 BC), Buddha also returned the religious thinking of his time back to fundamentals. Buddha stressed meditation, contemplation as well as the middle way. To Buddha, desire and attachment was the basis of all human suffering, because the impermanence of nature meant that everything craved for, would eventually crumble away. When Buddhism reached Japan, a country already strong in blue energy, Zen was one of the results. Zen is simplicity and stillness in the present. Zen is blue.

## The red period 1650 to 1800 AD

### Circular motion – growth

Life themes during the red period were:

- confusion
- linear thinking
- solutions
- obstacles
- capture
- growth
- restlessness
- anger
- appearance
- romance
- work

During the blue time the focus was on fundamentals. Even renaissance art was a return to the way things had been. In 1650 AD the red time began and replaced the reformation with the enlightenment and age of reason. Circular motion must make ends meet and red must find solutions. The esoteric left too many questions unexplained. Emphasis shifted from trying to understand the next world to trying to explain this one. Red turned away from religion and into scientific exploration.

When an obstacle gets in the way of circular motion it must push its way through. To red the world had so many problems that prayer had never changed, it was time to find new solutions away from magic and religion. Society under the influence of red turned magic into measurements, astrology into astronomy and alchemy into chemistry.

Scientific thinking became established during the red time because its process is like circular motion. Its purpose is to achieve reproducible results by performing the same actions. The same process for the same result is the circle going around. Science like red is linear. The eighteenth century became the age of reason because the eighteenth century was red. Newton changed knowledge forever, while Linnaeus catalogued nature. Questions that had troubled the world were answered during the red period, because circular motion must have a solution.

The church was an impediment to science because of its religious restrictions. It inhibited freedom of thought in an effort to keep alive the power that comes from mystery. During the red time many intellectuals moved to the north of Europe, where Protestantism encouraged ambition and did not interfere with experimentation.

The enlightenment was a time when everything was labelled. Circular motion is revolution. Politically, revolution was a word first used to describe the disturbance Galileo created, when he claimed the earth revolved around the sun. Revolution was common during the red period because of its need for freedom and liberty. Freedom is a part of the human condition but red emphasise it more because of the serf and the slave. The largest and most well known uprisings were the American Revolution that began with the Declaration of Independence in 1776, and the French revolution from 1789 to 1799.

French revolutionaries cried for Liberty, Equality, Fraternity! The Americans began their Declaration of Independence with, 'We hold these truths to be self-evident, that all men are created equal, that they are endowed by their Creator with certain unalienable Rights, that among these are Life, Liberty and the pursuit of Happiness.'

Social hierarchy and pre-revolutionary laws gave justice to the few, not the many, but that was soon to change. In France revolutionaries cut off the heads of more than thirteen hundred 'threats to the revolution' in one six-week period alone. In Russia, Peter the Great created the opportunity to earn rank by ability rather than by birth.

The slave trade of the 18th century created more human misery than in any other period before it. Slavery had existed since the dawn of time taking many guises and names. The Trans-Atlantic slave trade where it is estimated that between ten and fifteen million Africans were transported as labour, began in earnest in 1698 when the slave trade was officially opened to private traders. It has been estimated from mortality rates that while ten to fifteen million souls were brought into the Americas, at least twenty million must have been stolen. The rights of the individual during the red time obviously did not extend to everyone. The need for red to use work as proof of self-worth caused slaves to be taken from Africa, in never before heard of numbers in order to be worked to death. At the same time in Europe the machine was invented and the industrial revolution began.

In the previous red time 600 to 750 AD, smallpox first entered Europe. In the later red period 1650 to 1800 AD, smallpox would mutate into Europe's most feared disease, killing almost half a million Europeans a year, during the eighteenth century. Jenner developed the smallpox vaccine in 1796, as the red time came to an end.

Epidemic diseases do not end when a colour completes its period but they do lose their fear and social influence. Cancer has existed for as long as mankind but never with the fear it creates now. Tuberculosis continues to infect large numbers of people but it no longer captures the mind of the First World. Understanding illness from a colour group perspective means examining disease in terms of social impact, not by the numbers infected.

Mohammed started receiving messages from the angel Gabriel in 610 AD, ten years after the beginning of the previous red period. Islam, like circular motion, became a cradle for culture by joining what had been scattered tribes. Mohammed was a man of his time, uniting tribes and implementing religious and secular revolution.

# The green period 1800 to 1950 AD

## Outward and inward motion – reaction

Life themes during the green period were:

- adrenalin
- fight or flight
- reactivity
- sensitivity
- dissatisfaction
- freedom
- skill
- stimulation
- intellect

As Napoleon marched across Europe no-one could have known that this would be the first of four major wars, all to occur during the green time; the Napoleonic Wars, the American Civil War, World War One and World War Two. War fever spread through the green time as it did during the crusades of orange. With green however the objective for the average soldier was travel and adventure rather than salvation.

The green time had its positive and negative consequences. In between wars, many parts of the world found time to abolish slavery and serfdom, make significant advances in physics and biology as well as turn colonies into fully fledged countries.

Many artists believed the world had become dull, flattened by facts and figures. To some like Emerson it had lost its romance and charm and needed some mystery returned. Romanticism was the green response and was an artistic way of viewing the world that emphasised the uniqueness of the individual, showing there was more to life than reason.

Séances and spiritualism flourished because it suited the green temperament to find out first hand what happens after death. After World War One, séances became even more popular due to the need for parents to make contact with sons they had lost in the war.

The European populations of America, Canada, Australia, South Africa and New Zealand had remained relatively small until the green time. Australia for example was a penal colony where no-one wanted to go, until gold was found and people came from everywhere to turn a colony into a nation. Economic boom and bust was common in the nineteenth and early twentieth centuries because of the reactive energy of green. This reactivity of inward and outward motion culminated in the great depression.

The hunter is either at work or at leisure. Boom or bust is another expression of this same reactive motion. America exploded in a wave of adventure seekers looking for a home and freedom. The gold rushes of Australia and the United States like that of the Klondike in Canada were fuelled by the same reactive energy that lives inside the hunter.

For the hunter the bigger their kill, the more time they can spend relaxing afterwards. The 'fortune hunter' of the green time lived life exactly the same way. Each dreamt of that one big strike that would allow them to spend the rest of their lives in idleness and luxury. Immigration was popular in the green time because immigration meant freedom, a chance to start over and one more adventure.

In the previous green period, 750 to 900 AD, Charlemagne liberated Christendom and revived learning. He established schools and became a patron of the sciences and arts emphasising the weight that green places on thinking.

In Baghdad a fully funded educational institute called the House of Wisdom was built. The House of Wisdom was the world's unsurpassed centre for learning and remained so until it was destroyed during the Mongol invasions. It was said that the waters of the Tigris turned black from the ink of the huge number of books that the Mongols threw into the river.

# The brown period 1950 to 2100 AD

## Outward, circular and inward motion – unity
Life themes during the brown period are:

- perfection
- anxiety
- unity
- synthetic
- replication
- control
- breakdown
- building
- balance

Unity is the essence of brown. The brown time started at the end of the Second World War. Immediately the world began a concerted effort to find common ground and agreement and the United Nations was formed. Alliances between continents, such as NATO, were put in place to display a unified front against any threatening force.

Like matter struggling to secure itself against the ravages of the environment, regional agreements attempted to unify nations as a protection against outside forces. The communist block built a wall to shield itself from the influence of the western world.

During the Cold War the world lived in fear of nuclear destruction, the ultimate internal breakdown. While the West braced itself for total annihilation the communist block placed spies and cameras into every nook and cranny to pry into the lives of its citizens.

Anxiety underlies contemporary brown culture making the need for antidepressants and anxiety medications widespread. As communism fell terrorism took its place, another internal fear. Unable to block off the outside world the worst brown fear was realised, when nations started being attacked by threats from inside their borders.

During the green time armies fought like hunters, lying concealed before suddenly attacking, a tactic mimicked in the Blitzkrieg. In the brown time terror cells are as feared as cancer cells creating panic that cripples infrastructure.

The craftsman ensures that every product is as successful as the last. They try and follow a reproducible pattern so the outcome is always the same. The craftsman does not like anything substandard and they continually improve their design. Once their product is the way they want it each reproduction must be as good as the original. Take-away food is an example of brown as is mass production of any kind.

Internal unity cannot exist in brown when social disparity is blatant. In the past the division between rich and poor was obvious, but in the lucky First World this problem under the brown influence has come a long way to being solved. In the first world today the standard of living for the average person is at a level that only the rich of the past could afford.

Organic breakdown is built into the design of brown so matter can rebuild itself into new forms. This occurs when stress becomes too much for the old form to continue. The earth, due to the impact of the brown time is subject to the same influences, making the potential for internal breakdown under stress a real possibility.

For the planet, organic breakdown implies environmental collapse, but it does not have to be this way. Breakdown in brown occurs because of exhaustion but fatigue can be fixed. The planet, like an individual, will replenish and repair when conditions are right. Exhaustion can be remedied but not when it is total. Enough energy must remain for the body to be able to heal itself. Total exhaustion is irreparable and death will soon occur, but there are many stages before energy reaches its end, where recovery is still possible.

Individuals display this recuperative quality all the time. After being diagnosed with cancer or some other destructive disease, many people turn their lives around to become stronger than ever. A change of lifestyle and a shift in attitude, eliminating the stresses that bought them to this point, has helped many people in this dire position beat the odds and return to health. When this occurs the person who survives is often stronger, more confident and grateful. With the help of brown, the planet, like a butterfly from a chrysalis, can be the same as the individual survivor and emerge with a new appreciation of life; wiser, healthier and glad to be alive.

# ACKNOWLEDGEMENTS

The concept of traditional roles and the techniques of facial analysis have taken over eight years to develop. More than a thousand people who were willing to share their personal stories form the basis of the information in this book.

*Soul and Survival* is observation, not religion or science. It takes at face value the beliefs of others without clarification or judgement. It accepts personal experience as truth. *Soul and Survival* has a spiritual foundation but does not try to define God.

Accepting life stories without prejudice led to classifying patterns of behaviour. It is with heartfelt gratitude that I thank all the patients and students who contributed.

Thanks once again to Allan Cornwall for making the first print book a reality, and to *nishnish* for the cover design.

Thank you to those involved with the Remedy Group for their loyalty and support, and to Heather Betts for her artwork which is found on our website www.soulandsurvival.com.

To Samuel Hahnemann (1755–1843) whose discovery of homeopathy is the foundation of this book. *Soul and Survival* would never exist without his *Organon of Rational Medicine* or *Chronic Diseases*. To Herbert Roberts (1868–1950) and John Henry Allen (1854–1925) for making the first link to facial features, and James Tyler Kent (1849–1916) for thinking in a conceptual way.

To my children and stepchildren whose curiosity and enthusiasm made me aware that others would be interested in these ideas. My children are everything to me, and I thank them for the meaning they give to my life.

Finally to my wife Louise – without her this book would be just an idea. Her continuous effort and belief in this project has been inspirational. Louise has contributed many important additions to the traditional roles and facial features, as well as to the layout, development and creativity of the book. This book is for you Louise, with all my love and all my thanks.

Made in the USA
Columbia, SC
24 June 2019